# Business Plans Handbook

# Business Plans

A COMPILATION
OF BUSINESS
PLANS DEVELOPED
BY INDIVIDUALS
THROUGHOUT
NORTH AMERICA

# Handbook

**VOLUME**

# 30

Sonya D. Hill,
Project Editor

GALE
CENGAGE Learning

Farmington Hills, Mich • San Francisco • New York • Waterville, Maine
Meriden, Conn • Mason, Ohio • Chicago

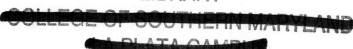

**Business Plans Handbook, Volume 30**

Project Editor: Sonya D. Hill

Project Editor: Michelle Lee

Content Developer: Michele P. LaMeau

Product Design: Jennifer Wahi

Composition and Electronic Prepress: Evi Seoud

Manufacturing: Rita Wimberley

*Gale, a part of Cengage Learning*
27500 Drake Rd.
Farmington Hills, MI 48331-3535

ISBN-13: 978-1-5699-5841-4
ISBN-10: 1-5699-5841-6
1084-4473

Printed in Mexico
1 2 3 4 5 6 7 18 17 16 15 14

# Contents

v

# CONTENTS

# Highlights

*Business Plans Handbook, Volume 30 (BPH-30)* is a collection of business plans compiled by entrepreneurs seeking funding for small businesses throughout North America. For those looking for examples of how to approach, structure, and compose their own business plans, *BPH-30* presents 20 sample plans, including plans for the following businesses:

- Angel Investor Network
- Biodiesel Plant
- Bioterrorism Prevention Organization
- Detective Agency
- Event Planner
- Factoring Company
- General Construction Business
- Graphic Designer
- Healthcare Advocacy Business
- Home Inspection Business
- Import and Export Company
- Medical Billing Business
- Mobile Mini Putt Putt Business
- Personal Chef Service
- Pet Aftercare Business
- Photo Retouching Service
- Residential Cleaning Service
- Senior Errand Service
- Senior Transportation Service
- Specialty Retail Business

## FEATURES AND BENEFITS

*BPH-30* offers many features not provided by other business planning references including:

- Twenty business plans, each of which represent an attempt at clarifying (for themselves and others) the reasons that the business should exist or expand and why a lender should fund the enterprise.
- Two fictional plans that are used by business counselors at a prominent small business development organization as examples for their clients. (You will find these in the Business Plan Template Appendix.)

- A directory section that includes listings for venture capital and finance companies, which specialize in funding start-up and second-stage small business ventures, and a comprehensive listing of Service Corps of Retired Executives (SCORE) offices. In addition, the Appendix also contains updated listings of all Small Business Development Centers (SBDCs); associations of interest to entrepreneurs; Small Business Administration (SBA) Regional Offices; and consultants specializing in small business planning and advice. It is strongly advised that you consult supporting organizations while planning your business, as they can provide a wealth of useful information.

- A Small Business Term Glossary to help you decipher the sometimes confusing terminology used by lenders and others in the financial and small business communities.

- A cumulative index, outlining each plan profiled in the complete Business Plans Handbook series.

- A Business Plan Template which serves as a model to help you construct your own business plan. This generic outline lists all the essential elements of a complete business plan and their components, including the Summary, Business History and Industry Outlook, Market Examination, Competition, Marketing, Administration and Management, Financial Information, and other key sections. Use this guide as a starting point for compiling your plan.

- Extensive financial documentation required to solicit funding from small business lenders. You will find examples of Cash Flows, Balance Sheets, Income Projections, and other financial information included with the textual portions of the plan.

# Introduction

Perhaps the most important aspect of business planning is simply doing it. More and more business owners are beginning to compile business plans even if they don't need a bank loan. Others discover the value of planning when they must provide a business plan for the bank. The sheer act of putting thoughts on paper seems to clarify priorities and provide focus. Sometimes business owners completely change strategies when compiling their plan, deciding on a different product mix or advertising scheme after finding that their assumptions were incorrect. This kind of healthy thinking and re-thinking via business planning is becoming the norm. The editors of *Business Plans Handbook, Volume 30 (BPH-30)* sincerely hope that this latest addition to the series is a helpful tool in the successful completion of your business plan, no matter what the reason for creating it.

This thirtieth volume, like each volume in the series, offers business plans used and created by real people. *BPH-30* provides 20 business plans. The business and personal names and addresses and general locations have been changed to protect the privacy of the plan authors.

## NEW BUSINESS OPPORTUNITIES

As in other volumes in the series, *BPH-30* finds entrepreneurs engaged in a wide variety of creative endeavors. Examples include a Graphic Design Business, a Healthcare Advocacy Business, and Senior Transportation Service. In addition, several other plans are provided, including a Photo Retouching Service, a Personal Chef Service, and a Detective Agency, among others.

Comprehensive financial documentation has become increasingly important as today's entrepreneurs compete for the finite resources of business lenders. Our plans illustrate the financial data generally required of loan applicants, including Income Statements, Financial Projections, Cash Flows, and Balance Sheets.

## ENHANCED APPENDIXES

In an effort to provide the most relevant and valuable information for our readers, we have updated the coverage of small business resources. For instance, you will find a directory section, which includes listings of all of the Service Corps of Retired Executives (SCORE) offices; an informative glossary, which includes small business terms; and a cumulative index, outlining each plan profiled in the complete *Business Plans Handbook* series. In addition we have updated the list of Small Business Development Centers (SBDCs); Small Business Administration Regional Offices; venture capital and finance companies, which specialize in funding start-up and second-stage small business enterprises; associations of interest to entrepreneurs; and consultants, specializing in small business advice and planning. For your reference, we have also reprinted the business plan template, which provides a comprehensive overview of the essential components of a business plan and two fictional plans used by small business counselors.

## SERIES INFORMATION

If you already have the first twenty-nine volumes of *BPH*, with this thirtieth volume, you will now have a collection of over 594 business plans (not including the updated plans); contact information for hundreds of organizations and agencies offering business expertise; a helpful business plan template; more than 1,500 citations to valuable small business development material; and a comprehensive glossary of terms to help the business planner navigate the sometimes confusing language of entrepreneurship.

## ACKNOWLEDGEMENTS

The Editors wish to sincerely thank the contributors to *BPH-30*, including:

- BizPlanDB.com
- Fran Fletcher
- Paul Greenland
- Brenda Kubiac
- Claire Moore
- Zuzu Enterprises

## COMMENTS WELCOME

Your comments on *Business Plans Handbook* are appreciated. Please direct all correspondence, suggestions for future volumes of *BPH*, and other recommendations to the following:

Managing Editor, Business Product
*Business Plans Handbook*
Gale, a part of Cengage Learning
27500 Drake Rd.
Farmington Hills, MI 48331-3535
Phone: (248)699-4253
Fax: (248)699-8052
Toll-Free: 800-347-GALE
E-mail: BusinessProducts@gale.com

# Angel Investor Network

Horan Investments

PO Box 34123
New York, New York 11022

*BizPlanDB.com*

*Horan Investments is a New York-based corporation that will provide investments into startup and expanding businesses throughout the United States. The Company was founded by Brady Horan.*

## 1.0 EXECUTIVE SUMMARY

The purpose of this business plan is to raise $10,000,000 for the development of an angel investor firm while showcasing the expected financials and operations over the next three years. Horan Investments ("the Company") is a New York-based corporation that will provide investments into startup and expanding businesses throughout the United States. The Company was founded by Brady Horan.

### 1.1 The Services

Horan Investments will specialize in making private investments into companies that show great promise in regards to revenue growth and Horan Investments' ability to take these businesses public (or divest them through private sale) to third parties throughout the United States. Specifically, Horan Investments will focus on making investments into new businesses that have promising technology or an innovative business concept, or existing businesses that are seeking rapid growth within their field.

Horan Investments will generate revenues by levying fees equal to 2 percent of the aggregate assets under management coupled with a 20 percent incentive fee on all profits generated by the business. This will be further discussed throughout the business plan.

The third section of the business plan will further describe the services offered by Horan Investments.

### 1.2 Financing

Mr. Horan is seeking to raise $10 million from a number of investors via a private placement offering that will be used to make investments into third party companies. The business will use a number of limited partnerships in order to effectively make investments into subsidiary businesses that hold a significant amount of promise. Primarily the financing will be used for the following:

- Development of the Company's location

- Financing for the first six months of operation

- Financing for the investments to be made by Horan Investments

### 1.3 Mission Statement

Horan Investment's mission is to provide potential investors access to fast growing companies that can provide substantial capital appreciation over a three to five year period once the firm divests its interest in the business.

### 1.4 Management Team

The Company was founded by Brady Horan. Mr. Horan has more than 10 years of experience in the investment industry. Through his expertise, he will be able to bring the operations of the business to profitability within its first year of operations.

### 1.5 Sales Forecasts

Mr. Horan expects a strong rate of growth at the start of operations. Below are the expected financials over the next three years.

**Proforma profit and loss (yearly)**

| Year | 1 | 2 | 3 |
|---|---|---|---|
| Sales | $4,796,778 | $5,180,520 | $5,594,962 |
| Operating costs | $1,469,297 | $1,576,979 | $1,690,210 |
| EBITDA | $2,847,803 | $3,085,489 | $3,345,255 |
| Taxes, interest, and depreciation | $1,978,951 | $2,069,271 | $2,167,983 |
| Net profit | $ 868,852 | $1,016,217 | $1,177,273 |

**Sales, operating costs, and profit forecast**

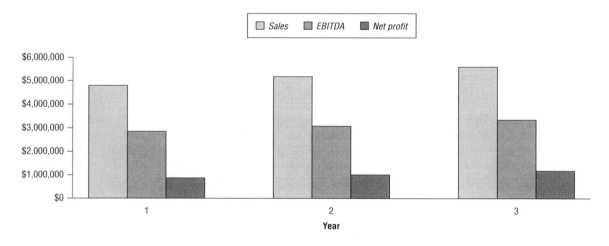

### 1.6 Expansion Plan

The Founder expects that the business will aggressively expand during the first three years of operation. Mr. Horan intends to implement marketing campaigns that will effectively target investors and companies seeking investment within the target market.

## 2.0 COMPANY AND FINANCING SUMMARY

### 2.1 Registered Name and Corporate Structure

Horan Investments is registered as a corporation in the State of New York. All shares of investments will be held through limited partnerships arranged by the Company.

## 2.2 Required Funds

At this time, Horan Investments requires $10 million of investment funds. Below is a breakdown of how these funds will be used:

**Projected startup costs**

| | |
|---|---:|
| Initial lease payments and deposits | $ 100,000 |
| Working capital | $ 350,000 |
| FF&E | $ 230,000 |
| Leasehold improvements | $ 120,000 |
| Security deposits | $ 50,000 |
| Insurance | $ 25,000 |
| Portfolio companies | $ 9,000,000 |
| Marketing budget | $ 75,000 |
| Miscellaneous and unforeseen costs | $ 50,000 |
| **Total startup costs** | **$10,000,000** |

## 2.3 Investor Equity

Mr. Horan is seeking to raise capital via the Company's private placement memorandum. He will retain a 100 percent ownership interest in the investment management company that will oversee the firm's angel investor's investments.

## 2.4 Management Equity

This will be further discussed in the Company's private placement memorandum.

## 2.5 Exit Strategy

If the business is very successful, Mr. Horan may seek to sell the business to a third party for a significant earnings multiple. In all likeliness, a qualified investment bank would be hired to manage the complex aspects of selling Horan Investments to a third party for a significant earnings multiple.

# 3.0 PRODUCTS AND SERVICES

Below is a description of the capital investment services offered by the Horan Investments.

## 3.1 Investments into New Businesses

The primary revenue center for the business will come from capital appreciation and dividends tied to investments in new businesses, innovative startup businesses, and existing businesses that are seeking expansion capital. The center of this revenue unit will come from the capital appreciation that is realized when a business in which Horan Investments has a stake is sold privately or via an initial public offering.

The business will hire a number of highly educated investment professionals that can provide insight into the economic viability of any business that is reviewed by Horan Investments for a potential investment.

## 3.2 Royalty Based Financing

The business will also make royalty based financing investments into new businesses with the intent to generate revenues both from capital appreciation as well as guaranteed payments based on the revenues of the business in which Horan Investments provides capital. This is a new and innovative form of financing that substantially reduces the risks associated with angel capital investing. A full royalty based financing model is accompanied with this business plan.

# 4.0 STRATEGIC AND MARKET ANALYSIS

### 4.1 Economic Outlook

This section of the analysis will detail the economic climate, the angel and venture capital industry, the customer profile, and the competition that the business will face as it progresses through its business operations.

Currently, the economic market condition in the United States is moderate. The meltdown of the subprime mortgage market coupled with increasing gas prices has led many people to believe that the U.S. is on the cusp of a double dip economic recession. However, Horan Investments should be able to continue to realize substantial profits from its investments as many of these companies' revenues are not dependent on the ongoing economic climate.

### 4.2 Industry Analysis

Within the United States, there are 1,000 registered investment companies that specifically engage in the activity of providing early stage growth capital to new and existing businesses. At this time, there is approximately $600 billion invested directly in angel investor networks and companies and venture capital limited partnerships. There are approximately 25,000 people working within this industry.

The angel/venture capital industry has recently undergone some legislative changes in regards to the individuals operating angel investor networks. Any manager of pooled funds who is overseeing more than $25 million is now required to be registered by the Securities and Exchange Commission.

### 4.3 Customer Profile

Horan Investments will not directly have customers. The business intends to solicit a substantial amount of capital from wealthy individuals, pension funds, insurance companies, and other investment companies that specialize in angel firm capital. As such, the customer profile will generally be equivalent to the requirements set forth by the rules regarding private placement memorandums.

### 4.4 Competition

As stated above, there are approximately 1,000 firms that are dedicated to providing financing to new businesses and innovative startups. As such, it is hard to quantify the competition that the business will continue to face as it progresses through its operations. However, Horan Investments intends to maintain a competitive advantage via its royalty based financing programs that produce immediate returns for the business once a portfolio company becomes profitable.

# 5.0 MARKETING PLAN

Horan Investments intends to develop a marketing campaign that will attract both investors and potential investment companies to the brand name of the firm. Below is an overview of these strategies.

### 5.1 Marketing Objectives

- Develop relationships with private placement brokers throughout the United States
- Develop a strong presence among other angel capital firms and funds
- Remain within the letter of law regarding the advertisements and marketing campaigns carried out by Horan Investments

### 5.2 Marketing Strategies

Marketing for Horan Investments will be limited as there are limits as to what can be printed when it comes to private investment partnerships. However, with the assistance of the Company's law firm, the business will become prominent in industry circulations that focus on angel capital and angel capital investments.

Horan Investments will also maintain an interactive website that showcases the operations of the firm, its principals, its portfolio investments, and the site will feature a login system where accredited investors can view their accounts and other information that is restricted to them.

As stated above, Horan Investments will also make it known that it is in the business of investing in new startups with innovative concepts, existing businesses that need growth capital, and technology businesses. This will ensure that the business can make investments quickly into profitable businesses.

## 6.0 ORGANIZATIONAL PLAN AND PERSONNEL SUMMARY

### 6.1 Corporate Organization

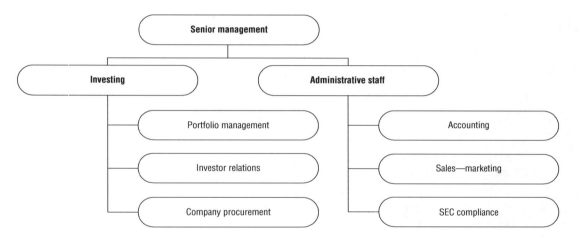

### 6.2 Organizational Budget

**Personnel plan—yearly**

| Year | 1 | 2 | 3 |
|---|---|---|---|
| Senior management | $250,000 | $257,500 | $ 265,225 |
| Principals | $250,000 | $257,500 | $ 265,225 |
| Analysts | $100,000 | $103,000 | $ 106,090 |
| Administrative | $135,000 | $185,400 | $ 238,703 |
| Accountant | $150,000 | $154,500 | $ 159,135 |
| **Total** | **$885,000** | **$957,900** | **$1,034,378** |

**Numbers of personnel**

| | | | |
|---|---|---|---|
| Senior management | 1 | 1 | 1 |
| Principals | 2 | 2 | 2 |
| Analysts | 1 | 1 | 1 |
| Administrative | 3 | 4 | 5 |
| Accountant | 2 | 2 | 2 |
| **Totals** | **9** | **10** | **11** |

**Personnel expense breakdown**

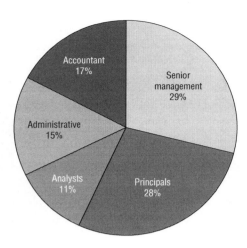

# 7.0 FINANCIAL PLAN

## 7.1 Underlying Assumptions

The Company has based its proforma financial statements on the following:

• Horan Investments will have an annual revenue growth rate of 16 percent per year

• The Owner will acquire $10,000,000 of equity funds

• The business will generate annual returns of approximately 35 percent compounded in unrealized gains

## 7.2 Sensitivity Analysis

As Horan Investments will have many portfolio investments, economic risks will be spread out among a number of businesses. As such, any type of economic recession will not have an impact on the Company's profitability or cash flow.

## 7.3 Source of Funds

**Financing**

| Equity contributions | |
|---|---|
| Investor(s) | $ 10,000,000.00 |
| **Total equity financing** | **$10,000,000.00** |
| Banks and lenders | |
| **Total debt financing** | **$      0.00** |
| **Total financing** | **$10,000,000.00** |

## 7.4 General Assumptions

**General assumptions**

| Year | 1 | 2 | 3 |
|---|---|---|---|
| Short term interest rate | 9.5% | 9.5% | 9.5% |
| Long term interest rate | 10.0% | 10.0% | 10.0% |
| Federal tax rate | 33.0% | 33.0% | 33.0% |
| State tax rate | 5.0% | 5.0% | 5.0% |
| Personnel taxes | 15.0% | 15.0% | 15.0% |

## 7.5 Profit and Loss Statements

**Proforma profit and loss (yearly)**

| Year | 1 | 2 | 3 |
|---|---|---|---|
| **Sales** | **$4,796,778** | **$5,180,520** | **$5,594,962** |
| Cost of goods sold | $ 479,678 | $ 518,052 | $ 559,496 |
| Gross margin | 90.00% | 90.00% | 90.00% |
| **Operating income** | **$4,317,100** | **$4,662,468** | **$5,035,466** |
| **Expenses** | | | |
| Payroll | $ 885,000 | $ 957,900 | $1,034,378 |
| General and administrative | $ 145,200 | $ 151,008 | $ 157,048 |
| Marketing expenses | $ 23,984 | $ 25,903 | $ 27,975 |
| Professional fees and licensure | $ 55,219 | $ 56,876 | $ 58,582 |
| Insurance costs | $ 21,987 | $ 23,086 | $ 24,241 |
| Travel and vehicle costs | $ 27,596 | $ 30,356 | $ 33,391 |
| Rent and utilities | $ 120,000 | $ 126,000 | $ 132,300 |
| Miscellaneous costs | $ 57,561 | $ 62,166 | $ 67,140 |
| Payroll taxes | $ 132,750 | $ 143,685 | $ 155,157 |
| **Total operating costs** | **$1,469,297** | **$1,576,979** | **$1,690,210** |
| **EBITDA** | **$2,847,803** | **$3,085,489** | **$3,345,255** |
| Federal income tax | $ 939,775 | $1,018,211 | $1,103,934 |
| State income tax | $ 142,390 | $ 154,274 | $ 167,263 |
| Interest expense | $ 0 | $ 0 | $ 0 |
| Depreciation expenses | $ 896,786 | $ 896,786 | $ 896,786 |
| **Net profit** | **$ 868,852** | **$1,016,217** | **$1,177,273** |
| **Profit margin** | **18.11%** | **19.62%** | **21.04%** |

**Sales, operating costs, and profit forecast**

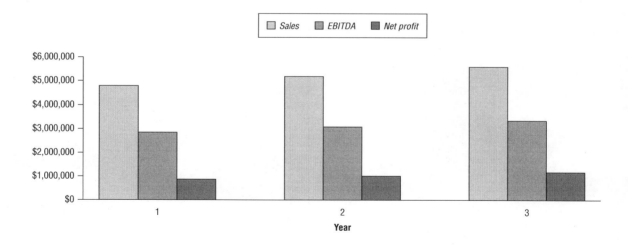

## 7.6 Cash Flow Analysis

**Proforma cash flow analysis—yearly**

| Year | 1 | 2 | 3 |
|---|---|---|---|
| Cash from operations | $ 1,765,638 | $ 1,913,003 | $ 2,074,058 |
| Cash from receivables | $ 0 | $ 0 | $ 0 |
| **Operating cash inflow** | **$ 1,765,638** | **$1,913,003** | **$2,074,058** |
| **Other cash inflows** | | | |
| Equity investment | $ 10,000,000 | $ 0 | $ 0 |
| Increased borrowings | $ 0 | $ 0 | $ 0 |
| Sales of business assets | $ 0 | $ 0 | $ 0 |
| A/P increases | $ 37,902 | $ 43,587 | $ 50,125 |
| **Total other cash inflows** | **$10,037,902** | **$ 43,587** | **$ 50,125** |
| **Total cash inflow** | **$11,803,540** | **$1,956,590** | **$2,124,184** |
| **Cash outflows** | | | |
| Repayment of principal | $ 0 | $ 0 | $ 0 |
| A/P decreases | $ 24,897 | $ 29,876 | $ 35,852 |
| A/R increases | $ 0 | $ 0 | $ 0 |
| Asset purchases | $ 9,405,000 | $ 286,950 | $ 311,109 |
| Dividends | $ 1,412,510 | $ 1,530,402 | $ 1,659,247 |
| **Total cash outflows** | **$10,842,407** | **$1,847,229** | **$2,006,207** |
| **Net cash flow** | **$ 961,133** | **$ 109,361** | **$ 117,977** |
| **Cash balance** | **$ 961,133** | **$1,070,494** | **$1,188,470** |

**Proforma cash flow (yearly)**

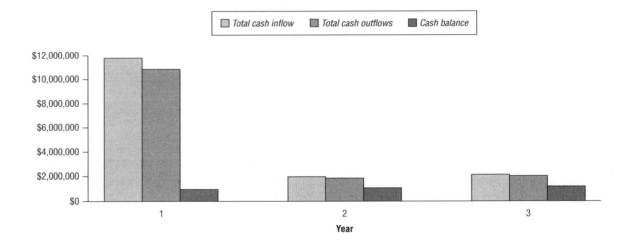

## 7.7 Balance Sheet

**Proforma balance sheet—yearly**

| Year | 1 | 2 | 3 |
|---|---|---|---|
| **Assets** | | | |
| Cash | $ 961,133 | $ 1,070,494 | $ 1,188,470 |
| Amortized development/expansion costs | $ 175,000 | $ 203,695 | $ 234,806 |
| Portfolio companies | $ 12,150,000 | $ 16,693,037 | $ 22,850,598 |
| FF&E | $ 230,000 | $ 273,043 | $ 319,709 |
| Accumulated depreciation | ($ 896,786) | ($ 1,793,571) | ($ 2,690,357) |
| **Total assets** | **$12,619,347** | **$16,446,697** | **$21,903,226** |
| **Liabilities and equity** | | | |
| Accounts payable | $ 13,005 | $ 26,716 | $ 40,990 |
| Long term liabilities | $ 0 | $ 0 | $ 0 |
| Other liabilities | $ 0 | $ 0 | $ 0 |
| **Total liabilities** | **$ 13,005** | **$ 26,716** | **$ 40,990** |
| **Net worth** | **$12,606,342** | **$16,419,981** | **$21,862,236** |
| **Total liabilities and equity** | **$12,619,347** | **$16,446,697** | **$21,903,226** |

**Proforma balance sheet**

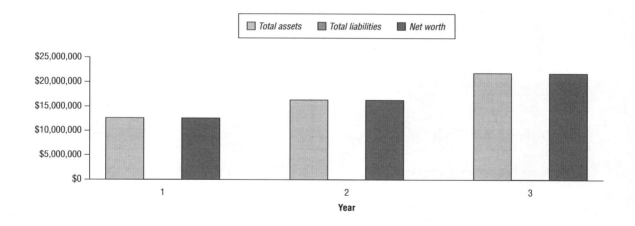

## 7.8 Breakeven Analysis

**Monthly break even analysis**

| Year | 1 | 2 | 3 |
|---|---|---|---|
| Monthly revenue | $ 136,046 | $ 146,017 | $ 156,501 |
| Yearly revenue | $1,632,552 | $1,752,199 | $1,878,012 |

**Break even analysis**

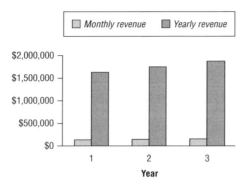

## 7.9 Business Ratios

**Business ratios—yearly**

| Year | 1 | 2 | 3 |
|---|---|---|---|
| **Sales** | | | |
| Sales growth | 0.00% | 8.00% | 8.00% |
| Gross margin | 90.00% | 90.00% | 90.00% |
| **Financials** | | | |
| Profit margin | 18.11% | 19.62% | 21.04% |
| Assets to liabilities | 970.35 | 615.61 | 534.36 |
| Equity to liabilities | 969.35 | 614.61 | 533.36 |
| Assets to equity | 1.00 | 1.00 | 1.00 |
| **Liquidity** | | | |
| Acid test | 73.90 | 40.07 | 28.99 |
| Cash to assets | 0.08 | 0.07 | 0.05 |

## 7.10 Three Year Profit and Loss Statement

**Profit and loss statement (first year)**

| Months | 1 | 2 | 3 | 4 | 5 | 6 | 7 |
|---|---|---|---|---|---|---|---|
| **Sales** | **$399,000** | **$399,133** | **$399,266** | **$399,399** | **$399,532** | **$399,665** | **$399,798** |
| Cost of goods sold | $ 39,900 | $ 39,913 | $ 39,927 | $ 39,940 | $ 39,953 | $ 39,967 | $ 39,980 |
| Gross margin | 90.00% | 90.00% | 90.00% | 90.00% | 90.00% | 90.00% | 90.00% |
| **Operating income** | **$359,100** | **$359,220** | **$359,339** | **$359,459** | **$359,579** | **$359,699** | **$359,818** |
| **Expenses** | | | | | | | |
| Payroll | $ 73,750 | $ 73,750 | $ 73,750 | $ 73,750 | $ 73,750 | $ 73,750 | $ 73,750 |
| General and administrative | $ 12,100 | $ 12,100 | $ 12,100 | $ 12,100 | $ 12,100 | $ 12,100 | $ 12,100 |
| Marketing expenses | $ 1,999 | $ 1,999 | $ 1,999 | $ 1,999 | $ 1,999 | $ 1,999 | $ 1,999 |
| Professional fees and licensure | $ 4,602 | $ 4,602 | $ 4,602 | $ 4,602 | $ 4,602 | $ 4,602 | $ 4,602 |
| Insurance costs | $ 1,832 | $ 1,832 | $ 1,832 | $ 1,832 | $ 1,832 | $ 1,832 | $ 1,832 |
| Travel and vehicle costs | $ 2,300 | $ 2,300 | $ 2,300 | $ 2,300 | $ 2,300 | $ 2,300 | $ 2,300 |
| Rent and utilities | $ 10,000 | $ 10,000 | $ 10,000 | $ 10,000 | $ 10,000 | $ 10,000 | $ 10,000 |
| Miscellaneous costs | $ 4,797 | $ 4,797 | $ 4,797 | $ 4,797 | $ 4,797 | $ 4,797 | $ 4,797 |
| Payroll taxes | $ 11,063 | $ 11,063 | $ 11,063 | $ 11,063 | $ 11,063 | $ 11,063 | $ 11,063 |
| **Total operating costs** | **$122,441** | **$122,441** | **$122,441** | **$122,441** | **$122,441** | **$122,441** | **$122,441** |
| **EBITDA** | **$236,659** | **$236,778** | **$236,898** | **$237,018** | **$237,137** | **$237,257** | **$237,377** |
| Federal income tax | $ 78,171 | $ 78,197 | $ 78,223 | $ 78,249 | $ 78,275 | $ 78,302 | $ 78,328 |
| State income tax | $ 11,844 | $ 11,848 | $ 11,852 | $ 11,856 | $ 11,860 | $ 11,864 | $ 11,868 |
| Interest expense | $ 0 | $ 0 | $ 0 | $ 0 | $ 0 | $ 0 | $ 0 |
| Depreciation expense | $ 74,732 | $ 74,732 | $ 74,732 | $ 74,732 | $ 74,732 | $ 74,732 | $ 74,732 |
| **Net profit** | **$ 71,911** | **$ 72,001** | **$ 72,090** | **$ 72,180** | **$ 72,270** | **$ 72,359** | **$ 72,449** |

## Profit and loss statement (first year cont.)

| Month | 8 | 9 | 10 | 11 | 12 | 1 |
|---|---|---|---|---|---|---|
| Sales | $399,931 | $400,064 | $400,197 | $400,330 | $400,463 | $4,796,778 |
| Cost of goods sold | $ 39,993 | $ 40,006 | $ 40,020 | $ 40,033 | $ 40,046 | $ 479,678 |
| Gross margin | 90.00% | 90.00% | 90.00% | 90.00% | 90.00% | 90.00% |
| Operating income | $359,938 | $360,058 | $360,177 | $360,297 | $360,417 | $4,317,100 |
| Expenses | | | | | | |
| Payroll | $ 73,750 | $ 73,750 | $ 73,750 | $ 73,750 | $ 73,750 | $ 885,000 |
| General and administrative | $ 12,100 | $ 12,100 | $ 12,100 | $ 12,100 | $ 12,100 | $ 145,200 |
| Marketing expenses | $ 1,999 | $ 1,999 | $ 1,999 | $ 1,999 | $ 1,999 | $ 23,984 |
| Professional fees and licensure | $ 4,602 | $ 4,602 | $ 4,602 | $ 4,602 | $ 4,602 | $ 55,219 |
| Insurance costs | $ 1,832 | $ 1,832 | $ 1,832 | $ 1,832 | $ 1,832 | $ 21,987 |
| Travel and vehicle costs | $ 2,300 | $ 2,300 | $ 2,300 | $ 2,300 | $ 2,300 | $ 27,596 |
| Rent and utilities | $ 10,000 | $ 10,000 | $ 10,000 | $ 10,000 | $ 10,000 | $ 120,000 |
| Miscellaneous costs | $ 4,797 | $ 4,797 | $ 4,797 | $ 4,797 | $ 4,797 | $ 57,561 |
| Payroll taxes | $ 11,063 | $ 11,063 | $ 11,063 | $ 11,063 | $ 11,063 | $ 132,750 |
| Total operating costs | $122,441 | $122,441 | $122,441 | $122,441 | $122,441 | $1,469,297 |
| EBITDA | $237,496 | $237,616 | $237,736 | $237,856 | $237,975 | $2,847,803 |
| Federal income tax | $ 78,354 | $ 78,380 | $ 78,406 | $ 78,432 | $ 78,458 | $ 939,775 |
| State income tax | $ 11,872 | $ 11,876 | $ 11,880 | $ 11,884 | $ 11,888 | $ 142,390 |
| Interest expense | $ 0 | $ 0 | $ 0 | $ 0 | $ 0 | $ 0 |
| Depreciation expense | $ 74,732 | $ 74,732 | $ 74,732 | $ 74,732 | $ 74,732 | $ 896,786 |
| Net profit | $ 72,539 | $ 72,629 | $ 72,718 | $ 72,808 | $ 72,898 | $ 868,852 |

## Profit and loss statement (second year)

| Quarter | Q1 | 2 Q2 | Q3 | Q4 | 2 |
|---|---|---|---|---|---|
| Sales | $1,036,104 | $1,295,130 | $1,398,740 | $1,450,546 | $5,180,520 |
| Cost of goods sold | $ 103,610 | $ 129,513 | $ 139,874 | $ 145,055 | $ 518,052 |
| Gross margin | 90.00% | 90.00% | 90.00% | 90.00% | 90.00% |
| Operating income | $ 932,494 | $1,165,617 | $1,258,866 | $1,305,491 | $4,662,468 |
| Expenses | | | | | |
| Payroll | $ 191,580 | $ 239,475 | $ 258,633 | $ 268,212 | $ 957,900 |
| General and administrative | $ 30,202 | $ 37,752 | $ 40,772 | $ 42,282 | $ 151,008 |
| Marketing expenses | $ 5,181 | $ 6,476 | $ 6,994 | $ 7,253 | $ 25,903 |
| Professional fees and licensure | $ 11,375 | $ 14,219 | $ 15,356 | $ 15,925 | $ 56,876 |
| Insurance costs | $ 4,617 | $ 5,772 | $ 6,233 | $ 6,464 | $ 23,086 |
| Travel and vehicle costs | $ 6,071 | $ 7,589 | $ 8,196 | $ 8,500 | $ 30,356 |
| Rent and utilities | $ 25,200 | $ 31,500 | $ 34,020 | $ 35,280 | $ 126,000 |
| Miscellaneous costs | $ 12,433 | $ 15,542 | $ 16,785 | $ 17,407 | $ 62,166 |
| Payroll taxes | $ 28,737 | $ 35,921 | $ 38,795 | $ 40,232 | $ 143,685 |
| Total operating costs | $ 315,396 | $ 394,245 | $ 425,784 | $ 441,554 | $1,576,979 |
| EBITDA | $ 617,098 | $ 771,372 | $ 833,082 | $ 863,937 | $3,085,489 |
| Federal income tax | $ 203,642 | $ 254,553 | $ 274,917 | $ 285,099 | $1,018,211 |
| State income tax | $ 30,855 | $ 38,569 | $ 41,654 | $ 43,197 | $ 154,274 |
| Interest expense | $ 0 | $ 0 | $ 0 | $ 0 | $ 0 |
| Depreciation expense | $ 224,196 | $ 224,196 | $ 224,196 | $ 224,196 | $ 896,786 |
| Net profit | $ 158,404 | $ 254,054 | $ 292,314 | $ 311,444 | $1,016,217 |

## Profit and loss statement (third year)

| Quarter | Q1 | 3 Q2 | Q3 | Q4 | 3 |
|---|---|---|---|---|---|
| **Sales** | **$1,118,992** | **$1,398,740** | **$1,510,640** | **$1,566,589** | **$5,594,962** |
| Cost of goods sold | $ 111,899 | $ 139,874 | $ 151,064 | $ 156,659 | $ 559,496 |
| Gross margin | 90.00% | 90.00% | 90.00% | 90.00% | 90.00% |
| **Operating income** | **$1,007,093** | **$1,258,866** | **$1,359,576** | **$1,409,930** | **$5,035,466** |
| **Expenses** | | | | | |
| Payroll | $ 206,876 | $ 258,594 | $ 279,282 | $ 289,626 | $1,034,378 |
| General and administrative | $ 31,410 | $ 39,262 | $ 42,403 | $ 43,974 | $ 157,048 |
| Marketing expenses | $ 5,595 | $ 6,994 | $ 7,553 | $ 7,833 | $ 27,975 |
| Professional fees and licensure | $ 11,716 | $ 14,645 | $ 15,817 | $ 16,403 | $ 58,582 |
| Insurance costs | $ 4,848 | $ 6,060 | $ 6,545 | $ 6,787 | $ 24,241 |
| Travel and vehicle costs | $ 6,678 | $ 8,348 | $ 9,016 | $ 9,350 | $ 33,391 |
| Rent and utilities | $ 26,460 | $ 33,075 | $ 35,721 | $ 37,044 | $ 132,300 |
| Miscellaneous costs | $ 13,428 | $ 16,785 | $ 18,128 | $ 18,799 | $ 67,140 |
| Payroll taxes | $ 31,031 | $ 38,789 | $ 41,892 | $ 43,444 | $ 155,157 |
| **Total operating costs** | **$ 338,042** | **$ 422,553** | **$ 456,357** | **$ 473,259** | **$1,690,210** |
| **EBITDA** | **$ 669,051** | **$ 836,314** | **$ 903,219** | **$ 936,671** | **$3,345,255** |
| Federal income tax | $ 220,787 | $ 275,984 | $ 298,062 | $ 309,102 | $1,103,934 |
| State income tax | $ 33,453 | $ 41,816 | $ 45,161 | $ 46,834 | $ 167,263 |
| Interest expense | $ 0 | $ 0 | $ 0 | $ 0 | $ 0 |
| Depreciation expense | $ 224,196 | $ 224,196 | $ 224,196 | $ 224,196 | $ 896,786 |
| **Net profit** | **$ 190,615** | **$ 294,318** | **$ 335,799** | **$ 356,540** | **$1,177,273** |

## 7.11 Three Year Cash Flow Analysis

## Cash flow analysis (first year)

| Month | 1 | 2 | 3 | 4 | 5 | 6 | 7 |
|---|---|---|---|---|---|---|---|
| Cash from operations | $ 146,643 | $146,733 | $ 146,823 | $ 146,912 | $ 147,002 | $ 147,092 | $ 147,181 |
| Cash from receivables | $ 0 | $ 0 | $ 0 | $ 0 | $ 0 | $ 0 | $ 0 |
| **Operating cash inflow** | **$ 146,643** | **$146,733** | **$ 146,823** | **$ 146,912** | **$ 147,002** | **$ 147,092** | **$ 147,181** |
| **Other cash inflows** | | | | | | | |
| Equity investment | $10,000,000 | $ 0 | $ 0 | $ 0 | $ 0 | $ 0 | $ 0 |
| Increased borrowings | $ 0 | $ 0 | $ 0 | $ 0 | $ 0 | $ 0 | $ 0 |
| Sales of business assets | $ 0 | $ 0 | $ 0 | $ 0 | $ 0 | $ 0 | $ 0 |
| A/P increases | $ 3,159 | $ 3,159 | $ 3,159 | $ 3,159 | $ 3,159 | $ 3,159 | $ 3,159 |
| **Total other cash inflows** | **$10,003,159** | **$ 3,159** | **$ 3,159** | **$ 3,159** | **$ 3,159** | **$ 3,159** | **$ 3,159** |
| **Total cash inflow** | **$10,149,802** | **$149,891** | **$ 149,981** | **$ 150,071** | **$ 150,160** | **$ 150,250** | **$ 150,340** |
| **Cash outflows** | | | | | | | |
| Repayment of principal | $ 0 | $ 0 | $ 0 | $ 0 | $ 0 | $ 0 | $ 0 |
| A/P decreases | $ 2,075 | $ 2,075 | $ 2,075 | $ 2,075 | $ 2,075 | $ 2,075 | $ 2,075 |
| A/R increases | $ 0 | $ 0 | $ 0 | $ 0 | $ 0 | $ 0 | $ 0 |
| Asset purchases | $ 9,405,000 | $ 0 | $ 0 | $ 0 | $ 0 | $ 0 | $ 0 |
| Dividends | $ 0 | $ 0 | $ 0 | $ 0 | $ 0 | $ 0 | $ 0 |
| **Total cash outflows** | **$ 9,407,075** | **$ 2,075** | **$ 2,075** | **$ 2,075** | **$ 2,075** | **$ 2,075** | **$ 2,075** |
| **Net cash flow** | **$ 742,727** | **$147,817** | **$ 147,906** | **$ 147,996** | **$ 148,086** | **$ 148,175** | **$ 148,265** |
| **Cash balance** | **$ 742,727** | **$890,544** | **$1,038,450** | **$1,186,446** | **$1,334,532** | **$1,482,707** | **$1,630,972** |

## Cash flow analysis (first year cont.)

| Month | 8 | 9 | 10 | 11 | 12 | 1 |
|---|---|---|---|---|---|---|
| Cash from operations | $ 147,271 | $ 147,361 | $ 147,450 | $ 147,540 | $ 147,630 | $ 1,765,638 |
| Cash from receivables | $ 0 | $ 0 | $ 0 | $ 0 | $ 0 | $ 0 |
| **Operating cash inflow** | **$ 147,271** | **$ 147,361** | **$ 147,450** | **$ 147,540** | **$ 147,630** | **$1,765,638** |
| **Other cash inflows** | | | | | | |
| Equity investment | $ 0 | $ 0 | $ 0 | $ 0 | $ 0 | $ 10,000,000 |
| Increased borrowings | $ 0 | $ 0 | $ 0 | $ 0 | $ 0 | $ 0 |
| Sales of business assets | $ 0 | $ 0 | $ 0 | $ 0 | $ 0 | $ 0 |
| A/P increases | $ 3,159 | $ 3,159 | $ 3,159 | $ 3,159 | $ 3,159 | $ 37,902 |
| **Total other cash inflows** | **$ 3,159** | **$ 3,159** | **$ 3,159** | **$ 3,159** | **$ 3,159** | **$10,037,902** |
| **Total cash inflow** | **$ 150,430** | **$ 150,519** | **$ 150,609** | **$ 150,699** | **$ 150,788** | **$11,803,540** |
| **Cash outflows** | | | | | | |
| Repayment of principal | $ 0 | $ 0 | $ 0 | $ 0 | $ 0 | $ 0 |
| A/P decreases | $ 2,075 | $ 2,075 | $ 2,075 | $ 2,075 | $ 2,075 | $ 24,897 |
| A/R increases | $ 0 | $ 0 | $ 0 | $ 0 | $ 0 | $ 0 |
| Asset purchases | $ 0 | $ 0 | $ 0 | $ 0 | $ 0 | $ 9,405,000 |
| Dividends | $ 0 | $ 0 | $ 0 | $ 0 | $1,412,510 | $ 1,412,510 |
| **Total cash outflows** | **$ 2,075** | **$ 2,075** | **$ 2,075** | **$ 2,075** | **$1,414,585** | **$10,842,407** |
| **Net cash flow** | **$ 148,355** | **$ 148,444** | **$ 148,534** | **$ 148,624** | **−$1,263,796** | **$ 961,133** |
| **Cash balance** | **$1,779,327** | **$1,927,771** | **$2,076,305** | **$2,224,929** | **$ 961,133** | **$ 961,133** |

## Cash flow analysis (second year)

| Quarter | Q1 | 2 Q2 | Q3 | Q4 | 2 |
|---|---|---|---|---|---|
| Cash from operations | $382,601 | $ 478,251 | $ 516,511 | $ 535,641 | $1,913,003 |
| Cash from receivables | $ 0 | $ 0 | $ 0 | $ 0 | $ 0 |
| **Operating cash inflow** | **$382,601** | **$ 478,251** | **$ 516,511** | **$ 535,641** | **$1,913,003** |
| **Other cash inflows** | | | | | |
| Equity investment | $ 0 | $ 0 | $ 0 | $ 0 | $ 0 |
| Increased borrowings | $ 0 | $ 0 | $ 0 | $ 0 | $ 0 |
| Sales of business assets | $ 0 | $ 0 | $ 0 | $ 0 | $ 0 |
| A/P increases | $ 8,717 | $ 10,897 | $ 11,769 | $ 12,204 | $ 43,587 |
| **Total other cash inflows** | **$ 8,717** | **$ 10,897** | **$ 11,769** | **$ 12,204** | **$ 43,587** |
| **Total cash inflow** | **$391,318** | **$ 489,148** | **$ 528,279** | **$ 547,845** | **$1,956,590** |
| **Cash outflows** | | | | | |
| Repayment of principal | $ 0 | $ 0 | $ 0 | $ 0 | $ 0 |
| A/P decreases | $ 5,975 | $ 7,469 | $ 8,067 | $ 8,365 | $ 29,876 |
| A/R increases | $ 0 | $ 0 | $ 0 | $ 0 | $ 0 |
| Asset purchases | $ 57,390 | $ 71,738 | $ 77,477 | $ 80,346 | $ 286,950 |
| Dividends | $306,080 | $ 382,601 | $ 413,209 | $ 428,513 | $1,530,402 |
| **Total cash outflows** | **$369,446** | **$ 461,807** | **$ 498,752** | **$ 517,224** | **$1,847,229** |
| **Net cash flow** | **$ 21,872** | **$ 27,340** | **$ 29,527** | **$ 30,621** | **$ 109,361** |
| **Cash balance** | **$983,005** | **$1,010,345** | **$1,039,873** | **$1,070,494** | **$1,070,494** |

## Cash flow analysis (third year)

| Quarter | Q1 | Q2 | Q3 | Q4 | 3 |
|---|---|---|---|---|---|
| Cash from operations | $ 414,812 | $ 518,515 | $ 559,996 | $ 580,736 | $2,074,058 |
| Cash from receivables | $ 0 | $ 0 | $ 0 | $ 0 | $ 0 |
| **Operating cash inflow** | **$ 414,812** | **$ 518,515** | **$ 559,996** | **$ 580,736** | **$2,074,058** |
| **Other cash inflows** | | | | | |
| Equity investment | $ 0 | $ 0 | $ 0 | $ 0 | $ 0 |
| Increased borrowings | $ 0 | $ 0 | $ 0 | $ 0 | $ 0 |
| Sales of business assets | $ 0 | $ 0 | $ 0 | $ 0 | $ 0 |
| A/P increases | $ 10,025 | $ 12,531 | $ 13,534 | $ 14,035 | $ 50,125 |
| **Total other cash inflows** | **$ 10,025** | **$ 12,531** | **$ 13,534** | **$ 14,035** | **$ 50,125** |
| **Total cash inflow** | **$ 424,837** | **$ 531,046** | **$ 573,530** | **$ 594,771** | **$2,124,184** |
| **Cash outflows** | | | | | |
| Repayment of principal | $ 0 | $ 0 | $ 0 | $ 0 | $ 0 |
| A/P decreases | $ 7,170 | $ 8,963 | $ 9,680 | $ 10,038 | $ 35,852 |
| A/R increases | $ 0 | $ 0 | $ 0 | $ 0 | $ 0 |
| Asset purchases | $ 62,222 | $ 77,777 | $ 83,999 | $ 87,110 | $ 311,109 |
| Dividends | $ 331,849 | $ 414,812 | $ 447,997 | $ 464,589 | $1,659,247 |
| **Total cash outflows** | **$ 401,241** | **$ 501,552** | **$ 541,676** | **$ 561,738** | **$2,006,207** |
| **Net cash flow** | **$ 23,595** | **$ 29,494** | **$ 31,854** | **$ 33,033** | **$ 117,977** |
| **Cash balance** | **$1,094,089** | **$1,123,583** | **$1,155,437** | **$1,188,470** | **$1,188,470** |

# Biodiesel Plant

Worthington Biofuels

11234 W. 53rd St.
New York, New York 10012

*BizPlanDB.com*

*Worthington Biofuels is a New York-based corporation that will produce and distribute biodiesel made from waste vegetable oils to its customers in its targeted market. The company was founded by Tad Worthington.*

## 1.0 EXECUTIVE SUMMARY

The purpose of this business plan is to raise $1,000,000 for the development of a biodiesel production facility while showcasing the expected financials and operations over the next three years. Worthington Biofuels is a New York-based corporation that will produce and distribute biodiesel made from waste vegetable oils to its customers in its targeted market. The company was founded by Tad Worthington.

### 1.1 The Biodiesel Products

As stated above, Worthington Biofuels will operate among two primary alternative energy units: biofuel production and delivery. The first aspect of the business operation, biofuel production, is readily becoming the number one alternative to standard diesel in the United States. Within many parts of the world, biofuel (also known as biodiesel) is a readily available diesel alternative that has gained wide acceptance. It is no secret that the world is facing an impending energy crisis and, now more than ever, it is imperative for countries and for-profit enterprises to develop methods for converting useable vegetables, oils, and feedstock for the production of usable (and easily transmittable) energies.

With the capital sought in this business plan, Worthington Biofuels will be able to develop its production and distribution capabilities with an expected output of 140,000 gallons per month.

The third section of the business plan will further describe the services offered by Worthington Biofuels.

### 1.2 Financing

Mr. Worthington is seeking to raise $1,000,000 from an investor for the development of Worthington Biofuels. On a preliminary basis, the investor will receive a 40 percent equity interest in the business along with a seat on the board of directors and regular dividend disbursements. The financing will be used for the following:

• Development of the Company's location

• Financing for the first six months of operation

• Capital to purchase the equipment and materials necessary to produce biodiesel

15

### 1.3 Mission Statement

The Company's goal is to develop and establish the methodology, technology, and physical plant required to process and convert large quantities of used oil into biodiesel. The Company is dedicated to providing the open market with a clean alternative form of energy for daily use among consumers.

### 1.4 Management Team

The company was founded by Tad Worthington. Mr. Worthington has more than 10 years of experience in the alternative energy industry. Through his expertise, he will be able to bring the operations of the business to profitability within its first year of operations.

### 1.5 Sales Forecasts

Mr. Worthington expects a strong rate of growth at the start of operations. Below are the expected financials over the next three years.

**Proforma profit and loss (yearly)**

| Year | 1 | 2 | 3 |
| --- | --- | --- | --- |
| Sales | $4,400,052 | $5,280,062 | $6,177,673 |
| Operating costs | $1,209,758 | $1,350,325 | $1,497,002 |
| EBITDA | $ 290,587 | $ 450,090 | $ 609,483 |
| Taxes, interest, and depreciation | $ 159,173 | $ 219,784 | $ 280,354 |
| Net profit | $ 131,414 | $ 230,306 | $ 329,130 |

**Sales, operating costs, and profit forecast**

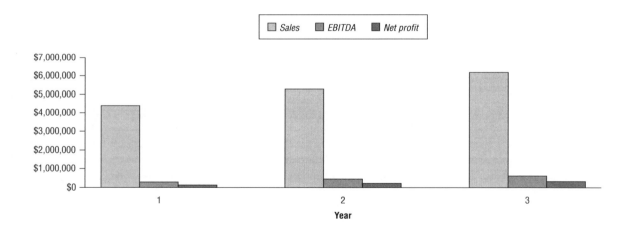

### 1.6 Expansion Plan

The Founder expects that the business will aggressively expand during the first three years of operation. Mr. Worthington intends to implement marketing campaigns that will effectively target individuals (that use diesel engines) and companies with large diesel fuel needs within the target market.

## 2.0 COMPANY AND FINANCING SUMMARY

### 2.1 Registered Name and Corporate Structure

Worthington Biofuels is registered as a corporation in the State of New York.

## 2.2 Required Funds

At this time, Worthington Biofuels requires $1,000,000 of equity funds. Below is a breakdown of how these funds will be used:

**Projected startup costs**

| | |
|---|---|
| Initial lease payments and deposits | $ 50,000 |
| Working capital | $ 300,000 |
| FF&E | $ 10,000 |
| Leasehold improvements | $ 75,000 |
| Security deposits | $ 25,000 |
| Insurance | $ 20,000 |
| Biodiesel producing equipment | $ 500,000 |
| Marketing budget | $ 17,500 |
| Miscellaneous and unforeseen costs | $ 2,500 |
| **Total startup costs** | **$1,000,000** |

**Use of funds**

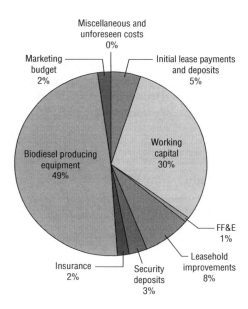

## 2.3 Investor Equity

At this time, Mr. Worthington is seeking to sell a 40 percent equity stake in exchange for the capital sought in this business plan. The investor will also receive a regular stream of dividends and a seat on the board of directors.

## 2.4 Management Equity

Tad Worthington currently owns 100 percent of Worthington Biofuels.

## 2.5 Exit Strategy

If the business is very successful, Mr. Worthington may seek to sell the business to a third party for a significant earnings multiple. Most likely, the Company will hire a qualified business broker to sell the business on behalf of Worthington Biofuels. Based on historical numbers, the business could fetch a sales premium of up to 10 times earnings.

## 3.0 PRODUCTS AND SERVICES

Below is a description of the biodiesel products offered by Worthington Biofuels.

### 3.1 Production of Biodiesel

After acquiring the input materials for biodiesel production, Management's plant employees will place them into a large reactor tank that is heated to 150 degrees Fahrenheit. Once the mixture of oil has been heated, it is transferred to a second reactor unit where the introduction of methanol occurs. These chemical injections are remotely controlled by the process computer. Methanol is added to the mix as a catalyst. Once the catalyst process is complete, glycerin is a gradually removed from the bottom of the tank while the biodiesel is allowed to react for two hours. From there, the final sediment is released.

The Company intends to produce 1,700,000 gallons or more of high purity biodiesel fuel per year at its facility, and Management anticipates that the total cost of production will be substantially less than the cost of conventional fossil fuels. Profits will be reinvested into the company to increase capacity as rapidly as possible. From the Company's initial production of biodiesel, the business was able to receive certification that the product produced by the Company complied with all ATSM D6751 standards, which is the benchmark set by the industry regarding the purity and quality of saleable biodiesel.

It should also be noted that at all times, the Company will adhere to all federal, state, and local laws regarding the safety of its facility. The Company will outsource a safety inspector that will regularly certify that all equipment and procedures used by the Company are to OSHA and state imposed safety standards. This is one of the top priorities of Management. The operational flow chart, procedural manuals, and other technical specifications/schematics are available upon request. For brevity, these items are documents separate to the business plan.

### 3.2 Distribution of Biodiesel Products

The secondary source of revenue will come from the distribution of biodiesel to farmers, government agencies, and businesses that have large diesel fuel needs. The Company will work with a contractor to deliver these products to their customers. The business will earn contribution margins of 20 percent on this aspect of the Company's distribution and logistics operations.

## 4.0 STRATEGIC AND MARKET ANALYSIS

### 4.1 Economic Outlook

This section of the analysis will detail the economic climate, the alternative fuel production industry, the customer profile, and the competition that the business will face as it progresses through its business operations.

The current geopolitical environment has led Management to believe that energy prices will continue to increase in the near future. The war in Iraq, faltering nuclear production talks with Iran, and general Middle Eastern instability has led many economists to believe that there is a fifteen to twenty percent risk premium now associated with the price of crude oil. While these issues bring worry to the general economy, Management sees a significant opportunity to enter the market with a source of alternative energy. Many politicians and special interest groups have promoted the development of alternative energy solutions to combat the continually increasing energy prices in the United States. As of 2014, the cost of energy products has reached all-time highs with moderate retractions in energy prices. Additionally, the fast growth of Asian nations (namely India and China) has prompted further increases in the global demand for energy. This trend is expected to continue in perpetuity.

Inflation is also concern for the company. As the inflation rate decreases, the purchasing power parity of the American dollar decreases in relation to other currencies. This may pose a significant risk to the company should rampant inflation, much like the inflation experienced in the late 1970s, occur again. This could negatively impact the cost of biodiesel.

As the company expands, Management intends to enact a number of strategies that will seek to protect the value of the biodiesel produced by the business. In the event that the cost of petrol based diesel fuel begins to fall and becomes cheaper in comparison to biofuel, the company may have trouble divesting its fuel inventories.

### 4.2 Industry Analysis

Biodiesel is completely interchangeable with conventional diesel fuel and heating oil, and the company's products will enter the existing energy market, perhaps the largest and most lucrative markets in the world. Over 55 billion gallons of diesel fuel were consumed in the United States last year, and demand is only increasing. As the prices of agricultural products continue to decline and the costs of fossil fuels continue to rise, it is natural to expect that an increasing share of the energy market will consider biofuel alternatives, and biodiesel is an efficient and economical substitute for diesel fuel.

Biodiesel energy can also be used for the direct heating of homes or the production of electricity via generators. As time continues, Management intends to inform the general public of biodiesel's ability to be used as for everyday energy consumption.

### 4.3 Customer Profile

The demand for Biofuel and biodiesel has risen among many industries as companies and government agencies look to reduce their energy expenditures. As such, the demand for these products is broad, and Management expects that it will receive biodiesel purchase orders from a number of transportation companies, transportation government agencies, farmers, and individuals seeking alternatives to traditional heating fuel.

### 4.4 Competition

At present time, biodiesel is available in the United States in limited quantities. However, several large oil refining and oil producing companies are beginning to enter the market with the development of expansive biodiesel production capabilities. As more agents enter the market, the company anticipates that pricing competition may occur.

Additional competition will stem from smaller farmers that intend to make moderate capital investments into developing small scale biodiesel production capabilities. However, many of these competitors will provide a very limited quantity of biodiesel, and they will not be able to benefit from the economies of scale that will be implemented by the company.

## 5.0 MARKETING PLAN

Worthington Biofuels intends to maintain an extensive marketing campaign that will ensure maximum visibility for the business in its targeted market. Below is an overview of the marketing strategies and objectives of Worthington Biofuels.

### 5.1 Marketing Objectives

- Develop an online presence by developing a website and placing the company's name and contact information with online directories

- Develop ongoing purchase order relationships with companies and government agencies that have large diesel fuel needs

## 5.2 Marketing Strategies

Currently, there are a number of organizations, including the National Biodiesel Board, that are pushing initiatives, lobbying legislatures, and informing the general public about the benefits about alternative biofuel-based energy products. Management feels that it is important to invest in these public relations campaigns (even though they will not affect direct sales) because in the future, the company may develop distribution networks that provide biodiesel directly to end users. Additionally, the increased awareness of biodiesel, its lower emissions, and ability to wean the United States off of foreign energy sources may prompt consumers and lawmakers to further expand the rebates, tax credits, and other incentive programs available for making biodiesel an economy viable energy product now and in the future. Approximately $10,000 per year will be spent to support these causes.

Mr. Worthington will regularly attend industry conventions, energy product trade shows, and other public relations campaigns will be enacted in order to promote the understanding of biodiesel to the general and business public.

Timely coverage of the company's alternative energy products will be further directed through ongoing press relations, news releases and feature stories targeted at key scientific and energy industry professionals.

## 5.3 Pricing

The company anticipates that it will receive approximately $70 per barrel of biodiesel produced. However, energy products, especially consumable fuel, are price elastic and volatile. The prices for energy are determined by a free market method, in most countries, and contracts representing an underlying amount of energy are traded on several international and national exchanges. This is accomplished through the sale of futures, options, and spot and forward contracts. Market shocks occur on a frequent basis with minor incidents causing tremendous volatility in the price of energy. The price of consumable fuel and related energy products is expected to continually increase as supplies and reserves of the resource are finite. Additionally, the fast growing Asian markets have driven up the price of energy significantly over the last two years. A moderate risk to the company is currency risk. Currently, almost all energy contracts are traded in denominations based on U.S. dollars and should this change, the company will have to develop strategies and methods that will reduce the currency exposure.

# 6.0 ORGANIZATIONAL PLAN AND PERSONNEL SUMMARY

## 6.1 Corporate Organization

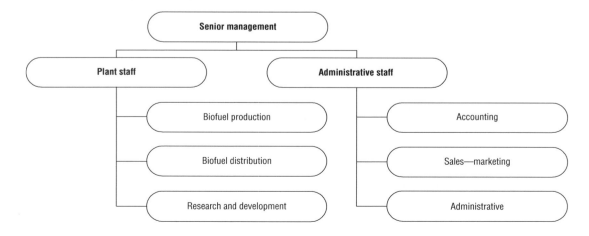

## 6.2 Organizational Budget

**Personnel plan—yearly**

| Year | 1 | 2 | 3 |
|------|---|---|---|
| Owner | $100,000 | $103,000 | $106,090 |
| Plant manager | $130,000 | $133,900 | $137,917 |
| Biodiesel plant employees | $232,000 | $298,700 | $369,193 |
| R&D and scientific staff | $130,000 | $133,900 | $137,917 |
| Administrative and accounting | $ 70,000 | $ 72,100 | $ 74,263 |
| **Total** | **$662,000** | **$741,600** | **$825,380** |

**Numbers of personnel**

| | | | |
|------|---|---|---|
| Owner | 1 | 1 | 1 |
| Plant manager | 2 | 2 | 2 |
| Biodiesel plant employees | 8 | 10 | 12 |
| R&D and scientific staff | 2 | 2 | 2 |
| Administrative and accounting | 2 | 2 | 2 |
| **Totals** | **15** | **17** | **19** |

**Personnel expense breakdown**

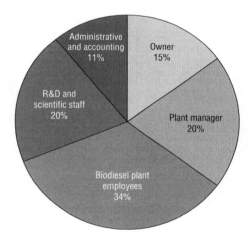

# 7.0 FINANCIAL PLAN

## 7.1 Underlying Assumptions

The company has based its proforma financial statements on the following:

- Worthington Biofuels will have an annual revenue growth rate of 16 percent per year.

- The owner will acquire $1,000,000 to develop the business.

- The investor(s) will receive a 40 percent equity interest in the business.

## 7.2 Sensitivity Analysis

The company's revenues are moderately sensitive to changes in the general economy. Biodiesel products are comparatively priced with their petroleum based counterparts, and in the event that oil prices decline, the company may have issues divesting its inventory of biodiesel products. However, the price of oil is expected to continue to climb as reserves are limited and the price of oil has increased significantly over the last two years. Only in the event of a steep drop in the price of petrol-based energy products does Management anticipate that the company will have issues regarding top line income.

## 7.3 Source of Funds

**Financing**

| | |
|---|---|
| **Equity contributions** | |
| Investor(s) | $ 1,000,000.00 |
|     **Total equity financing** | **$1,000,000.00** |
| **Banks and lenders** | |
|     **Total debt financing** | **$ 0.00** |
|     **Total financing** | **$1,000,000.00** |

## 7.4 General Assumptions

**General assumptions**

| Year | 1 | 2 | 3 |
|---|---|---|---|
| Short term interest rate | 9.5% | 9.5% | 9.5% |
| Long term interest rate | 10.0% | 10.0% | 10.0% |
| Federal tax rate | 33.0% | 33.0% | 33.0% |
| State tax rate | 5.0% | 5.0% | 5.0% |
| Personnel taxes | 15.0% | 15.0% | 15.0% |

## 7.5 Profit and Loss Statements

**Proforma profit and loss (yearly)**

| Year | 1 | 2 | 3 |
|---|---|---|---|
| **Sales** | **$4,400,052** | **$5,280,062** | **$6,177,673** |
| Cost of goods sold | $ 2,899,706 | $ 3,479,648 | $ 4,071,188 |
| Gross margin | 34.10% | 34.10% | 34.10% |
| **Operating income** | **$1,500,346** | **$1,800,415** | **$2,106,485** |
| **Expenses** | | | |
| Payroll | $ 662,000 | $ 741,600 | $ 825,380 |
| General and administrative | $ 61,200 | $ 63,648 | $ 66,194 |
| Marketing expenses | $ 44,001 | $ 52,801 | $ 61,777 |
| Professional fees and licensure | $ 25,219 | $ 25,976 | $ 26,755 |
| Insurance costs | $ 51,987 | $ 54,586 | $ 57,316 |
| Production expenses | $ 88,001 | $ 105,601 | $ 123,553 |
| Rent and utilities | $ 125,250 | $ 131,513 | $ 138,088 |
| Miscellaneous costs | $ 52,801 | $ 63,361 | $ 74,132 |
| Payroll taxes | $ 99,300 | $ 111,240 | $ 123,807 |
|     **Total operating costs** | **$1,209,758** | **$1,350,325** | **$1,497,002** |
| **EBITDA** | **$ 290,587** | **$ 450,090** | **$ 609,483** |
| Federal income tax | $ 95,894 | $ 148,530 | $ 201,129 |
| State income tax | $ 14,529 | $ 22,504 | $ 30,474 |
| Interest expense | $ 0 | $ 0 | $ 0 |
| Depreciation expenses | $ 48,750 | $ 48,750 | $ 48,750 |
| **Net profit** | **$ 131,414** | **$ 230,306** | **$ 329,130** |
| **Profit margin** | **2.99%** | **4.36%** | **5.33%** |

**Sales, operating costs, and profit forecast**

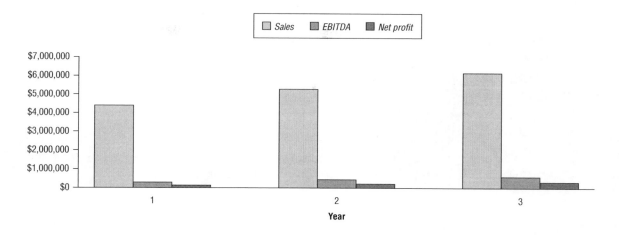

## 7.6 Cash Flow Analysis

**Proforma cash flow analysis—yearly**

| Year | 1 | 2 | 3 |
|---|---|---|---|
| Cash from operations | $ 180,164 | $279,056 | $377,880 |
| Cash from receivables | $ 0 | $ 0 | $ 0 |
| **Operating cash inflow** | **$ 180,164** | **$279,056** | **$377,880** |
| **Other cash inflows** | | | |
| Equity investment | $1,000,000 | $ 0 | $ 0 |
| Increased borrowings | $ 0 | $ 0 | $ 0 |
| Sales of business assets | $ 0 | $ 0 | $ 0 |
| A/P increases | $ 37,902 | $ 43,587 | $ 50,125 |
| **Total other cash inflows** | **$1,037,902** | **$ 43,587** | **$ 50,125** |
| **Total cash inflow** | **$1,218,066** | **$322,643** | **$428,005** |
| **Cash outflows** | | | |
| Repayment of principal | $ 0 | $ 0 | $ 0 |
| A/P decreases | $ 24,897 | $ 29,876 | $ 35,852 |
| A/R increases | $ 0 | $ 0 | $ 0 |
| Asset purchases | $ 682,500 | $ 69,764 | $ 94,470 |
| Dividends | $ 108,099 | $167,433 | $226,728 |
| **Total cash outflows** | **$ 815,496** | **$267,074** | **$357,049** |
| **Net cash flow** | **$ 402,571** | **$ 55,569** | **$ 70,956** |
| **Cash balance** | **$ 402,571** | **$458,140** | **$529,096** |

**Proforma cash flow (yearly)**

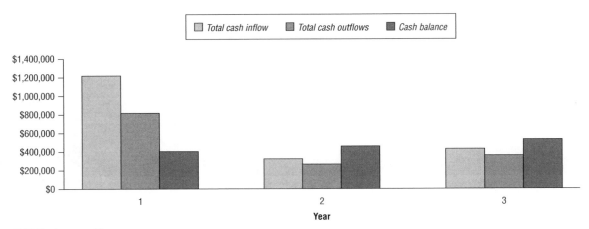

## 7.7 Balance Sheet

**Proforma balance sheet—yearly**

| Year | 1 | 2 | 3 |
|---|---|---|---|
| **Assets** | | | |
| Cash | $ 402,571 | $ 458,140 | $ 529,096 |
| Amortized development—expansion costs | $ 172,500 | $ 179,476 | $ 188,923 |
| Biofuel production assets | $ 500,000 | $ 552,323 | $ 623,175 |
| FF&E | $ 10,000 | $ 20,465 | $ 34,635 |
| Accumulated depreciation | ($ 48,750) | ($ 97,500) | ($ 146,250) |
| **Total assets** | **$1,036,321** | **$1,112,904** | **$1,229,579** |
| **Liabilities and equity** | | | |
| Accounts payable | $ 13,005 | $ 26,716 | $ 40,990 |
| Long term liabilities | $ 0 | $ 0 | $ 0 |
| Other liabilities | $ 0 | $ 0 | $ 0 |
| **Total liabilities** | **$ 13,005** | **$ 26,716** | **$ 40,990** |
| **Net worth** | **$1,023,316** | **$1,086,188** | **$1,188,590** |
| **Total liabilities and equity** | **$1,036,321** | **$1,112,904** | **$1,229,579** |

**Proforma balance sheet**

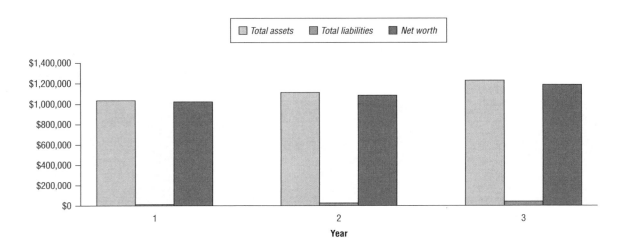

## 7.8 Breakeven Analysis

**Monthly break even analysis**

| Year | 1 | 2 | 3 |
|---|---|---|---|
| Monthly revenue | $ 295,654 | $ 330,007 | $ 365,854 |
| Yearly revenue | $3,547,849 | $3,960,088 | $4,390,246 |

**Break even analysis**

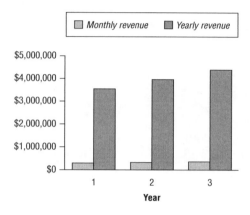

## 7.9 Business Ratios

**Business ratios—yearly**

| Year | 1 | 2 | 3 |
|---|---|---|---|
| **Sales** | | | |
| Sales growth | 0.00% | 20.00% | 17.00% |
| Gross margin | 34.10% | 34.10% | 34.10% |
| **Financials** | | | |
| Profit margin | 2.99% | 4.36% | 5.33% |
| Assets to liabilities | 79.69 | 41.66 | 30.00 |
| Equity to liabilities | 78.69 | 40.66 | 29.00 |
| Assets to equity | 1.01 | 1.02 | 1.03 |
| **Liquidity** | | | |
| Acid test | 30.96 | 17.15 | 12.91 |
| Cash to assets | 0.39 | 0.41 | 0.43 |

## 7.10 Three Year Profit and Loss Statement

### Profit and loss statement (first year)

| Months | 1 | 2 | 3 | 4 | 5 | 6 | 7 |
|---|---|---|---|---|---|---|---|
| **Sales** | **$366,000** | **$366,122** | **$366,244** | **$366,366** | **$366,488** | **$366,610** | **$366,732** |
| Cost of goods sold | $241,200 | $241,280 | $241,361 | $241,441 | $241,522 | $241,602 | $241,682 |
| Gross margin | 34.10% | 34.10% | 34.10% | 34.10% | 34.10% | 34.10% | 34.10% |
| **Operating income** | **$124,800** | **$124,842** | **$124,883** | **$124,925** | **$124,966** | **$125,008** | **$125,050** |
| **Expenses** | | | | | | | |
| Payroll | $ 55,167 | $ 55,167 | $ 55,167 | $ 55,167 | $ 55,167 | $ 55,167 | $ 55,167 |
| General and administrative | $ 5,100 | $ 5,100 | $ 5,100 | $ 5,100 | $ 5,100 | $ 5,100 | $ 5,100 |
| Marketing expenses | $ 3,667 | $ 3,667 | $ 3,667 | $ 3,667 | $ 3,667 | $ 3,667 | $ 3,667 |
| Professional fees and licensure | $ 2,102 | $ 2,102 | $ 2,102 | $ 2,102 | $ 2,102 | $ 2,102 | $ 2,102 |
| Insurance costs | $ 4,332 | $ 4,332 | $ 4,332 | $ 4,332 | $ 4,332 | $ 4,332 | $ 4,332 |
| Production expenses | $ 7,333 | $ 7,333 | $ 7,333 | $ 7,333 | $ 7,333 | $ 7,333 | $ 7,333 |
| Rent and utilities | $ 10,438 | $ 10,438 | $ 10,438 | $ 10,438 | $ 10,438 | $ 10,438 | $ 10,438 |
| Miscellaneous costs | $ 4,400 | $ 4,400 | $ 4,400 | $ 4,400 | $ 4,400 | $ 4,400 | $ 4,400 |
| Payroll taxes | $ 8,275 | $ 8,275 | $ 8,275 | $ 8,275 | $ 8,275 | $ 8,275 | $ 8,275 |
| **Total operating costs** | **$100,813** | **$100,813** | **$100,813** | **$100,813** | **$100,813** | **$100,813** | **$100,813** |
| **EBITDA** | **$ 23,987** | **$ 24,028** | **$ 24,070** | **$ 24,112** | **$ 24,153** | **$ 24,195** | **$ 24,236** |
| Federal income tax | $ 7,977 | $ 7,979 | $ 7,982 | $ 7,985 | $ 7,987 | $ 7,990 | $ 7,992 |
| State income tax | $ 1,209 | $ 1,209 | $ 1,209 | $ 1,210 | $ 1,210 | $ 1,211 | $ 1,211 |
| Interest expense | $ 0 | $ 0 | $ 0 | $ 0 | $ 0 | $ 0 | $ 0 |
| Depreciation expense | $ 4,063 | $ 4,063 | $ 4,063 | $ 4,063 | $ 4,063 | $ 4,063 | $ 4,063 |
| **Net profit** | **$ 10,739** | **$ 10,778** | **$ 10,816** | **$ 10,855** | **$ 10,893** | **$ 10,932** | **$ 10,970** |

### Profit and loss statement (first year cont.)

| Month | 8 | 9 | 10 | 11 | 12 | 1 |
|---|---|---|---|---|---|---|
| **Sales** | **$366,854** | **$366,976** | **$367,098** | **$367,220** | **$367,342** | **$4,400,052** |
| Cost of goods sold | $241,763 | $241,843 | $241,924 | $242,004 | $242,084 | $2,899,706 |
| Gross margin | 34.10% | 34.10% | 34.10% | 34.10% | 34.10% | 34.10% |
| **Operating income** | **$125,091** | **$125,133** | **$125,174** | **$125,216** | **$125,258** | **$1,500,346** |
| **Expenses** | | | | | | |
| Payroll | $ 55,167 | $ 55,167 | $ 55,167 | $ 55,167 | $ 55,167 | $ 662,000 |
| General and administrative | $ 5,100 | $ 5,100 | $ 5,100 | $ 5,100 | $ 5,100 | $ 61,200 |
| Marketing expenses | $ 3,667 | $ 3,667 | $ 3,667 | $ 3,667 | $ 3,667 | $ 44,001 |
| Professional fees and licensure | $ 2,102 | $ 2,102 | $ 2,102 | $ 2,102 | $ 2,102 | $ 25,219 |
| Insurance costs | $ 4,332 | $ 4,332 | $ 4,332 | $ 4,332 | $ 4,332 | $ 51,987 |
| Production expenses | $ 7,333 | $ 7,333 | $ 7,333 | $ 7,333 | $ 7,333 | $ 88,001 |
| Rent and utilities | $ 10,438 | $ 10,438 | $ 10,438 | $ 10,438 | $ 10,438 | $ 125,250 |
| Miscellaneous costs | $ 4,400 | $ 4,400 | $ 4,400 | $ 4,400 | $ 4,400 | $ 52,801 |
| Payroll taxes | $ 8,275 | $ 8,275 | $ 8,275 | $ 8,275 | $ 8,275 | $ 99,300 |
| **Total operating costs** | **$100,813** | **$100,813** | **$100,813** | **$100,813** | **$100,813** | **$1,209,758** |
| **EBITDA** | **$ 24,278** | **$ 24,320** | **$ 24,361** | **$ 24,403** | **$ 24,444** | **$ 290,587** |
| Federal income tax | $ 7,995 | $ 7,998 | $ 8,000 | $ 8,003 | $ 8,006 | $ 95,894 |
| State income tax | $ 1,211 | $ 1,212 | $ 1,212 | $ 1,213 | $ 1,213 | $ 14,529 |
| Interest expense | $ 0 | $ 0 | $ 0 | $ 0 | $ 0 | $ 0 |
| Depreciation expense | $ 4,063 | $ 4,063 | $ 4,063 | $ 4,063 | $ 4,063 | $ 48,750 |
| **Net profit** | **$ 11,009** | **$ 11,048** | **$ 11,086** | **$ 11,125** | **$ 11,163** | **$ 131,414** |

**Profit and loss statement (second year)**

| Quarter | Q1 | 2 Q2 | Q3 | Q4 | 2 |
|---|---|---|---|---|---|
| **Sales** | **$1,056,012** | **$1,320,016** | **$1,425,617** | **$1,478,417** | **$5,280,062** |
| Cost of goods sold | $ 695,930 | $ 869,912 | $ 939,505 | $ 974,301 | $ 3,479,648 |
| Gross margin | 34.10% | 34.10% | 34.10% | 34.10% | 34.10% |
| **Operating income** | **$ 360,083** | **$ 450,104** | **$ 486,112** | **$ 504,116** | **$1,800,415** |
| **Expenses** | | | | | |
| Payroll | $ 148,320 | $ 185,400 | $ 200,232 | $ 207,648 | $ 741,600 |
| General and administrative | $ 12,730 | $ 15,912 | $ 17,185 | $ 17,821 | $ 63,648 |
| Marketing expenses | $ 10,560 | $ 13,200 | $ 14,256 | $ 14,784 | $ 52,801 |
| Professional fees and licensure | $ 5,195 | $ 6,494 | $ 7,013 | $ 7,273 | $ 25,976 |
| Insurance costs | $ 10,917 | $ 13,647 | $ 14,738 | $ 15,284 | $ 54,586 |
| Production expenses | $ 21,120 | $ 26,400 | $ 28,512 | $ 29,568 | $ 105,601 |
| Rent and utilities | $ 26,303 | $ 32,878 | $ 35,508 | $ 36,824 | $ 131,513 |
| Miscellaneous costs | $ 12,672 | $ 15,840 | $ 17,107 | $ 17,741 | $ 63,361 |
| Payroll taxes | $ 22,248 | $ 27,810 | $ 30,035 | $ 31,147 | $ 111,240 |
| **Total operating costs** | **$ 270,065** | **$ 337,581** | **$ 364,588** | **$ 378,091** | **$1,350,325** |
| **EBITDA** | **$ 90,018** | **$ 112,522** | **$ 121,524** | **$ 126,025** | **$ 450,090** |
| Federal income tax | $ 29,706 | $ 37,132 | $ 40,103 | $ 41,588 | $ 148,530 |
| State income tax | $ 4,501 | $ 5,626 | $ 6,076 | $ 6,301 | $ 22,504 |
| Interest expense | $ 0 | $ 0 | $ 0 | $ 0 | $ 0 |
| Depreciation expense | $ 12,188 | $ 12,188 | $ 12,188 | $ 12,188 | $ 48,750 |
| **Net profit** | **$ 43,624** | **$ 57,576** | **$ 63,158** | **$ 65,948** | **$ 230,306** |

**Profit and loss statement (third year)**

| Quarter | Q1 | 3 Q2 | Q3 | Q4 | 3 |
|---|---|---|---|---|---|
| **Sales** | **$1,235,535** | **$1,544,418** | **$1,667,972** | **$1,729,748** | **$6,177,673** |
| Cost of goods sold | $ 814,238 | $ 1,017,797 | $ 1,099,221 | $ 1,139,933 | $ 4,071,188 |
| Gross margin | 34.10% | 34.10% | 34.10% | 34.10% | 34.10% |
| **Operating income** | **$ 421,297** | **$ 526,621** | **$ 568,751** | **$ 589,816** | **$2,106,485** |
| **Expenses** | | | | | |
| Payroll | $ 165,076 | $ 206,345 | $ 222,853 | $ 231,106 | $ 825,380 |
| General and administrative | $ 13,239 | $ 16,548 | $ 17,872 | $ 18,534 | $ 66,194 |
| Marketing expenses | $ 12,355 | $ 15,444 | $ 16,680 | $ 17,297 | $ 61,777 |
| Professional fees and licensure | $ 5,351 | $ 6,689 | $ 7,224 | $ 7,491 | $ 26,755 |
| Insurance costs | $ 11,463 | $ 14,329 | $ 15,475 | $ 16,048 | $ 57,316 |
| Production expenses | $ 24,711 | $ 30,888 | $ 33,359 | $ 34,595 | $ 123,553 |
| Rent and utilities | $ 27,618 | $ 34,522 | $ 37,284 | $ 38,665 | $ 138,088 |
| Miscellaneous costs | $ 14,826 | $ 18,533 | $ 20,016 | $ 20,757 | $ 74,132 |
| Payroll taxes | $ 24,761 | $ 30,952 | $ 33,428 | $ 34,666 | $ 123,807 |
| **Total operating costs** | **$ 299,400** | **$ 374,251** | **$ 404,191** | **$ 419,161** | **$1,497,002** |
| **EBITDA** | **$ 121,897** | **$ 152,371** | **$ 164,560** | **$ 170,655** | **$ 609,483** |
| Federal income tax | $ 40,226 | $ 50,282 | $ 54,305 | $ 56,316 | $ 201,129 |
| State income tax | $ 6,095 | $ 7,619 | $ 8,228 | $ 8,533 | $ 30,474 |
| Interest expense | $ 0 | $ 0 | $ 0 | $ 0 | $ 0 |
| Depreciation expense | $ 12,188 | $ 12,188 | $ 12,188 | $ 12,188 | $ 48,750 |
| **Net profit** | **$ 63,388** | **$ 82,282** | **$ 89,840** | **$ 93,619** | **$ 329,130** |

## 7.11 Three Year Cash Flow Analysis

### Cash flow analysis (first year)

| Month | 1 | 2 | 3 | 4 | 5 | 6 | 7 |
|---|---|---|---|---|---|---|---|
| Cash from operations | $ 14,802 | $ 14,840 | $ 14,879 | $ 14,917 | $ 14,956 | $ 14,994 | $ 15,033 |
| Cash from receivables | $ 0 | $ 0 | $ 0 | $ 0 | $ 0 | $ 0 | $ 0 |
| **Operating cash inflow** | **$ 14,802** | **$ 14,840** | **$ 14,879** | **$ 14,917** | **$ 14,956** | **$ 14,994** | **$ 15,033** |
| **Other cash inflows** | | | | | | | |
| Equity investment | $1,000,000 | $ 0 | $ 0 | $ 0 | $ 0 | $ 0 | $ 0 |
| Increased borrowings | $ 0 | $ 0 | $ 0 | $ 0 | $ 0 | $ 0 | $ 0 |
| Sales of business assets | $ 0 | $ 0 | $ 0 | $ 0 | $ 0 | $ 0 | $ 0 |
| A/P increases | $ 3,159 | $ 3,159 | $ 3,159 | $ 3,159 | $ 3,159 | $ 3,159 | $ 3,159 |
| **Total other cash inflows** | **$1,003,159** | **$ 3,159** | **$ 3,159** | **$ 3,159** | **$ 3,159** | **$ 3,159** | **$ 3,159** |
| **Total cash inflow** | **$1,017,960** | **$ 17,999** | **$ 18,037** | **$ 18,076** | **$ 18,114** | **$ 18,153** | **$ 18,191** |
| **Cash outflows** | | | | | | | |
| Repayment of principal | $ 0 | $ 0 | $ 0 | $ 0 | $ 0 | $ 0 | $ 0 |
| A/P decreases | $ 2,075 | $ 2,075 | $ 2,075 | $ 2,075 | $ 2,075 | $ 2,075 | $ 2,075 |
| A/R increases | $ 0 | $ 0 | $ 0 | $ 0 | $ 0 | $ 0 | $ 0 |
| Asset purchases | $ 682,500 | $ 0 | $ 0 | $ 0 | $ 0 | $ 0 | $ 0 |
| Dividends | $ 0 | $ 0 | $ 0 | $ 0 | $ 0 | $ 0 | $ 0 |
| **Total cash outflows** | **$ 684,575** | **$ 2,075** | **$ 2,075** | **$ 2,075** | **$ 2,075** | **$ 2,075** | **$ 2,075** |
| **Net cash flow** | **$ 333,385** | **$ 15,924** | **$ 15,963** | **$ 16,001** | **$ 16,040** | **$ 16,078** | **$ 16,117** |
| **Cash balance** | **$ 333,385** | **$349,309** | **$365,272** | **$381,273** | **$397,313** | **$413,391** | **$429,508** |

### Cash flow analysis (first year cont.)

| Month | 8 | 9 | 10 | 11 | 12 | 1 |
|---|---|---|---|---|---|---|
| Cash from operations | $ 15,071 | $ 15,111 | $ 15,149 | $ 15,187 | $ 15,226 | $ 180,164 |
| Cash from receivables | $ 0 | $ 0 | $ 0 | $ 0 | $ 0 | $ 0 |
| **Operating cash inflow** | **$ 15,071** | **$ 15,111** | **$ 15,149** | **$ 15,187** | **$ 15,226** | **$ 180,164** |
| **Other cash inflows** | | | | | | |
| Equity investment | $ 0 | $ 0 | $ 0 | $ 0 | $ 0 | $1,000,000 |
| Increased borrowings | $ 0 | $ 0 | $ 0 | $ 0 | $ 0 | $ 0 |
| Sales of business assets | $ 0 | $ 0 | $ 0 | $ 0 | $ 0 | $ 0 |
| A/P increases | $ 3,159 | $ 3,159 | $ 3,159 | $ 3,159 | $ 3,159 | $ 37,902 |
| **Total other cash inflows** | **$ 3,159** | **$ 3,159** | **$ 3,159** | **$ 3,159** | **$ 3,159** | **$1,037,902** |
| **Total cash inflow** | **$ 18,230** | **$ 18,270** | **$ 18,307** | **$ 18,346** | **$ 18,384** | **$1,218,066** |
| **Cash outflows** | | | | | | |
| Repayment of principal | $ 0 | $ 0 | $ 0 | $ 0 | $ 0 | $ 0 |
| A/P decreases | $ 2,075 | $ 2,075 | $ 2,075 | $ 2,075 | $ 2,075 | $ 24,897 |
| A/R increases | $ 0 | $ 0 | $ 0 | $ 0 | $ 0 | $ 0 |
| Asset purchases | $ 0 | $ 0 | $ 0 | $ 0 | $ 0 | $ 682,500 |
| Dividends | $ 0 | $ 0 | $ 0 | $ 0 | $108,099 | $ 108,099 |
| **Total cash outflows** | **$ 2,075** | **$ 2,075** | **$ 2,075** | **$ 2,075** | **$110,174** | **$ 815,496** |
| **Net cash flow** | **$ 16,155** | **$ 16,195** | **$ 16,232** | **$ 16,271** | **−$ 91,790** | **$ 402,571** |
| **Cash balance** | **$445,663** | **$461,858** | **$478,090** | **$494,361** | **$402,571** | **$ 402,571** |

## Cash flow analysis (second year)

| Quarter | Q1 | 2<br>Q2 | Q3 | Q4 | 2 |
|---|---|---|---|---|---|
| Cash from operations | $ 55,811 | $ 69,764 | $ 75,345 | $ 78,136 | $279,056 |
| Cash from receivables | $ 0 | $ 0 | $ 0 | $ 0 | $ 0 |
| **Operating cash inflow** | **$ 55,811** | **$ 69,764** | **$ 75,345** | **$ 78,136** | **$279,056** |
| **Other cash inflows** | | | | | |
| Equity investment | $ 0 | $ 0 | $ 0 | $ 0 | $ 0 |
| Increased borrowings | $ 0 | $ 0 | $ 0 | $ 0 | $ 0 |
| Sales of business assets | $ 0 | $ 0 | $ 0 | $ 0 | $ 0 |
| A/P increases | $ 8,717 | $ 10,897 | $ 11,769 | $ 12,204 | $ 43,587 |
| **Total other cash inflows** | **$ 8,717** | **$ 10,897** | **$ 11,769** | **$ 12,204** | **$ 43,587** |
| **Total cash inflow** | **$ 64,529** | **$ 80,661** | **$ 87,114** | **$ 90,340** | **$322,643** |
| **Cash outflows** | | | | | |
| Repayment of principal | $ 0 | $ 0 | $ 0 | $ 0 | $ 0 |
| A/P decreases | $ 5,975 | $ 7,469 | $ 8,067 | $ 8,365 | $ 29,876 |
| A/R increases | $ 0 | $ 0 | $ 0 | $ 0 | $ 0 |
| Asset purchases | $ 13,953 | $ 17,441 | $ 18,836 | $ 19,534 | $ 69,764 |
| Dividends | $ 33,487 | $ 41,858 | $ 45,207 | $ 46,881 | $167,433 |
| **Total cash outflows** | **$ 53,415** | **$ 66,768** | **$ 72,110** | **$ 74,781** | **$267,074** |
| **Net cash flow** | **$ 11,114** | **$ 13,892** | **$ 15,004** | **$ 15,559** | **$ 55,569** |
| **Cash balance** | **$413,685** | **$427,577** | **$442,581** | **$458,140** | **$458,140** |

## Cash flow analysis (third year)

| Quarter | Q1 | 3<br>Q2 | Q3 | Q4 | 3 |
|---|---|---|---|---|---|
| Cash from operations | $ 75,576 | $ 94,470 | $102,027 | $105,806 | $377,880 |
| Cash from receivables | $ 0 | $ 0 | $ 0 | $ 0 | $ 0 |
| **Operating cash inflow** | **$ 75,576** | **$ 94,470** | **$102,027** | **$105,806** | **$377,880** |
| **Other cash inflows** | | | | | |
| Equity investment | $ 0 | $ 0 | $ 0 | $ 0 | $ 0 |
| Increased borrowings | $ 0 | $ 0 | $ 0 | $ 0 | $ 0 |
| Sales of business assets | $ 0 | $ 0 | $ 0 | $ 0 | $ 0 |
| A/P increases | $ 10,025 | $ 12,531 | $ 13,534 | $ 14,035 | $ 50,125 |
| **Total other cash inflows** | **$ 10,025** | **$ 12,531** | **$ 13,534** | **$ 14,035** | **$ 50,125** |
| **Total cash inflow** | **$ 85,601** | **$107,001** | **$115,561** | **$119,841** | **$428,005** |
| **Cash outflows** | | | | | |
| Repayment of principal | $ 0 | $ 0 | $ 0 | $ 0 | $ 0 |
| A/P decreases | $ 7,170 | $ 8,963 | $ 9,680 | $ 10,038 | $ 35,852 |
| A/R increases | $ 0 | $ 0 | $ 0 | $ 0 | $ 0 |
| Asset purchases | $ 18,894 | $ 23,617 | $ 25,507 | $ 26,452 | $ 94,470 |
| Dividends | $ 45,346 | $ 56,682 | $ 61,216 | $ 63,484 | $226,728 |
| **Total cash outflows** | **$ 71,410** | **$ 89,262** | **$ 96,403** | **$ 99,974** | **$357,049** |
| **Net cash flow** | **$ 14,191** | **$ 17,739** | **$ 19,158** | **$ 19,868** | **$ 70,956** |
| **Cash balance** | **$472,331** | **$490,070** | **$509,228** | **$529,096** | **$529,096** |

# Bioterrorism Prevention Organization

Bioterrorism & Infections Prevention Organization

2307 Lincoln Ave., Suite 14
Charlottesville, Virginia 22902

*The BIPO is a private not-for-profit organization dedicated to the education and training of the public regarding bioterrorism prevention and response plans. The goal of the organization is to minimize the advantage of the potential effective use of any biological pathogen by terrorists through cultivating and enhancing our nation's public health infrastructure to ensure prompt identification of a threat and an appropriate response.*

*This business plan appeared in Business Plans Handbook, Volume 3. It has been updated for this volume.*

---

## EXECUTIVE SUMMARY

### Mission

The BIPO's (Bioterrorism & Infections Prevention Organization) mission is "to provide public health and healthcare facilities with the tools needed for preparedness, response, recovery, and mitigation of intentional or naturally occurring outbreaks."

### Organization Overview

The BIPO, a private not-for-profit organization dedicated to the education and training of the public regarding bioterrorism prevention and response plans, has been preparing for bioterrorism-type infections long before the events of September 11, 2001. However, after the events of September 11, 2001, bioterrorism awareness skyrocketed. It is for these reasons the Bioterrorism Department decided to expand its operations. The goal of the organization is to minimize the advantage of the potential effective use of any biological pathogen by terrorists through cultivating and enhancing our nation's public health infrastructure to ensure prompt identification of a threat and an appropriate response.

### Business Objectives

The primary objective is to come up with a marketing plan for multimedia informational software entitled, "Be Prepared for Bioterrorism." The marketing plan takes into consideration a multi-distribution channel approach, including e-commerce, along with partnering with other professional organizations in an attempt to get this information into the hands of as many public health professionals as possible.

### Current Product

The current product is narrative software which contains a bioterrorism preparation kit with a checklist for bioterrorism "readiness." The toolkit is customized by state and includes important emergency phone numbers along with other information on what to do in the case of a terrorist attack or viral outbreak.

### Advertising & Promotion

Advertising and promotion efforts will focus primarily on prospective customers over the Internet through various public health organizations such as the Professional Epidemiology Network, the National Disaster Medical Systems, the Infectious Disease Society of America, along with others. Promotions also will include ways to increase website traffic and will utilize mass mailings to target potential customers.

## PRESENT SITUATION

Currently the University of Virginia Bioterrorism Center is looking for a Business Plan or e-commerce solution for the University of Virginia School of Public Health that incorporates the delivery and sales of digital multimedia presentations that include information regarding bioterrorism preparation and response plans relayed over the Internet. This may include software downloads and apps for both Android and Apple products.

Presently, the School of Public Health is working with the Professional Epidemiology Network (PEN). PEN is a nonprofit, international organization that worked with the School of Public Health in putting together informational software on bioterrorism. It is being distributed as "Be Prepared for the Unexpected" and is currently available from PEN for $16 for members or $30 for non-members.

### Vision

Our vision is to provide a comprehensive and coordinated training and preparedness program across the full continuum of public health activities in the United States to protect Americans from both the intentional use of biological agents and emerging infections.

### Goals & Objectives

The objective of the plan will include documenting the necessary processes to distribute digital multi-media information through multiple distribution channels, including an "in-house" e-Commerce solution as well as apps for both Android and Apple devices.

The plan will include everything from the reproduction of the media, the presence on the Internet, to the plans for the distribution of product through various methods. Initial plans include what is necessary to distribute the media via Amazon.com, while researching other possible markets, and E-Commerce solutions.

## PRODUCT STRATEGY

Overall the product strategy is to deliver digital documentation and multimedia presentations via software and/or app downloads regarding bioterrorism preparedness and reaction plans. The initial product focuses on targeting public health professionals, infection control professionals, nurses, and physicians. Response plans address bioterrorism agents such as anthrax, smallpox, and plague and will include history, signs, symptoms, diagnosis, isolation, treatment, prophylaxis, and vaccination.

### Current Product Description

The current product is multimedia software/app that includes information and documents regarding bioterrorism readiness and response plans. The product includes clinical fact sheets on anthrax, smallpox, botulism, and plague. It also has fact sheets from the Center of Disease Control and information from the Department of Defense, as well as a Mass Casualty Disaster Plan Checklist.

PEN and the University of Virginia's School of Public Health estimate that over 90 percent of the population can view information on their computer, tablet, or phone. All forms of the software/apps also include downloadable files that should be printed so in the event of an actual bioterrorism attack, in which the Internet, telephones, libraries, or other means of gathering data may not be available, one would still have a hard copy of the pertinent information. This download includes some history and several photos of the various diseases themselves.

Maps are also included on the software/app with customized templates for bioterrorism readiness plans or "Templates for Healthcare Professionals." By clicking on a state, it will bring up a customized template for each state including important phone numbers such as the FBI and CDC emergency response offices.

## Upcoming New Products

The first title listed below is the first product in this effort and includes a collection of resources to assist a healthcare facility in bioterrorism preparedness. The others listed are new components in the pipeline, some of them recently completed. The primary focus and strategy of the other modules is to target other audiences with specific information pertaining to their area of expertise. Some of the modules are specific to a particular disease and include history, signs and symptoms, diagnosis, isolation, treatment, prophylaxis, and vaccination. See the chart below for specific information.

| Title | Audience | Content | Length of Completion | Estimated Date |
|---|---|---|---|---|
| Be Prepared for Bioterrorism | Infection control professionals | Collection of resources to assist a healthcare facility in bioterrorism preparedness. | N/A | Completed |
| Bioterrorism Agent Epidemiology: Anthrax Smallpox, and Plague | Nurses and infections control professionals | Bioterrorism preparedness and the epidemiology of three of CDC's category A agents: anthrax, smallpox, and plague. | 1 hour | Completed |
| Epidemiology of Anthrax | Physicians and nurse practitioners | History, signs and symptoms, diagnosis, isolation, treatment, prophylaxis, and vaccination. | 1 hour | 4/15/14 |
| Epidemiology of Smallpox | Physicians and nurse practitioners | History, signs and symptoms, diagnosis, isolation, treatment, prophylaxis and vaccination. | 1 hour | Undetermined (Summer 2014) |
| Epidemiology of Botulism and Tularemia | Physicians and nurse practitioners | History, signs and symptoms, diagnosis, isolation, treatment, prophylaxis and vaccination. | 1 hour | Undetermined (Fall 2014) |
| Epidemiology of Plague and Viral Hemorrhagic Fevers | Physicians and nurse practitioners | History, signs and symptoms, diagnosis, isolation, treatment, prophylaxis and vaccination. | 1 hour | Undetermined (Spring 2015) |
| Public Health preparedness | General public | Description of the role of the public health in the community and in bioterrorism preparedness. | 30 minutes | Completed |
| Bioterrorism Preparedness | Public health professionals | Bioterrorism threat analysis and history. | 1 hour | Completed |

## Research & Development

*Obtain Copyrights*—Information that is the exclusive property of the university is already covered by copyright law. However, it is not a bad idea to obtain an official copyright statement to have one on file.

For the modules that contain public data as well as that of the university, it may be possible to add value to the public information to the point a copyright can be obtained based on a "derivative work." That is if you "add value" to the product by perhaps adding an indexing system, or other way to retrieve the data through some sort of software or enhanced interface, the information as well as the software/app may be eligible to obtain an official copyright.

The current copyright filing fee is $65. See the United States Copyright Library of Congress at http://www.loc.gov/copyright/ for more information on copyrights.

### Delivery Modes

#### Digital Download of Software

The primary method of delivery will be through digital download through a dedicated web site. The website will be advertised on Google as well as on the University and PEN websites.

#### Apps available for Download

Apps for all Android and Apple products will also be available. The android version will be available via Google Play and those with Apple products will be able to purchase and download the app via the Apple Store.

Having all versions of the software available electronically will allow for easy and quick updates in both functionality and data. People will be able to have access to the most up-to-the-minute information available.

## MARKET ANALYSIS

The market will vary with the actual data that resides on the individual module. For the purposes of this plan we are focusing on "Be Prepared for Bioterrorism." As the other products are completed, it will need to be decided which of the following markets the product fits in and which markets to target. There will always be some overlap.

We have identified three distinct markets from which to work. The goal should be to work from the primary market and then expand into the secondary and tertiary markets as the organization evolves.

### General Market Definitions and Customer Profiles

#### Primary Market

This would include Infection Control Professionals, along with everyone directly involved in the Public Health Industry.

*Infection Control Professionals*— There are currently approximately 5,700 hospitals in the United States. Each one is by law required to have an Infection Control Professional on staff. Some of the smaller hospitals may share the position, whereas some of the larger hospitals may have more than one. On average it is about one per hospital. This is PEN's primary customer base.

*Public Health Professionals*—There are approximately 6,500 Public Health officers in the United States. The bioterrorism department has a list of the officers as many of them were involved in the initial technology survey sent out.

#### Secondary Market

This would include a subset of the entire Healthcare Industry. Since the Healthcare Industry is so broad, it would have to be segregated. It would include, but not be limited to, nurses, especially nurses within the Infection Control area. It would include first response Healthcare workers such as doctors and nurses that work in the emergency department. Furthermore, it would include students of infection control. Many of these individuals are members of the organizations listed in the Marketing Plan, and for the sake of concentration should be pursued directly through those organizations.

### Tertiary Market

Special modules could be tailored toward fire fighters, police officers, and other public "first" responders.

For fire fighters, the IAFF (International Association of Fire Fighters) would be an excellent place to pursue (http://www.iaff.org/). The IAFF represents more than 300,000 professional fire fighters and emergency medical personnel in the United States and Canada.

For police officers the best resource would be NAPO, or National Association of Police Officers, http://www.napo.org/. The NAPO is now the strongest unified voice supporting law enforcement officers in the United States. NAPO represents more than 240,000 sworn law enforcement officers.

This market also would include the general public. The general public should be pursued through ads and distribution on major websites, and good placement in Google and Bing.

## Competition

The primary competition for this software/app is the Center for Disease Control public domain data. However, this software/app does add value and puts all of the data in one place so you do not have to sift through the information. The CDC also does not offer information in video format.

## Risks

The "Be Prepared for Bioterrorism" software/app is not yet copyrighted. If you copyright it, then people shouldn't copy it, except in accordance with applicable laws. This risk will be mitigated as soon as the copyright is approved.

## Technology Access Survey Information

A survey by Philip J. Ferguson, Ph.D., and M.P.H. Associate Director of Science, was conducted to find out how many physicians have access to technology and the Internet, and how the physicians prefer to train. The results indicated that 98 percent of the healthcare workers surveyed had access to a computer/tablet and/or Android phone/iPhone.

The survey also indicated approximately 60 percent prefer training using computer software, and 40 percent preferred training on apps their other devices.

# MARKETING PLAN

The marketing plan proposed a multi-channel distribution approach. This means that BIPO will sell its products through a variety of outlets or channels in order to most efficiently get its products before the key markets. This initially includes direct sales through PEN and other professional organizations, as well as the BIPO e-commerce website, and sales through distribution on Google Play and Apple Store.

## Direct Sales Marketing Information

The goal of the direct marketing plan is to partner with other organizations that are "already in the business." This will give the university direct contact with the primary, secondary, and tertiary markets, and those most apt to purchase these types of materials.

The following organizations need to be contacted directly to find out about possible partnerships, web links, newsletter, and conference information. Many of these organizations hold regular conferences and exhibits. Information needs to be gathered as to what is necessary to get the software/apps promoted, possible product demonstrations, or trial versions.

Each of these organizations also has websites and it may be possible to add links from their website to the School of Public Health's Bioterrorism website.

| Organization | Description | Market | Numbers |
|---|---|---|---|
| PEN—Professional Epidemiology Network | Primary customer base is Infection Control Professionals and those interested in the Infection Control field. | Primary | Approximately 14,000 members. |
| APHA—American Public Health Association http://www.apha.org/ | An association of individuals and organizations working to improve the public's health and to achieve equity in health status for all. | Primary and secondary | 50,000 members from over 50 occupations of public health. |
| NDMS—National Disaster Medical System http://www.oep-ndms. dhhs.gov/index.html | The overall purpose of the NDMS is to establish a single, integrated national medical response capability for assisting state and local authorities in dealing with the medical and health effects of major disasters. | Primary, secondary, and tertiary | More than 7,000 physicians, nurses, paramedics, pharmacists, and other allied healthcare personnel serve as members of the NDMS disaster response teams. |
| IDSA—Infectious Disease Society of America http://www.idsociety.org/ | IDSA's mission is to promote and recognize excellence in patient care, education, research, public health, and the prevention of infectious diseases. | Primary and secondary | Annual conference held in October. October 2013 attendance approximately 3,500. |
| OPHS—Office of Public Health and Science, Department of Health and Human Services Services. http://www.surgeongeneral .gov/ophs/resource | OPHS serves as the Senior Advisor on U.S. public health and science issues to the Secretary of Health and Human This site has links to many public health office and organizations. | Primary, secondary, and tertiary | Many links and addresses to other public health offices. Emergency preparedness offices, etc. could be excellent for mass mailings. |
| NACCHO—National Association of County City Health Officials http://www.naccho.org/ | NACCHO provides education, information, and research, and technical assistance to local health departments and facilitates partnerships among local, state, and federal agencies in order to promote and strengthen public health. | Primary, secondary, and tertiary | Serves all of the nearly 3,000 local health departments nationwide. Approximately 500 attend the annual conference. |
| MMRS—Metropolitan Medical Response System. http://www.mmrs.hhs.gov/ | Managed by the Office of Emergency Preparedness (OEP). The primary focus is to develop or enhance existing emergency preparedness systems. The goal is to coordinate the efforts of local law enforcement, fire, HAZMAT, EMS, hospital, public health, and other personnel to improve response capabilities in the event of a terrorist attack. The number one goal is to integrate biological preparedness into the overall planning process. | Primary, secondary, and tertiary | Membership unknown, however, various events are held every month. Bioterrorism preparedness is a primary focus. |

## Commerce Marketing Strategy

This strategy depends on getting the BIPO name to individuals who are surfing the Internet and interested in bioterrorism. To give an indication of the current size of this audience, www.bioterrorism.uv.edu recorded 3,758 page views in the month of February. Of those, 2,7 81 were unique visitors and the average time spent looking was 2 minutes and 29 seconds (Information supplied by John Masterson, Webmaster, University of Virginia). Since the majority of page referrals come from search engines, especially from the first few entries returned from a search engine, it is important to be one of the first sites returned. At this point BIPO is doing quite well. See the results listed below when you search on the term "Bioterrorism" with the following search engines:

- Google.com—The Center for Disease Control comes up first and University of Virginia's website comes up as the second link on the search list

- Bing.com—University of Virginia comes up first

- Yahoo.com—University of Virginia comes up fourth

There are several techniques the center could use to build on this strategy, like finding similar words to search on to generate hits. See the examples below.

- Biological Warfare—Searched Google, first 50 hits and none of them were from the University of Virginia

- Anthrax—Searched Google, first 50 hits and none of them were from the University of Virginia

- Small Pox—Searched Google, first 50 hits had a University of Virginia pdf file posted; however, there was not a link to the university's website

The center also could partner with other organization websites with similar interests to set up links to the University of Virginia's website. Examples may include:

- Department of Defense

- Centers of Disease Control

- Other universities

- American Medical Association—This URL is an Index to Bioterrorism Resources and contains links to other Bioterrorism related sites. http://www.ama-assn.org/resources/doc/mss/toolkit_ bioterrorism.pdf

- Office of Public Health and Science—http://www.surgeongeneral.gov/ophs/

- Office of Emergency Preparedness—http://ndms.dhhs.gov/

**Google Play**
Requirements

- Register for a Google Play publisher account

- Set up a Google Wallet Merchant Account

- Test app quality

- Determine app's content rating, country distribution, and app size; app size cannot exceed 50 MB

- Confirm app's platform and screen compatibility ranges

- Determine cost and set prices

- Prepare promotional graphics, screenshots, and videos

- Build and upload the release

- Plan a beta release

- Complete the app's product details

- Publish the app

- Provide user support after launch

Pros

- No variable cost

- We are able to provide valuable updates quickly

- App will be available to large number of people

- We determine the price

- Payments are received monthly

- No credit card fees, hosting fees, or marketing fees

Cons

- Google only pays 70% of sales price

- There is a $25 fee to register an account

- You must deal on "their" terms

**Apple Store**
Requirements

- Register for the iOS Developer Program

- Develop the application with the iOS SDK

- Determine cost and set prices

- Test and debug the app on various devices to finalize the application

- Prepare promotional graphics, screenshots, and videos

- Distribute the app via the App Store

- Provide user support after launch

Pros

- No variable cost

- We are able to provide valuable updates quickly

- App will be available to large number of people

- We determine the price

- Payments are received monthly

- No credit card fees, hosting fees, or marketing fees

Cons

- Apple only pays 70% of sales price

- The iOS Developer Program costs $99/year

- You must deal on "their" terms

## Production

The School of Public Health's Bioterrorism department is working with PEN in programming the various versions of the information (software download, Google app and Apple app).

## SALES PROJECTIONS & PRICING STRATEGY

See below the multi-tiered pricing strategy and sales projection strategy. The current pricing strategy is priced somewhat low, and revolves a lot around PEN's current pricing structure. It is designed to try and get a fair price for the software/app, while offering discounts and quantity pricing to individuals that belong to professional health organizations.

### Pricing Strategy

This pricing strategy is based on attracting individuals that belong to various professional healthcare associations. Also included is "conference pricing," whereas it may be possible to give conference attendees promotional discounts. This would give the university an opportunity to get its name out there and generate more business for future products.

With the exception of the "conference pricing," the prices below are the same prices PEN is charging. However, as long as the products are not identical, it would be possible to have a higher base price. Since at this point the products are identical, it is recommended the university charge the same price as PEN.

| Pricing Method | Price | Description |
|---|---|---|
| Base price/nonmembership | $30.00 | This is the price to be charged to all individuals who are not members of the predetermined organizations. The Bioterrorism department will need to come up with the list of the organizations to which it wants to give the discount. |
| Membership pricing | $16.00 | Again, the Bioterrorism department will need to decide what organizations it wants to give discounts. It is recommended to give discounts to all organizations it is interested in partnering with. |
| Conference pricing | $12.00 | This is designed to sell the software/app in bulk. This will allow the department to make a profit, along with the hope of gaining a customer that will purchase future products such as CME credits, etc. |

## Sales Projection Method

Given there is not any historical data to project sales, a theoretical method was applied to all groups in the multi-distribution channel. That is a hypothetical "group member"/reachable ratio or "web visits"/sales ratio was used. That was based on a theoretical number of individuals that might possibly be reached within a given organization.

For instance, organizations such as APHA that have 50,000 members, the individuals are very spread out, thus harder to reach all 50,000. Therefore it was assigned a lower member/reachable ratio. Markets that are dense were assigned higher percentages, as it is easier to hit the masses all at once (i.e., if you could show your product at a conference, it would "hit" a very high percentage of the people).

From here an arbitrary number of 3 percent was assigned across the board. This number could be high for some markets, but is probably low for most. The theory is that of all the qualified individuals that actually see the product, 3 percent of them would buy it. In some of the organizations membership was unknown, therefore a conservative arbitrary number was applied. Again, this is a very conservative approach and focuses on making back expenditures, however, retains the flexibility for higher sales.

Please note: These numbers are based on one product only, "Be Prepared for Bioterrorism." As the product line expands, so will the markets and, therefore, so will the sales. Consequently, it is imperative to target the markets based on the current product line. See Appendix A for the actual numbers that were assigned.

## Sales Projection Summary

The sales projection summary in Appendix A totaled 1,818. This is the number of this particular software/app that is being used as a first-year baseline. Also, scenarios for various amounts of sales can be found in Appendix B.

For the purposes of this plan a baseline price of $20.00 per module has been established. That is an average sale price of the $30.00, $16.00 and $12.00 price points.

*Again, the reason for the above prices is because this is the exact price PEN is charging for the exact same software/app that in turn contains PEN references. If the Bioterrorism department modifies the software whereas it is a different software/app, and can obtain a copyright, the department will have much more flexibility over the price and how the software/app is sold.

## ORGANIZATION OVERVIEW

### Location

University of Virginia, School of Public Health

Center for the Study of Bioterrorism and Emerging Infections

Charlottesville, VA 22902

### Legal Business Description

University of Virginia, School of Public Health Center for the Study of Bioterrorism and Emerging Infections is a private not-for-profit organization dedicated to the education and training of the public regarding the Bioterrorism prevention and response plans.

### Management Team

Edward Delgado

Business Plan Developer

E-mail: edelgado@comcast.net

Pat Clebe, RN, MSN, CIC

Infectious Disease Specialist

E-mail: pclebe@uv.edu

R. John Kletcha, Ph.D., M.P.H.

Director

E-mail: rjkletcha@uv.edu

Amy Ruler, B.S.B.A.

Web Development Specialist/Business Manager

E-mail: aruler@uv.edu

Jerry S. Rutgers, M.P.H.

Associate Director of Management and Training

E-mail: jrutgers@uv.edu

James White, B.A.

Multimedia Developer

E-mail: jwhite@uv.edu

Philip J. Ferguson, Ph.D., M.P.H.

Associate Director of Science

E-mail: pjferguson@uv.edu

Lakeisha Walker, B.A.

Research Assistant

E-mail: lwalker@uv.edu

Daniel B. Portnoy, Ph.D., C.I.H.

Associate Professor in Environmental and Occupational Health

E-mail: portnoy@uv.edu

Tayanna Brown

Secretary/Receptionist

E-mail: tbrown@uv.edu

Michael V. Jennings, M.D.

Infectious Disease Consultant

Roy Jorgenson, Financial Coordinator

rjorgenson@uv.edu

## Strategic Alliances

PEN—Professional Epidemiology Network

1595 M Street, SW, Suite 400, Washington, D.C. 20005-4006, Telephone: 202-789-4590

Fax: 202-789-4599

PEN Company Overview—PEN is a multi-disciplinary, voluntary, international organization. PEN promotes wellness and prevents illness and infection worldwide by advancing healthcare epidemiology through education, collaboration, research, practice, and credentialing. PEN also offers courses that count towards Continuing Education (CE) credits.

PEN is also in the business of marketing information regarding healthcare and infection control. PEN handed out approximately 4,000 free "Be Prepared for Bioterrorism" module downloads at their 2013 "Annual Educational Conference." At this conference there was actually a specified section on Bioterrorism. This year's conference will be held in June and will include many of the same people that attended last year's conference; however, it will not contain a section on Bioterrorism.

The Director of Marketing at PEN, Jessica Blaine, has agreed to share marketing numbers and information with University of Virginia as both organizations have a common interest in marketing Education.

## APPENDIX A

Sales Projections from Sales Projection Summary. Results of Exact Sales Projection Method Used.

## 1st Year Sales Projections from Various Distribution Channels for "Be Prepared for Bioterrorism" module only

| Organization | Total number of members | Arbitrary estimated percentage to actually reach in market | Number of members actually reached based on the estimated % | Estimated number of projected sales based on sales of 3% of the market reached |
| --- | --- | --- | --- | --- |
| PEN—Approx. 4,000 members already have the software from the conference, this number has been deducted from the "Actual Number to Reach." | 14,000 | 75% | 7,500 | 225 |
| APHA—50,000 members from over 50 occupations of public health. Note: Not as much of a primary market as PEN. | 50,000 | 20% | 10,000 | 300 |
| NDMS—7,000+ physicians, nurses, paramedics, pharmacists, and other allied healthcare personnel serve as members of the NDMS disaster response teams. | 7,000 | 50% | 3,500 | 105 |
| IDSA—Annual Conference held in October. October 2013 attendance approx. 3,300. | 3,300 | 100% | 3,300 | 99 |
| OPHS—Serves as the Senior Advisor on public health and science issues to the Secretary of Health and Human Services. This site has links to many public health office and organizations. | unknown | unknown | unknown | 100 |
| NACCHO—Serves all of the nearly 3,000 local health departments nationwide. Approximately 500 attend the annual conference. | 3,000 | 100% | 3,000 | 90 |
| MMRS—Membership unknown; however, various events are held every month. Bioterrorism Preparedness is a primary focus. | unknown | unknown | unknown | 100 |
| BIPO—E-Commerce Marketing Strategy, based on web visits per month, total "visits" were multiplied by 12 to come up with an annual amount. Increased visits would mean increased sales. | 24,972 | 100% | 24,972 | 749 |
| Amazon.com | unknown | unknown | unknown | 50 |
| | | | **Total** | **1,818** |

## APPENDIX B

### Break Even/Profit Point Based on 1st Year's Estimated Sales

**Sales breakeven summary for initial module**

| | |
|---|---:|
| U-V's estimated average gross sale per module | $ 20.00 |
| **Total estimated gross sale per module** | **$ 20.00** |
| Less U-V's estimated cost per module (30% fees) | $ 6.00 |
| **Initial gross profit per module** | **$ 14.00** |
| **Less university expenses** | |
| Less 10% of gross profit per module goes to the school | 1.40 |
| Less 12% gross profit per module goes to the university | $ 1.68 |
| **78% goes to the School of Public Health = gross profit per module** | **10.92** |
| **Initial start-up cost** | |
| Estimated programming cost | $ 15,250.00 |
| Merchant's fees | $ 125.00 |
| **Total start-up cost** | **$15,375.00** |
| Number of modulesales necessary for the School of Public Health to break even | 1,408 |
| Initial number of estimated modules to be sold | 1,818 |
| Difference | +410 |
| **Net profit** | **$ 4,477.20** |

## APPENDIX C

### Profit/Loss Scenarios Based on Number of Modules Sold

| Profit/loss vs. sales | | 500 | 1,000 | 2,000 | 3,000 | 5,000 |
|---|---:|---:|---:|---:|---:|---:|
| U-V's estimated average gross sales per module | $ 20.00 | $ 10,000 | $20,000 | $40,000 | $60,000 | $100,000 |
| Total estimated gross sales per module | $ 20.00 | $ 10,000 | $20,000 | $40,000 | $60,000 | $100,000 |
| Less U-V's estimated cost per module | | | | | | |
| Initial gross profit per module | $ 14.00 | $ 7,000 | $14,000 | $28,000 | $42,000 | $ 70,000 |
| **Less university expenses** | | | | | | |
| Less 10% gross profit per module goes to the school | $ 1.40 | $ 700 | $ 1,400 | $ 2,800 | $ 4,200 | $ 7,000 |
| Less 12% gross profit per module goes to the university | $ 1.68 | $ 840 | $ 1,680 | $ 3,360 | $ 5,040 | $ 8,400 |
| 78% goes to the School of Public Health = gross profit per module | $ 10.92 | $ 5,460 | $10,920 | $21,840 | $32,760 | $ 54,600 |
| **Less initial start-up cost** | | | | | | |
| Estimated programming cost | $ 15,250 | $ 15,250 | $15,250 | $15,250 | $15,250 | $ 15,250 |
| Merchant's fees | $ 125 | $ 125 | $ 125 | $ 125 | $ 125 | $ 125 |
| **Profit/loss** | **−$15,364.08** | **−$9,915.00** | **−$ 4,455** | **$ 6,465** | **$17,385** | **$ 39,255** |

## APPENDIX D

### Website Disaster Recovery Considerations

Disaster Recovery—A contingency plan for the Bioterrorism website needs to be looked at. After all, we are talking about disasters. Various "what if" scenarios need to be taken into account and The School of

Public Health needs to decide what is mission critical and what still needs to function in a time of disaster. From there the school can decide the best option to pursue in the case of a disaster. Scenarios that should be taken into consideration are:

What if the website was hacked by a terrorist at the same time biological agents are released?

What if the data center or point where the server resides in Charlottesville is gone via a natural or intentional disaster?

What if Charlottesville, or the University of Virginia were gone? This also pertains to the CDC. Where would the public turn to for direction?

Although these are scenarios that may be unlikely, they need to be addressed and at least the appropriate risk assigned to them. People thought the World Trade Center bombing was unlikely as well. If it were not for contingency plan regulations mandated by the SEC, many of those companies may have not been able to do business for weeks or months.

Possible options could include a second data center or server setup at another site out-of-state. This could reside at another U-V location. This server could be used to do load balancing, or just used as a fail-over server in case of emergency.

Many third-party companies offer facilities that you can go to with your backups and restore your setup in a disaster mode. These types of companies supply floor space, servers, and network connections out-of-state that can be accessed in case of a disaster.

Either way the university needs to decide how important this is, research the cost, and do a cost benefit analysis for the various options.

## APPENDIX E

Summary of "To Do's" and Recommendations

1. Research the possibility of obtaining a copyright. This would require re-programming the software, removing the PEN segments and replacing them with the Bioterrorism department's material.

2. Add "hot links" to the software and apps that take the user back to the Bioterrorism website. This will help keep the website in front of the customer and allow them to view additional products.

3. Contact the organizations listed in Direct Sales and Marketing Information. Inquire about: Getting hot links from their website to the University of Virginia's Bioterrorism website. It may be necessary to add a link from your website to theirs; get key individuals sample copies of the software and apps and find out if their membership would be interested; see if they will sponsor something in their newsletters; inquire about upcoming conferences and find out what is necessary to exhibit the product.

4. Work on getting more words recognized on search engines. See BIPO E-Commerce Marketing Strategy.

5. Add another module to the product line tailored toward the "Tertiary" market, which includes fire fighters, police officers, and other public first responders. See General Market Definitions and Customer Profiles.

# Detective Agency

Barr Detective Agency

PO Box 2001
Grand Haven, MI 45533

*This business plan offers an excellent consideration of factors involved in starting an investigative practice. Unlike many other entrepreneurial ventures, this field needs to keep abreast of the changing legal climate. Changing regulations reform the marketplace, making it necessary for investigators to be aware of each new piece of legislation that impacts their clients and industry practices.*

*This business plan appeared in Business Plans Handbook, Volume 5. It has been updated for this volume.*

## BACKGROUND OF BUSINESS

Barr Detective Agency has been in business in various formats since October of 2008. The business name has changed several times to reflect the incorporation of the business and its partners. The name reverted back to Barr Detective Agency in 2013 and is currently operated as a sole proprietorship with the exclusive owner of the business being Glenn A. Barr. The business has been largely inactive for the last couple of years and is undergoing retooling of its sales efforts in order to become more active and profitable.

## BACKGROUND OF OWNER

The current owner of Barr Detective Agency is Glenn A. Barr. Mr. Barr is licensed as both a private investigator and security guard director in the State of Michigan. His background includes two years as a U.S. Army Military Police officer, three years as a practice investigator and district manager for Pinkerton's, Inc., and eight years of private practice investigation. His education includes graduating with honors from Central Michigan University and extensive graduate level training in both psychology and legal studies.

## MISSION AND STRATEGY

The mission of Barr Detective Agency is to offer first class corporate investigative and security services to the private sector in accordance with all applicable provisions of state law and the licensure authority of the Michigan State Police. The business is currently licensed and licensure itself is a valuable commodity within the state. The strategy of Barr Detective Agency will be to outsell its investigative counterparts through an innovative sales process that will be revealed in the marketing section of this plan.

## REGULATORY CONSIDERATIONS AND INSURANCE

In addition to the thorough screening that is required of all potential applicants, each business is required by statute to be bonded. The bonding for Barr Detective Agency currently exceeds the state mandated minimum and is set at $20,000. Liability insurance is also easily obtainable and affordable for this business because of the low exposure to litigation in the industry. There is one exception to this rule, however, and that is in loss prevention. Physically detaining shoplifters carries a high degree of risk and injury and lawsuits are more common in this one investigative service than in all others combined. Invasion of privacy lawsuits are minimal and are usually easily defeated if the investigator stays within prescribed guidelines. The granting of weapons permits is a significant factor in driving up the costs of liability insurance and should be avoided except for the most outstanding and reliable personnel in the organization. Even then, weapons training and restricted use will prevent a large number of liability problems down the road. Armed accounts only account for a small fraction of the investigative market and therefore should not be considered a significant weighting factor in terms of coverage.

## LICENSING AND MARKET EXCLUSIVITY

The competition among licensed private investigators is less than in many other businesses. The rigorous licensing and approval process is slow and arduous. Therefore, a dearth of would-be private investigators is kept from the market. Only the more serious individuals stand a realistic chance of surviving the screening process, which focuses heavily on provable experience dealing with the investigative laws in this state. The Private Investigator Licensing Act of 1963 erects a formidable barrier to licensing by requiring that each individual is separately licensed for either security or investigations, and not both. That means that each process is separate from the other and requires a completely different set of qualifications and experience. The main prerequisite for becoming a licensed private investigator is to have three years of investigative experience in the field prior to application. The same prerequisite applies to the security process as well. After this is accomplished, a thorough background check is performed on the individual seeking to become licensed. Very high standards are applied. In fact, the process is so stringent that a majority of licensed private investigators are ex-law enforcement officers of varying degrees. This is an advantage that I shall address more fully in the next section.

## GENERAL COMPETITIVE ANALYSIS

The competitive advantage alluded to in the previous section is simple. Since so many applicants and licensees in this state are ex-law enforcement officers, there is an utter lack of experienced business personnel in this field. Most law enforcement training is not geared towards business and the amount of inexperience in this aspect of the field is shocking. Since my skills were learned in a business environment, there is a decided edge in my favor in regard to business planning and development. Another distinct advantage is that because so much of the competition has already served in a career capacity, many of the investigators in the field are only part-time at best and do not take either the cases or the business seriously. There are other investigators in the field who come from either a loss prevention or private security background, and these competitors are more difficult to challenge.

## SPECIFIC COMPETITIVE ANALYSIS

The Knoll Group of New York City and Business Risk International the two premier investigative companies in the United States. Other national companies such as Pinkerton and Burns International provide investigative services to their manufacturing clients, but mostly on an ad hoc basis and not with investigative services being the beneficiary, but more as a peripheral service that helps them sell security services. There is surprisingly little in the way of national competition because the laws are so complex and difficult to apply on a broad scope. Further, there is the notion that the field of private investigation should be a small one, similar to a law firm. As such, most companies tend to be local and regional, covering three or fewer states. Here in Grand Haven, there are currently 7 agencies licensed to do business. Although that number appears quite high, there are very few agencies doing high volume work. With the exception of one agency, none of the other agencies are noteworthy. The one agency that is noteworthy is Fatmans. He has a well-run agency with an international reputation. He specializes primarily in marital investigations and is not considered a keen competitor.

## SERVICE OVERVIEW AND MARKET CONSIDERATIONS

Any private investigative company will usually offer a mix of services. Developing a portfolio of different services is especially helpful when laws change and enhance or eliminate the need for certain types of investigations. The field of private investigation offers a large array of possible services, which are explained in detail in the section that follows.

## STRENGTHS AND WEAKNESSES OF SERVICES OFFERED

### Insurance Investigations

The bread and butter of investigators throughout the United States. Barr Detective Agency is no exception. Worker's Compensation fraud referrals are the most common form of investigation that insurance companies request; however, there is still a great need for liability, fire, and accident reinvestigation cases as well. My agency is most experienced in the injury fraud type of case and it is so commonly requested that it should be considered a specialization.

### Background Investigations

Commonly only requested by corporations looking to hire applicants without a strong sense of who they are besides what is listed on their resume, background investigations can be lucrative assignments if obtained in volume. They are virtually useless sources of revenue as stand-alone cases. The reason for this is that a background check has a natural component of cost. To do a national criminal search requires an upfront cost as well as several other forms of credential verification. For this reason, only large background volume will produce decent net profile. The companies using background checks, to a large degree, also perform them in-house via their human resources department.

### Loss Prevention

Commonly known as store detective work. Many companies hire their own in-house investigator to perform this task, but there are still large chains that subcontract out this type of work. From the client's view, this is an advantageous relationship because the liability for a false arrest can be significantly shifted to a properly insured private investigation company. The work tends to be on an hourly basis, therefore earnings are limited. A large account, however, can generate sufficient revenue to allow for decent profit margins.

### Personal Protection

These accounts are accounts of opportunity. When developed, these are high paying accounts that can make up a significant portion of revenue in a short period of time. What is so appealing is that the person being protected needs a high degree of protection usually around the clock. Therefore, the rate of pay is high and is continuous as long as the individual needs protection. Some positions are full time, as with a celebrity, but most often personal protection assignments are short-lived and deal with a specific threat by some individual that provides a period of uncertainty that the target must endure. After the threat has been ended or minimized, the assignment is usually ended or phased out and the revenue stream is terminated. Sometimes, the perpetrator is apprehended immediately and no significant revenue is obtained. In either situation personal protection accounts are lucrative, but inherently unstable and it is best to avoid this type of assignment as a source for long-term gain. However, in the short-term, they are highly profitable.

## Store Testing

Also known as "mystery shopping." An excellent service comparable to background checks. Testing is performed by an operative working undercover as a normal customer. The store and its operations are reported on and a score affixed to determine the comparative value of the store. Testing must be performed in volume if it is to be profitable in any meaningful sense. Large accounts are known to exist in this field; however, they are difficult accounts to obtain by anything less than a national corporation.

## Domestics

This term refers to the type of cases that cover a broad array of individually ordered, noncommercial type of investigation. Also known as marital or spousal investigations, these are occasional sources of intermittent revenue. They have fallen out of favor in Michigan for a couple of reasons. One, because they are noncommercial, domestics are often simple information gathering, but sometimes clients wish the investigator to perform surveillance in an unlawful manner, such as tapping phones or harassing the individual. Because of this, liability exposure is greatly enhanced, in addition to the added threat posed by a hostile spouse who may act irrationally.

Secondly, the laws of this state preclude using evidence gathered in a divorce case because Michigan has no-fault divorce laws. In those states that still have partial fault divorce laws, the domestic market is seen as a key market. Until or unless the legal climate changes in Michigan, domestic cases should not be considered a strong source of revenue.

## Electronic Countermeasures and Debugging

This is an excellent side business with enormous profit potential. Here, the largest problem stems from the fact that a great deal of equipment is needed to perform this kind of high-tech electronic work. A spectrum frequency analyzer, a wall sweep unit, and a phone line tracer system are just some of the pieces of equipment needed to do a thorough job in this field. Some investigators have been known to buy a few gadgets and try to pass themselves off as electronic countermeasures specialists, but with limited success. This is an elite field and difficult to break into; average equipment costs approach $75,000. The one key factor which makes this field so attractive is the fact that billing for this type of service is in the $8,000 to $15,000 range per assignment and assignments are usually completed in a matter of two to three days.

## Process Serving

Process serving involves tracking down and giving individuals notice of court actions that are pending against them. They can be either very time-consuming or quick and easy, depending on the subject being served. These cases can be a profitable portion of any company's repertoire of investigative services. However, this service requires tremendous volume to be profitable and assignments have to be procured on an individual law firm basis. There are no national accounts for process serving anywhere in the country at the present time. Laws for each state are different and hence process serving is a local type of account, limiting the revenue which is capable of being generated.

## Internal Surveys/Undercover Investigations

Usually performed for large manufacturing companies that have internal drug or theft problems. As a source of revenue, these types of cases can be considered profitable; however, the true worth of a manufacturing client is not the revenue derived from this one form of limited investigation, but from the steady stream of other investigations that can springboard from a strong client relationship. Manufacturing companies need background checks, employee honesty determinations and host of smaller investigative services. Further, the manufacturing client is an ideal market for security services.

### Legal Investigations

Usually performed for litigators in large law firms. These types of investigations usually involve reconstructing accident scenes, as with insurance companies, or finding evidence to refute the opposing counsel's legal strategy. Evidence may be in the form of written statements or in the form of actual proof subject to chain of evidence requirements. These cases are usually profitable, but difficult to come by. They are cases of opportunity like some of the other cases mentioned here and that limits their usefulness.

## APPROACH TO THE MARKET

Considering all of the aforementioned market opportunities, it should be clear that the best approach to the market is through selling insurance investigative services. Therefore, the concentration of effort will take place in that market. The most common manner of approaching insurance agents is through direct sales. Sales letters followed up with phone contact serve as the best method of contacting those companies most likely to need investigative services. The S.I.U. unit of an insurance company is the ideal contact source and those companies which are most prone to use vendor private investigators can be located through the insurance underwriter's handbook. Direct sales will account for most of the sales effort of Barr Detective Agency.

## ADVERTISING

The advertising budget for Barr Detective Agency is small compared to some other service businesses for a good reason. Investigative clients are clients of opportunity. Normal retail advertising is not a solid approach, because most clients are gotten through word-of-mouth and only when they have a problem. Similar to the legal profession, the best cases are derived through the referral system. There are a couple of exceptions to this rule, and those exceptions are legal and insurance clientele. Insurance companies and law firms have a pressing need for investigative services on a regular basis. In fact, they are the only groups of commercial clients in the business. Therefore, any advertising strategy has to incorporate this factor as the main principle for advertising. Targeting law firms and insurance companies through trade publications provides an inherent advantage in strategic advertising because it allows the focus to be on two select groups and nowhere else. All other investigative accounts can have minimal advertising efforts directed at them without a significant impact on revenue.

## BUSINESS LOGISTICS

### Location

Barr Detective Agency can be run from a home office located in Grand Haven, Michigan. The office will be large enough to accommodate all the needs for running a medium-size investigative firm.

### Benefit

The advantages to working out of a home office are enormous. Without the expenditure of rent for office space, the business has a greatly improved chance for success.

### Minimal Overhead

Besides phone usage and other minor costs, overhead can be kept to an absolute minimum. There is no reason for any significant expenditure of revenue except for the cost of occasional equipment updates.

### Benefit

Having minimal overhead maximizes the chance for success.

### Equipment

All necessary equipment has been purchased and is available for use. The one equipment deficit would be in the area of surveillance camera equipment. The equipment on hand could be upgraded to utilize better technology that is now available.

### Benefit

A significant capital outlay can be avoided because the necessary equipment has already been procured.

## NOTES ON FINANCIAL INFORMATION

### Introduction

The following financial information is accurate as of fiscal year 2013. The information presented was prepared by an accounting firm using standard accounting principles. These figures have not been audited, but do represent the best information available at the time that it was gathered. Barr Detective Agency makes no other representations as to its value.

### Balance Sheet

The balance sheet statement is based on the third quarter performance of 2013 and includes the year ending statement as well.

### Profit and Loss Statement

The P and L statement is based on the third quarter performance of 2013 and includes the year ending statement as well.

# THIRD QUARTER AND YEAR END STATEMENTS

## Balance Sheet—Third Quarter July

**Current assets:**

| | | | |
|---|---|---|---|
| Cash in bank—checking | 4,083.651 | | |
| Cash in bank—payroll | 1,527.163 | | |
| Cash in bank—savings | 0.076 | | |
| **Total current assets** | | 8,923.464 | |

**Property and equipment:**

| | | | |
|---|---|---|---|
| Equipment | 8,856.147 | | |
| Accum. deprec—equipment | 5,969.667 | | |
| Furniture & fixtures | 815.936 | | |
| Accum. deprec—furn. & fix. | 815.936 | | |
| Vehicles | 19,000.000 | | |
| Accum. deprec.—vehicles | 7,590.500 | | |
| **Total property and equipment** | | 14,295.980 | |

**Other assets:**

| | | | |
|---|---|---|---|
| Photographic equipment | 1,482.627 | | |
| **Total other assets** | | 1,482.627 | |
| **Total assets** | | | 24,702.07 |

**Current liabilities:**

| | | | |
|---|---|---|---|
| American express | 1,799.490 | | |
| Payroll taxes payable | 7,506.558 | | |
| **Total current liabilities** | | 9,306.048 | |

**Non-current liabilities:**

| | | | |
|---|---|---|---|
| Note payable—beneficial nat'l | 765.757 | | |
| Note payable—Whirlpool fin. | 451.535 | | |
| Note payable—first of America | 668.648 | | |
| Note payable—officer | 437.000 | | |
| **Total non-current liabilities** | | 2,322.940 | |

**Equity:**

| | | | |
|---|---|---|---|
| Capital | 6,112.110 | | |
| Additional PIC—Barr | 10,483.330 | | |
| Additional PIC—Kearney | 3,998.797 | | |
| **Net income (loss)** | 12,700.660 | | |
| **Total equity** | | 13,073.080 | |
| **Total liabilities and equity** | | | 24,702.07 |

## Balance Sheet—Third Quarter August

**Current assets:**

| | | |
|---|---|---|
| Cash in bank—checking | $ 176.530 | |
| Cash in bank—payroll | 7,069.710 | |
| Cash in bank—savings | 0.076 | |
| Employee advances | 6,366.900 | |
| **Total current assets** | | **$13,613.22** |

**Property and equipment:**

| | | |
|---|---|---|
| Equipment | $9,346.350 | |
| Accum. deprec.—equipment | 5,969.670 | |
| Furniture & fixtures | 815.936 | |
| Accum. deprec.—furn. & fix. | 815.936 | |
| Vehicles | 19,000.000 | |
| Accum. deprec.—vehicles | 7,590.500 | |
| **Total property and equipment** | | **$14,786.18** |

**Other assets:**

| | | |
|---|---|---|
| Photographic equipment | $1,482.630 | |
| **Total other assets** | **$1,482.630** | |
| **Total assets** | | **$29,882.02** |

**Current liabilities:**

| | | |
|---|---|---|
| American express | $1,799.490 | |
| Payroll taxes payable | 9,515.410 | |
| **Total current liabilities** | | **$11,314.90** |

**Non-current liabilities:**

| | | |
|---|---|---|
| Note payable—beneficial nat'l | $ 765.760 | |
| Note payable—Whirlpool fin. | 352.735 | |
| Note payable—first of America | 668.648 | |
| Note payable—officer | 437.000 | |
| **Total non-current liabilities** | | **$ 2,224.14** |

**Equity:**

| | | | |
|---|---|---|---|
| Capital | −$6,112.110 | | |
| Additional PIC—Barr | 10,483.330 | | |
| Additional PIC—Kearney | −3,998.800 | | |
| **Net income (loss)** | 15,970.560 | | |
| **Total equity** | | **$16,342.98** | |
| **Total liabilities & equity** | | | **$29,882.02** |

## Balance Sheet—Third Quarter September

**Current assets:**

| | | | |
|---|---|---|---|
| Cash in bank—checking | $ 167.390 | | |
| Cash in bank—payroll | 244.340 | | |
| Cash in bank—savings | 0.076 | | |
| Employee advances | 6,366.900 | | |
| **Total current assets** | | $ 6,778.71 | |

**Property and equipment:**

| | | | |
|---|---|---|---|
| Equipment | $9,346.330 | | |
| Accum. deprec.—equipment | 5,969.670 | | |
| Furniture & fixtures | 815.936 | | |
| Accum. deprec.—furn. & fix. | 815.936 | | |
| Vehicles | 19,000.000 | | |
| Accum. deprec.—vehicles | 7,590.500 | | |
| **Total property and equipment** | | $14,786.18 | |

**Other assets:**

| | | | |
|---|---|---|---|
| Photographic equipment | $1,482.630 | | |
| **Total other assets** | | $ 1,482.63 | |
| **Total assets** | | | $23,047.51 |

**Current liabilities:**

| | | | |
|---|---|---|---|
| American express | $1,799.490 | | |
| Payroll taxes payable | 9,231.020 | | |
| **Total current liabilities** | | $11,030.51 | |

**Non-current liabilities:**

| | | | |
|---|---|---|---|
| Note payable—beneficial nat'l | 765.757 | | |
| Note payable—Whirlpool fin. | −27.265 | | |
| Note payable—first of America | 668.648 | | |
| Note payable—officer | 437.000 | | |
| **Total non-current liabilities** | | $ 1,844.14 | |

**Equity:**

| | | | |
|---|---|---|---|
| Capital | −$6,112.110 | | |
| Additional PIC—Barr | 11,171.130 | | |
| Additional PIC—Kearney | −3,998.800 | | |
| **Net income (loss)** | 9,112.650 | | |
| **Total equity** | | 10,172.87 | |
| **Total liabilities and equity** | | | $23,047.51 |

## Profit & Loss Statement—Third Quarter July

| | Current period | | Year to date | |
|---|---|---|---|---|
| **Sales:** | | | | |
| Sales | $22,790.330 | 100.00% | $130,952.140 | 100.00% |
| **Total sales** | **22,790.330** | **100.00** | **130,952.140** | **100.00** |
| **Selling expenses:** | | | | |
| Licenses, fees, & permits | 66.500 | 0.30 | 532.494 | 0.40 |
| Surveillance expense | 3,971.860 | 17.40 | 18,491.770 | 14.10 |
| **Total selling expenses** | **4,038.360** | **17.70** | **19,024.260** | **14.50** |
| **General & administrative:** | | | | |
| Wages | 6,240.930 | 27.40 | $ 27,835.820 | 21.30 |
| Auto expense | 4,446.000 | 19.50 | 13,411.470 | 10.20 |
| Bank charges | 225.454 | 1.00 | 597.854 | 0.50 |
| Advertising | | | 1,722.958 | 1.30 |
| Dues & subscriptions | | | 201.400 | 0.20 |
| Equipment rental | 570.000 | 2.50 | 3,261.450 | 2.50 |
| Lease payments | | | 76.000 | 0.10 |
| Insurance—workmans comp | 617.975 | 2.70 | 1,746.575 | 1.30 |
| Insurance—general | 334.400 | 1.50 | 2,604.620 | 2.00 |
| Insurance—auto | | | 1,143.876 | 0.90 |
| Legal & accounting | 313.500 | 1.40 | 3,183.600 | 2.40 |
| Miscellaneous expense | 587.518 | 2.60 | 2,391.760 | 1.80 |
| Office | 123.101 | 0.50 | 2,558.100 | 2.00 |
| Contract labor | 6,049.920 | 26.50 | 12,539.070 | 9.60 |
| Postage | | | 313.177 | 0.20 |
| Uniforms | 574.636 | 2.50 | 1,896.618 | 1.40 |
| Rent | | | 1553.250 | 1.20 |
| Repairs & maintenance | | | 766.973 | 0.60 |
| Supplies | 474.620 | 2.10 | 2,354.210 | 1.80 |
| Taxes—FICA & medicare | 477.470 | 2.10 | 2,124.010 | 1.60 |
| Taxes—MESC | 168.511 | 0.70 | 751.621 | 0.60 |
| Taxes—FUTA | 49.932 | 0.20 | 222.661 | 0.20 |
| Telephone | 1,226.108 | 5.40 | 11,639.740 | 8.90 |
| Answering service | | | 281.580 | 0.20 |
| Travel | | | 3,097.550 | 2.40 |
| Meals | | | 810.369 | 0.60 |
| **Total general & admin.** | **22,481.030** | **98.60** | **99,086.310** | **75.70** |
| **Net operating income (loss)** | **3,729.050** | **16.40** | **12,841.570** | **9.80** |
| **Other (income) and expenses:** | | | | |
| Fines & penalties | | | 140.980 | 0.10 |
| Interest income | | | ($ 0.080) | |
| **Total other (income) and exp** | | | **140.904** | **0.10** |
| **Net income (loss)** | | | | |
| **Before tax** | **(3,729.050)** | **(16.40)** | **12,700.660** | **9.70** |
| **Net income (loss)** | **(3,729.050)** | **(16.40)** | **$ 12,700.660** | **9.70%** |

## Profit & Loss Statement—Third Quarter August

| | Current period | | Year to date | |
|---|---|---|---|---|
| **Sales:** | | | | |
| Sales | $26,582.520 | 100.00% | $157,534.660 | 100.00% |
| **Total sales** | **26,582.520** | **100.00** | **157,534.660** | **100.00** |
| **Selling expenses:** | | | | |
| Licenses, fees, & permits | 38.000 | 0.10 | 570.494 | 0.40 |
| Surveillance expense | 3,504.490 | 13.20 | 21,996.260 | 14.00 |
| **Total selling expenses** | **3,542.493** | **13.30** | **22,566.760** | **14.30** |
| **General & administrative:** | | | | |
| Wages | 6,748.800 | 25.40 | 34,584.620 | 22.00 |
| Auto expense | 1,798.065 | 6.80 | 15,209.540 | 9.70 |
| Bank charges | 59.622 | 0.20 | 657.476 | 0.40 |
| Advertising | 190.000 | 0.70 | 1,912.960 | 1.20 |
| Dues & subscriptions | | | 201.400 | 0.10 |
| Equipment rental | 140.600 | 0.50 | 3,402.050 | 2.20 |
| Lease payments | | | 76.000 | |
| Insurance—workmans comp | | | 1,746.575 | 1.10 |
| Insurance—general | 334.172 | 1.30 | 2,938.790 | 1.90 |
| Insurnace—auto | | | 1,143.876 | 0.70 |
| Legal & accounting | 1,377.500 | 5.20 | 4,561.100 | 2.90 |
| Miscellaneous expense | 1,549.849 | 5.80 | 3,941.610 | 2.50 |
| Office | 366.624 | 1.40 | 2,924.730 | 1.90 |
| Contract labor | 2,969.700 | 11.20 | 15,508.770 | 9.80 |
| Postage | 56.430 | 0.20 | 369.607 | 0.20 |
| Uniforms | 874.000 | 3.30 | 2,770.620 | 1.80 |
| Rent | | | 1,553.250 | 1.00 |
| Repairs & maintenance | | | 766.973 | 0.50 |
| Supplies | 141.854 | 0.50 | 2,496.070 | 1.60 |
| Taxes—FICA & medicare | 516.325 | 1.90 | 2,640.340 | 1.70 |
| Taxes—MESC | 182.210 | 0.70 | 933.831 | 0.60 |
| Taxes—FUTA | 53.960 | 0.20 | 276.621 | 0.20 |
| Telephone | 1,621.194 | 6.10 | 13,260.940 | 8.40 |
| Answering service | | | 281.580 | 0.20 |
| Travel | | | 3,097.550 | 2.00 |
| Meals | | | 810.369 | 0.50 |
| **Total general & admin.** | **18,980.910** | **71.40** | **118,067.220** | **74.90** |
| **Net operating income (loss)** | **4,059.120** | **15.30** | **16,900.690** | **10.70** |
| **Other (income) and expenses:** | | | | |
| Fines & penalties | 789.222 | 3.00 | 930.202 | 0.60 |
| Interest income | | | ($ 0.080) | |
| **Total other (income) and expense** | **789.222** | **3.00** | **930.126** | **0.60** |
| **Net income (loss)** | | | | |
| **Before tax** | **3,269.900** | **12.30** | **15,970.560** | **10.10** |
| **Net income (loss)** | **$ 3,269.900** | **12.30%** | **$ 15,970.560** | **10.10%** |

## Profit & Loss Statement—Third Quarter September

| | Current period | | Year to date | |
|---|---|---|---|---|
| **Sales:** | | | | |
| Sales | $17,516.540 | 100.00% | 175,051.200 | 100.00% |
| **Total sales** | **17,516.540** | **100.00** | **175,051.200** | **100.00** |
| **Selling expenses:** | | | | |
| licenses, fees, & permits | | | 570.494 | 0.30 |
| Surveillance expense | 5,011.920 | 28.60 | 27,008.180 | 15.40 |
| **Total selling expenses** | **5,011.920** | **28.60** | **27,578.670** | **15.80** |
| **General & administrative:** | | | | |
| Wages | 5,878.130 | 33.60 | 40,462.740 | 23.10 |
| Auto expense | 1,319.455 | 7.50 | 16,528.990 | 9.40 |
| Bank charges | 128.459 | 0.70 | 785.935 | 0.40 |
| Advertising | | | 1,912.960 | 1.10 |
| Dues & subscriptions | | | 201.400 | 0.10 |
| Equipment rental | 274.075 | 1.60 | 3,676.120 | 2.10 |
| Lease payments | | | 76.000 | |
| Insurance—workmans comp | 1,260.175 | 7.20 | 3,006.750 | 1.70 |
| Insurance—general | 334.400 | 1.90 | 3,273.190 | 1.90 |
| Insurance—auto | | | 1,143.876 | 0.70 |
| Legal & accounting | 226.385 | 1.30 | 4,787.490 | 2.70 |
| Miscellaneous expense | 915.230 | 5.20 | 4,856.840 | 2.80 |
| Office | 341.962 | 20.00 | 3,266.690 | 1.90 |
| Contract labor | 1,686.630 | 9.60 | 17,195.400 | 9.80 |
| Postage | 95.513 | 0.50 | 465.120 | 0.30 |
| Uniforms | 115.311 | 0.70 | 2,885.930 | 1.60 |
| Rent | | | 1,553.250 | 0.90 |
| Repairs & maintenance | | | 766.973 | 0.40 |
| Supplies | 279.357 | 1.60 | 2,775.430 | 1.60 |
| Taxes—FICA & medicare | 449.673 | 2.60 | 3,090.010 | 1.80 |
| Taxes—MESC | 158.707 | 0.90 | 1,092.538 | 0.60 |
| Taxes—FUTA | 47.025 | 0.30 | 323.646 | 0.20 |
| Telephone | 3,038.690 | 17.30 | 16,299.630 | 9.30 |
| Answering service | | | 281.580 | 0.20 |
| Travel | 604.447 | 3.50 | 3,702.000 | 2.10 |
| Meals | 72.333 | 0.40 | 882.702 | 0.50 |
| **Total general & admin.** | **17,225.950** | **98.30** | **135,293.170** | **77.30** |
| **Net operating income (loss)** | **4,721.330** | **27.00** | **12,179.360** | **7.00** |
| **Other (income) and expenses:** | | | | |
| Fines & penalties | 2,136.590 | 12.20 | 3,066.790 | 1.80 |
| Interest income | | | ($0.080) | |
| **Total other (income) and exp** | **2,136.590** | **12.20** | **3,066.710** | **1.80** |
| **Net income (loss)** | | | | |
| **Before tax** | **−6,857.920** | **−39.20** | **9,112.650** | **5.20** |
| **Net income (loss)** | **−6,857.920** | **−39.20%** | **6,857.920** | **5.20%** |

## Balance Sheet Year Ending

**Current assets:**

| | | | |
|---|---|---|---|
| Cash in bank—checking | $ 62.590 | | |
| Cash in bank—payroll | 739.366 | | |
| Cash in bank—savings | 0.076 | | |
| Employee advances | 6,366.900 | | |
| **Total current assets** | | $ 7,168.93 | |

**Property and equipment:**

| | | | |
|---|---|---|---|
| Equipment | $9,346.350 | | |
| Accum. deprec.—equipment | 5,969.670 | | |
| Furniture & fixtures | 815.936 | | |
| Accum. deprec.—furn. & fix. | 815.936 | | |
| Vehicles | 19,000.000 | | |
| Accum. deprec.—vehicles | 7,590.500 | | |
| **Total property and equipment** | | $14,786.18 | |

**Other assets:**

| | | | |
|---|---|---|---|
| Notes receivable—Kearney | $6,786.690 | | |
| Suspense | $1,482.630 | | |
| **Total other assets** | | $ 8,269.31 | |
| **Total assets** | | | $30,224.42 |

**Liabilities and equity:**

**Current liabilities:**

| | | | |
|---|---|---|---|
| American express | $1,799.490 | | |
| Payroll taxes payable | 13,462.790 | | |
| **Total current liabilities** | | $15,262.28 | |

**Non-current liabilities:**

| | | | |
|---|---|---|---|
| Note payable—beneficial nat'l | 765.757 | | |
| Note payable—Whirlpool fin. | −232.465 | | |
| Note payable—first of America | 668.648 | | |
| Note payable—officer | 20,007.000 | | |
| **Total non-current liabilities** | | $21,208.94 | |

**Equity:**

| | | | |
|---|---|---|---|
| Capital | ($6,112.110) | | |
| Additional PIC—Barr | 11,459.740 | | |
| Additional PIC—Kearney | 2,787.890 | | |
| **Net income (loss)** | −14,382.320 | | |
| **Total equity** | | −6,246.80 | |
| **Total liabilities and equity** | | | $30,224.42 |

## Profit & Loss Year Ending

| | Current period | | Year to date | |
|---|---|---|---|---|
| **Sales:** | | | | |
| Sales | $17,703.540 | 100.00% | 203,754.400 | 100.00% |
| **Total sales** | **17,703.540** | **100.00** | **203,754.400** | **100.00** |
| **Selling expenses:** | | | | |
| Licenses, fees, & permits | 19.665 | 0.10 | 916.104 | 0.40 |
| Surveillance expense | 6,059.580 | 34.20 | 42,004.400 | 20.60 |
| **Total selling expenses** | **6,079.240** | **34.30** | **42,920.510** | **21.10** |
| **General & administrative:** | | | | |
| Wages | | | 53,783.700 | 26.40 |
| Auto expense | 1,406.000 | 7.90 | 19,606.990 | 9.60 |
| Bank charges | 147.250 | 0.80 | 983.269 | 0.50 |
| Advertising | | | 2,202.140 | 1.10 |
| Dues & subscriptions | | | 201.400 | 0.10 |
| Equipment rental | | | 3,801.520 | 1.90 |
| Lease payments | | | 76.000 | |
| Insurance—workman's comp. | | | 3,006.750 | 1.50 |
| Insurance—general | | | 3,282.000 | 1.60 |
| Insurance—auto | | | 1,143.876 | 0.60 |
| Legal & accounting | | | 5,167.490 | 2.50 |
| Miscellaneous expense | 245.100 | 0.30 | 5,344.760 | 2.60 |
| Office | 550.962 | 3.10 | 4,355.200 | 2.10 |
| Contract labor | 3,534.890 | 20.00 | 27,652.960 | 13.60 |
| Postage | 25.403 | 0.10 | 528.333 | 0.30 |
| Uniforms | 277.552 | 1.60 | 3,433.280 | 1.70 |
| Rent | | | 1,553.250 | 0.80 |
| Repairs & maintenance | | | 964.573 | 0.50 |
| Supplies | | | 3,394.010 | 1.70 |
| Taxes—FICA & medicare | | | 3,715.410 | 1.80 |
| Taxes—MESC | | | 1,452.208 | 0.70 |
| Taxes—FUTA | | | 1,225.823 | 0.60 |
| Telephone | 1,240.776 | 7.00 | 20,243.280 | 9.90 |
| Answering service | | | 281.580 | 0.10 |
| Travel | | | 4,449.020 | 2.20 |
| Meals | 52.060 | 0.30 | 1,096.262 | 0.50 |
| **Total general & admin.** | **7,290.000** | **41.20** | **173,285.040** | **85.00** |
| **Net operating income (loss)** | **4,334.300** | **24.50** | **−12,451.140** | **−6.10** |
| **Other (income) and expenses:** | | | | |
| Fines & penalties | | | 1,931.260 | 0.90 |
| Interest income | | | −$0.080 | |
| **Total other (income) and exp** | | | **1,931.180** | **0.90** |
| **Net income (loss)** | | | | |
| **Before tax** | **4,334.30** | **24.50** | **−14,382.320** | **−7.10** |
| **Net income (loss)** | **4,334.30** | **24.50%** | **−$14,382.320** | **−7.10%** |

# Event Planner

Ultimate Events

87712 E. Washington St.
New York, New York 11022

*BizPlanDB.com*

*Ultimate Events is a New York-based corporation that will provide event planning, design, and management services to customers in its targeted market. The company was founded by Doug Woods*

## 1.0 EXECUTIVE SUMMARY

The purpose of this business plan is to raise $100,000 for the development of an event planning and consulting firm while showcasing the expected financials and operations over the next three years. Ultimate Events is a New York-based corporation that will provide event planning, design, and management services to customers in its targeted market. The company was founded by Doug Woods.

### 1.1 The Services

As state above, Mr. Woods intends to arrange events that range from $7,500 to over $100,000. Ultimate Events will develop and manage each step and aspect of a client's event. Mr. Woods will personally manage every event that is hosted by the company.

For each event, the company will receive ten to twenty five percent of the aggregate budget for the event. This is a sliding scale, and as the event becomes more costly, the percentage fees received by Ultimate Events will decrease. The business will also receive per hour fees for services related to design and large scale event consulting.

The third section of the business plan will further describe the services offered by Ultimate Events.

### 1.2 Financing

Mr. Woods is seeking to raise $100,000 from a bank loan. The interest rate and loan agreement are to be further discussed during negotiation. This business plan assumes that the business will receive a 10-year loan with a 9 percent fixed interest rate. The financing will be used for the following:

• Development of the company's office and event planning location

• Financing for the first six months of operation

• Capital to purchase a company vehicle

Mr. Woods will contribute $10,000 to the venture.

### 1.3 Mission Statement

Mr. Woods's mission is to develop Ultimate Events into a premier event planning business within the target market.

### 1.4 Management Team

The company was founded by Doug Woods. Mr. Woods has more than 10 years of experience in the event management industry. Through his expertise, he will be able to bring the operations of the business to profitability within its first year of operations.

### 1.5 Sales Forecasts

Mr. Woods expects a strong rate of growth at the start of operations. Below are the expected financials over the next three years.

**Proforma profit and loss (yearly)**

| Year | 1 | 2 | 3 |
|---|---|---|---|
| Sales | $327,978 | $393,574 | $460,481 |
| Operating costs | $234,278 | $243,562 | $253,204 |
| EBITDA | $ 60,903 | $110,654 | $161,229 |
| Taxes, interest, and depreciation | $ 36,488 | $ 51,697 | $ 70,505 |
| Net profit | $ 24,415 | $ 58,957 | $ 90,725 |

**Sales, operating costs, and profit forecast**

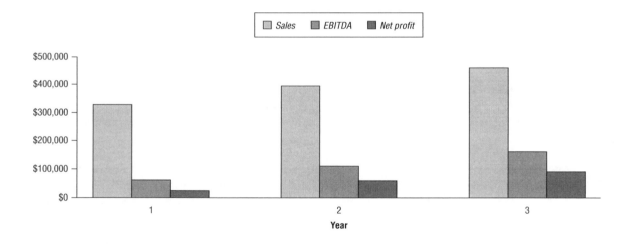

### 1.6 Expansion Plan

The Founder expects that the business will aggressively expand during the first three years of operation. Mr. Woods intends to implement marketing campaigns that will effectively target individuals, small businesses, and large corporations within the target market.

## 2.0 COMPANY AND FINANCING SUMMARY

### 2.1 Registered Name and Corporate Structure

Ultimate Events, Inc. is registered as a corporation in the State of New York.

## 2.2 Required Funds

At this time, Ultimate Events requires $100,000 of debt funds. Below is a breakdown of how these funds will be used:

**Projected startup costs**

| | |
|---|---|
| Initial lease payments and deposits | $ 10,000 |
| Working capital | $ 28,000 |
| FF&E | $ 17,000 |
| Leasehold improvements | $ 5,000 |
| Security deposits | $ 5,000 |
| Insurance | $ 2,500 |
| Company vehicle | $ 30,000 |
| Marketing budget | $ 7,500 |
| Miscellaneous and unforeseen costs | $ 5,000 |
| **Total startup costs** | **$110,000** |

**Use of funds**

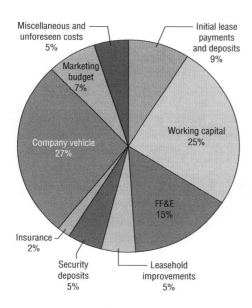

## 2.3 Investor Equity

Mr. Woods is not seeking an investment from a third party at this time.

## 2.4 Management Equity

Doug Woods owns 100 percent of Ultimate Events.

## 2.5 Exit Strategy

If the business is very successful, Mr. Woods may seek to sell the business to a third party for a significant earnings multiple. Most likely, the company will hire a qualified business broker to sell the business on behalf of Ultimate Events. Based on historical numbers, the business could fetch a sales premium of up to 4 times earnings.

# 3.0 PRODUCTS AND SERVICES

Below is a description of the planning and consulting services offered by Ultimate Events.

## 3.1 Event Planning and Management Services

The primary revenue source for the business will come from services related to planning and managing events including weddings, major anniversaries, Bar/Bat Mitzvahs, Sweet Sixteen parties, and corporate events. Mr. Woods will charge a percentage fee (10 to 25 percent on a sliding scale) depending on the size and scope of the event. Each aspect of the event will be managed by Mr. Woods and his staff. These services include the following:

- Catering selection and oversight

- Event management

- Music selection and management

- Payment arrangements

## 3.2 Consulting

The company will also generate secondary revenues from per hour consulting fees for people that are seeking general advice for their event. Management expects that 15 percent of the company's revenues will come from these services.

# 4.0 STRATEGIC AND MARKET ANALYSIS

## 4.1 Economic Outlook

This section of the analysis will detail the economic climate, the event planning industry, the customer profile, and the competition that the business will face as it progresses through its business operations.

Currently, the economic market condition in the United States is moderate. Many economists expect that this slower growth will continue for three years, at which point the economy will begin a prolonged normal growth period. This may present certain difficulties with revenue generation as people will spend less on their large scale events.

## 4.2 Industry Analysis

The U.S. Economic Census indicates that there are approximately 5,000 companies that specialize in event management. Each year, these businesses aggregately generate more than $5 billion dollars a year of revenue and provide jobs for more than 40,000 people. The growth of this industry has remained in lockstep with the growth of the economy in general. The number of businesses operating within this industry has increased 15 percent over last five years while gross receipts have increased almost two fold.

This industry has exploded as the economic tastes of Americans have changed significantly over the last five years as the overall wealth of the country has grown. As Americans now have more access to capital and an increased borrowing capacity, their ability to spend money on luxury items/services has also increased. With this, the number of people having extravagant and expensive events (including weddings) has had a marked increase over the last five years. In 2005, the average wedding (excluding transportation costs) exceeded $25,000. In the same year, Americans spend nearly $125 billion dollars on weddings. This trend is expected to continue as the economy remains strong.

## 4.3 Customer Profile

Ultimate Events anticipates that its average client will be a couple seeking to get married, a family planning a large gathering, or a corporation planning a large scale event for clients/employees. Management has outlined several demographics among its target client market, including the following:

- Has an annual household income of $50,000 or more

- Is seeking to spend approximately $20,000 on their event

- Between the ages of 21 and 60

- Among businesses, has revenues aggregately exceeding $1,000,00+ per year

### 4.4 Competition

Event planning is one of the most competitive business markets. This is primarily due to the fact that many people are interested in this field, and the high gross margins generated from these services draw many agents into the market. Ultimate Events, Inc. will benefit greatly from the highly experienced nature of its Owner, Doug Woods. Additionally, at the onset of operations, the business will reduce its fees in order to drive clients to the business.

## 5.0 MARKETING PLAN

Ultimate Events intends to maintain an extensive marketing campaign that will ensure maximum visibility for the business in its targeted market. Below is an overview of the marketing strategies and objectives of Ultimate Events.

### 5.1 Marketing Objectives

- Develop an online presence by developing a website and placing the company's name and contact information with online directories

- Implement a local campaign with the company's targeted market via the use of flyers, local newspaper advertisements, and word of mouth

- Establish relationships with banquet halls and country clubs within the target market

### 5.2 Marketing Strategies

Mr. Woods will promote the business through a number of traditional marketing and advertising channels. The foremost marketing strategy that the business will use is to develop connections with local banquet halls and hotels that outsource their event planning to third party event planners like the company. This will greatly decrease the amount of advertising required by the business as once a rapport is established with these vendors they will continually refer business to Mr. Woods.

The company will also maintain a strong level of print and media advertising among local newspapers, event planning publications, wedding publications, and other news medium. The business will also maintain listings in the local Yellow Books.

Ultimate Events will also use an Internet-based strategy. This is very important as many people seeking local services, such as event planners, now use the Internet to conduct their preliminary searches. Mr. Woods will register Ultimate Events with online portals so that potential customers can easily reach the business. The company will also develop its own online website, which will showcase the elegance of events that Ultimate Events can provide to its clients.

### 5.3 Pricing

Management anticipates that each event managed by the business will generate $2,500 to $20,000 for the business.

# 6.0 ORGANIZATIONAL PLAN AND PERSONNEL SUMMARY

## 6.1 Corporate Organization

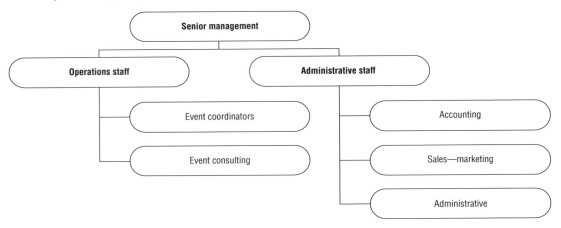

## 6.2 Organizational Budget

**Personnel plan—yearly**

| Year | 1 | 2 | 3 |
|---|---|---|---|
| Owner | $ 40,000 | $ 41,200 | $ 42,436 |
| Assistant manager | $ 29,000 | $ 29,870 | $ 30,766 |
| Event coordinators | $ 48,000 | $ 49,440 | $ 50,923 |
| Bookkeeper (P/T) | $ 9,000 | $ 9,270 | $ 9,548 |
| Administrative (P/T) | $ 17,000 | $ 17,510 | $ 18,035 |
| **Total** | **$143,000** | **$147,290** | **$151,709** |

**Numbers of personnel**

| | | | |
|---|---|---|---|
| Owner | 1 | 1 | 1 |
| Assistant manager | 1 | 1 | 1 |
| Event coordinators | 2 | 2 | 2 |
| Bookkeeper (P/T) | 1 | 1 | 1 |
| Administrative (P/T) | 1 | 1 | 1 |
| **Totals** | **6** | **6** | **6** |

**Personnel expense breakdown**

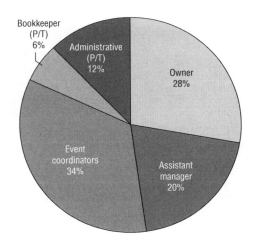

# 7.O FINANCIAL PLAN

## 7.1 Underlying Assumptions

The company has based its proforma financial statements on the following:

- Ultimate Events will have an annual revenue growth rate of 16 percent per year

- The Owner will acquire $100,000 of debt funds to develop the business

- The loan will have a 10 year term with a 9 percent interest rate

## 7.2 Sensitivity Analysis

The business's revenues are somewhat sensitive to the overall condition of the economic markets. In the event of a steep economic decline, Management expects that its revenue will decrease as people host smaller scale events at less expensive venues. In the event of a decline in revenues, the business will be able to maintain profitability because the business generates significantly high gross margins.

## 7.3 Source of Funds

**Financing**

| | |
|---|---|
| **Equity contributions** | |
| Management investment | $  10,000.00 |
| **Total equity financing** | **$  10,000.00** |
| **Banks and lenders** | |
| Banks and lenders | $100,000.00 |
| **Total debt financing** | **$100,000.00** |
| **Total financing** | **$110,000.00** |

## 7.4 General Assumptions

**General assumptions**

| Year | 1 | 2 | 3 |
|---|---|---|---|
| Short term interest rate | 9.5% | 9.5% | 9.5% |
| Long term interest rate | 10.0% | 10.0% | 10.0% |
| Federal tax rate | 33.0% | 33.0% | 33.0% |
| State tax rate | 5.0% | 5.0% | 5.0% |
| Personnel taxes | 15.0% | 15.0% | 15.0% |

## 7.5 Profit and Loss Statements

**Proforma profit and loss (yearly)**

| Year | 1 | 2 | 3 |
|---|---|---|---|
| **Sales** | **$327,978** | **$393,574** | **$460,481** |
| Cost of goods sold | $ 32,798 | $ 39,357 | $ 46,048 |
| Gross margin | 90.00% | 90.00% | 90.00% |
| **Operating income** | **$295,180** | **$354,216** | **$414,433** |
| **Expenses** | | | |
| Payroll | $143,000 | $147,290 | $151,709 |
| General and administrative | $ 25,200 | $ 26,208 | $ 27,256 |
| Marketing expenses | $ 1,640 | $ 1,968 | $ 2,302 |
| Professional fees and licensure | $ 5,219 | $ 5,376 | $ 5,537 |
| Insurance costs | $ 11,987 | $ 12,586 | $ 13,216 |
| Travel and vehicle costs | $ 7,596 | $ 8,356 | $ 9,191 |
| Rent and utilities | $ 14,250 | $ 14,963 | $ 15,711 |
| Miscellaneous costs | $ 3,936 | $ 4,723 | $ 5,526 |
| Payroll taxes | $ 21,450 | $ 22,094 | $ 22,756 |
| **Total operating costs** | **$234,278** | **$243,562** | **$253,204** |
| **EBITDA** | **$ 60,903** | **$110,654** | **$161,229** |
| Federal income tax | $ 20,098 | $ 33,832 | $ 50,741 |
| State income tax | $ 3,045 | $ 5,126 | $ 7,688 |
| Interest expense | $ 8,738 | $ 8,131 | $ 7,468 |
| Depreciation expenses | $ 4,607 | $ 4,607 | $ 4,607 |
| **Net profit** | **$ 24,415** | **$ 58,957** | **$ 90,725** |
| **Profit margin** | **7.44%** | **14.98%** | **19.70%** |

**Sales, operating costs, and profit forecast**

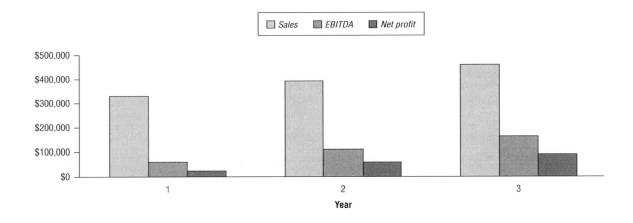

## 7.6 Cash Flow Analysis

**Proforma cash flow analysis—yearly**

| Year | 1 | 2 | 3 |
|---|---|---|---|
| Cash from operations | $ 29,022 | $ 63,564 | $ 95,332 |
| Cash from receivables | $ 0 | $ 0 | $ 0 |
| **Operating cash inflow** | **$ 29,022** | **$ 63,564** | **$ 95,332** |
| **Other cash inflows** | | | |
| Equity investment | $ 10,000 | $ 0 | $ 0 |
| Increased borrowings | $100,000 | $ 0 | $ 0 |
| Sales of business assets | $ 0 | $ 0 | $ 0 |
| A/P increases | $ 37,902 | $ 43,587 | $ 50,125 |
| Total other cash inflows | **$147,902** | **$ 43,587** | **$ 50,125** |
| Total cash inflow | **$176,924** | **$107,151** | **$145,457** |
| **Cash outflows** | | | |
| Repayment of principal | $ 6,463 | $ 7,070 | $ 7,733 |
| A/P decreases | $ 24,897 | $ 29,876 | $ 35,852 |
| A/R increases | $ 0 | $ 0 | $ 0 |
| Asset purchases | $ 64,500 | $ 8,474 | $ 13,140 |
| Dividends | $ 18,047 | $ 45,195 | $ 70,079 |
| Total cash outflows | **$113,907** | **$ 90,616** | **$126,804** |
| **Net cash flow** | **$ 63,017** | **$ 16,536** | **$ 18,654** |
| **Cash balance** | **$ 63,017** | **$ 79,552** | **$ 98,206** |

**Proforma cash flow (yearly)**

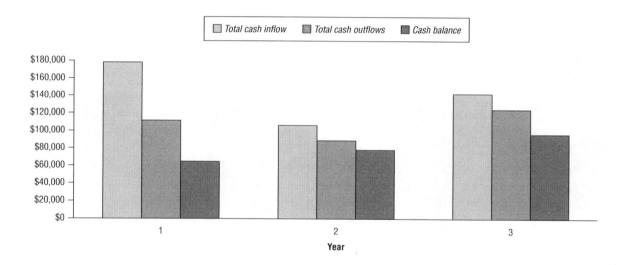

## 7.7 Balance Sheet

**Proforma balance sheet—yearly**

| Year | 1 | 2 | 3 |
|---|---|---|---|
| **Assets** | | | |
| Cash | $ 63,017 | $ 79,552 | $ 98,206 |
| Amortized development/expansion costs | $ 17,500 | $ 22,584 | $ 30,468 |
| Company vehicle | $ 30,000 | $ 32,119 | $ 35,403 |
| FF&E | $ 17,000 | $ 18,271 | $ 20,242 |
| Accumulated depreciation | ($ 4,607) | ($ 9,214) | ($ 13,821) |
| **Total assets** | **$122,910** | **$143,312** | **$170,499** |
| **Liabilities and equity** | | | |
| Accounts payable | $ 13,005 | $ 26,716 | $ 40,990 |
| Long term liabilities | $ 93,537 | $ 86,467 | $ 79,397 |
| Other liabilities | $ 0 | $ 0 | $ 0 |
| **Total liabilities** | **$106,542** | **$113,183** | **$120,387** |
| **Net worth** | **$ 16,368** | **$ 30,129** | **$ 50,112** |
| **Total liabilities and equity** | **$122,910** | **$143,312** | **$170,499** |

**Proforma balance sheet**

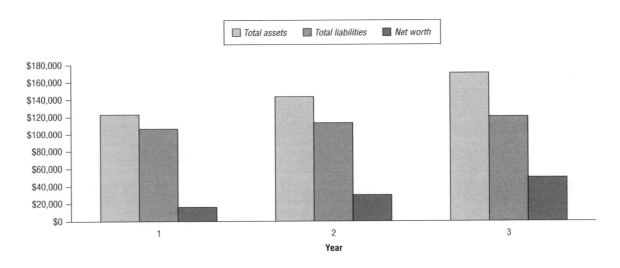

## 7.8 Breakeven Analysis

**Monthly break even analysis**

| Year | 1 | 2 | 3 |
|---|---|---|---|
| Monthly revenue | $ 21,692 | $ 22,552 | $ 23,445 |
| Yearly revenue | $260,308 | $270,625 | $281,338 |

**Break even analysis**

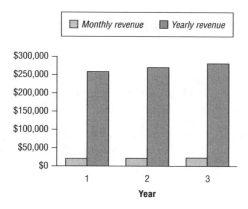

## 7.9 Business Ratios

**Business ratios—yearly**

| Year | 1 | 2 | 3 |
|---|---|---|---|
| **Sales** | | | |
| Sales growth | 00.00% | 20.00% | 17.00% |
| Gross margin | 90.00% | 90.00% | 90.00% |
| **Financials** | | | |
| Profit margin | 7.44% | 14.98% | 19.70% |
| Assets to liabilities | 1.15 | 1.27 | 1.42 |
| Equity to liabilities | 0.15 | 0.27 | 0.42 |
| Assets to equity | 7.51 | 4.76 | 3.40 |
| **Liquidity** | | | |
| Acid test | 0.59 | 0.70 | 0.82 |
| Cash to assets | 0.51 | 0.56 | 0.58 |

## 7.10 Three Year Profit and Loss Statement

**Profit and loss statement (first year)**

| Months | 1 | 2 | 3 | 4 | 5 | 6 | 7 |
|---|---|---|---|---|---|---|---|
| **Sales** | **$26,600** | **$ 26,733** | **$26,866** | **$26,999** | **$27,132** | **$ 27,265** | **$27,398** |
| Cost of goods sold | $ 2,660 | $ 2,673 | $ 2,687 | $ 2,700 | $ 2,713 | $ 2,727 | $ 2,740 |
| Gross margin | 90.0% | 90.00% | 90.00% | 90.00% | 90.00% | 90.00% | 90.00% |
| **Operating income** | **$23,940** | **$24,060** | **$24,179** | **$24,299** | **$24,419** | **$24,539** | **$24,658** |
| **Expenses** | | | | | | | |
| Payroll | $11,917 | $ 11,917 | $11,917 | $11,917 | $11,917 | $ 11,917 | $11,917 |
| General and administrative | $ 2,100 | $ 2,100 | $ 2,100 | $ 2,100 | $ 2,100 | $ 2,100 | $ 2,100 |
| Marketing expenses | $ 137 | $ 137 | $ 137 | $ 137 | $ 137 | $ 137 | $ 137 |
| Professional fees and licensure | $ 435 | $ 435 | $ 435 | $ 435 | $ 435 | $ 435 | $ 435 |
| Insurance costs | $ 999 | $ 999 | $ 999 | $ 999 | $ 999 | $ 999 | $ 999 |
| Travel and vehicle costs | $ 633 | $ 633 | $ 633 | $ 633 | $ 633 | $ 633 | $ 633 |
| Rent and utilities | $ 1,188 | $ 1,188 | $ 1,188 | $ 1,188 | $ 1,188 | $ 1,188 | $ 1,188 |
| Miscellaneous costs | $ 328 | $ 328 | $ 328 | $ 328 | $ 328 | $ 328 | $ 328 |
| Payroll taxes | $ 1,788 | $ 1,788 | $ 1,788 | $ 1,788 | $ 1,788 | $ 1,788 | $ 1,788 |
| **Total operating costs** | **$19,523** | **$ 19,523** | **$19,523** | **$19,523** | **$19,523** | **$19,523** | **$19,523** |
| **EBITDA** | **$ 4,417** | **$ 4,537** | **$ 4,656** | **$ 4,776** | **$ 4,896** | **$ 5,015** | **$ 5,135** |
| Federal income tax | $ 1,630 | $ 1,638 | $ 1,646 | $ 1,654 | $ 1,663 | $ 1,671 | $ 1,679 |
| State income tax | $ 247 | $ 248 | $ 249 | $ 251 | $ 252 | $ 253 | $ 254 |
| Interest expense | $ 750 | $ 746 | $ 742 | $ 738 | $ 734 | $ 730 | $ 726 |
| Depreciation expense | $ 384 | $ 384 | $ 384 | $ 384 | $ 384 | $ 384 | $ 384 |
| **Net profit** | **$ 1,406** | **$ 1,520** | **$ 1,634** | **$ 1,749** | **$ 1,863** | **$ 1,977** | **$ 2,092** |

## Profit and loss statement (first year cont.)

| Month | 8 | 9 | 10 | 11 | 12 | 1 |
|---|---|---|---|---|---|---|
| **Sales** | **$27,531** | **$27,664** | **$27,797** | **$27,930** | **$28,063** | **$327,978** |
| Cost of goods sold | $ 2,753 | $ 2,766 | $ 2,780 | $ 2,793 | $2,806 | $ 32,798 |
| Gross margin | 90.00% | 90.00% | 90.00% | 90.00% | 90.00% | 90.00% |
| **Operating income** | **$24,778** | **$24.898** | **$25,017** | **$25,137** | **$25,257** | **$295,180** |
| **Expenses** | | | | | | |
| Payroll | $11,917 | $11,917 | $11,917 | $11,917 | $11,917 | $143,000 |
| General and administrative | $ 2,100 | $ 2,100 | $ 2,100 | $ 2,100 | $ 2,100 | $ 25,200 |
| Marketing expenses | $ 137 | $ 137 | $ 137 | $ 137 | $ 137 | $ 1,640 |
| Professional fees and licensure | $ 435 | $ 435 | $ 435 | $ 435 | $ 435 | $ 5,219 |
| Insurance costs | $ 999 | $ 999 | $ 999 | $ 999 | $ 999 | $ 11,987 |
| Travel and vehicle costs | $ 633 | $ 633 | $ 633 | $ 633 | $ 633 | $ 7,596 |
| Rent and utilities | $ 1,188 | $ 1,188 | $ 1,188 | $ 1,188 | $ 1,188 | $ 14,250 |
| Miscellaneous costs | $ 328 | $ 328 | $ 328 | $ 328 | $ 328 | $ 3,936 |
| Payroll taxes | $ 1,788 | $ 1,788 | $ 1,788 | $ 1,788 | $ 1,788 | $ 21,450 |
| **Total operating costs** | **$19,523** | **$19,523** | **$19,523** | **$19,523** | **$19,523** | **$234,278** |
| **EBITDA** | **$ 5,255** | **$ 5,374** | **$ 5,494** | **$ 5,614** | **$ 5,734** | **$ 60,903** |
| Federal income tax | $ 1,687 | $ 1,695 | $ 1,703 | $ 1,711 | $ 1,720 | $ 20,098 |
| State income tax | $ 256 | $ 257 | $ 258 | $ 259 | $ 261 | $ 3,045 |
| Interest expense | $ 722 | $ 718 | $ 714 | $ 710 | $ 706 | $ 8,738 |
| Depreciation expense | $ 384 | $ 384 | $ 384 | $ 384 | $ 384 | $ 4,607 |
| **Net profit** | **$ 2,206** | **$ 2,320** | **$ 2,435** | **$ 2,549** | **$ 2,664** | **$ 24,415** |

## Profit and loss statement (second year)

| Quarter | Q1 | 2<br>Q2 | Q3 | Q4 | 2 |
|---|---|---|---|---|---|
| **Sales** | **$78,715** | **$98,393** | **$106,265** | **$110,201** | **$393,574** |
| Cost of goods sold | $ 7,871 | $ 9,839 | $ 10,626 | $ 11,020 | $ 39,357 |
| Gross margin | 90.00% | 90.00% | 90.00% | 90.00% | 90.00% |
| **Operating income** | **$70,843** | **$88,554** | **$ 95,638** | **$ 99,181** | **$354,216** |
| **Expenses** | | | | | |
| Payroll | $29,458 | $36,823 | $ 39,768 | $ 41,241 | $147,290 |
| General and administrative | $ 5,242 | $ 6,552 | $ 7,076 | $ 7,338 | $ 26,208 |
| Marketing expenses | $ 394 | $ 492 | $ 531 | $ 551 | $ 1,968 |
| Professional fees and licensure | $ 1,075 | $ 1,344 | $ 1,451 | $ 1,505 | $ 5,376 |
| Insurance costs | $ 2,517 | $ 3,147 | $ 3,398 | $ 3,524 | $ 12,586 |
| Travel and vehicle costs | $ 1,671 | $ 2,089 | $ 2,256 | $ 2,340 | $ 8,356 |
| Rent and utilities | $ 2,993 | $ 3,741 | $ 4,040 | $ 4,190 | $ 14,963 |
| Miscellaneous costs | $ 945 | $ 1,181 | $ 1,275 | $ 1,322 | $ 4,723 |
| Payroll taxes | $ 4,419 | $ 5,523 | $ 5,965 | $ 6,186 | $ 22,094 |
| **Total operating costs** | **$48,712** | **$60,891** | **$ 65,762** | **$ 68,197** | **$243,562** |
| **EBITDA** | **$22,131** | **$27,663** | **$ 29,877** | **$ 30,983** | **$110,654** |
| Federal income tax | $ 6,766 | $ 8,458 | $ 9,135 | $ 9,473 | $ 33,832 |
| State income tax | $ 1,025 | $ 1,282 | $ 1,384 | $ 1,435 | $ 5,126 |
| Interest expense | $ 2,092 | $ 2,053 | $ 2,013 | $ 1,973 | $ 8,131 |
| Depreciation expense | $ 1,152 | $ 1,152 | $ 1,152 | $ 1,152 | $ 4,607 |
| **Net profit** | **$11,095** | **$14,719** | **$ 16,192** | **$ 16,950** | **$ 58,957** |

**Profit and loss statement (third year)**

| Quarter | Q1 | 3<br>Q2 | Q3 | Q4 | 3 |
|---|---|---|---|---|---|
| **Sales** | **$92,096** | **$115,120** | **$124,330** | **$128,935** | **$460,481** |
| Cost of goods sold | $ 9,210 | $ 11,512 | $ 12,433 | $ 12,893 | $ 46,048 |
| Gross margin | 90.00% | 90.00% | 90.00% | 90.00% | 90.00% |
| **Operating income** | **$82,887** | **$103,608** | **$111,897** | **$116,041** | **$414,433** |
| **Expenses** | | | | | |
| Payroll | $30,342 | $ 37,927 | $ 40,961 | $ 42,478 | $151,709 |
| General and administrative | $ 5,451 | $ 6,814 | $ 7,359 | $ 7,632 | $ 27,256 |
| Marketing expenses | $ 460 | $ 576 | $ 622 | $ 645 | $ 2,302 |
| Professional fees and licensure | $ 1,107 | $ 1,384 | $ 1,495 | $ 1,550 | $ 5,537 |
| Insurance costs | $ 2,643 | $ 3,304 | $ 3,568 | $ 3,700 | $ 13,216 |
| Travel and vehicle costs | $ 1,838 | $ 2,298 | $ 2,482 | $ 2,574 | $ 9,191 |
| Rent and utilities | $ 3,142 | $ 3,928 | $ 4,242 | $ 4,399 | $ 15,711 |
| Miscellaneous costs | $ 1,105 | $ 1,381 | $ 1,492 | $ 1,547 | $ 5,526 |
| Payroll taxes | $ 4,551 | $ 5,689 | $ 6,144 | $ 6,372 | $ 22,756 |
| **Total operating costs** | **$50,641** | **$ 63,301** | **$ 68,365** | **$ 70,897** | **$253,204** |
| **EBITDA** | **$32,246** | **$ 40,307** | **$ 43,532** | **$ 45,144** | **$161,229** |
| Federal income tax | $10,148 | $ 12,685 | $ 13,700 | $ 14,208 | $ 50,741 |
| State income tax | $ 1,538 | $ 1,922 | $ 2,076 | $ 2,153 | $ 7,688 |
| Interest expense | $ 1,932 | $ 1,889 | $ 1,846 | $ 1,802 | $ 7,468 |
| Depreciation expense | $ 1,152 | $ 1,152 | $ 1,152 | $ 1,152 | $ 4,607 |
| **Net profit** | **$17,477** | **$ 22,659** | **$ 24,758** | **$ 25,831** | **$ 90,725** |

## 7.11 Three Year Cash Flow Analysis

**Cash flow analysis (first year)**

| Month | 1 | 2 | 3 | 4 | 5 | 6 | 7 |
|---|---|---|---|---|---|---|---|
| Cash from operations | $ 1,790 | $ 1,904 | $ 2,018 | $ 2,133 | $ 2,247 | $ 2,361 | $ 2,475 |
| Cash from receivables | $ 0 | $ 0 | $ 0 | $ 0 | $ 0 | $ 0 | $ 0 |
| **Operating cash inflow** | **$ 17,790** | **$ 1,904** | **$ 2,018** | **$ 2,133** | **$ 2,247** | **$ 2,361** | **$ 2,475** |
| **Other cash inflows** | | | | | | | |
| Equity investment | $ 10,000 | $ 0 | $ 0 | $ 0 | $ 0 | $ 0 | $ 0 |
| Increased borrowings | $100,000 | $ 0 | $ 0 | $ 0 | $ 0 | $ 0 | $ 0 |
| Sales of business assets | $ 0 | $ 0 | $ 0 | $ 0 | $ 0 | $ 0 | $ 0 |
| A/P increases | $ 3,159 | $ 3,159 | $ 3,159 | $ 3,159 | $ 3,159 | $ 3,159 | $ 3,159 |
| **Total other cash inflows** | **$113,159** | **$ 3,159** | **$ 3,159** | **$ 3,159** | **$ 3,159** | **$ 3,159** | **$ 3,159** |
| **Total cash inflow** | **$114,948** | **$ 5,063** | **$ 5,177** | **$ 5,291** | **$ 5,405** | **$ 5,520** | **$ 5,634** |
| **Cash outflows** | | | | | | | |
| Repayment of principal | $ 517 | $ 521 | $ 525 | $ 528 | $ 532 | $ 536 | $ 540 |
| A/P decreases | $ 2,075 | $ 2,075 | $ 2,075 | $ 2,075 | $ 2,075 | $ 2,075 | $ 2,075 |
| A/R increases | $ 0 | $ 0 | $ 0 | $ 0 | $ 0 | $ 0 | $ 0 |
| Asset purchases | $ 64,500 | $ 0 | $ 0 | $ 0 | $ 0 | $ 0 | $ 0 |
| Dividends | $ 0 | $ 0 | $ 0 | $ 0 | $ 0 | $ 0 | $ 0 |
| **Total cash outflows** | **$ 67,092** | **$ 2,595** | **$ 2,599** | **$ 2,603** | **$ 2,607** | **$ 2,611** | **$ 2,615** |
| **Net cash flow** | **$ 47,857** | **$ 2,467** | **$ 2,578** | **$ 2,688** | **$ 2,798** | **$ 2,908** | **$ 3,019** |
| **Cash balance** | **$ 47,857** | **$50,324** | **$52,902** | **$55,589** | **$58,388** | **$61,296** | **$64,315** |

## Cash flow analysis (first year cont.)

| Month | 8 | 9 | 10 | 11 | 12 | 1 |
|---|---|---|---|---|---|---|
| Cash from operations | $ 2,590 | $ 2,704 | $ 2,819 | $ 2,933 | $ 3,048 | $ 29,022 |
| Cash from receivables | $ 0 | $ 0 | $ 0 | $ 0 | $ 0 | $ 0 |
| **Operating cash inflow** | **$ 2,590** | **$ 2,704** | **$ 2,819** | **$ 2,933** | **$ 3,048** | **$ 29,022** |
| **Other cash inflows** | | | | | | |
| Equity investment | $ 0 | $ 0 | $ 0 | $ 0 | $ 0 | $ 10,000 |
| Increased borrowings | $ 0 | $ 0 | $ 0 | $ 0 | $ 0 | $ 100,000 |
| Sales of business assets | $ 0 | $ 0 | $ 0 | $ 0 | $ 0 | $ 0 |
| A/P increases | $ 3,159 | $ 3,159 | $ 3,159 | $ 3,159 | $ 3,159 | $ 37,902 |
| **Total other cash inflows** | **$ 3,159** | **$ 3,159** | **$ 3,159** | **$ 3,159** | **$ 3,159** | **$ 147,902** |
| **Total cash inflow** | **$ 5,748** | **$ 5,863** | **$ 5,977** | **$ 6,092** | **$ 6,206** | **$ 176,924** |
| **Cash outflows** | | | | | | |
| Repayment of principal | $ 545 | $ 549 | $ 553 | $ 557 | $ 561 | $ 6,463 |
| A/P decreases | $ 2,075 | $ 2,075 | $ 2,075 | $ 2,075 | $ 2,075 | $ 24,897 |
| A/R increases | $ 0 | $ 0 | $ 0 | $ 0 | $ 0 | $ 0 |
| Asset purchases | $ 0 | $ 0 | $ 0 | $ 0 | $ 0 | $ 64,500 |
| Dividends | $ 0 | $ 0 | $ 0 | $ 0 | $18,047 | $ 18,047 |
| **Total cash outflows** | **$ 2,619** | **$ 2,623** | **$ 2,627** | **$ 2,632** | **$20,683** | **$ 113,907** |
| **Net cash flow** | **$ 3,129** | **$ 3,239** | **$ 3,350** | **$ 3,460** | **−$14,477** | **$ 63,017** |
| **Cash balance** | **$67,444** | **$70,683** | **$74,033** | **$77,493** | **$63,017** | **$ 63,017** |

## Cash flow analysis (second year)

| Quarter | Q1 | 2 Q2 | Q3 | Q4 | 2 |
|---|---|---|---|---|---|
| Cash from operations | $12,713 | $15,891 | $17,162 | $17,798 | $ 63,564 |
| Cash from receivables | $ 0 | $ 0 | $ 0 | $ 0 | $ 0 |
| **Operating cash inflow** | **$12,713** | **$15,891** | **$ 7,162** | **$17,798** | **$ 63,564** |
| **Other cash inflows** | | | | | |
| Equity investment | $ 0 | $ 0 | $ 0 | $ 0 | $ 0 |
| Increased borrowings | $ 0 | $ 0 | $ 0 | $ 0 | $ 0 |
| Sales of business assets | $ 0 | $ 0 | $ 0 | $ 0 | $ 0 |
| A/P increases | $ 8,717 | $10,897 | $11,769 | $12,204 | $ 43,587 |
| **Total other cash inflows** | **$ 8,717** | **$10,897** | **$11,769** | **$12,204** | **$ 43,587** |
| **Total cash inflow** | **$21,430** | **$26,788** | **$28,931** | **$30,002** | **$107,151** |
| **Cash outflows** | | | | | |
| Repayment of principal | $ 1,708 | $ 1,747 | $ 1,787 | $ 1,827 | $ 7,070 |
| A/P decreases | $ 5,975 | $ 7,469 | $ 8,067 | $ 8,365 | $ 29,876 |
| A/R increases | $ 0 | $ 0 | $ 0 | $ 0 | $ 0 |
| Asset purchases | $ 1,695 | $ 2,119 | $ 2,288 | $ 2,373 | $ 8,474 |
| Dividends | $ 9,039 | $11,299 | $12,203 | $12,655 | $ 45,195 |
| **Total cash outflows** | **$18,418** | **$22,634** | **$24,344** | **$25,220** | **$ 90,616** |
| **Net cash flow** | **$ 3,013** | **$ 4,154** | **$ 4,587** | **$ 4,782** | **$ 16,536** |
| **Cash balance** | **$66,029** | **$70,183** | **$74,770** | **$79,552** | **$ 79,552** |

## Cash flow analysis (third year)

| Quarter | Q1 | 3 Q2 | Q3 | Q4 | 3 |
|---|---|---|---|---|---|
| Cash from operations | $19,066 | $23,833 | $25,740 | $26,693 | $ 95,332 |
| Cash from receivables | $     0 | $     0 | $     0 | $     0 | $     0 |
| **Operating cash inflow** | **$19,066** | **$23,833** | **$25,740** | **$26,693** | **$ 95,332** |
| **Other cash inflows** | | | | | |
| Equity investment | $     0 | $     0 | $     0 | $     0 | $     0 |
| Increased borrowings | $     0 | $     0 | $     0 | $     0 | $     0 |
| Sales of business assets | $     0 | $     0 | $     0 | $     0 | $     0 |
| A/P increases | $10,025 | $12,531 | $13,534 | $14,035 | $ 50,125 |
| **Total other cash inflows** | **$10,025** | **$12,531** | **$13,534** | **$14,035** | **$ 50,125** |
| **Total cash inflow** | **$29,091** | **$36,364** | **$39,273** | **$40,728** | **$145,457** |
| **Cash outflows** | | | | | |
| Repayment of principal | $ 1,869 | $ 1,911 | $ 1,954 | $ 1,999 | $  7,733 |
| A/P decreases | $ 7,170 | $ 8,963 | $ 9,680 | $10,038 | $ 35,852 |
| A/R increases | $     0 | $     0 | $     0 | $     0 | $     0 |
| Asset purchases | $ 2,628 | $ 3,285 | $ 3,548 | $ 3,679 | $ 13,140 |
| Dividends | $14,016 | $17,520 | $18,921 | $19,622 | $ 70,079 |
| **Total cash outflows** | **$25,683** | **$31,679** | **$34,103** | **$35,338** | **$126,804** |
| **Net cash flow** | **$ 3,409** | **$ 4,686** | **$ 5,170** | **$ 5,390** | **$ 18,654** |
| **Cash balance** | **$82,961** | **$87,646** | **$92,816** | **$98,206** | **$ 98,206** |

# Factoring Company
R e g i s   F i n a n c i a l

PO Box 5567
New York, New York 10123

*BizPlanDB.com*

*Regis Financial, Inc. is a New York-based corporation that will provide financing based on accounts receivables to companies within the target market. The company was founded by Andrew Regis.*

## 1.0 EXECUTIVE SUMMARY

The purpose of this business plan is to raise $550,000 for the development of a factoring company while showcasing the expected financials and operations over the next three years. Regis Financial, Inc. is a New York-based corporation that will provide financing based on accounts receivables to companies within the target market. The company was founded by Andrew Regis.

### 1.1 The Services

Regis Financial will make advances to businesses that carry extensive accounts receivables from businesses within the target market. On each invoice, the business will provide financing equal to 90 percent of the total amount of the invoice. The business will earn substantial fees for providing this financing to businesses that carry extensive accounts receivables.

Regis Financial, from time to time, will make divestitures of these investments as they become profitable and will produce tax friendly returns. Management is currently working with an attorney to determine the most appropriate structure of the factoring company.

The third section of the business plan will further describe the services offered by Regis Financial.

### 1.2 Financing

Mr. Regis will make a $550,000 investment into the business. Primarily the financing will be used for the following:

- Financing for the first six months of operation
- Financing for the investments to be made by Regis Financial

Again, an attorney has been retained in order to make sure that the structure of Regis Financial is appropriate.

### 1.3 Mission Statement

Regis Financial's mission is to provide ongoing returns for the aggregated portfolios of accounts receivables held by the business.

## 1.4 Management Team

The company was founded by Andrew Regis. Mr. Regis has more than 10 years of experience in the finance industry. Through his expertise, he will be able to bring the operations of the business to profitability within its first year of operations.

## 1.5 Sales Forecasts

Mr. Regis expects a strong rate of growth at the start of operations. Below are the expected financials over the next three years.

**Proforma profit and loss (yearly)**

| Year | 1 | 2 | 3 |
|------|-----|-----|-----|
| Sales | $327,978 | $354,216 | $382,554 |
| Operating costs | $136,288 | $144,911 | $149,886 |
| EBITDA | $158,892 | $173,883 | $194,412 |
| Taxes, interest, and depreciation | $ 97,150 | $102,847 | $110,648 |
| Net profit | $ 61,742 | $ 71,036 | $ 83,764 |

**Sales, operating costs, and profit forecast**

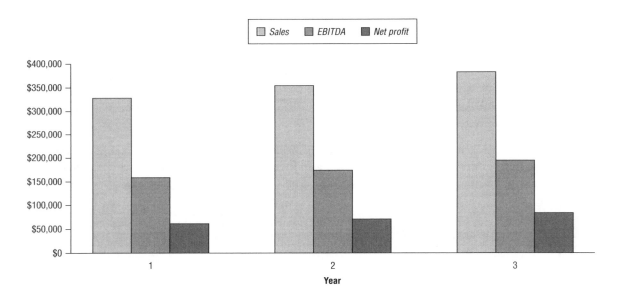

## 1.6 Expansion Plan

The Founder expects that the business will aggressively expand during the first three years of operation. Mr. Regis intends to implement marketing campaigns effectively target both investors that want higher than average returns on their investments as well as companies that carry an extensive amount of accounts receivables.

# 2.0 COMPANY AND FINANCING SUMMARY

## 2.1 Registered Name and Corporate Structure

Regis Financial, Inc. is registered as a for profit company in the State of New York.

## 2.2 Required Funds

At this time, Regis Financial requires $550,000 of investment funds. Below is a breakdown of how these funds will be used:

**Projected startup costs**

| | |
|---|---|
| Initial lease payments and deposits | $ 10,000 |
| Working capital | $ 35,000 |
| FF&E | $ 23,000 |
| Leasehold improvements | $ 12,000 |
| Security deposits | $ 5,000 |
| Insurance | $ 2,500 |
| Factoring portfolio | $450,000 |
| Marketing budget | $ 7,500 |
| Miscellaneous and unforeseen costs | $ 5,000 |
| **Total startup costs** | **$550,000** |

## 2.3 Investor Equity

This will be discussed during negotiations. However, Management anticipates that the Investor will receive a large equity participation interest in the business in exchange for the capital sought in this business plan.

## 2.4 Management Equity

This will be discussed during negotiations.

## 2.5 Exit Strategy

Factoring companies are extremely profitable. As such, in the event that Management wishes to divest the business to a third party entity, the company will hire a business broker or small mergers/ acquisitions oriented investment bank to handle the transaction. Based on historical sales figures of similar businesses, Regis Financial could receive a sales premium of seven to ten times earnings based on the profitability of the business.

# 3.0 PRODUCTS AND SERVICES

Below is a description of the services offered by Regis Financial.

## 3.1 Factoring Operations

As stated in the executive summary, Regis Financial will focus heavily on acquiring discounted accounts receivable portfolios with the intent to generate substantial returns on investment as other businesses pay their invoices directly to Regis Financial. On each investment, the business will generate annualized returns of nearly 100 percent as invoices will be held for approximately 30 days to 60 days depending on the credit quality of the individual business that has received an invoice from one of the company's corporate customers.

The business will enact strong credit protocols to ensure that defaults on invoices are kept to an absolute minimum.

# 4.0 STRATEGIC AND MARKET ANALYSIS

## 4.1 Economic Outlook

This section of the analysis will detail the economic climate, the financial intermediation and factoring industry, the customer profile, and the competition that the business will face as it progresses through its business operations.

Currently, the economic market condition in the United States is moderate. The meltdown of the subprime mortgage market coupled with increasing gas prices has led many people to believe that the U.S. is on the cusp of a double dip economic recession. However, Regis Financial will be able to remain profitable and cash flow positive given the very high return on investment that comes from managing and servicing a portfolio of accounts receivables.

### 4.2 Industry Analysis

According to the U.S. Economic Census, there are approximately 1,500 companies that are actively engaged in the purchase, collection, and sale of accounts receivables as it relates to factoring financing. Each year, these firms generate more than $32 billion of revenues while providing jobs for approximately 35,000 people. Annual payrolls in each of the last five years have exceeded $2 billion. This is a mature industry, and the future expected growth rate is expected to equal that of the general economy.

Due to the continually changing nature of SEC regulations, factoring companies that accept third party investments from investors may need to alter their structures as many scandals lately have tightened regulations regarding aggregated funding pools that invest in accounts receivables portfolios.

### 4.3 Customer Profile

Management anticipates that the clients of Regis Financial, Inc. will be small- to medium-sized businesses within the company's targeted market. Below is a profile of individuals that are expected to become clients of Regis Financial:

- Operates a business that is within 50 miles of the company's location

- Has $5,000 to $50,000 of receivables to divest with the business

- EBITDA in excess of $50,000+

Within the greater New York metropolitan area and New York State (where the company is to be licensed), there are approximately 200,000 businesses that could potentially hypothecate their invoices with Regis Financial on an ongoing basis.

### 4.4 Competition

As stated above, there are more than 1,500 businesses within the United States that focus on providing invoice factoring services. As such, it is difficult to gauge the competition that the business will face as it progresses through its operations. However, Management intends to maintain a competitive advantage by offering extremely fast factoring decisions and disbursement of capital to customers.

## 5.0 MARKETING PLAN

Regis Financial intends to develop a marketing campaign that will attract both investors and potential clients to the brand name of the firm. Below is an overview of these marketing strategies.

### 5.1 Marketing Objectives
- Develop an online presence by developing a website and placing the company's name and contact information with online directories

- Implement a local campaign with the company's targeted market via the use of flyers, local newspaper advertisements, and word of mouth advertising

- Establish relationships with referring business advisories within the targeted market

## 5.2 Marketing Strategies

Mr. Regis intends on using a number of marketing strategies that will allow Regis Financial to easily target small- and medium-sized businesses within the target market. These strategies include traditional print advertisements and ads placed on search engines on the Internet. Below is a description of how the business intends to market its services to the general public.

The company will also use an Internet-based strategy. This is very important as many people seeking local services, such as factoring companies and specialized financing companies, now use the Internet to conduct their preliminary searches. Mr. Regis will register the practice with online portals so that potential customers can easily reach the business. The company will also develop its own online website showcasing the company's financing capabilities, Regis Financial's location, hours of operation, and accepted accounts receivables that can be financed by the business.

The company will maintain a sizable amount of print and traditional advertising methods within local markets to promote the accounts receivables financing services that the company is selling.

## 5.3 Pricing

The company will receive a fee equal to 10 percent of the factored invoice.

# 6.0 ORGANIZATIONAL PLAN AND PERSONNEL SUMMARY

### 6.1 Corporate Organization

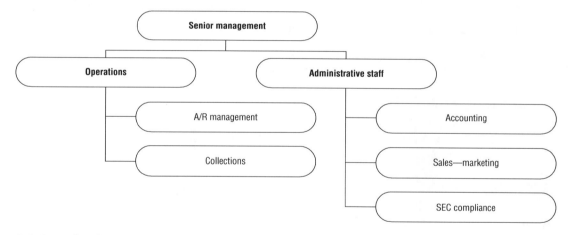

### 6.2 Organizational Budget

**Personnel plan—yearly**

| Year | 1 | 2 | 3 |
|---|---|---|---|
| Senior management | $ 30,000 | $ 30,900 | $ 31,827 |
| Analysts | $ 25,000 | $ 25,750 | $ 26,523 |
| Administrative | $ 25,000 | $ 25,750 | $ 26,523 |
| Accountant | $ 25,000 | $ 25,750 | $ 26,523 |
| **Total** | **$105,000** | **$108,150** | **$111,395** |

**Numbers of personnel**

| | | | |
|---|---|---|---|
| Senior management | 1 | 1 | 1 |
| Analysts | 1 | 1 | 1 |
| Administrative | 1 | 1 | 1 |
| Accountant | 1 | 1 | 1 |
| **Totals** | **4** | **4** | **4** |

**Personnel expense breakdown**

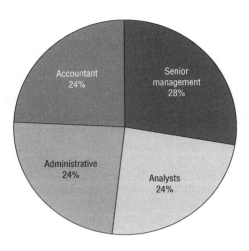

---

# 7.0 FINANCIAL PLAN

### 7.1 Underlying Assumptions

The company has based its proforma financial statements on the following:

- Regis Financial will have an annual revenue growth rate of 16 percent per year

- The Founder will invest $550,000 of equity funds

- The business will generate annual returns of approximately 10 percent compounded in unrealized gains

### 7.2 Sensitivity Analysis

As Regis Financial will have many investments in accounts receivables portfolios, economic risks will be spread out among a number of businesses. As such, any type of economic recession will not have an impact on the company's profitability or cash flow.

### 7.3 Source of Funds

**Financing**

| | |
|---|---|
| **Equity contributions** | |
| Investor(s) | $10,000,000.00 |
| **Total equity financing** | **$10,000,000.00** |
| **Banks and lenders** | |
| **Total debt financing** | **$       0.00** |
| **Total financing** | **$10,000,000.00** |

## 7.4 General Assumptions

**General assumptions**

| Year | 1 | 2 | 3 |
|---|---|---|---|
| Short term interest rate | 9.5% | 9.5% | 9.5% |
| Long term interest rate | 10.0% | 10.0% | 10.0% |
| Federal tax rate | 33.0% | 33.0% | 33.0% |
| State tax rate | 5.0% | 5.0% | 5.0% |
| Personnel taxes | 15.0% | 15.0% | 15.0% |

## 7.5 Profit and Loss Statements

**Proforma profit and loss (yearly)**

| Year | 1 | 2 | 3 |
|---|---|---|---|
| **Sales** | **$327,978** | **$354,216** | **$382,554** |
| Cost of goods sold | $ 32,798 | $ 35,422 | $ 38,255 |
| Gross margin | 90.00% | 90.00% | 90.00% |
| **Operating income** | **$295,180** | **$318,795** | **$344,298** |
| **Expenses** | | | |
| Payroll | $105,000 | $108,150 | $111,395 |
| General and administrative | $ 4,800 | $ 4,992 | $ 5,192 |
| Marketing expenses | $ 1,640 | $ 1,771 | $ 1,913 |
| Professional fees and licensure | $ 2,500 | $ 2,575 | $ 2,652 |
| Insurance costs | $ 1,000 | $ 1,050 | $ 1,103 |
| Travel and vehicle costs | $ 2,500 | $ 2,750 | $ 3,025 |
| Rent and utilities | $ 3,000 | $ 3,150 | $ 3,308 |
| Miscellaneous costs | $ 98 | $ 4,251 | $ 4,591 |
| Payroll taxes | $ 15,750 | $ 16,223 | $ 16,709 |
| **Total operating costs** | **$136,288** | **$144,911** | **$149,886** |
| **EBITDA** | **$158,892** | **$173,883** | **$194,412** |
| Federal income tax | $ 52,434 | $ 57,382 | $ 64,156 |
| State income tax | $ 7,945 | $ 8,694 | $ 9,721 |
| Interest expense | $ 0 | $ 0 | $ 0 |
| Depreciation expenses | $ 36,771 | $ 36,771 | $ 36,771 |
| **Net profit** | **$ 61,742** | **$ 71,036** | **$ 83,764** |
| **Profit margin** | **18.82%** | **20.05%** | **21.90%** |

**Sales, operating costs, and profit forecast**

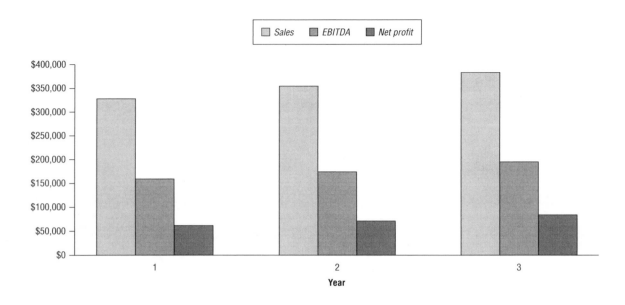

## 7.6 Cash Flow Analysis

**Proforma cash flow analysis—yearly**

| Year | 1 | 2 | 3 |
|---|---|---|---|
| Cash from operations | $ 98,513 | $107,808 | $120,536 |
| Cash from receivables | $ 0 | $ 0 | $ 0 |
| **Operating cash inflow** | **$ 98,513** | **$107,808** | **$120,536** |
| **Other cash inflows** | | | |
| Equity investment | $550,000 | $ 0 | $ 0 |
| Increased borrowings | $ 0 | $ 0 | $ 0 |
| Sales of business assets | $ 0 | $ 0 | $ 0 |
| A/P increases | $ 37,902 | $ 43,587 | $ 50,125 |
| **Total other cash inflows** | **$587,902** | **$ 43,587** | **$ 50,125** |
| **Total cash inflow** | **$686,415** | **$151,395** | **$170,661** |
| **Cash outflows** | | | |
| Repayment of principal | $ 0 | $ 0 | $ 0 |
| A/P decreases | $ 24,897 | $ 29,876 | $ 35,852 |
| A/R increases | $ 0 | $ 0 | $ 0 |
| Asset purchases | $469,800 | $ 16,171 | $ 18,080 |
| Dividends | $ 78,810 | $ 86,246 | $ 96,428 |
| **Total cash outflows** | **$573,507** | **$132,294** | **$150,360** |
| **Net cash flow** | **$112,908** | **$ 19,101** | **$ 20,300** |
| **Cash balance** | **$112,908** | **$132,009** | **$152,309** |

**Proforma cash flow (yearly)**

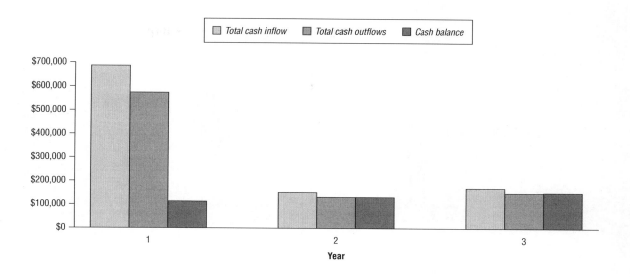

## 7.7 Balance Sheet

**Proforma balance sheet—yearly**

| Year | 1 | 2 | 3 |
|---|---|---|---|
| **Assets** | | | |
| Cash | $112,908 | $132,009 | $152,309 |
| Amortized development/expansion costs | $ 17,500 | $ 19,117 | $ 20,925 |
| Portfolio | $495,000 | $557,841 | $628,542 |
| FF&E | $ 2,300 | $ 4,726 | $ 7,438 |
| Accumulated depreciation | ($ 36,771) | ($ 73,543) | ($110,314) |
| **Total assets** | **$590,936** | **$640,150** | **$698,900** |
| **Liabilities and equity** | | | |
| Accounts payable | $ 13,005 | $ 26,716 | $ 40,990 |
| Long term liabilities | $ 0 | $ 0 | $ 0 |
| Other liabilities | $ 0 | $ 0 | $ 0 |
| **Total liabilities** | **$ 13,005** | **$ 26,716** | **$ 40,990** |
| **Net worth** | **$577,931** | **$613,434** | **$657,910** |
| **Total liabilities and equity** | **$590,936** | **$640,150** | **$698,900** |

**Proforma balance sheet**

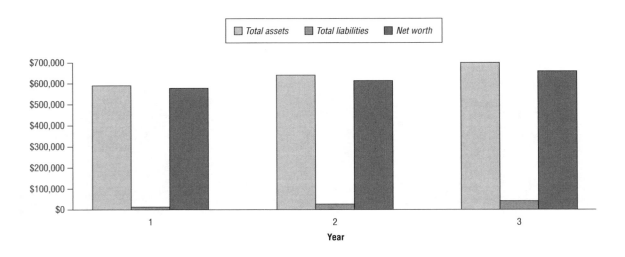

## 7.8 Breakeven Analysis

**Monthly break even analysis**

| Year | 1 | 2 | 3 |
|---|---|---|---|
| Monthly revenue | $ 12,619 | $ 13,418 | $ 13,878 |
| Yearly revenue | $151,431 | $161,012 | $166,540 |

**Break even analysis**

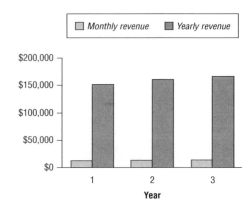

## 7.9 Business Ratios

**Business ratios—yearly**

| Year | 1 | 2 | 3 |
|---|---|---|---|
| **Sales** | | | |
| Sales growth | 0.00% | 8.00% | 8.00% |
| Gross margin | 90.00% | 90.00% | 90.00% |
| **Financials** | | | |
| Profit margin | 18.82% | 20.05% | 21.90% |
| Assets to liabilities | 45.44 | 23.96 | 17.05 |
| Equity to liabilities | 44.44 | 22.96 | 16.05 |
| Assets to equity | 1.02 | 1.04 | 1.06 |
| **Liquidity** | | | |
| Acid test | 8.68 | 4.94 | 3.72 |
| Cash to assets | 0.19 | 0.21 | 0.22 |

## 7.10 Three Year Profit and Loss Statement

**Profit and loss statement (first year)**

| Months | 1 | 2 | 3 | 4 | 5 | 6 | 7 |
|---|---|---|---|---|---|---|---|
| **Sales** | **$26,600** | **$26,733** | **$26,866** | **$26,999** | **$27,132** | **$27,265** | **$27,398** |
| Cost of goods sold | $ 2,660 | $ 2,673 | $ 2,687 | $ 2,700 | $ 2,713 | $ 2,727 | $ 2,740 |
| Gross margin | 90.00% | 90.00% | 90.00% | 90.00% | 90.00% | 90.00% | 90.00% |
| **Operating income** | **$23,940** | **$24,060** | **$24,179** | **$24,299** | **$24,419** | **$24,539** | **$24,658** |
| **Expenses** | | | | | | | |
| Payroll | $ 8,750 | $ 8,750 | $ 8,750 | $ 8,750 | $ 8,750 | $ 8,750 | $ 8,750 |
| General and administrative | $ 400 | $ 400 | $ 400 | $ 400 | $ 400 | $ 400 | $ 400 |
| Marketing expenses | $ 137 | $ 137 | $ 137 | $ 137 | $ 137 | $ 137 | $ 137 |
| Professional fees and licensure | $ 208 | $ 208 | $ 208 | $ 208 | $ 208 | $ 208 | $ 208 |
| Insurance costs | $ 83 | $ 83 | $ 83 | $ 83 | $ 83 | $ 83 | $ 83 |
| Travel and vehicle costs | $ 208 | $ 208 | $ 208 | $ 208 | $ 208 | $ 208 | $ 208 |
| Rent and utilities | $ 250 | $ 50 | $ 250 | $ 205 | $ 250 | $ 250 | $ 250 |
| Miscellaneous costs | $ 8 | $ 8 | $ 8 | $ 8 | $ 8 | $ 8 | $ 8 |
| Payroll taxes | $ 1,313 | $ 1,313 | $ 1,313 | $ 1,313 | $ 1,313 | $ 1,313 | $ 1,313 |
| **Total operating costs** | **$11,357** | **$11,357** | **$11,357** | **$11,357** | **$11,357** | **$11,357** | **$11,357** |
| **EBITDA** | **$12,583** | **$12,702** | **$12,822** | **$12,942** | **$13,061** | **$ 13,181** | **$ 13,301** |
| Federal income tax | $ 4,253 | $ 4,274 | $ 4,295 | $ 4,316 | $ 4,338 | $ 4,359 | $ 4,380 |
| State income tax | $ 644 | $ 648 | $ 651 | $ 654 | $ 657 | $ 660 | $ 664 |
| Interest expense | $ 0 | $ 0 | $ 0 | $ 0 | $ 0 | $ 0 | $ 0 |
| Depreciation expense | $ 3,064 | $ 3,064 | $ 3,064 | $ 3,064 | $ 3,064 | $ 3,064 | $ 3,064 |
| **Net profit** | **$ 4,621** | **$ 4,717** | **$ 4,812** | **$ 4,907** | **$ 5,002** | **$ 5,098** | **$ 5,193** |

## Profit and loss statement (first year cont.)

| Month | 8 | 9 | 10 | 11 | 12 | 1 |
|---|---|---|---|---|---|---|
| Sales | $27,531 | $27,664 | $27,797 | $ 27,930 | $28,063 | $327,978 |
| Cost of goods sold | $ 2,753 | $ 2,766 | $ 2,780 | $ 2,793 | $ 2,806 | $ 32,798 |
| Gross margin | 90.00% | 90.00% | 90.00% | 90.00% | 90.00% | 90.00% |
| Operating income | $24,778 | $24,898 | $25,017 | $ 25,137 | $25,257 | $295,180 |
| Expenses | | | | | | |
| Payroll | $ 8,750 | $ 8,750 | $ 8,750 | $ 8,750 | $ 8,750 | $105,000 |
| General and administrative | $ 400 | $ 400 | $ 400 | $ 400 | $ 400 | $ 4,800 |
| Marketing expenses | $ 137 | $ 137 | $ 137 | $ 137 | $ 137 | $ 1,640 |
| Professional fees and licensure | $ 208 | $ 208 | $ 208 | $ 208 | $ 208 | $ 2,500 |
| Insurance costs | $ 83 | $ 83 | $ 83 | $ 83 | $ 83 | $ 1,000 |
| Travel and vehicle costs | $ 208 | $ 208 | $ 208 | $ 208 | $ 208 | $ 2,500 |
| Rent and utilities | $ 250 | $ 250 | $ 250 | $ 250 | $ 250 | $ 3,000 |
| Miscellaneous costs | $ 8 | $ 8 | $ 8 | $ 8 | $ 8 | $ 98 |
| Payroll taxes | $ 1,313 | $ 1,313 | $ 1,313 | $ 1,313 | $ 1,313 | $ 15,750 |
| Total operating costs | $11,357 | $11,357 | $11,357 | $ 11,357 | $11,357 | $136,288 |
| EBITDA | $13,421 | $13,540 | $13,660 | $ 13,780 | $13,899 | $158,892 |
| Federal income tax | $ 4,401 | $ 4,423 | $ 4,444 | $ 4,465 | $ 4,486 | $ 52,434 |
| State income tax | $ 667 | $ 670 | $ 673 | $ 677 | $ 680 | $ 7,945 |
| Interest expense | $ 0 | $ 0 | $ 0 | $ 0 | $ 0 | $ 0 |
| Depreciation expense | $ 3,064 | $ 3,064 | $ 3,064 | $ 3,064 | $ 3,064 | $ 36,771 |
| Net profit | $ 5,288 | $ 5,383 | $ 5,478 | $ 5,574 | $ 5,669 | $ 61,742 |

## Profit and loss statement (second year)

| Quarter | Q1 | 2 Q2 | Q3 | Q4 | 2 |
|---|---|---|---|---|---|
| Sales | $70,843 | $88,554 | $95,638 | $99,181 | $354,216 |
| Cost of goods sold | $ 7,084 | $ 8,855 | $ 9,564 | $ 9,918 | $ 35,422 |
| Gross margin | 90.00% | 90.00% | 90.00% | 90.00% | 90.00% |
| Operating income | $63,759 | $79,699 | $86,075 | $89,262 | $318,795 |
| Expenses | | | | | |
| Payroll | $21,630 | $27,038 | $29,201 | $30,282 | $108,150 |
| General and administrative | $ 998 | $ 1,248 | $ 1,348 | $ 1,398 | $ 4,992 |
| Marketing expenses | $ 354 | $ 443 | $ 478 | $ 496 | $ 1,771 |
| Professional fees and licensure | $ 515 | $ 644 | $ 695 | $ 721 | $ 2,575 |
| Insurance costs | $ 210 | $ 263 | $ 284 | $ 294 | $ 1,050 |
| Travel and vehicle costs | $ 550 | $ 688 | $ 743 | $ 770 | $ 2,750 |
| Rent and utilities | $ 630 | $ 788 | $ 851 | $ 882 | $ 3,150 |
| Miscellaneous costs | $ 850 | $ 1,063 | $ 1,148 | $ 1,190 | $ 4,251 |
| Payroll taxes | $ 3,245 | $ 4,056 | $ 4,380 | $ 4,542 | $ 16,223 |
| Total operating costs | $28,982 | $36,228 | $39,126 | $40,575 | $144,911 |
| EBITDA | $34,777 | $43,471 | $46,949 | $48,687 | $173,883 |
| Federal income tax | $11,476 | $14,345 | $15,493 | $16,067 | $ 57,382 |
| State income tax | $ 1,739 | $ 2,174 | $ 2,347 | $ 2,434 | $ 8,694 |
| Interest expense | $ 0 | $ 0 | $ 0 | $ 0 | $ 0 |
| Depreciation expense | $ 9,193 | $ 9,193 | $ 9,193 | $ 9,193 | $ 36,771 |
| Net profit | $12,369 | $17,759 | $19,915 | $20,993 | $ 71,036 |

**Profit and loss statement (third year)**

| Quarter | Q1 | 3<br>Q2 | Q3 | Q4 | 3 |
|---|---|---|---|---|---|
| **Sales** | **$76,511** | **$95,638** | **$103,289** | **$107,115** | **$382,554** |
| Cost of goods sold | $ 7,651 | $ 9,564 | $ 10,329 | $ 10,711 | $ 38,255 |
| Gross margin | 90.00% | 90.00% | 90.00% | 90.00% | 90.00% |
| **Operating income** | **$68,860** | **$86,075** | **$ 92,961** | **$ 96,403** | **$344,298** |
| **Expenses** | | | | | |
| Payroll | $22,279 | $27,849 | $ 30,077 | $ 31,190 | $111,395 |
| General and administrative | $ 1,038 | $ 1,298 | $ 1,402 | $ 1,454 | $ 5,192 |
| Marketing expenses | $ 383 | $ 478 | $ 516 | $ 536 | $ 1,913 |
| Professional fees and licensure | $ 530 | $ 663 | $ 716 | $ 743 | $ 2,652 |
| Insurance costs | $ 221 | $ 276 | $ 298 | $ 309 | $ 1,103 |
| Travel and vehicle costs | $ 605 | $ 756 | $ 817 | $ 847 | $ 3,025 |
| Rent and utilities | $ 662 | $ 827 | $ 893 | $ 926 | $ 3,308 |
| Miscellaneous costs | $ 918 | $ 1,148 | $ 1,239 | $ 1,285 | $ 4,591 |
| Payroll taxes | $ 3,342 | $ 4,177 | $ 4,511 | $ 4,679 | $ 16,709 |
| **Total operating costs** | **$29,977** | **$37,472** | **$ 40,469** | **$ 41,968** | **$149,886** |
| **EBITDA** | **$38,882** | **$48,603** | **$ 52,491** | **$ 54,435** | **$194,412** |
| Federal income tax | $12,831 | $16,039 | $ 17,322 | $ 17,964 | $ 64,156 |
| State income tax | $ 1,944 | $ 2,430 | $ 2,625 | $ 2,722 | $ 9,721 |
| Interest expense | $ 0 | $ 0 | $ 0 | $ 0 | $ 0 |
| Depreciation expense | $ 9,193 | $ 9,193 | $ 9,193 | $ 9,193 | $ 36,771 |
| **Net profit** | **$14,914** | **$20,941** | **$ 23,352** | **$ 24,557** | **$ 83,764** |

## 7.11 Three Year Cash Flow Analysis

**Cash flow analysis (first year)**

| Month | 1 | 2 | 3 | 4 | 5 | 6 | 7 |
|---|---|---|---|---|---|---|---|
| Cash from operations | $ 7,686 | $ 7,781 | $ 7,876 | $ 7,971 | $ 8,067 | $ 8,162 | $ 8,257 |
| Cash from receivables | $ 0 | $ 0 | $ 0 | $ 0 | $ 0 | $ 0 | $ 0 |
| **Operating cash inflow** | **$ 7,686** | **$ 7,781** | **$ 7,876** | **$ 7,971** | **$ 8,067** | **$ 8,162** | **$ 8,257** |
| **Other cash inflows** | | | | | | | |
| Equity investment | $550,000 | $ 0 | $ 0 | $ 0 | $ 0 | $ 0 | $ 0 |
| Increased borrowings | $ 0 | $ 0 | $ 0 | $ 0 | $ 0 | $ 0 | $ 0 |
| Sales of business assets | $ 0 | $ 0 | $ 0 | $ 0 | $ 0 | $ 0 | $ 0 |
| A/P increases | $ 3,159 | $ 3,159 | $ 3,159 | $ 3,159 | $ 3,159 | $ 3,159 | $ 3,159 |
| **Total other cash inflows** | **$553,159** | **$ 3,159** | **$ 3,159** | **$ 3,159** | **$ 3,159** | **$ 3,159** | **$ 3,159** |
| **Total cash inflow** | **$560,844** | **$10,939** | **$ 11,035** | **$ 11,130** | **$ 11,225** | **$ 11,320** | **$ 11,416** |
| **Cash outflows** | | | | | | | |
| Repayment of principal | $ 0 | $ 0 | $ 0 | $ 0 | $ 0 | $ 0 | $ 0 |
| A/P decreases | $ 2,075 | $ 2,075 | $ 2,075 | $ 2,075 | $ 2,075 | $ 2,075 | $ 2,075 |
| A/R increases | $ 0 | $ 0 | $ 0 | $ 0 | $ 0 | $ 0 | $ 0 |
| Asset purchases | $469,800 | $ 0 | $ 0 | $ 0 | $ 0 | $ 0 | $ 0 |
| Dividends | $ 0 | $ 0 | $ 0 | $ 0 | $ 0 | $ 0 | $ 0 |
| **Total cash outflows** | **$471,875** | **$ 2,075** | **$ 2,075** | **$ 2,075** | **$ 2,075** | **$ 2,075** | **$ 2,075** |
| **Net cash flow** | **$ 88,969** | **$ 8,865** | **$ 8,960** | **$ 9,055** | **$ 9,150** | **$ 9,246** | **$ 9,341** |
| **Cash balance** | **$ 88,969** | **$97,834** | **$106,794** | **$115,849** | **$125,000** | **$134,245** | **$143,586** |

## Cash flow analysis (first year cont.)

| Month | 8 | 9 | 10 | 11 | 12 | 1 |
|---|---|---|---|---|---|---|
| Cash from operations | $ 8,352 | $ 8,447 | $ 8,543 | $ 8,638 | $ 8,733 | $ 98,513 |
| Cash from receivables | $ 0 | $ 0 | $ 0 | $ 0 | $ 0 | $ 0 |
| **Operating cash inflow** | **$ 8,352** | **$ 8,447** | **$ 8,543** | **$ 8,638** | **$ 8,733** | **$ 98,513** |
| **Other cash inflows** | | | | | | |
| Equity investment | $ 0 | $ 0 | $ 0 | $ 0 | $ 0 | $ 550,000 |
| Increased borrowings | $ 0 | $ 0 | $ 0 | $ 0 | $ 0 | $ 0 |
| Sales of business assets | $ 0 | $ 0 | $ 0 | $ 0 | $ 0 | $ 0 |
| A/P increases | $ 3,159 | $ 3,159 | $ 3,159 | $ 3,159 | $ 3,159 | $ 37,902 |
| **Total other cash inflows** | **$ 3,159** | **$ 3,159** | **$ 3,159** | **$ 3,159** | **$ 3,159** | **$ 587,902** |
| **Total cash inflow** | **$ 11,511** | **$ 11,606** | **$ 11,701** | **$ 11,796** | **$ 11,892** | **$ 686,415** |
| **Cash outflows** | | | | | | |
| Repayment of principal | $ 0 | $ 0 | $ 0 | $ 0 | $ 0 | $ 0 |
| A/P decreases | $ 2,075 | $ 2,075 | $ 2,075 | $ 2,075 | $ 2,075 | $ 24,897 |
| A/R increases | $ 0 | $ 0 | $ 0 | $ 0 | $ 0 | $ 0 |
| Asset purchases | $ 0 | $ 0 | $ 0 | $ 0 | $ 0 | $ 469,800 |
| Dividends | $ 0 | $ 0 | $ 0 | $ 0 | $ 78,810 | $ 78,810 |
| **Total cash outflows** | **$ 2,075** | **$ 2,075** | **$ 2,075** | **$ 2,075** | **$ 80,885** | **$ 573,507** |
| **Net cash flow** | **$ 9,436** | **$ 9,531** | **$ 9,626** | **$ 9,722** | **−$ 68,993** | **$ 112,908** |
| **Cash balance** | **$153,022** | **$162,553** | **$172,180** | **$181,901** | **$112,908** | **$112,908** |

## Cash flow analysis (second year)

| Quarter | Q1 | 2<br>Q2 | Q3 | Q4 | 2 |
|---|---|---|---|---|---|
| Cash from operations | $ 21,562 | $ 26,952 | $ 29,108 | $ 30,186 | $107,808 |
| Cash from receivables | $ 0 | $ 0 | $ 0 | $ 0 | $ 0 |
| **Operating cash inflow** | **$ 21,562** | **$ 26,952** | **$ 29,108** | **$ 30,186** | **$107,808** |
| **Other cash inflows** | | | | | |
| Equity investment | $ 0 | $ 0 | $ 0 | $ 0 | $ 0 |
| Increased borrowings | $ 0 | $ 0 | $ 0 | $ 0 | $ 0 |
| Sales of business assets | $ 0 | $ 0 | $ 0 | $ 0 | $ 0 |
| A/P increases | $ 8,717 | $ 10,897 | $ 11,769 | $ 12,204 | $ 43,587 |
| **Total other cash inflows** | **$ 8,717** | **$ 10,897** | **$ 11,769** | **$ 12,204** | **$ 43,587** |
| **Total cash inflow** | **$ 30,279** | **$ 37,849** | **$ 40,877** | **$ 42,391** | **$151,395** |
| **Cash outflows** | | | | | |
| Repayment of principal | $ 0 | $ 0 | $ 0 | $ 0 | $ 0 |
| A/P decreases | $ 5,975 | $ 7,469 | $ 8,067 | $ 8,365 | $ 29,876 |
| A/R increases | $ 0 | $ 0 | $ 0 | $ 0 | $ 0 |
| Asset purchases | $ 3,234 | $ 4,043 | $ 4,366 | $ 4,528 | $ 16,171 |
| Dividends | $ 17,249 | $ 21,562 | $ 23,286 | $ 24,149 | $ 86,246 |
| **Total cash outflows** | **$ 26,459** | **$ 33,073** | **$ 35,719** | **$ 37,042** | **$132,294** |
| **Net cash flow** | **$ 3,820** | **$ 4,775** | **$ 5,157** | **$ 5,348** | **$ 19,101** |
| **Cash balance** | **$116,728** | **$121,503** | **$126,661** | **$132,009** | **$132,009** |

## Cash flow analysis (third year)

| Quarter | Q1 | 3 Q2 | Q3 | Q4 | 3 |
|---|---|---|---|---|---|
| Cash from operations | $ 24,107 | $ 30,134 | $ 32,545 | $ 33,750 | $120,536 |
| Cash from receivables | $ 0 | $ 0 | $ 0 | $ 0 | $ 0 |
| **Operating cash inflow** | **$ 24,107** | **$ 30,134** | **$ 32,545** | **$ 33,750** | **$120,536** |
| **Other cash inflows** | | | | | |
| Equity investment | $ 0 | $ 0 | $ 0 | $ 0 | $ 0 |
| Increased borrowings | $ 0 | $ 0 | $ 0 | $ 0 | $ 0 |
| Sales of business assets | $ 0 | $ 0 | $ 0 | $ 0 | $ 0 |
| A/P increases | $ 10,025 | $ 12,531 | $ 13,534 | $ 14,035 | $ 50,125 |
| **Total other cash inflows** | **$ 10,025** | **$ 12,531** | **$ 13,534** | **$ 14,035** | **$ 50,125** |
| **Total cash inflow** | **$ 34,132** | **$ 42,665** | **$ 46,078** | **$ 47,785** | **$170,661** |
| **Cash outflows** | | | | | |
| Repayment of principal | $ 0 | $ 0 | $ 0 | $ 0 | $ 0 |
| A/P decreases | $ 7,170 | $ 8,963 | $ 9,680 | $ 10,038 | $ 35,852 |
| A/R increases | $ 0 | $ 0 | $ 0 | $ 0 | $ 0 |
| Asset purchases | $ 3,616 | $ 4,520 | $ 4,882 | $ 5,062 | $ 18,080 |
| Dividends | $ 19,286 | $ 24,107 | $ 26,036 | $ 27,000 | $ 96,428 |
| **Total cash outflows** | **$ 30,072** | **$ 37,590** | **$ 40,597** | **$ 42,101** | **$150,360** |
| **Net cash flow** | **$ 4,060** | **$ 5,075** | **$ 5,481** | **$ 5,684** | **$ 20,300** |
| **Cash balance** | **$136,069** | **$141,144** | **$146,625** | **$152,309** | **$152,309** |

# General Construction Company

Riley Contracting, LLC

6734 Robin Lane
Lansing, MI 48917

*Brenda Kubiac*

*Riley Contracting, LLC is a general contracting and home improvement company.*

## 1.0 EXECUTIVE SUMMARY

### 1.1 Business Overview

Riley Contracting is a limited liability general contracting company based out of Lansing, Michigan. The company is licensed, bonded, and insured. Riley Contracting is fully versed on building codes and requirements and therefore can ensure that customers receive their permits and inspections in a timely manner, keeping the job running smoothly. The company will also strive to have great working relationships with the local building departments. Additionally, Riley Contracting has set in place reliable and qualified sub-contractors who will take care of their customer's needs and arrive on schedule.

Now is an ideal time to be part of the remodeling industry. "Residential remodeling will continue a gradual climb back up in 2014 from a dramatic fall during the economic downturn," according to the National Association of Home Builders. They also report that "[r]emodelers from around the country agreed with the forecast, citing increased demand from home owners for upgrades to existing bathrooms and kitchens" (http://www.nahb.org/news_details.aspx?sectionID=2286&newsID=16635). The National Association of Home Builders reported the home improvement industry is valued at $214 billion.

The company plans to target homeowners in the greater Lansing, Michigan area including Okemos, East Lansing, Haslett, Dewitt, Grand Ledge, Lansing, Holt, Charlotte, Mason, Williamston, St. Johns and all other mid-Michigan cities.

Owner Cameron Riley is also classified as a Certified Green Building Professional (CGP), and Riley Contracting is featured online in Build it Green's Certified Green Professionals Directory.

Cameron also took part in the Certified Aging-in-Place Specialist (CAPS) designation program through the National Association of Home Builders program. CAPS professionals are trained in common remodeling projects and costs, accessibility issues, product recommendations, codes and standards, and the process and resources needed to provide a complete aging-in-place solution.

Cameron Riley is a member of both the Lansing Home Builders & Remodelers Association and the Building Trades Association and the National Kitchen & Bath Association (NKBA).

### 1.2 Mission

Riley Contracting will handle all projects with a diligent commitment to customer satisfaction and will complete all projects within budget and on schedule.

### 1.3 Goals and Objectives

Riley Contracting's goal is to become a Better Business Bureau Accredited Business. To reach this goal the company will deliver what it promises and in turn the company receives customer satisfaction ensuring repeat business.

## 2.0 INDUSTRY AND MARKET ANALYSIS

### 2.1 Industry Analysis

According to the Remodeling Futures Program at the Joint Center (http://www.jchs.harvard.edu/sites/jchs.harvard.edu/files/harvard_jchs_remodeling_report_2013.pdf, 2013), "Foreclosed properties are being rehabilitated, sustainable home improvements are gaining popularity, older homeowners are retrofitting their homes to accommodate their evolving needs, and the future market potential is immense, as the emerging echo boom generation is projected to be the largest in our nation's history."

Also, according to experts at a press conference hosted by the National Association of Home Builders (NAHB) Remodelers at the International Builders' Show (IBS) in Las Vegas (http://www.nahb.org/news_details.aspx?newsID=16635&fromGSA=1), "Residential remodeling will continue a gradual climb back up in 2014 from a dramatic fall during the economic downturn." Remodelers from around the country agree with the forecast, citing increased demand from home owners for upgrades to existing bathrooms and kitchens.

### 2.2 Market Analysis

Riley Contracting has an estimated 113,996 potential customers scattered throughout Lansing, including the individuals that reside in the 54,181 housing units. The company shares the market with countless other construction companies whose construction services can vary widely from roof contractors to home builders to window installers.

Other potential customers who can benefit from my Aging-in-Place training are the 14,772 individuals that are 45 to 54 years old; the 4,770 residents 55 to 59 years old; the 6,210 residents 60 to 64 years old; the 4,121 residents 75 to 84 years; and the 1,274 residents 85 years old and over.

### 2.3 Competition

Riley Contracting is a new company entering the market; the company believes word-of-mouth and repeat business will go a long way when it comes to proving itself.

## 3.0 MANAGEMENT SUMMARY

Cameron Riley was employed with Abbot Contractors, located in Lansing, Michigan, for 8 years. The company specialized in kitchens and baths. Cameron brought innovative ideas to the table earning the company millions of dollars while there. Other areas of strength Cameron possesses are budgeting and scheduling. These qualities will prove to be beneficial while running his general contracting company.

## 4.0 PROFESSIONAL AND ADVISORY SUPPORT

Cameron Riley shared his business plan with Mr. Platt at Lakeside Commercial Bank in an effort to begin and maintain a good working relationship. In doing so, goals and objectives are clear. A line of credit was established by Riley Contracting that periodically may need cash to support daily operations. The company also established a merchant account for accepting credit cards. Day-to-day bookkeeping will be done in-house. For added accounting and financial functions, Riley Contracting has retained the services of Semco Financial Services. For all legal aspects relating the business, the company has retained the services of Samson Law, LLP, who initially prepared a basic contract format that the company plans to use. For all of its insurance needs, Riley Contracting has retained the services of Anchor Insurance Group.

## 5.0 STRATEGIES

### 5.1 Business strategy

Riley Contracting plans to offer free in-home consultations at which time the company will provide a written estimate to reduce risk of confusion about pricing with customers and present a more professional image. The company will also provide written specifications to avoid problems with customers regarding materials and equipment planned to be installed in their homes.

A business binder, presented to clients will contain the following:

- Background info on myself and Riley Contracting
- Copy of business license
- Copy of certificate of insurance
- Copy of bond
- Blank contract and estimate forms
- Change order forms
- List of services
- Price list for standard services
- Photos of past jobs
- References
- Any testimonial letters from past customers

A product book containing marketing materials for products company installs and uses including the following:

- Flooring
- Vanities
- Windows and screens
- Tile and countertops
- Storage systems
- Cabinetry
- Decking
- Carpentry

### 5.2 Growth strategy

- Keep promises
- Return phone calls promptly
- Maintain an open and honest relationship

- Be punctual

- Always do quality work

- Never overcharge customer

- Stand behind workmanship

- Be professional at all times

- Prioritize warranty work

- When possible, give customers more than they expect

- Regularly update website and answer emails

- Diversify company if necessary

- Salesman lined up if needed

- Use a compiled customer database to send a monthly newsletter, reminders of seasonal maintenance, announcements of new services offered, and discount coupons

## 6.0 PRODUCTS AND SERVICES

Our general contracting capabilities include the following:

- Additions & Renovations

- Interior & Exterior

- Kitchens & Bathrooms

- Patios & Decks

- Sheet Rocking

- Doors

- Aging-in-Place Modifications

- Fire & Water Damage

- Green building

### 6.1 Other services include the following:

1. On-demand workshops starting at $50 per hour with a minimum of 4 hours

2. Accommodates those over the age of 50 who want to modify their home to age-in-place

3. Trained in green building

### 6.2 Pricing

Payment schedule includes one-third of the contract amount when the contract is signed, one-third at the halfway point of the job, and the balance upon completion.

The company will use a standard software program for estimating the costs of just about any type of building or repair job.

HomeTech Kitchen & Bath Cost Estimator Software will be used for pricing kitchen and baths.

## 7.0 MARKETING & SALES

### 7.1 Advertising and promotion

Advertising and promotion efforts below will be based on a trial and error format:

- Advertise in the phone directory with small ad

- Direct mail

- Door hangers

- Web presence listing contact information, services, special offer, location with map, photo gallery of work as completed, and client testimonials

- Order some inexpensive yard signs to place outside while on the job

- Get a sign with the company name and phone number to attach to vehicle

- Write articles offering tips in the Sunday home improvement section of the local newspaper

- Offer free services to local nonprofit organizations within the community to help them raise money or donate discount coupons for services

- Local periodicals

- Door-to-door solicitation

- Telemarketing

- Build a database file of customers and potential customers to print mailing labels to send out flyers or announcements to current and potential customers

- Signs

- Notices hung in local businesses and public bulletin boards

- Newsletters or brochures

- Imprinted clothing

- Social media sites Facebook, etc.

- Senior discounts

- Printable Internet discount coupon to receive 10% off estimated prices

- Post instructional videos

## 8.0 OPERATIONS

### 8.1 Customers

Riley Contracting will target the 114,947 residents who reside in the 54,464 housing units located in Lansing, Michigan.

### 8.2 Suppliers

1. Neighborhood Builders & Supply Co.

2. Jays Rent-it-All

3. Wyley Lumber

4. Hanover Kitchen & Bath, Inc.

5.  Bentley's Hardware

6.  Jackson Contractors Supply

### 8.3 Equipment

1.  As a new business, Riley Residential Contracting plans to keep inventory basically on an as-needed basis

2.  Buy in quantity for everyday items whenever feasible

3.  Rent expensive tools

### 8.4 Hours

Riley Residential Contracting will remain flexible when it comes to hours of operation. Hours will depend on project and customer preference. In general hours of operation will be 8:00 a.m. until 9:00 p.m. Monday through Saturday unless otherwise discussed.

### 8.5 Facility and Location

The company will conduct its business out of home office located at 6734 Robin Lane in Lansing, Michigan, where Cameron converted a room to designate as his office. A home office is an ideal location since a pole barn on the premises allows for more than enough storage for tools and materials that may be acquired. The barn also has a space for building if necessary.

### 8.6 Legal Environment

Below is a list of essential elements in Riley Contracting's contract compiled by Samson Law, LLP:

1.  The scope of work being contracted

2.  The cost of the work that has been accepted for the work described and the method of payment and the dates of when payments are to be made

3.  The time frame in which the work will take place—the start date, duration, and completion date

4.  Other terms relating to changes in the work, acceptable delays, and miscellaneous provisions unique to this project and how they will be handled

5.  Signatures attesting to acceptance of the agreement, along with the date of the signing of the contract

Note: When changes to the scope of work are requested by customer the company plans to document changes with a change order.

Note: Will use one contract format for sub-contractors and one for homebuyers.

Service orders: will be used to document acceptance of some minor work repair.

## 9.0 FINANCIAL ANALYSIS

### 9.1 2014 Balance Sheet

**Revenue**

| | |
|---|---|
| General construction | $78,000 |
| Workshops | $13,500 |
| **Total revenue** | **$91,500** |

**Expenses**

| | |
|---|---|
| Materials | $ 4,000 |
| Accounting | $ 550 |
| Legal | $ 900 |
| Advertising | $ 1,000 |
| Office equipment | $ 1,500 |
| Office supplies | $ 400 |
| Computer software | $ 100 |
| Magnetic sign with company name and phone number to attach to truck | $ 100 |
| Answering machine with ability to check messages remotely | $ 100 |
| Auto (used) | $12,000 |
| License | $ 150 |
| General liability and auto/rental equipment insurance | $ 300 |
| Association fees | $ 399 |
| Miscellaneous | $ 500 |
| **Total expenses** | **$21,999** |
| **Net income** | **$69,501** |

# Graphic Designer

Patterson Design LLC

2835 Charlotte Pkwy.
Stevens Point, NC 27000

*Paul Greenland*

*Patterson Design LLC is a new graphic design business established by Bill Patterson. Patterson Design is located in the mid-sized city of Stevens Point, North Carolina.*

## EXECUTIVE SUMMARY

Patterson Design LLC is a new graphic design business established by Bill Patterson. A stay-at-home dad for the past five years, Patterson has been preparing to establish his own business by completing graphic design and traditional art courses online and from Rockton Community College. This applied coursework has provided him with the training needed to use graphic design software applications such as Adobe Creative Suite (Photoshop, Illustrator, Dreamweaver, and InDesign). Patterson has been an artistic person from a young age. Forming Patterson Design will allow him to fulfill his creative spirit while providing a service needed by businesses in a wide range of industries. Steady, measured growth is projected for the business, as outlined in the Growth Strategy section of this plan.

## MARKET ANALYSIS

Patterson Design is located in the mid-sized city of Stevens Point, North Carolina. In 2014 the community was home to about 5,000 organizations and businesses, and 135,000 residents. Bill Patterson will target his services toward organizations in the following sub-categories:

### Retail Trade

Auto Dealers & Gas Stations (143)

Bars (29)

Building Materials, Hardware & Garden (31)

Clothing Stores (48)

Convenience Stores (15)

Drugstores (12)

Electronics & Computer Stores (26)

Food Markets (28)

Furniture Stores (19)

General Merchandise Stores (28)

Home Furnishings (22)

Liquor Stores (18)

Music Stores (4)

Food Service Providers (59)

Restaurants (193)

Specialty Stores (180)

## Services

Advertising Agencies (29)

Churches (198)

Colleges & Universities (3)

Conference & Convention Centers (2)

Entertainment & Recreation Services (73)

Health & Medical Service Providers (380)

Hospitals (2)

Hotels & Lodging (19)

Insurance Agencies (98)

Legal Services (179)

Membership Organizations (143)

Museums & Zoos (3)

Printers (13)

Professional Services (197)

Realtors (119)

*Market data obtained from Johnson & Irwin Research LLC.

## Competition

Patterson Design's primary source of competition will be other independent graphic designers and advertising agencies. As of 2014 there were 29 advertising agencies located in Stevens Point, and approximately 18 independent graphic designers. Because some organizations within the community utilize the services of advertising agencies and graphic designers located in other cities, these figures are likely somewhat higher. These competitors also represent potential business partners, since agencies and designers occasionally utilize independent contractors to handle project overflow during high-volume periods.

## INDUSTRY ANALYSIS

According to data from the U.S. Bureau of Labor Statistics (BLS), approximately 279,200 graphic designers were employed in 2010. About 37,300 new jobs were expected to be created within the industry by 2020, representing an average growth rate of 13 percent. Many graphic designers work "in-house" and are employed by public relations firms, advertising agencies, publishing companies, newspapers, magazines, digital media companies, and large organizations, while others work independently. The BLS estimates that 29 percent of graphic designers were self-employed in 2010.

The graphic design industry is represented by several industry associations, including AIGA, "the professional association for design." With more than 23,000 members and 67 chapters, the association was established in 1914 as the American Institute of Graphic Arts. According to the organization, "AIGA advances design as a professional craft, strategic advantage and vital cultural force. As the largest community of design advocates, we bring together practitioners, enthusiasts and patrons to amplify the voice of design and create the vision for a collective future. We define global standards and ethical practices, guide design education, inspire designers and the public, enhance professional development, and make powerful tools and resources accessible to all."

## GROWTH STRATEGY

Because Patterson Design is new to the market and does not yet have extensive experience, Bill Patterson is projecting steady, measured growth for his business. The following annual targets have been established for the first five years of operations:

**2014:** Achieve 825 billable hours ($41,250). Focus on marketing Patterson Design to local small/mid-sized businesses, large organizations, non-profit agencies, and advertising agencies.

**2015:** Achieve 1,040 billable hours ($52,000). Continue to focus strongly on mass marketing the business to build awareness. Break even after sustaining a modest net loss during the first year.

**2016:** Achieve 1,352 billable hours ($67,600). Continue to focus strongly on mass marketing the business to build awareness. Attempt to secure one "flagship" customer (accounting for up to 25 percent of business). Consider beginning to concentrate on serving a specific industry/industry niche. Generate profits of $12,900.

**2017:** Achieve 1,664 billable hours ($83,200). Begin to focus marketing efforts on relationship building with larger customers, taking a more targeted approach. Attempt to secure a second "flagship" customer (accounting for up to 25 percent of business). Generate profits of $16,000.

**2018:** Achieve 1,768 billable hours ($88,400). Continue to focus marketing efforts on relationship building with larger customers. Generate profits of $11,200 and consider growing the business via the addition of a second graphic designer. Continue to operate as a virtual/home-based operation.

*Patterson acknowledges that additional non-billable hours will be required to manage administrative aspects of his business (e.g., marketing, billing, record keeping, project estimating, etc.).

The following graph illustrates projected revenues and net profit/loss for Patterson Design during the business' first five years of operations:

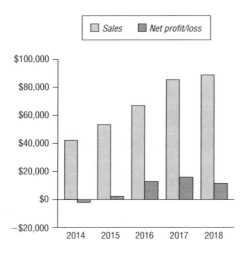

## PERSONNEL

Bill Patterson has been a creative person from a young age. During his youth he served on the high school newspaper and yearbook committee, gaining fundamental experience with page layout, developing advertisements, and taking photos. Patterson attended Rockton Community College, where he gained similar experience helping to lay out the college newspaper. After earning an associate's degree, Patterson then became a stay-at-home dad, enabling his wife to continue working for Stevens Point Solutions, her family's office equipment business.

At the same time Patterson began preparing to establish his own business by completing graphic design and traditional art courses online and from Rockton Community College. This applied coursework has provided him with the training needed to use graphic design software applications such as Adobe Creative Suite (Photoshop, Illustrator, Dreamweaver, and InDesign). By establishing Patterson Design, Bill Patterson will be able to fulfill his creative spirit while providing a service needed by businesses in a wide range of industries.

### Professional & Advisory Support

Patterson Design has established a business banking account with Stevens Point Bank, including a merchant account for accepting credit card payments. Tax advisement is provided by Winfield & Associates Accounting LLC. Patterson utilized a popular online legal document service to establish his limited liability company.

## SERVICES

Patterson Design will interact with a wide range of customers, including business owners (typically at small- and medium-sized businesses) and marketing/communications professionals (at larger companies), editors (at book publishers and magazines), and art directors (at advertising agencies).

Especially in the case of publications, the graphic design services provided by Patterson Design are often part of a larger process. For example, before the graphic design phase begins, a client already may have engaged in activities such as planning/market research, writing, approving/correcting copy, editing, proofreading, and photography. Ideally, a customer has all of the elements needed for their particular design project, and is aware of their goals and objectives, before contacting Patterson Design (although this will not always be the case).

When working with clients, Patterson Design typically will approach graphic design projects in the following phases:

1. **Concept Development:** Initially, Bill Patterson will meet with clients to discuss specific details regarding the project. He will ask questions about what the customer's goals and objectives are and who the target audience(s) is. If appropriate, he will offer suggestions for the client's consideration. For example, if the customer desires a new brochure, Patterson might suggest developing a companion piece, such as a refrigerator magnet, panel card, or envelope. At this time Patterson also will ask the customer to identify the content elements that will be included in the project (e.g., text, photos, illustrations, charts, graphs, logos, etc.) and specify how they will be provided (e.g., on a CD/DVD or USB mass storage device, via e-mail, via FTP, etc.). He also will ask questions regarding the approval process and project deadlines.

2. **Application:** During this phase Patterson simply will develop several rough sketches/approaches for the customer to consider. Significant effort will not be devoted to any one approach, as the goal is to provide the customer with several different general directions to consider for a look/design. This stage may involve the selection of colors, text styles, possibly stock images/illustrations, and the identification of several different potential layouts.

3. **Feedback:** Patterson will share rough sketches/approaches with the customer, in order to gain feedback and suggestions.

4. **Adjustment:** Information gained during the feedback phase will then be used to arrive at the best design approach for a particular project. This phase typically is time intensive and may involve a detailed focus on elements such as size, color, type/font selection, etc.

5. **Production:** The production phase involves making final modifications/enhancements to the design, providing the customer with an opportunity for final review, gathering information regarding quantity, identifying the best printing approach (e.g., digital press, offset press, etc.), providing digital files to the printer of choice, performing press checks, and ensuring delivery of the finished product to the customer.

The timeframe for this entire five-phase process typically is 6-8 weeks, with approximately 1.5 weeks specifically devoted to creative/graphic design work.

Too extensive to list in their entirety, Patterson Design will handle a wide variety of graphic design projects. Some of the more common examples include:

- Ads
- Articles
- Backlit Displays
- Binders
- Booklets
- Brochures
- Business Cards
- Calendars
- Catalogs
- CD/DVD Cases
- CD/DVD Labels
- Data Sheets

- Directories
- Exterior Signage
- Interior Signage
- Invitations
- Invoices & Forms
- Labels
- Letterhead
- Logos
- Manuals
- Memo Sheets
- Menus
- Newsletters
- Notepads
- Postcards
- Posters
- Presentation Folders
- Programs
- Proposals
- Questionnaires
- Reports
- Social Media Page Design
- Tip Sheets
- Tradeshow Exhibits
- Vehicle Wraps
- Web Sites

## MARKETING & SALES

Patterson Design has developed a marketing plan that includes the following primary tactics:

1. A Web site that prominently features an online portfolio of Bill Patterson's work. Although many of the portfolio items will be sample projects (e.g., work not done for actual clients), Patterson will include brochures and other items he has developed for local non-profit agencies and his wife's family business, Stevens Point Solutions. He will feature several testimonials on his site to convey confidence and trust. The site will include a simple intake form, providing prospective customers with an opportunity to submit basic project details to Patterson Design at any time.

2. A series of four-color glossy postcards, showcasing Bill Patterson's design skills and basic information about the services provided by Patterson Design. These will be used for a regularly scheduled direct mail campaign targeting the 2,300 prospects referenced in the Market Analysis section of this plan (detailed list available upon request). Stevens Point Letter Service, a local mail house, will

handle the mailings and secure the local business mailing list needed for the campaign. Patterson design will send postcard mailings to each prospect twice throughout the course of the year and will follow-up mailings with phone calls in order to maximize the campaign's success.

3. An e-mail marketing campaign targeting members of the Stevens Point Chamber of Commerce. Patterson will utilize a popular e-mail marketing service to send messages on behalf of Patterson Design. Patterson will follow-up mailings with phone calls in order to maximize the campaign's success.

4. A social media strategy involving Twitter, Facebook, and LinkedIn. These social media platforms will be integrated with Patterson Design's Web site.

5. Membership in the Stevens Point Chamber of Commerce, in order to gain and maintain visibility among local businesses.

6. A customer referral program, providing existing clients with a 15 percent project discount for every referral.

## OPERATIONS

One main advantage to this business is that there is virtually no overhead. All design work is performed in Bill Patterson's home office. Patterson will meet with clients at their place of business to discuss projects and share design concepts. When appropriate, he will perform press checks at local printers, ensuring the quality of the finished piece.

Patterson also will share proofs, concepts, and other project-related information with clients digitally, via e-mail, CD/DVD, or FTP.

### Location

Patterson Design will operate from a home office in Bill Patterson's residence, located at 2835 Charlotte Pkwy. in Stevens Point, North Carolina.

### Fees

Unless customers specifically request to be charged by the hour, Patterson Design will provide customers with a flat project estimate, based on an hourly rate of $50. Bill Patterson will require all new customers to provide 50 percent of the project fee in advance. Although Patterson Design will obtain bids from different printers for a project, customers will be required to pay printers separately; Patterson Design will only invoice its customers for graphic design and related services.

### Telecommunications/Internet

Bill Patterson has contracted for broadband Internet service from a local service provider. This service package also includes an Internet-based business telephone line.

### Insurance

A liability insurance policy has been obtained to cover the scope of services provided.

### Equipment

Patterson Design will require the following equipment and computer software prior to start-up ($1,679):

- Adobe Creative Suite 6 Design Standard - Mac - DVD-ROM - Universal English ($579)
- Apple iMac - 21.5" - 8 GB RAM - 1 TB HDD - 2.7 GHz Core i5 Processor ($1,100)

### Hours of Operation

As an independent contractor, Patterson has the ability to work a flexible schedule, depending on the needs of customers and specific projects. He will respond to customer requests and inquiries as quickly as possible, including evening and weekend hours when needed. As a rule, Patterson has chosen not to work on the following major holidays:

- Christmas Day

- Christmas Eve

- July 4

- Labor Day

- Memorial Day

- New Year's Day

- Thanksgiving Day

## FINANCIAL ANALYSIS

Bill Patterson will cover the aforementioned startup costs of $1,679 from his own personal savings. The following table shows Patterson Design's projected profit and loss for the first five years of operations:

**2014–18 Pro forma profit and loss statement**

|  | 2014 | 2015 | 2016 | 2017 | 2018 |
|---|---|---|---|---|---|
| **Sales** | $41,250 | $52,000 | $67,600 | $83,200 | $88,400 |
| **Expenses** | | | | | |
| Salary | $30,000 | $35,000 | $40,000 | $55,000 | $65,000 |
| Accounting & legal | $ 1,000 | $ 1,000 | $ 1,000 | $ 1,000 | $ 1,000 |
| Marketing | $ 7,500 | $ 7,500 | $ 7,500 | $ 5,000 | $ 5,000 |
| Insurance | $ 2,750 | $ 2,750 | $ 2,750 | $ 2,750 | $ 2,750 |
| Software/software upgrades | $ 0 | $ 500 | $ 500 | $ 500 | $ 500 |
| Equipment | $ 0 | $ 750 | $ 750 | $ 750 | $ 750 |
| Internet/telecommunications | $ 1,500 | $ 1,500 | $ 1,500 | $ 1,500 | $ 1,500 |
| Miscellaneous | $ 700 | $ 700 | $ 700 | $ 700 | $ 700 |
| **Total operating costs** | $43,450 | $49,700 | $54,700 | $67,200 | $77,200 |
| **Net profit/loss** | −$ 2,200 | $ 2,300 | $12,900 | $16,000 | $11,200 |

## SWOT ANALYSIS

**Strengths:** Patterson Design is a home-based business with minimal overhead.

**Weaknesses:** Bill Patterson has a limited portfolio and virtually no awareness of his services in the local marketplace.

**Opportunities:** Local demand for graphic design services is high.

**Threats:** Patterson Design's ability to operate rests solely upon Bill Patterson, meaning that the business could be jeopardized in the event of injury or illness.

# Healthcare Advocacy Business

Lewis Health Consultants LLC

5782 Wyman St.
Columbus, OH 43000

*Paul Greenland*

*Lewis Health Consultants LLC is a new consulting practice that helps consumers to navigate the often confusing healthcare industry landscape.*

## EXECUTIVE SUMMARY

Lewis Health Consultants LLC is a new consulting practice that helps consumers to navigate the rapidly changing and often confusing healthcare industry landscape. The practice provides services such as assisting with complicated insurance claims; helping individuals file and win insurance appeals; performing healthcare research and general education; and helping to resolve problems between individuals, healthcare providers, and insurance companies. The practice is being established by Beth Lewis, who has 15 years of insurance industry experience in areas such as customer service and claims processing. She is establishing her own firm to provide a service that is in great demand and fulfill her entrepreneurial spirit.

## INDUSTRY ANALYSIS

In January of 2014 millions of Americans began receiving healthcare coverage under the Affordable Care Act, one of the most sweeping pieces of healthcare legislation in U.S. history. An immediate concern was that a large number of citizens were unfamiliar with basic health insurance concepts and terms, such as deductibles, premiums, provider networks, and co-pays. This lack of education presented a concern to many industry players. For example, organizations such as the American College of Physicians counseled members to expect problems assisting newly insured patients.

At the same time, major changes were taking place within the healthcare industry itself. New compensation models that focused on quality instead of quantity were being implemented at hospitals and healthcare systems. This pay-for-performance approach resulted in a stronger focus on wellness and prevention and more focused management of patients with chronic health conditions. Other trends, including a growing shortage of family physicians, resulted in an increase in healthcare provided by so-called mid-level providers such as physician assistants and nurse practitioners.

## MARKET ANALYSIS

Lewis Health Consultants will provide healthcare consulting services in the state of Ohio, and mainly in the Columbus metropolitan area. In 2014 the Ohio Hospital Association served 213 hospitals and 22 health systems statewide. That year, 22,000 physicians, residents, medical students, and practice managers were members of the Ohio State Medical Association.

According to the *Ohio Department of Insurance 2013 Annual Report,* Ohio is one of the world's top insurance marketplaces, with about 110,000 people directly employed by insurance agencies, insurance companies, and related businesses, as well as 106,000 jobs indirectly connected to the industry. According to the department, Ohio is home to more than 250 insurance companies. By 2018 strong demand within the industry is expected to result in the need for an additional 17,000 insurance-related jobs.

Within Columbus, specifically, there were 962,620 households in 2013, with an average household income of $68,913. That year, average annual household expenditures for healthcare totaled $3,603. Of this amount, $2,080 was attributed to healthcare insurance. Another $893 was attributed to medical services. By 2018 annual household healthcare expenditures are expected to reach $4,226, according to Experian and Alteryx.

As the general population continues to age, increased healthcare services demand and utilization is expected. The following tables summarize the Columbus population in 2013 and 2018 (projected), by age:

**2013**

| Population | 2,461,518 |
|---|---|
| Age 0–4 | 6.50% |
| Age 5–9 | 6.60% |
| Age 10–14 | 6.70% |
| Age 15–19 | 6.90% |
| Age 20–24 | 7.50% |
| Age 25–34 | 14.00% |
| Age 35–44 | 13.50% |
| Age 45–54 | 14.30% |
| Age 55–64 | 11.90% |
| Age 65–74 | 6.50% |
| Age 75–84 | 3.60% |
| Age 85+ | 1.40% |

**2018**

| Population | 2,566,524 |
|---|---|
| Age 0–4 | 6.60% |
| Age 5–9 | 6.50% |
| Age 10–14 | 6.50% |
| Age 15–19 | 6.60% |
| Age 20–24 | 7.20% |
| Age 25–34 | 14.10% |
| Age 35–44 | 13.10% |
| Age 45–54 | 13.20% |
| Age 55–64 | 12.40% |
| Age 65–74 | 7.80% |
| Age 75–84 | 3.80% |
| Age 85+ | 1.50% |

## GROWTH STRATEGY

Lewis Health Consultants has developed the following growth targets for the practice's first three years of operations:

### Year One:

Begin operations with two consultants (including owner Beth Lewis). Achieve 2,704 billable hours and generate revenues of $202,800.

### Year Two:

Expand operations to include three consultants. Achieve 4,462 billable hours and generate revenues of $334,650.

### Year Three:

Expand operations to include four consultants. Achieve 6,483 billable hours and generate revenues of $486,225.

The following tables illustrate Lewis Health Consultants' projected billable hours and gross revenues for the first three years of operations:

**Billable hours**

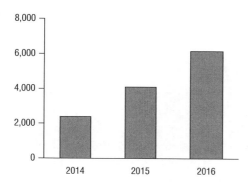

**Gross revenue**

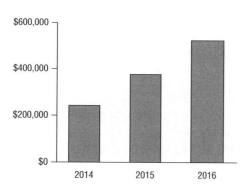

# PERSONNEL

### Beth Lewis, Owner

Beth Lewis has 15 years of health insurance industry experience in areas such as customer service and claims processing. Most recently, she served as the claims supervisor for Northern Ridge Insurance Company. Lewis holds an undergraduate business degree from Ohio State University. She is establishing Lewis Health Consultants to provide a service that is in great demand and will fulfill her entrepreneurial spirit.

### Shelley Spear, Consultant

Like Lewis, Shelley Spear also has considerable healthcare experience. Prior to joining Lewis Health Consultants, she worked as a clinic operations manager for Greenfield Health System in northern Ohio.

In that role, she was responsible for managing a clinic that included five family practice physicians and a number of different specialists. She frequently worked with patients, physicians, staff, and insurance companies to resolve a wide variety of billing, insurance coverage, and healthcare-related issues. Spear holds an undergraduate business degree from the University of Toledo.

### Professional & Advisory Support

Lewis Health Consultants has established a business banking account with Central Columbus Bank, including a merchant account for accepting credit card payments. Tax advisement is provided by Berkeley & Lane Accounting LLC. Lewis utilized a popular online legal document service to establish her limited liability company.

## SERVICES

Lewis Health Consultants will offer a number of different services. As a rule, an hourly rate of $75 will be used when calculating cost estimates for potential clients.

1. **Complex Claims Assessments:** This will involve working in partnership with/on behalf of consumers trying to understand why their insurance company has denied a particular claim. In some cases, denied claims are the result of insurance company errors, healthcare providers' incorrect use of procedure codes, etc. Sometimes, the denied claim is the result of an insured individual not accessing their benefit plan properly. Lewis Health Consultants will help clients sort out all of the facts and ensure that their claim has indeed been processed correctly. Assistance also will be provided for Medicaid and Medicare-related claims.

2. **Insurance Appeals:** When a healthcare claim is denied, consumers can appeal the decision. Lewis Health Consultants will help clients to understand their rights and guide them through this often confusing process. Beth Lewis and her team will help clients to write appeals that state information factually, objectively, and respectively, in order to maximize their chance of a successful appeal. This often is difficult for people to do, because benefit denials can be highly charged emotional situations when someone's health is at stake.

3. **Healthcare Research:** This service involves working with clients to obtain detailed information regarding medical conditions and diagnoses. Lewis Health Consultants also will help clients to identify the best treatment options, doctors, and hospitals for their specific situation. The practice will work with clients' insurance companies to ensure the availability of coverage for all potential treatments and providers. If coverage is not available, Lewis Health Consultants will present the client with available alternatives.

4. **Problem Resolution:** Most healthcare consumers will encounter a challenge with their healthcare provider or insurance company. These may include billing errors, incorrectly processed claims, or concerns with poor service. Lewis Health Consultants work with clients to identify specific issues and resolve them as quickly as possible. This may involve writing letters to physicians or hospitals on behalf of clients, seeking some form of service recovery or billing adjustment.

5. **General Education:** Lewis Health Consultants will provide general consultations to clients to help them understand benefit plan options. This will involve reviewing summary plan documents and other information provided by the client's employer or insurance company. Beth Lewis will teach clients how to collect and organize documentation when communicating with the insurance company. General education services also will involve helping clients learn to read and understand account statements and medical bills, which can be very confusing.

6. **Educational Seminars:** Lewis Health Consultants will host affordable educational seminars to help consumers understand the basics of healthcare coverage, and how industry changes could potentially impact them or their loved ones. A primary objective of these seminars will be to gain new clients.

## Process

When first meeting with new clients, Lewis Health Consultants will identify their specific goals and objectives. Based on this information, the customer will be provided with a time and cost estimate for the services they need. In addition, a privacy release will be obtained, giving Lewis Health Consultants access to the client's health information, including medical records, claim forms, explanation of benefits, account numbers, contact information, and other documents.

# MARKETING & SALES

Lewis Health Consultants has developed a marketing plan that includes the following primary tactics:

1. A tri-fold brochure describing the business and services offered.

2. A Web site with complete details about the practice and the services it offers.

3. A social media strategy involving Facebook (for consumers) and LinkedIn (for professionals).

4. Ongoing direct mail campaigns to households within a 50-mile radius of Columbus, Ohio. Because females aged 45 to 64 often are the primary health care decision-makers for their families, mailings will be targeted toward this demographic group. Because disposable income is needed for the services provided by our firm, mailings will target consumers with household incomes of $65,000 and above.

5. Monthly seminars to educate consumers about the benefits of having a personal health advocate. These will be promoted heavily via direct mail, targeting households with incomes of $65,000 and above. The objective of these seminars will be to gain new clients.

6. A public relations campaign that involves the submission of "success stories, " in the form of press releases, to local print and broadcast media.

7. Relationship-building efforts (e.g., lunch meetings, department meeting presentations, etc.) targeting counselors, operations managers, social workers, nurses, and discharge planners at area hospitals and clinics. The objective of these efforts will be to generate referrals.

# OPERATIONS

## Location

Suitable office space for Lewis Health Consultants has been secured at 5782 Wyman Street in Columbus. Beth Lewis has negotiated a three-year lease for space that includes four offices. Two of the offices are large enough to accommodate two people, providing capacity for as many as six consultants. The office also includes a small waiting area and a conference room. Utilities are included in the lease.

## Fees

As a rule, an hourly rate of $75 will be used when calculating cost estimates for potential clients.

### Telecommunications/Internet

Lewis Health Consultants' lease includes four office telephones and business class Internet-based voice service, along with a standard broadband connection for Web and e-mail access.

### Insurance

A liability insurance policy has been obtained to cover the scope of services provided. In addition, Lewis Health Consultants will provide its employees with health insurance.

### Equipment

Lewis Health Consultants will lease a networked multi-function device (copier/scanner/printer/fax machine) from Columbus Office Associates. In addition, the business will purchase two IBM PCs during the first year, along with additional computers as more consultants are added during years two and three.

### Hours of Operation

Lewis Health Consultants will operate during regular business hours (Monday-Friday, 8 AM-5 PM). The business will be closed on the following major holidays:

- Christmas Day
- Christmas Eve
- July 4
- Labor Day
- Memorial Day
- New Year's Day
- Thanksgiving Day

## FINANCIAL ANALYSIS

The following table shows Lewis Health Consultants' projected profit for the first three years of operations:

**2014–18 Pro forma profit and loss statement**

|  | 2014 | 2015 | 2016 |
|---|---|---|---|
| **Sales** | **$202,800** | **$334,650** | **$486,225** |
| **Expenses** | | | |
| Payroll | $110,000 | $165,000 | $225,000 |
| Office lease | $ 15,000 | $ 15,000 | $ 15,000 |
| Marketing | $ 20,000 | $ 20,000 | $ 20,000 |
| Licenses & fees | $ 400 | $ 400 | $ 400 |
| Business loan | $ 12,777 | $ 12,777 | $ 12,778 |
| Accounting & legal | $ 2,250 | $ 1,200 | $ 1,200 |
| Business insurance | $ 850 | $ 950 | $ 1,050 |
| Software | $ 1,000 | $ 500 | $ 500 |
| Telecommunications | $ 3,000 | $ 3,250 | $ 3,500 |
| Equipment | $ 2,000 | $ 2,250 | $ 2,500 |
| Employee benefits | $ 18,408 | $ 27,612 | $ 36,816 |
| Payroll taxes | $ 5,500 | $ 8,250 | $ 11,250 |
| Office supplies | $ 2,250 | $ 2,250 | $ 2,250 |
| Miscellaneous | $ 1,000 | $ 1,000 | $ 1,000 |
| **Total operating costs** | **$194,435** | **$260,439** | **$333,244** |
| **Net profit** | **$ 8,365** | **$ 74,211** | **$152,981** |

The following graph provides a visual snapshot of Lewis Health Consultants' projected net profits from 2014 to 2016:

**Net profit**

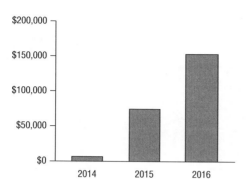

Beth Lewis will invest $15,000 of her own money into the business. She is seeking $35,000 in additional financing in the form of a three-year business loan to cover initial operating and startup costs. Lewis projects that she will recoup her personal investment during the first half of year two.

After year three, Lewis anticipates that the business will have amassed net profits of $235,557. With guidance from a financial advisor, she plans to invest a portion of these proceeds in stocks, providing the business with a source of investment income. A percentage of net profits also will be used for potential growth and expansion.

## EVALUATION & ADJUSTMENT

This plan will be evaluated every six months during Lewis Health Consultants' first three years of operations.

# Home Inspection Business

Pinnacle Inspection Services, LLC

1517 Winding Way
Colorado Springs, CO 80917

*Fran Fletcher*

*Pinnacle Inspection Services, LLC is a home inspection business based in Colorado Springs, Colorado. Pinnacle Inspection Services provides a variety of home inspection and testing services to current and potential homeowners.*

## EXECUTIVE SUMMARY

Pinnacle Inspection Services, LLC is a home inspection business based in Colorado Springs, Colorado. Pinnacle Inspection Services provides a variety of home inspection and testing services to current and potential homeowners.

Owner Bobby Wommack has 20 years of experience in the home construction business. He has many established business relationships with local regulatory agencies and realtors. Mr. Wommack recently attained national home inspection and radon certification, and therefore has the expertise necessary to run a successful home inspection service.

The home inspection industry is expected to increase at a rate of 12 percent over a ten-year period, which is considered average growth. Colorado Springs is home to over 170,000 households, which provides a large customer base for the business.

Pinnacle Inspection Services will equally market its home inspection and environmental testing services. Mr. Wommack expects that 45 percent of the company's income will be generated from basic real estate inspections and 45 percent from radon testing.

There are several other home inspection businesses in the area but Mr. Wommack is confident that Pinnacle Inspection Services will stand out from its competitors. Mr. Wommack plans to partner with a local realty and will offer their clients a discounted rate for general home inspections.

Referrals are vital in the home inspection business, and Mr. Wommack will work hard to gain the respect of clients by providing impeccable customer service. Pinnacle Inspection Services will also advertise through local real estate magazines, the yellow pages, the Chamber of Commerce, and local newspapers.

Pinnacle Inspection Services expects to see small profits almost immediately. Mr. Wommack is not seeking financing at this time. He owns a truck that he will convert to business use and he will use personal savings to cover start-up costs and monthly expenses until the business becomes profitable.

# COMPANY DESCRIPTION

### Location

Pinnacle Inspection Services is located in Colorado Springs, Colorado. Mr. Wommack plans to work out of his home office.

### Hours of Operations

Monday-Friday 9 AM-6 PM

Saturday-Sunday by appointment only

### Personnel

**Bobby Wommack (Owner/Inspector)**

Mr. Wommack will provide all home inspection services. He has 20 years of experience in the home construction industry. He holds national radon certification and national home inspection certification. He will also perform all accounting duties associated with the business.

**Inspection Assistant**

An assistant will be hired as the business grows. The assistant will be given on the job training and will obtain radon certification and any other certifications deemed necessary to provide competent testing and thorough inspections.

### Products and Services

**Products**

- Carbon monoxide detectors

- Soil meters

**Inspection Services**

- General

- Structural

- Water damage using thermal imaging

- Energy efficiency

**Testing Services**

- Radon (short and long term)

- Mold

- Carbon monoxide

- Expansive soil

# MARKET ANALYSIS

### Industry Overview

According to National Labor Statistics, jobs in the home inspection industry are expected to increase by 12 percent from 2012 to 2022. The growth of this industry is somewhat determined by local real estate markets since a large portion of business is generated from real estate inspections.

According to demographic data, there were 170,000 households in Colorado Springs in 2010. Colorado law dictates that all real estate transactions must include radon testing and that all homes must be equipped with carbon monoxide detectors. This means that there are over 170,000 potential residential clients in the area in need of services provided by Pinnacle Inspection Services.

## Target Market

Pinnacle Inspection Services has a two-fold marketing strategy that will keep business going even if area real estate sales are in a slump.

The company's primary focus will be given to residents of Colorado Springs who are in the process of buying or selling a home and need a thorough inspection in order to negotiate a fair price.

The company's secondary focus will be on homeowners who want to have their homes monitored for radon gas, carbon monoxide gas, or require other types of testing services offered by the company. Most testing will not rely heavily on the real estate market and will generate revenue even during a real estate decline.

## Competition

There are currently four competitors in Colorado Springs. Two competitors offer a full range of home inspection services, one offers services to businesses only, and one specializes in roof inspection and repair. These competitors are listed below:

1. Walker Home Inspection Services, 24330 Pike Rd., offers full range of home inspection services

2. Inspection Connection, 4259 Glendale Ave., offers full range of home inspection services

3. A+ Inspection, 31333 N. Main St., provides inspection services to businesses

4. Rudy's Roof Repair, 5200 Wyoming Way, specializes in roof inspections and repair

# GROWTH STRATEGY

The overall strategy of the company is to offer great service at a fair price. Pinnacle Inspection Services wishes to achieve strong financial growth during the first three years of operation by making a name for itself as the best, most competent inspection service in Colorado Springs.

## Sales and Marketing

According to the Small Business Center, referrals serve as the main advertising method for home inspection services. Referrals will be extremely important to Mr. Wommack's marketing strategy. He plans to partner with Pike Realty and will offer their clients a discounted rate.

Mr. Wommack has identified key advertising avenues to bring in customers and build a reputation for quality.

- Same day service and 48-hour service
- Thermal imaging to identify water damage
- Radon testing
- Comprehensive report with photos and explanation of findings

## Advertising

Advertising will include the following:

- Pike Realty
- Colorado Springs newspaper
- Local real estate magazines

- Yellow pages

- Advertising on local television*

*Advertising on local television is expensive and will only be used to boost business for testing services if the housing market declines

## FINANCIAL ANALYSIS

### Start-up costs

Mr. Wommack plans to cover the start-up costs with his personal savings. Start-up costs are estimated at $2,450.

| | |
|---|---|
| Legal fees/business license | $ 550 |
| Initial advertising | $ 200 |
| CO detectors and moisture meters | $ 200 |
| Testing supplies | $ 200 |
| Digital camera | $ 200 |
| Infrared thermography camera | $ 900 |
| Office supplies | $ 200 |
| **Total** | **$2,450** |

### Estimated Monthly Income

Mr. Wommack believes that his time will be split into the following service segments:

**Service segments**

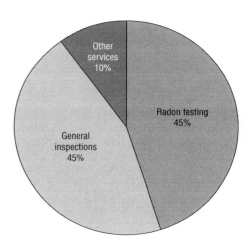

### Prices for Services

General home inspections for real estate generally take 2-2.5 hours to complete. Prices are determined based on square footage. The prices listed are based on a 2,500 sq. foot home.

| Service | Price |
|---|---|
| Same day real estate inspection | $ 100 + $100/hour |
| Inspection within 48 hours | $  50 + $100/hour |
| Short term radon testing | $ 150 |
| Long term radon testing | $ 300 |
| Mold testing | $ 150 |
| Carbon monoxide testing | $ 100/hour |
| Energy efficiency | $1,000/hour |
| Expansive soil | $ 100/hour |
| Water damage | $ 150/hour |
| Structural | $ 100/hour |

## Estimated Monthly Expenses

| | |
|---|---|
| Supplies | $ 200 |
| Phone/internet | $ 100 |
| Advertising | $ 100 |
| Insurance | $ 100 |
| Wages for Mr. Wommack | $3,200 |
| **Total** | **$3,700** |

## Profit/Loss

Mr. Wommack conservatively estimates that in the first month of operation, he will perform two general real estate inspections per week, perform two short-term radon tests each week, and one long-term radon test per month.

Mr. Wommack takes a conservative approach and estimates $3,100 income in the first month, and an increase by one general home inspection and one radon test each week, and one additional long-term radon test per month for Months 2 and 3. Then, income is estimated to remain constant with 4 general home inspections per week, 4 short-term radon tests per week, and 3 long-term radon tests per month for the next nine months. Mr. Wommack feels that this is the maximum amount of inspections that he can perform without hiring an additional employee. When an assistant is hired, the company's income will need to increase by approximately $3,200 per month to cover the assistant's salary.

**Estimated profits**

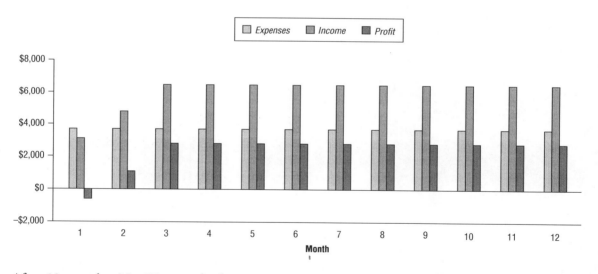

After 12 months, Mr. Wommack plans to increase his salary from $3,200 to $4,000 per month. If business continues to climb, he plans to hire an assistant during the second year, but will hire help within the first year in order to keep up with inspection requests. This will increase his monthly expenses by $4,000. He expects income to increase by 50 percent in Year 2 with the help of an assistant. Income is expected to increase an additional 25 percent in Year 3 while keeping expenses the same.

**Estimated profits years 1–3**

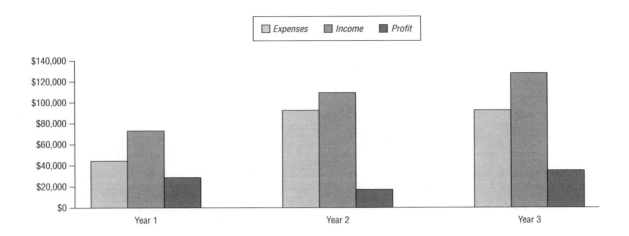

## Financing

Mr. Wommack is not seeking financing for this venture. Start-up costs are minimal and will be covered by personal savings.

# Import Export Company

Rotole Import Export Company, Inc.

90012 W. 57th St.
New York, New York 10012

*BizPlanDB.com*

*Rotole Import Export Company, Inc. is a New York-based corporation that will acquire inventories of in-demand domestic products with the intent to distribute them to wholesalers overseas. The business will also import in-demand products for distribution to wholesalers within the Domestic US market. The company was founded by Alex Rotole.*

## 1.0 EXECUTIVE SUMMARY

The purpose of this business plan is to raise $125,000 for the development of an import and export company while showcasing the expected financials and operations over the next three years. Rotole Import Export Company, Inc. is a New York-based corporation that will acquire inventories of in-demand domestic products with the intent to distribute them to wholesalers overseas. The business will also import in-demand products for distribution to wholesalers within the Domestic US market. The company was founded by Alex Rotole.

### 1.1 The Services

The primary operations of the business will be the acquisition of in-demand goods with the intent to export them to overseas countries. With the US dollar at an all-time valuation low, export businesses have thrived as overseas suppliers can purchase substantial inventories at relatively low prices.

The business' secondary revenue stream will come from the importation of in-demand foreign products with the intent to distribute them to wholesalers within the United States. As the strength of the dollar improves, Mr. Rotole will expand this segment of the business.

The third section of the business plan will further describe the services offered by Rotole Import Export Company.

### 1.2 Financing

Mr. Rotole is seeking to raise $125,000 from a bank loan. The interest rate and loan agreement are to be further discussed during negotiation. This business plan assumes that the business will receive a 10-year loan with a 9 percent fixed interest rate. The financing will be used for the following:

- Development of the company's office and warehouse location
- Financing for the first six months of operation
- Capital to purchase the initial inventories of the business

Mr. Rotole will contribute $25,000 to the venture.

### 1.3 Mission Statement

Management's mission is to develop Rotole Import Export Company into a profitable enterprise by sourcing in-demand products both domestically and internationally for sale and distribution to major wholesalers and retailers.

### 1.4 Management Team

The company was founded by Alex Rotole. Mr. Rotole has more than 10 years of experience in the import/export industry. Through his expertise, he will be able to bring the operations of the business to profitability within its first year of operations.

### 1.5 Sales Forecasts

Mr. Rotole expects a strong rate of growth at the start of operations. Below are the expected financials over the next three years.

**Proforma profit and loss (yearly)**

| Year | 1 | 2 | 3 |
|---|---|---|---|
| Sales | $1,823,400 | $2,188,080 | $2,560,054 |
| Operating costs | $ 644,337 | $ 727,628 | $ 815,164 |
| EBITDA | $ 267,363 | $ 366,412 | $ 464,863 |
| Taxes, interest, and depreciation | $ 119,484 | $ 152,503 | $ 189,400 |
| Net profit | $ 147,879 | $ 213,910 | $ 275,463 |

**Sales, operating costs, and profit forecast**

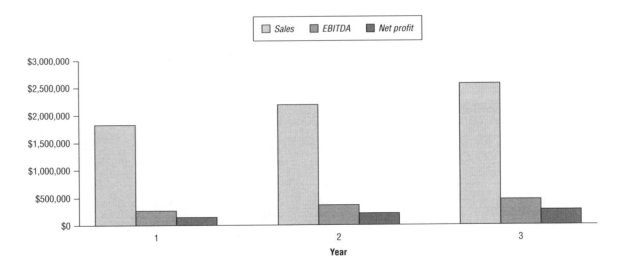

### 1.6 Expansion Plan

The Founder expects that the business will aggressively expand during the first three years of operation. Mr. Rotole intends to aggressively develop a network of wholesalers and major retailers that will purchase inventories of exported and imported goods both domestically and overseas.

## 2.0 COMPANY AND FINANCING SUMMARY

### 2.1 Registered Name and Corporate Structure

Rotole Import Export Company, Inc. is registered as a corporation in the State of New York.

## 2.2 Required Funds

At this time, Rotole Import Export Company requires $125,000 of debt funds. Below is a breakdown of how these funds will be used:

**Projected startup costs**

| | |
|---|---|
| Initial lease payments and deposits | $ 10,000 |
| Working capital | $ 35,000 |
| FF&E | $ 23,000 |
| Leasehold improvements | $ 5,000 |
| Security deposits | $ 5,000 |
| Insurance | $ 2,500 |
| Opening inventory | $ 57,000 |
| Marketing budget | $ 7,500 |
| Miscellaneous and unforeseen costs | $ 5,000 |
| **Total startup costs** | **$150,000** |

**Use of funds**

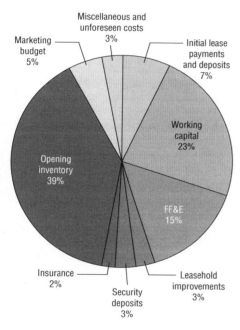

## 2.3 Investor Equity

Mr. Rotole is not seeking an investment from a third party at this time.

## 2.4 Management Equity

Alex Rotole owns 100% of Rotole Import Export Company, Inc.

## 2.5 Exit Strategy

If the business is very successful, Mr. Rotole may seek to sell the business to a third party for a significant earnings multiple. Most likely, the company will hire a qualified business broker to sell the business on behalf of Rotole Import Export Company. Based on historical numbers, the business could fetch a sales premium of up to 4 times earnings.

# 3.0 IMPORT AND EXPORT OPERATIONS

Below is a description of the importing and exporting operations of the company.

### 3.1 Exportation of In-Demand Products

As discussed in the executive summary, Management has identified an outstanding opportunity to acquire inventories of in-demand products produced domestically with the intent to distribute them overseas to wholesalers and major retailers. As the value of the U.S. dollar is now at an all-time low, many foreign buyers are seizing opportunities to purchase U.S. goods as the purchasing power parity in relation to their currency is very strong. Mr. Rotole intends to travel to Europe and Asia to find what American products are in-demand among consumers. He will then source U.S.-based manufacturers and distributors that will provide him with wholesale/distributor level pricing so that he can acquire bulk inventories.

### 3.2 Importation of In-Demand Products

At the moment, the secondary product line of the business will be the importation of in-demand goods among American consumers with the intent to resell and distribute these products to other wholesalers and retailers. As the U.S. dollar strengthens, this segment of the business will increase as the company will be able to more affordably purchase foreign produced goods for importation and distribution into the United States.

# 4.0 STRATEGIC AND MARKET ANALYSIS

### 4.1 Economic Outlook

This section of the analysis will detail the economic climate, the import/export industry, the customer profile, and the competition that the business will face as it progresses through its business operations.

Currently, the economic market condition in the United States is moderate. The meltdown of the subprime mortgage market coupled with increasing gas prices has led many people to believe that the U.S. is on the cusp of a double dip economic recession. This slowdown in the economy has also greatly impacted real estate sales, which has halted to historical lows.

Inflation is somewhat of a concern for the company. As the inflation rate decreases, the purchasing power parity of the American dollar decreases in relation to other currencies. This may pose a risk to the company should rampant inflation, much like the inflation experienced in the late 1970s, occur again. This event would significant weaken the company's ability to borrow funds, but it could also severely impact the gross margins of the business. After the business begins to generate in excess of $3,000,000 per year in revenues, the business may solicit a currency based investment bank to hedge against inflationary risks. This risk has been faced by many companies over the last five years as the value of the Euro/Yuan/Yen has appreciated significantly in its relation to the American dollar.

### 4.2 Industry Analysis

Each year more than $3 trillion dollars of products (and now services with the advent of the Internet) are traded with foreign countries. Currently, with the dollar at an all-time low, net exports are beginning to exceed imports as foreign buyers are recognizing tremendous bargains for American goods simply due to the condition of the U.S. dollar. Based on information from the U.S. Economic Census and the Bureau of Labor Statistics, there are more than 2 million businesses that are actively engaged in the importation or exportation of goods and services. Approximately 10 percent of these companies operate in a general importing and exporting capacity while the remaining businesses typically have a specific product focus.

During the next two years, Management expects that imports will become more in-demand as the dollar strengths as a result of natural growth in the U.S. economy and a return to more stable economy.

## 4.3 Customer Profile

As the company intends to purchase a number of in-demand products, both domestically and internationally, it is difficult to determine the end users of the company's product lines. However, Management has developed a demographic profile for the types of wholesalers and retailers of which Mr. Rotole intends to develop strategic partnerships. These demographics include, but are not limited to the following:

• Generates revenues in excess of $5,000,000

• Operates as a wholesaler or major retailer

• Has EBITDA in excess of $500,000

Although these demographics are broad, the business intends to carry extensive inventories of products ranging from household goods to state-of-the-art electronics.

## 4.4 Competition

As there are literally two million businesses engaged in imports/exports industry, it is very difficult to determine the competition that the business will continue to face as it progresses through operations. However, one of the ways that Rotole Import Export Company intends to maintain competitive operations is to operate a very lean operating infrastructure, which can ensure that costs savings are passed onto wholesalers, distributors, and retailers both domestically and abroad.

# 5.0 MARKETING PLAN

Rotole Import Export Company intends to maintain an extensive marketing campaign that will ensure maximum visibility for the business in its targeted market. Below is an overview of the marketing strategies and objectives of Rotole Import Export Company.

## 5.1 Marketing Objectives

• Develop an online presence by developing a website and placing the company's name and contact information with online directories

• Establish relationships with wholesalers, retailers, and distributors domestically and internationally

## 5.2 Marketing Strategies

The company will engage a number of traditional and experimental sales and marketing strategies in order to have a high inventory turnover. Rotole Import Export Company's advertising campaigns will be completed through Internet, print and media campaigns, word of mouth referral, and public relations.

At the onset of operations, the company will develop a number of relationships with domestic and internationally based trade brokers that will allow the business to immediately begin divesting inventories of products. As Mr. Rotole has had extensive experience and contacts within the industry, he will draw on these existing relationships to build a network of brokers that source products on behalf of Rotole Import Export Company.

The Management of Rotole Import Export Company also intends to use an online based marketing campaign to develop its sales. Primarily, the company will use search engine optimization techniques that will increase the company's visibility when selected key words regarding the importation and exportation of products are used among major search engines. The company's website will be an expansive online platform that showcases Rotole Import Export Company's operations, the product lines that it carries, how to become a trading partner with the business, and policies regarding trade and carrying terms.

### 5.3 Pricing

Pricing will range based on the products imported/exported by the business. Management anticipates that the business will generate gross margins of 50 percent on all sales made through the business.

# 6.0 ORGANIZATIONAL PLAN AND PERSONNEL SUMMARY

## 6.1 Corporate Organization

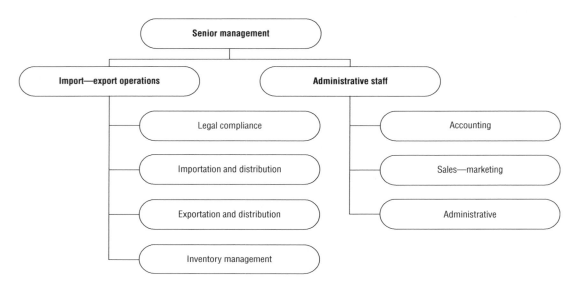

## 6.2 Organizational Budget

**Personnel plan—yearly**

| Year | 1 | 2 | 3 |
|---|---|---|---|
| Owner | $150,000 | $154,500 | $159,135 |
| Inventory manager | $ 55,000 | $ 56,650 | $ 58,350 |
| Distribution specialists | $ 35,000 | $ 36,050 | $ 37,132 |
| Legal compliance manager | $135,000 | $185,400 | $238,703 |
| Administrative and accounting | $ 55,000 | $ 56,650 | $ 58,350 |
| **Total** | **$430,000** | **$489,250** | **$551,668** |
| **Numbers of personnel** | | | |
| Owner | 2 | 2 | 2 |
| Inventory manager | 1 | 1 | 1 |
| Distribution specialists | 1 | 1 | 1 |
| Legal compliance manager | 3 | 4 | 5 |
| Administrative and accounting | 2 | 2 | 2 |
| **Totals** | **9** | **10** | **11** |

**Personnel expense breakdown**

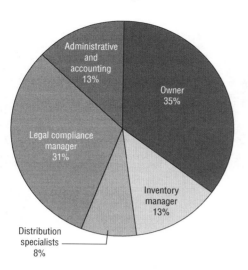

---

# 7.0 FINANCIAL PLAN

### 7.1 Underlying Assumptions

The company has based its proforma financial statements on the following:

- Rotole Import Export Company will have an annual revenue growth rate of 16% per year.

- The Owner will acquire $125,000 of debt funds to develop the business.

- The loan will have a 10-year term with a 9 percent interest rate.

### 7.2 Sensitivity Analysis

Rotole Import Export Company's revenues are sensitive to several changes in the general economy. Primarily, the risks associated with the company's operations revolve around the varying fluctuations of currency. However, as the business will operate as both an importer and exporter of products, the risks associated with a weak dollar vs. a strong dollar should cancel each other out.

### 7.3 Source of Funds

**Financing**

| | |
|---|---|
| **Equity contributions** | |
| Management investment | $ 25,000.00 |
| **Total equity financing** | **$ 25,000.00** |
| **Banks and lenders** | |
| Banks and lenders | $ 125,000.00 |
| **Total debt financing** | **$125,000.00** |
| **Total financing** | **$150,000.00** |

## 7.4 General Assumptions

**General assumptions**

| Year | 1 | 2 | 3 |
|---|---|---|---|
| Short term interest rate | 9.5% | 9.5% | 9.5% |
| Long term interest rate | 10.0% | 10.0% | 10.0% |
| Federal tax rate | 33.0% | 33.0% | 33.0% |
| State tax rate | 5.0% | 5.0% | 5.0% |
| Personnel taxes | 15.0% | 15.0% | 15.0% |

## 7.5 Profit and Loss Statements

**Proforma profit and loss (yearly)**

| Year | 1 | 2 | 3 |
|---|---|---|---|
| **Sales** | **$1,823,400** | **$2,188,080** | **$2,560,054** |
| Cost of goods sold | $ 911,700 | $ 1,094,040 | $ 1,280,027 |
| Gross margin | 50.00% | 50.00% | 50.00% |
| **Operating income** | **$ 911,700** | **$1,094,040** | **$1,280,027** |
| **Expenses** | | | |
| Payroll | $ 430,000 | $ 489,250 | $ 551,668 |
| General and administrative | $ 25,200 | $ 26,208 | $ 27,256 |
| Marketing expenses | $ 36,468 | $ 43,762 | $ 51,201 |
| Professional fees and licensure | $ 15,219 | $ 15,676 | $ 16,146 |
| Insurance costs | $ 11,987 | $ 12,586 | $ 13,216 |
| Travel and vehicle costs | $ 27,596 | $ 30,356 | $ 33,391 |
| Rent and utilities | $ 24,250 | $ 25,463 | $ 26,736 |
| Miscellaneous costs | $ 9,117 | $ 10,940 | $ 12,800 |
| Payroll taxes | $ 64,500 | $ 73,388 | $ 82,750 |
| **Total operating costs** | **$ 644,337** | **$ 727,628** | **$ 815,164** |
| **EBITDA** | **$ 267,363** | **$ 366,412** | **$ 464,863** |
| Federal income tax | $ 88,230 | $ 117,562 | $ 150,324 |
| State income tax | $ 13,368 | $ 17,812 | $ 22,776 |
| Interest expense | $ 10,922 | $ 10,164 | $ 9,335 |
| Depreciation expenses | $ 6,964 | $ 6,964 | $ 6,964 |
| **Net profit** | **$ 147,879** | **$ 213,910** | **$ 275,463** |
| **Profit margin** | **8.11%** | **9.78%** | **10.76%** |

**Sales, operating costs, and profit forecast**

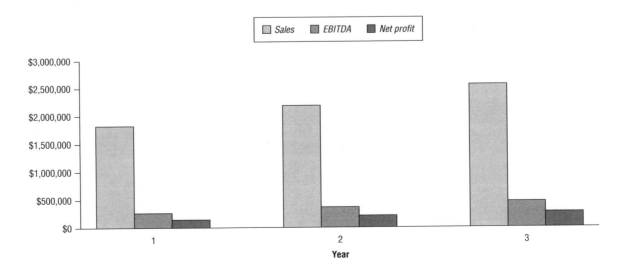

## 7.6 Cash Flow Analysis

**Proforma cash flow analysis—yearly**

| Year | 1 | 2 | 3 |
|---|---|---|---|
| Cash from operations | $154,843 | $220,874 | $282,427 |
| Cash from receivables | $    0 | $    0 | $    0 |
| **Operating cash inflow** | **$154,843** | **$220,874** | **$282,427** |
| **Other cash inflows** | | | |
| Equity investment | $ 25,000 | $    0 | $    0 |
| Increased borrowings | $125,000 | $    0 | $    0 |
| Sales of business assets | $    0 | $    0 | $    0 |
| A/P increases | $ 37,902 | $ 43,587 | $ 50,125 |
| **Total other cash inflows** | **$187,902** | **$ 43,587** | **$ 50,125** |
| **Total cash inflow** | **$342,745** | **$264,461** | **$332,552** |
| **Cash outflows** | | | |
| Repayment of principal | $  8,079 | $  8,837 | $  9,666 |
| A/P decreases | $ 24,897 | $ 29,876 | $ 35,852 |
| A/R increases | $    0 | $    0 | $    0 |
| Asset purchases | $ 97,500 | $ 55,218 | $ 70,607 |
| Dividends | $108,390 | $154,612 | $197,699 |
| **Total cash outflows** | **$238,866** | **$248,544** | **$313,823** |
| **Net cash flow** | **$103,879** | **$ 15,917** | **$ 18,729** |
| **Cash balance** | **$103,879** | **$119,796** | **$138,525** |

**Proforma cash flow (yearly)**

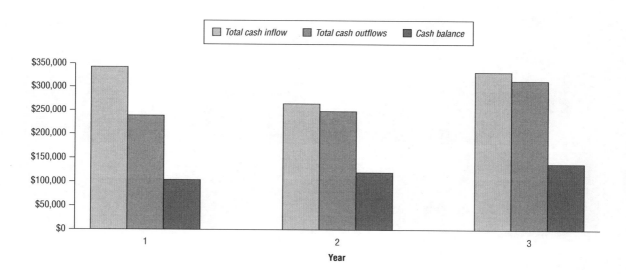

## 7.7 Balance Sheet

**Proforma balance sheet—yearly**

| Year | 1 | 2 | 3 |
|---|---|---|---|
| **Assets** | | | |
| Cash | $103,879 | $119,796 | $138,525 |
| Amortized development/expansion costs | $ 17,500 | $ 23,022 | $ 30,083 |
| Inventory | $ 57,000 | $ 84,609 | $119,913 |
| FF&E | $ 23,000 | $ 45,087 | $ 73,330 |
| Accumulated depreciation | ($ 6,964) | ($ 13,929) | ($ 20,893) |
| **Total assets** | **$194,414** | **$258,586** | **$340,957** |
| **Liabilities and equity** | | | |
| Accounts payable | $ 13,005 | $ 26,716 | $ 40,990 |
| Long term liabilities | $116,921 | $108,084 | $ 99,247 |
| Other liabilities | $ 0 | $ 0 | $ 0 |
| **Total liabilities** | **$129,926** | **$134,800** | **$140,236** |
| **Net worth** | **$ 64,489** | **$123,786** | **$200,721** |
| **Total liabilities and equity** | **$194,414** | **$258,586** | **$340,957** |

**Proforma balance sheet**

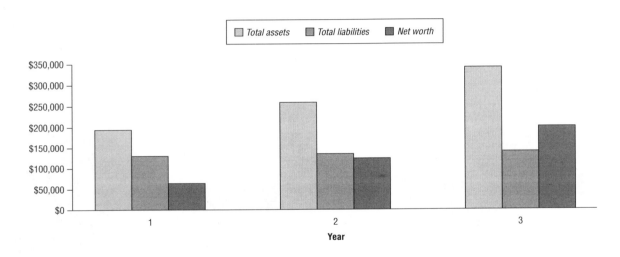

## 7.8 Breakeven Analysis

**Monthly break even analysis**

| Year | 1 | 2 | 3 |
|---|---|---|---|
| Monthly revenue | $ 107,390 | $ 121,271 | $ 135,861 |
| Yearly revenue | $1,288,674 | $1,455,255 | $1,630,328 |

**Break even analysis**

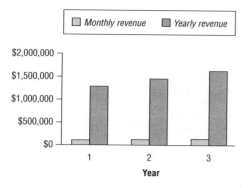

## 7.9 Business Ratios

**Business ratios—yearly**

| Year | 1 | 2 | 3 |
|---|---|---|---|
| **Sales** | | | |
| Sales growth | 0.00% | 20.00% | 17.00% |
| Gross margin | 50.00% | 50.00% | 50.00% |
| **Financials** | | | |
| Profit margin | 8.11% | 9.78% | 10.76% |
| Assets to liabilities | 1.50 | 1.92 | 2.43 |
| Equity to liabilities | 0.50 | 0.92 | 1.43 |
| Assets to equity | 3.01 | 2.09 | 1.70 |
| **Liquidity** | | | |
| Acid test | 0.80 | 0.89 | 0.99 |
| Cash to assets | 0.53 | 0.46 | 0.41 |

## 7.10 Three Year Profit and Loss Statement

**Profit and loss statement (first year)**

| Month | 1 | 2 | 3 | 4 | 5 | 6 | 7 |
|---|---|---|---|---|---|---|---|
| **Sales** | $150,300 | $150,600 | $150,900 | $151,200 | $151,500 | $151,800 | $152,100 |
| Cost of goods sold | $ 75,150 | $ 75,300 | $ 75,450 | $ 75,600 | $ 75,750 | $ 75,900 | $ 76,050 |
| Gross margin | 50.00% | 50.00% | 50.00% | 50.00% | 50.00% | 50.00% | 50.00% |
| **Operating income** | $ 75,150 | $ 75,300 | $ 75,450 | $ 75,600 | $ 75,750 | $ 75,900 | $ 76,050 |
| **Expenses** | | | | | | | |
| Payroll | $ 35,833 | $ 35,833 | $ 35,833 | $ 35,833 | $ 35,833 | $ 35,833 | $ 35,833 |
| General and administrative | $ 2,100 | $ 2,100 | $ 2,100 | $ 2,100 | $ 2,100 | $ 2,100 | $ 2,100 |
| Marketing expenses | $ 3,039 | $ 3,039 | $ 3,039 | $ 3,039 | $ 3,039 | $ 3,039 | $ 3,039 |
| Professional fees and licensure | $ 1,268 | $ 1,268 | $ 1,268 | $ 1,268 | $ 1,268 | $ 1,268 | $ 1,268 |
| Insurance costs | $ 999 | $ 999 | $ 999 | $ 999 | $ 999 | $ 999 | $ 999 |
| Travel and vehicle costs | $ 2,300 | $ 2,300 | $ 2,300 | $ 2,300 | $ 2,300 | $ 2,300 | $ 2,300 |
| Rent and utilities | $ 2,021 | $ 2,021 | $ 2,021 | $ 2,021 | $ 2,021 | $ 2,021 | $ 2,021 |
| Miscellaneous costs | $ 760 | $ 760 | $ 760 | $ 760 | $ 760 | $ 760 | $ 760 |
| Payroll taxes | $ 5,375 | $ 5,375 | $ 5,375 | $ 5,375 | $ 5,375 | $ 5,375 | $ 5,375 |
| **Total operating costs** | $ 53,695 | $ 53,695 | $ 53,695 | $ 53,695 | $ 53,695 | $ 53,695 | $ 53,695 |
| **EBITDA** | $ 21,455 | $ 21,605 | $ 21,755 | $ 21,905 | $ 22,055 | $ 22,205 | $ 22,355 |
| Federal income tax | $ 7,273 | $ 7,287 | $ 7,302 | $ 7,316 | $ 7,331 | $ 7,345 | $ 7,360 |
| State income tax | $ 1,102 | $ 1,104 | $ 1,106 | $ 1,109 | $ 1,111 | $ 1,113 | $ 1,115 |
| Interest expense | $ 938 | $ 933 | $ 928 | $ 923 | $ 918 | $ 913 | $ 908 |
| Depreciation expense | $ 580 | $ 580 | $ 580 | $ 580 | $ 580 | $ 580 | $ 580 |
| **Net profit** | $ 11,563 | $ 11,701 | $ 11,839 | $ 11,977 | $ 12,116 | $ 12,254 | $ 12,392 |

### Profit and loss statement (first year cont.)

| Month | 8 | 9 | 10 | 11 | 12 | 1 |
|---|---|---|---|---|---|---|
| Sales | $152,400 | $152,700 | $153,000 | $153,300 | $153,600 | $1,823,400 |
| Cost of goods sold | $ 76,200 | $ 76,350 | $ 76,500 | $ 76,650 | $ 76,800 | $ 911,700 |
| Gross margin | 50.00% | 50.00% | 50.00% | 50.00% | 50.00% | 50.00% |
| Operating income | $ 76,200 | $ 76,350 | $ 76,500 | $ 76,650 | $ 76,800 | $ 911,700 |
| Expenses | | | | | | |
| Payroll | $ 35,833 | $ 35,833 | $ 35,833 | $ 35,833 | $ 35,833 | $ 430,000 |
| General and administrative | $ 2,100 | $ 2,100 | $ 2,100 | $ 2,100 | $ 2,100 | $ 25,200 |
| Marketing expenses | $ 3,039 | $ 3,039 | $ 3,039 | $ 3,039 | $ 3,039 | $ 36,468 |
| Professional fees and licensure | $ 1,268 | $ 1,268 | $ 1,268 | $ 1,268 | $ 1,268 | $ 15,219 |
| Insurance costs | $ 999 | $ 999 | $ 999 | $ 999 | $ 999 | $ 11,987 |
| Travel and vehicle costs | $ 2,300 | $ 2,300 | $ 2,300 | $ 2,300 | $ 2,300 | $ 27,596 |
| Rent and utilities | $ 2,021 | $ 2,021 | $ 2,021 | $ 2,021 | $ 2,021 | $ 24,250 |
| Miscellaneous costs | $ 760 | $ 760 | $ 760 | $ 760 | $ 760 | $ 9,117 |
| Payroll taxes | $ 5,375 | $ 5,375 | $ 5,375 | $ 5,375 | $ 5,375 | $ 64,500 |
| Total operating costs | $ 53,695 | $ 53,695 | $ 53,695 | $ 53,695 | $ 53,695 | $ 644,337 |
| EBITDA | $ 22,505 | $ 22,655 | $ 22,805 | $ 22,955 | $ 23,105 | $ 267,363 |
| Federal income tax | $ 7,374 | $ 7,389 | $ 7,403 | $ 7,418 | $ 7,432 | $ 88,230 |
| State income tax | $ 1,117 | $ 1,120 | $ 1,122 | $ 1,124 | $ 1,126 | $ 13,368 |
| Interest expense | $ 903 | $ 898 | $ 893 | $ 887 | $ 882 | $ 10,922 |
| Depreciation expense | $ 580 | $ 580 | $ 580 | $ 580 | $ 580 | $ 6,964 |
| Net profit | $ 12,531 | $ 12,669 | $ 12,807 | $ 12,946 | $ 13,084 | $ 147,879 |

### Profit and loss statement (second year)

| Quarter | Q1 | 2 Q2 | Q3 | Q4 | 2 |
|---|---|---|---|---|---|
| Sales | $437,616 | $547,020 | $590,782 | $612,662 | $2,188,080 |
| Cost of goods sold | $218,808 | $273,510 | $295,391 | $306,331 | $1,094,040 |
| Gross margin | 50.00% | 50.00% | 50.00% | 50.00% | 50.00% |
| Operating income | $218,808 | $273,510 | $295,391 | $306,331 | $1,094,040 |
| Expenses | | | | | |
| Payroll | $ 97,850 | $122,313 | $132,098 | $136,990 | $ 489,250 |
| General and administrative | $ 5,242 | $ 6,552 | $ 7,076 | $ 7,338 | $ 26,208 |
| Marketing expenses | $ 8,752 | $ 10,940 | $ 11,816 | $ 12,253 | $ 43,762 |
| Professional fees and licensure | $ 3,135 | $ 3,919 | $ 4,232 | $ 4,389 | $ 15,676 |
| Insurance costs | $ 2,517 | $ 3,147 | $ 3,398 | $ 3,524 | $ 12,586 |
| Travel and vehicle costs | $ 6,071 | $ 7,589 | $ 8,196 | $ 8,500 | $ 30,356 |
| Rent and utilities | $ 5,093 | $ 6,366 | $ 6,875 | $ 7,130 | $ 25,463 |
| Miscellaneous costs | $ 2,188 | $ 2,735 | $ 2,954 | $ 3,063 | $ 10,940 |
| Payroll taxes | $ 14,678 | $ 18,347 | $ 19,815 | $ 20,549 | $ 73,388 |
| Total operating costs | $145,526 | $181,907 | $196,459 | $203,736 | $ 727,628 |
| EBITDA | $ 73,282 | $ 91,603 | $ 98,931 | $102,595 | $ 366,412 |
| Federal income tax | $ 23,512 | $ 29,390 | $ 31,742 | $ 32,917 | $ 117,562 |
| State income tax | $ 3,562 | $ 4,453 | $ 4,809 | $ 4,987 | $ 17,812 |
| Interest expense | $ 2,615 | $ 2,566 | $ 2,517 | $ 2,466 | $ 10,164 |
| Depreciation expense | $ 1,741 | $ 1,741 | $ 1,741 | $ 1,741 | $ 6,964 |
| Net profit | $ 41,852 | $ 53,452 | $ 58,122 | $ 60,483 | $ 213,910 |

## Profit and loss statement (third year)

| Quarter | Q1 | 3 Q2 | Q3 | Q4 | 3 |
|---|---|---|---|---|---|
| Sales | $512,011 | $640,013 | $691,214 | $716,815 | $2,560,054 |
| Cost of goods sold | $256,005 | $320,007 | $345,607 | $358,408 | $1,280,027 |
| Gross margin | 50.00% | 50.00% | 50.00% | 50.00% | 50.00% |
| Operating income | $256,005 | $320,007 | $345,607 | $358,408 | $1,280,027 |
| **Expenses** | | | | | |
| Payroll | $110,334 | $137,917 | $148,950 | $154,467 | $ 551,668 |
| General and administrative | $ 5,451 | $ 6,814 | $ 7,359 | $ 7,632 | $ 27,256 |
| Marketing expenses | $ 10,240 | $ 12,800 | $ 13,824 | $ 14,336 | $ 51,201 |
| Professional fees and licensure | $ 3,229 | $ 4,036 | $ 4,359 | $ 4,521 | $ 16,146 |
| Insurance costs | $ 2,643 | $ 3,304 | $ 3,568 | $ 3,700 | $ 13,216 |
| Travel and vehicle costs | $ 6,678 | $ 8,348 | $ 9,016 | $ 9,350 | $ 33,391 |
| Rent and utilities | $ 5,347 | $ 6,684 | $ 7,219 | $ 7,486 | $ 26,736 |
| Miscellaneous costs | $ 2,560 | $ 3,200 | $ 3,456 | $ 3,584 | $ 12,800 |
| Payroll taxes | $ 16,550 | $ 20,688 | $ 22,343 | $ 23,170 | $ 82,750 |
| **Total operating costs** | **$163,033** | **$203,791** | **$220,094** | **$228,246** | **$ 815,164** |
| **EBITDA** | **$ 92,973** | **$116,216** | **$125,513** | **$130,162** | **$ 464,863** |
| Federal income tax | $ 30,065 | $ 37,581 | $ 40,587 | $ 42,091 | $ 150,324 |
| State income tax | $ 4,555 | $ 5,694 | $ 6,150 | $ 6,377 | $ 22,776 |
| Interest expense | $ 2,414 | $ 2,361 | $ 2,307 | $ 2,252 | $ 9,335 |
| Depreciation expense | $ 1,741 | $ 1,741 | $ 1,741 | $ 1,741 | $ 6,964 |
| **Net profit** | **$ 54,197** | **$ 68,838** | **$ 74,727** | **$ 77,700** | **$ 275,463** |

# 7.11 Three Year Cash Flow Analysis

## Cash flow analysis (first year)

| Month | 1 | 2 | 3 | 4 | 5 | 6 | 7 |
|---|---|---|---|---|---|---|---|
| Cash from operations | $ 12,143 | $12,281 | $12,419 | $ 12,558 | $ 12,696 | $ 12,834 | $ 12,973 |
| Cash from receivables | $ 0 | $ 0 | $ 0 | $ 0 | $ 0 | $ 0 | $ 0 |
| **Operating cash inflow** | **$ 12,143** | **$12,281** | **$12,419** | **$ 12,558** | **$ 12,696** | **$ 12,834** | **$ 12,973** |
| **Other cash inflows** | | | | | | | |
| Equity investment | $ 25,000 | $ 0 | $ 0 | $ 0 | $ 0 | $ 0 | $ 0 |
| Increased borrowings | $125,000 | $ 0 | $ 0 | $ 0 | $ 0 | $ 0 | $ 0 |
| Sales of business assets | $ 0 | $ 0 | $ 0 | $ 0 | $ 0 | $ 0 | $ 0 |
| A/P increases | $ 3,159 | $ 3,159 | $ 3,159 | $ 3,159 | $ 3,159 | $ 3,159 | $ 3,159 |
| **Total other cash inflows** | **$153,159** | **$ 3,159** | **$ 3,159** | **$ 3,159** | **$ 3,159** | **$ 3,159** | **$ 3,159** |
| **Total cash inflow** | **$165,302** | **$15,440** | **$15,578** | **$ 15,716** | **$ 15,854** | **$ 15,993** | **$ 16,131** |
| **Cash outflows** | | | | | | | |
| Repayment of principal | $ 646 | $ 651 | $ 656 | $ 661 | $ 666 | $ 671 | $ 676 |
| A/P decreases | $ 2,075 | $ 2,075 | $ 2,075 | $ 2,075 | $ 2,075 | $ 2,075 | $ 2,075 |
| A/R increases | $ 0 | $ 0 | $ 0 | $ 0 | $ 0 | $ 0 | $ 0 |
| Asset purchases | $ 97,500 | $ 0 | $ 0 | $ 0 | $ 0 | $ 0 | $ 0 |
| Dividends | $ 0 | $ 0 | $ 0 | $ 0 | $ 0 | $ 0 | $ 0 |
| **Total cash outflows** | **$100,221** | **$ 2,726** | **$ 2,730** | **$ 2,735** | **$ 2,740** | **$ 2,745** | **$ 2,750** |
| **Net cash flow** | **$ 65,081** | **$12,714** | **$12,848** | **$ 12,981** | **$ 13,114** | **$ 13,247** | **$ 13,381** |
| **Cash balance** | **$ 65,081** | **$77,795** | **$90,643** | **$103,624** | **$116,738** | **$129,985** | **$143,366** |

## Cash flow analysis (first year cont.)

| Month | 8 | 9 | 10 | 11 | 12 | 1 |
|---|---|---|---|---|---|---|
| Cash from operations | $ 13,111 | $ 13,249 | $ 13,388 | $ 13,526 | $ 13,665 | $154,843 |
| Cash from receivables | $ 0 | $ 0 | $ 0 | $ 0 | $ 0 | $ 0 |
| **Operating cash inflow** | **$ 13,111** | **$ 13,249** | **$ 13,388** | **$ 13,526** | **$ 13,665** | **$154,843** |
| **Other cash inflows** | | | | | | |
| Equity investment | $ 0 | $ 0 | $ 0 | $ 0 | $ 0 | $ 25,000 |
| Increased borrowings | $ 0 | $ 0 | $ 0 | $ 0 | $ 0 | $125,000 |
| Sales of business assets | $ 0 | $ 0 | $ 0 | $ 0 | $ 0 | $ 0 |
| A/P increases | $ 3,159 | $ 3,159 | $ 3,159 | $ 3,159 | $ 3,159 | $ 37,902 |
| **Total other cash inflows** | **$ 3,159** | **$ 3,159** | **$ 3,159** | **$ 3,159** | **$ 3,159** | **$187,902** |
| **Total cash inflow** | **$ 16,269** | **$ 16,408** | **$ 16,546** | **$ 16,685** | **$ 16,823** | **$342,745** |
| **Cash outflows** | | | | | | |
| Repayment of principal | $ 681 | $ 686 | $ 691 | $ 696 | $ 701 | $ 8,079 |
| A/P decreases | $ 2,075 | $ 2,075 | $ 2,075 | $ 2,075 | $ 2,075 | $ 24,897 |
| A/R increases | $ 0 | $ 0 | $ 0 | $ 0 | $ 0 | $ 0 |
| Asset purchases | $ 0 | $ 0 | $ 0 | $ 0 | $ 0 | $ 97,500 |
| Dividends | $ 0 | $ 0 | $ 0 | $ 0 | $108,390 | $108,390 |
| **Total cash outflows** | **$ 2,755** | **$ 2,760** | **$ 2,766** | **$ 2,771** | **$111,166** | **$238,866** |
| **Net cash flow** | **$ 13,514** | **$ 13,647** | **$ 13,781** | **$ 13,914** | **−$ 94,343** | **$103,879** |
| **Cash balance** | **$156,880** | **$170,527** | **$184,308** | **$198,222** | **$103,879** | **$103,879** |

## Cash flow analysis (second year)

| Quarter | Q1 | 2 Q2 | Q3 | Q4 | 2 |
|---|---|---|---|---|---|
| Cash from operations | $ 44,175 | $ 55,218 | $ 59,636 | $ 61,845 | $220,874 |
| Cash from receivables | $ 0 | $ 0 | $ 0 | $ 0 | $ 0 |
| **Operating cash inflow** | **$ 44,175** | **$ 55,218** | **$ 59,636** | **$ 61,845** | **$220,874** |
| **Other cash inflows** | | | | | |
| Equity investment | $ 0 | $ 0 | $ 0 | $ 0 | $ 0 |
| Increased borrowings | $ 0 | $ 0 | $ 0 | $ 0 | $ 0 |
| Sales of business assets | $ 0 | $ 0 | $ 0 | $ 0 | $ 0 |
| A/P increases | $ 8,717 | $ 10,897 | $ 11,769 | $ 12,204 | $ 43,587 |
| **Total other cash inflows** | **$ 8,717** | **$ 10,897** | **$ 11,769** | **$ 12,204** | **$ 43,587** |
| **Total cash inflow** | **$ 52,892** | **$ 66,115** | **$ 71,405** | **$ 74,049** | **$264,461** |
| **Cash outflows** | | | | | |
| Repayment of principal | $ 2,136 | $ 2,184 | $ 2,233 | $ 2,284 | $ 8,837 |
| A/P decreases | $ 5,975 | $ 7,469 | $ 8,067 | $ 8,365 | $ 29,876 |
| A/R increases | $ 0 | $ 0 | $ 0 | $ 0 | $ 0 |
| Asset purchases | $ 11,044 | $ 13,805 | $ 14,909 | $ 15,461 | $ 55,218 |
| Dividends | $ 30,922 | $ 38,653 | $ 41,745 | $ 43,291 | $154,612 |
| **Total cash outflows** | **$ 50,077** | **$ 62,111** | **$ 66,954** | **$ 69,402** | **$248,544** |
| **Net cash flow** | **$ 2,815** | **$ 4,005** | **$ 4,450** | **$ 4,647** | **$ 15,917** |
| **Cash balance** | **$106,694** | **$110,699** | **$115,149** | **$119,796** | **$119,796** |

**Cash flow analysis (third year)**

| Quarter | Q1 | 3 Q2 | Q3 | Q4 | 3 |
|---|---|---|---|---|---|
| Cash from operations | $ 56,485 | $ 70,607 | $ 76,255 | $ 79,080 | $282,427 |
| Cash from receivables | $ 0 | $ 0 | $ 0 | $ 0 | $ 0 |
| **Operating cash inflow** | **$ 56,485** | **$ 70,607** | **$ 76,255** | **$ 79,080** | **$282,427** |
| **Other cash inflows** | | | | | |
| Equity investment | $ 0 | $ 0 | $ 0 | $ 0 | $ 0 |
| Increased borrowings | $ 0 | $ 0 | $ 0 | $ 0 | $ 0 |
| Sales of business assets | $ 0 | $ 0 | $ 0 | $ 0 | $ 0 |
| A/P increases | $ 10,025 | $ 12,531 | $ 13,534 | $ 14,035 | $ 50,125 |
| **Total other cash inflows** | **$ 10,025** | **$ 12,531** | **$ 13,534** | **$ 14,035** | **$ 50,125** |
| **Total cash inflow** | **$ 66,510** | **$ 83,138** | **$ 89,789** | **$ 93,115** | **$332,552** |
| **Cash outflows** | | | | | |
| Repayment of principal | $ 2,336 | $ 2,389 | $ 2,443 | $ 2,498 | $ 9,666 |
| A/P decreases | $ 7,170 | $ 8,963 | $ 9,680 | $ 10,038 | $ 35,852 |
| A/R increases | $ 0 | $ 0 | $ 0 | $ 0 | $ 0 |
| Asset purchases | $ 14,121 | $ 17,652 | $ 19,064 | $ 19,770 | $ 70,607 |
| Dividends | $ 39,540 | $ 49,425 | $ 53,379 | $ 55,356 | $197,699 |
| **Total cash outflows** | **$ 63,167** | **$ 78,428** | **$ 84,565** | **$ 87,662** | **$313,823** |
| **Net cash flow** | **$ 3,343** | **$ 4,710** | **$ 5,224** | **$ 5,452** | **$ 18,729** |
| **Cash balance** | **$123,139** | **$127,849** | **$133,073** | **$138,525** | **$138,525** |

# Medical Billing Business

Bottom Line Medical Billing, Inc.

357 Vallejo Street
Sacramento, CA 95833

*Claire Moore*

*Bottom Line Medical Billing, Inc. will provide clients with cloud-based electronic medical billing services. Our clients will realize increased cash flow as a result of outsourcing their billing tasks.*

---

## EXECUTIVE SUMMARY

One of the biggest challenges to those in the healing professions is navigating the complex systems of health insurers' systems. Thousands are spent each year in an attempt to collect the proper fees for services rendered. The Center for Information Technology Leadership, a nonprofit health-technology research group, estimates the total annual cost to medical providers to be as high as $10 billion.

One key to managing costs of processing claims is the use of electronic claims submission. In a 2006 report titled, "Follow That Claim," the American Medical Association (AMA) stated that the average cost of processing an error-free electronic claim would be $2.90 compared to $6.63 for a comparable manual claim. The report projected that the average health professional could save as much as 60 percent on funds spent to process claims transactions per year when using electronic processing.

Electronic claims submission reduces errors because it reduces the amount of manual data entry required. This reduction in errors shortens the turnaround time of claims.

Claims that are processed electronically are either submitted to a clearinghouse, or in the case of high-volume health insurers such as Medicare, they are sent directly to the health insurer.

Bottom Line Medical Billing, Inc. will provide clients with cloud-based electronic medical billing services. Our clients will realize increased cash flow as a result of outsourcing their billing tasks.

We have a combined total of 13 years of experience in medical billing, including electronic billing. Our expertise covers a variety of medical specialties and includes medical office, billing coding, and insurance and business experience.

This business plan is for internal use and is not intended for use in obtaining funding.

---

## OBJECTIVES

Bottom Line Medical Billing, Inc. will achieve the following objectives:

- We will acquire at least one additional account by the end of the second year in business

- We will process at least 800 claims a month by our second year in business
- We will become recognized as a trusted local provider of medical billing and reimbursement services

## MISSION

At Bottom Line Medical Billing, Inc. we help health professionals to increase their cash flow by maintaining an efficient system of claims submission, review, tracking, posting and follow up. We take over the responsibility of keeping up with the ever-changing requirements that are imposed by health insurers, government, and other agencies, thus saving our clients valuable time that they can devote to growing their practice.

## COMPANY SUMMARY

Bottom Line Medical Billing, Inc. is organized as a corporation. Articles of incorporation were filed with the California Secretary of State in February, 2014. The Law Office of John Smith is the agent for service of process.

A fictitious name statement has been filed with our city and county clerk and our logo has been trademarked through the United States Department of Commerce Patent and Trademark Office.

## COMPANY OWNERSHIP

Ownership in Bottom Line Medical Billing, Inc. is split equally between Sonya Martinez and Amber Smith.

Sonya worked for five years as a claims processor for a national health insurance company with offices in Sacramento. She is a graduate of American River College with an associate degree in business.

Amber Smith has worked for eight years as a billing manager for a 5- physician multi-specialty medical clinic in Sacramento. She received training in medical billing and coding by taking courses at Sierra Community College in Rocklin, CA. Upon completion of her training Amber earned Certified Professional Coder (CPC) certification as a professional coder through the American Association of Professional Coders (AAPC).

Both Sonya and Amber are members of the American Medical Billing Association (AMBA) and both have earned CMRS Certified Medical Reimbursement Specialist certification.

Both have years of experience in the following:

- Medical terminology
- International Statistical Classifications of Diseases ICD-9
- Healthcare Common Procedure Coding System (HCPCS)
- Current Procedural Terminology (CPT) coding
- Knowledge of California workers' compensation Regulations and Billing Guidelines
- Knowledge of Medicare and Medi-Cal HMO Regulations and Billing Guidelines
- Knowledge of commercial, PPO and HMO Regulations and Billing Guidelines
- Ability to code via document abstraction

- Experience in charge entry and review

- Electronic medical record experience

- Electronic claims submission

## STARTUP SUMMARY

During the first year of operation, Sonya Martinez will work in the business on a full-time basis while Amber will split her time between her office job and the business. Sonya will be paid $200 monthly for rental of her office space. She will also receive a salary of $1,500 per month during the first year of operation.

It is expected that in year two, Amber will transition to working part-time for the business and will be paid a salary to be determined at that time.

Sonya's main duties will be to service the current customers and work to add new customers. Bottom Line currently has one client office that has been developed through contacts of the owners. Because the volume of claims is not currently prohibitive, Sonya will be able to manage the duties of processing claims as well as marketing.

Amber will contribute to networking efforts by devoting several nights a month to attending local meetings of business groups and health professional providers and using social media to build a presence online.

Both Sonya and Amber are contributing $2,500 to the business for a total of $5,000 startup capital. Because the office will be located in Sonya's home no further investment is required at this time.

The startup capital will be used to purchase a computer and software, printer, scanner and fax, paper shredder, telephone system, supplies for the office, and marketing materials. Furniture for the office is being contributed by both Sonya and Amber and includes desks, chairs, lamps, a fireproof filing cabinet, bookshelves, and a table.

## COMPANY LOCATION

The business office will be located within Sonya Martinez's home in an extra bedroom. The office will house the computer and office equipment and all records for the business. The office will be used for all business activity including data entry, recordkeeping and clerical operations.

Sonya will add riders to her homeowner's and auto insurance to ensure coverage related to the business operations.

## SERVICES

Our service offerings include the following:

- Charge entry

- Electronic and paper claim submission

- Dedicated follow-up

- Claim correction and/or resubmission

- Government, commercial and private billing
- Weekly / monthly customized reports
- Patient statements
- Payment posting / adjustments
- Denial management
- Tracking / claims management
- Managing collections
- Patient inquires
- A/R recovery

Bottom Line Medical Billing will charge a fee from 6 to 10 percent depending on the specific services rendered. Percentages are based on monthly revenues collected and medical specialty.

We use the services of a medical claims clearinghouse that allows us to submit claims electronically to over 5,000 payers. We can access records at any time. This software service is HIPAA compliant and includes online claim history, detailed summary reports, and real-time status reports.

The practice management component of this service allows for code search to check the validity of ICD9, Place of Service and Modifier Codes, and the ability to fix claims that have been rejected.

## COMPETITION

Research of Sacramento area medical billing services shows that there are seven companies in the area of comparable size to Bottom Line. Moreover, services provided are similar. This is not surprising due to the nature of medical billing and the requirements of processing claims.

We believe that we can be competitive with other billing services both large and small because we will focus on serving local health professionals. Our broad experience in both billing and coding for various specialties gives us a competitive advantage over other billing services with limited experience.

Our services enable our clients to fulfill their insurance filing and billing needs more efficiently than they could by using in-house staff. Cost savings will be realized by our clients because our price structure combined with our streamlined processing gives them a higher return on investment.

## MARKET ANALYSIS

Because of the changes brought by health care reform, more Californians will be able to purchase health insurance. Many of these new insured will have Medi-Cal coverage. In a 2012 study conducted by the Sierra Health Foundation data showed that an estimated 16 million people will be eligible for Medi-Cal, a 133 percent increase. The Foundation stated that many of the newly insured are likely to have chronic conditions and limited experience in managing their health.

The report estimated that 167,257 uninsured individuals will obtain insurance in 2014. The majority, or 54 percent, are expected to receive Medi-Cal coverage and the remainder, or 46 percent are expected to find insurance in the individual health insurance exchange.

It is assumed that hospitals and health providers will gain more customers now that more Californians will be insured. The combination of an increase in customers (and claims) with tighter cost constraints means that health providers will have to become experts at retrieving every dime from health claims.

Health providers will no doubt be looking for ways to contain the costs associated with their front office. They will likely find that outsourcing claims processing and collection will prove to be more cost effective than keeping those duties in-house.

To get an idea of how many physicians practice in the Sacramento metro area we searched online. In a search for physicians by category in the Sacramento metro area, which consists of four counties, the following was found:

| Specialty | Number |
|---|---|
| General practioners | 1,123 |
| Ear, nose and throat | 54 |
| Endocrinologist | 32 |
| Urologist | 58 |
| Podiatrist | 72 |
| Pediatrician | 260 |

This is a partial list of physicians but it gives an idea of the potential market.

## MARKETING STRATEGY

Bottom Line will focus its marketing to those practices of up to 4 members. For the present we will not limit ourselves to serving any particular specialty. In addition to soliciting doctors and dentists, Bottom Line will explore the markets that are not usually pursued by medical billers which include:

- Social workers

- Nursing homes

- Ambulance services

- Pharmacists

- Home-health practitioners

A major selling point will be our ability to transition billing services with no disruption to their cash flow. Within two weeks of transition, billing with the prior system will discontinue. We will stress how our electronic filing service speeds up payment and decreases errors and denials.

Bottom Line has opened its doors for business already, having secured a contract with one Sacramento physician office housing two practicing physicians. By providing this client with excellent service, we plan to demonstrate to prospective clients our ability to increase their cash flow. Our marketing materials will include testimonials from our current client attesting to our competency and value.

We will ask our satisfied clients for referrals to other prospects who may benefit from our services. We will also get the word out by networking with other professionals who may work with physicians such as attorneys, accountants, and real insurance agents.

Our marketing materials will include business cards, tri-panel brochures and a website. All materials will bear our name and logo and will provide a listing of services and contact information.

Our marketing materials will stress the advantages of outsourcing medical billing to Bottom Line which include the following:

- Our expertise in claims filing and collection

- Our staff is trained

- No worries about turnover, vacation, sick leave

- We use the latest electronic methods to process claims

Because our clients no longer have to manage in-house staff for billing and shoulder the costs that go with having employees, their cash flows will increase. Moreover, they can dedicate their time to developing their practice instead of spending valuable time on administrative tasks.

## PERSONNEL PLAN

During the first two years in operation all duties will be performed by Sonya Martinez and Amber Smith. As more clients are added, staff will be increased. Interns and employee candidates can be recruited from local schools that have medical billing programs.

## STARTUP COSTS

Because Bottom Line will operate from the home of Sonya Martinez, costs will be low. Our cloud-based medical billing software does not charge for processing of claims.

The bulk of the startup costs is in the office setup and includes the following:

| | |
|---|---|
| Computer | $1,800 |
| Printer, fax, scanner | 400 |
| Software office | 300 |
| Reference manuals | 300 |
| Claim forms | 75 |
| Phone | 175 |
| Answering machine | 120 |
| Office supplies | 200 |
| Postage and miscellaneous | 400 |

## FINANCIALS

We currently serve one doctor who sees an average of 20 patients per day and works a five day week. Assuming an average claim of $70 and our fee at 6 percent we estimate annual gross revenue to be $21,840 or $1,820 per month.

Income projections for two years assuming one new client by year two.

| | 2014 | 2015 |
|---|---|---|
| Revenues | $43,680 | $65,520 |
| Expenses | | |
| Depreciation | $ 100 | $ 100 |
| Phone/internet | $ 1,360 | $ 1,760 |
| Insurance: liability | $ 650 | $ 650 |
| Insurance: life insurance | $ 2,500 | $ 2,500 |
| Advertising | $ 850 | $ 950 |
| Professional dues/memberships | $ 700 | $ 700 |
| Books/subscriptions | $ 450 | $ 500 |
| Office supplies | $ 350 | $ 450 |
| Processing fees | $ 2,621 | $ 3,931 |
| Office rent | $ 2,400 | $ 2,400 |
| Salaries | $16,500 | $16,500 |
| Payroll taxes | $ 1,485 | $ 1,485 |
| Other expenses | $ 1,200 | $ 1,600 |
| **Total expenses** | **$31,166** | **$33,526** |
| **Net income (loss)** | **$12,514** | **$31,994** |

## SOURCES

http://www.sacramentomedicalbilling.com/

http://www.sierrahealth.org/assets/SRHCP_Sacramento_County_Presentation_040212_Final.pdf

http://www.chcf.org/~/media/MEDIA%20LIBRARY%20Files/PDF/A/PDF%20AlmanacRegMktQRG Sacramento13.pdf

http://www.bplans.com/medical_billing_business_plan/executive_summary_fc.php#.UwuXFvk7uM4

http://www.entrepreneur.com/article/37890-1

http://www.thefinanceresource.com/free_business_plans/free_medical_billing_company_business_ plan.aspx

http://www.all-things-medical-billing.com/medical-billing-business-plan.html

http://medicalbillingbizhq.com/medical-billing-salary/

http://www.youtube.com/watch?v=DgaOxEQ2v-I&feature=youtu.be

http://www.medicalbillinglive.com/medical-billing-business.shtml

http://www.absystems.com/income-potential/billing-calculator.php

# Mobile Mini Putt Putt Business
Putts2You LLC

68 Forest Path Dr.
Lombard, IL 60148

*Paul Greenland*

*Putts2You LLC is a mobile mini putt putt business focused on the fund-raising and corporate event markets.*

## EXECUTIVE SUMMARY

High school economics teacher Brian Nelson spends a lot of time in the classroom. However, as a scratch golfer, his summer months involve many hours on the golf course. Two years ago Nelson combined his knack for economics and golf skills to create a unique fundraiser for a local charity's annual festival: A one-hole "beat the pro" mini putt putt game that gave participants a chance to win a portion of the cash proceeds.

The popularity of Nelson's "beat the pro" game gave him the idea for an innovative part-time business that has full-time potential. Putts2You LLC is a portable nine-hole mini putt putt course business focused on the fund-raising and corporate event markets. Using a revenue-sharing model, the business has strong potential to generate profits for the owner and raise funds for host locations/organizations (e.g., schools, churches, charities, corporate foundations, etc.).

## MARKET ANALYSIS

Putts2You LLC is located in DuPage County Illinois, in the suburban Chicago village of Lombard. Surrounding communities include Elmhurst, Downers Grove, Wheaton, Glendale Heights, Addison, Glen Ellyn, and Oak Brook. As illustrated in the following table, these communities represent a collective population of approximately 300,000 people. Modest growth is expected between 2013 and 2018.

|      | Addison | Downers Grove | Elmhurst | Glendale Heights | Glen Ellyn | Lombard | Oak Brook | Wheaton |
|------|---------|---------------|----------|------------------|------------|---------|-----------|---------|
| 2013 | 37,360  | 48,595        | 44,758   | 34,579           | 27,858     | 43,711  | 8,178     | 53,204  |
| 2018 | 37,551  | 48,944        | 44,891   | 35,001           | 28,302     | 44,213  | 8,279     | 53,264  |

### Target Markets

Putts2You will focus its marketing initiatives on schools, churches, charities, corporate foundations, organizations, and event planners. Specifically, the business will market its mobile mini putt putt course as an entertainment choice for group events, including:

- Business Meetings
- Conferences
- Conventions & Expos
- Networking Events
- Receptions
- Team-building Exercises
- Trade Shows
- Fairs & Festivals
- Fundraisers

Relying upon data from the research firm, Stenberg Riley & Hamilton, non-school prospects in the Lombard area market can be broken down as follows:

- Churches & Religious Organizations (1,497 establishments)
- Membership Organizations (1,127 establishments)
- Large Companies (216 establishments)
- Mid-sized Companies (543 establishments)

Significant opportunities exist with schools. For example, Lombard School District 44 consists of seven schools that serve more than 3,000 students in grades PK through 8:

- Glenn Westlake Middle School
- Madison Elementary School
- WM Hammerschmidt Elementary School
- Manor Hill Elementary School
- Pleasant Lane Elementary School
- Park View Elementary School
- Butterfield Elementary School

Beyond Lombard, other nearby schools include:

- Montini Catholic High School
- Glenbard East High School
- York Community High School
- Willowbrook High School
- College Preparatory School of America
- Jackson Middle School
- Immaculate Conception High School
- Hinsdale Central High School
- Timothy Christian High School
- Glenbard West High School
- Sacred Heart School
- Sandburg Middle School

- Jefferson Middle School

- Bryan Middle School

- Jackson Middle School

- Hadley Junior High School

- John E Albright Middle School

- Churchville Middle School

- Westmore Elementary School

- York Center Elementary School

- Sacred Heart School

- Stevenson School

- North Elementary School

- Brook Forest Elementary School

- Saint Alexander School

- St Pius X School

- Edison Elementary School

Additionally, there are approximately 60 colleges and universities located within close geographic proximity to Putts2You. Within this category, opportunities include fundraisers for alumni associations, athletic teams, academic departments, college/university foundations, scholarship programs, and more.

## INDUSTRY ANALYSIS

Mini putt putt has been a fixture in the United States since the late 1920s, when Garnet Carter created what some believe to be the nation's first miniature golf course at the Fairyland Inn near Chattanooga, Tennessee. According to Commerce Department figures, by 1930 approximately 25,000 mini-golf courses were in operation nationwide, many of which had opened that year. Something of a fad initially, by the 1950s mini putt putt had regained its popularity, marked by the formation of the Putt-Putt brand by Don Clayton.

In 2012 *The New York Times* reported that there were approximately 5,000 U.S. mini putt putt courses in operation. Popular permanent courses were in place in many communities, featuring elaborate obstacles such as 40-foot-high volcanoes. Miniature golf is more than a recreational activity for some. Beyond the United States, the World MiniGolf Sports Federation (WMSF) includes members from 30 different countries. The United States ProMiniGolf Association organizes tournaments domestically, and is the nation's only official member of the WMSF.

## SERVICES

Once a location/organization has selected Putts2You, Brian Nelson will work with a designated contact person in advance, to identify a specific site for placement of the business' nine-hole course. The course consists of nine different greens, providing participants with a variety of different fun, challenging scenarios. In addition to changing elevations, some greens feature stationery and moving (battery-powered) obstacles.

Brian Nelson will provide background music when requested, in order to create a fun and festive atmosphere at the event. In addition, Nelson will recommend reputable, independently owned and operated mobile food vendors (e.g., pizza, tacos, hot dogs, vegetarian cuisine, snacks, ice cream, beverages, etc.) when customers request food and/or beverage services.

On the agreed upon date(s), Nelson will personally handle course setup and operation. Participants typically pay $5 cash to play. This fee includes the use of a putter, golf ball, and one round on the nine-hole mini putt putt course. At the end of the event Nelson will provide the host organization/location with an agreed-upon percentage of the cash proceeds. Nelson will then handle tear down and removal of the course.

## MARKETING & SALES

Putts2You has developed a marketing plan that involves the following primary tactics:

1.  Magnetic business cards that include contact information for Brian Nelson. These will include Putts2You's Facebook, Twitter, and Web site information.

2.  A glossy, four-color flyer showcasing Putts2You's nine-hole course and describing potential fundraising benefits for a host location/organization. This can be used for direct mail campaigns and as a leave-behind after meetings with event planners and prospective organizations/locations.

3.  A Web site with complete details about Putts2You.

4.  A social media strategy involving Twitter and Facebook.

5.  Quarterly direct mailings to event planners and area organizations/locations. Mailing lists will be obtained from a reputable mailing list broker in the Chicago area. A suburban Chicago mail house has been identified for managing the mailings (e.g., labeling, affixing postage, bar coding, etc.).

6.  A media relations strategy that involves the submission of periodic press releases to local media outlets, showcasing Putts2You as a unique fundraiser.

7.  Presentations to local business organizations and service clubs, including the Rotary and Kiwanis.

8.  Large-format vehicle wrapping for Putts2You's cargo trailer, in order to provide the business with mobile advertising exposure.

9.  Membership in local business organizations, including the Lombard Chamber of Commerce.

## OPERATIONS

### Equipment

After considerable research, Putts2You selected a high-quality mini golf system from a leading vendor. The system is made from recycled composite plastic panels, which connect together to comprise the nine different putting greens. The panels' construction is such that they conform to any surface, indoors or outdoors, providing a realistic experience. Each green includes a border to keep golf balls in play. As opposed to wooden construction, the more lightweight plastic panel system provides added benefits of durability, weather resistance and low maintenance. Construction of the entire nine-hole course can be completed in approximately 15 minutes. Putts2You's operations also include an inventory of golf balls and putters in a variety of sizes. The business will utilize a 6 x 12 trailer to transport the portable mini putt putt course to various locations. When not in use, Brian Nelson will store the trailer at his home.

## Fees

Putts2You will employ a revenue sharing model, in which a portion of the proceeds raised will be split with the host location/organization, be it a church, school, foundation, special event planner, or shopping mall. Play generally is priced at $5 per round, with $1.50 typically going to the host location/organization. There is no charge for equipment setup/removal.

## Insurance

Putts2You has secured appropriate liability and business insurance. A copy of our policy is available upon request.

## PERSONNEL

### Brian Nelson, Owner

Brian Nelson has been a high school economics teacher near Lombard, Illinois, for 12 years. A scratch golfer, Nelson has a passion for the sport. When he's not in the classroom, he is often on the golf course. Nelson earned undergraduate education and economics degrees from Northern Illinois University, where he received a full athletic scholarship for golf. Nelson and his wife, Rose, have two sons: Stephen (age 16) and Toby (age 14).

### Professional & Advisory Support

Putts2You has established a business banking account with Lombard Community Bank, as well as a merchant account for accepting credit card payments. Vince Rodgers, a local accountant, will provide accounting and tax advisory services. Brian Nelson has as utilized a popular online legal document service to prepare the paperwork necessary for the establishment of the limited liability company.

## GROWTH STRATEGY

Brian Nelson is projecting that Putts2You will generate net income of $22,500 by year three, which will be used to fund the purchase of a second nine-hole course and 6 x 12 cargo trailer. After adding a second course, the business will generate projected net income of nearly $63,000 in years four and five. Brian's son, Stephen, will join the business in year four, while attending college, and will be responsible for managing the second nine-hole course.

The following table and bar graph illustrate Putts2You's steady financial and operational growth during its first five years of operations.

|  | Year 1 | Year 2 | Year 3 | Year 4 | Year 5 |
|---|---|---|---|---|---|
| Events served | 100 | 120 | 140 | 200 | 240 |
| Gross revenue | $75,000 | $90,000 | $105,000 | $150,000 | $180,000 |
| Net revenue | $52,500 | $63,000 | $ 73,500 | $105,000 | $126,000 |

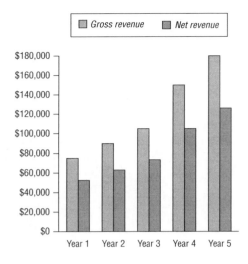

## FINANCIAL ANALYSIS

The following table provides a summary of the business' projected revenue and expenses for the first five years of operations. Additional financial statements have been prepared in partnership with accountant Vince Rodgers and are available upon request.

|  | Year 1 | Year 2 | Year 3 | Year 4 | Year 5 |
|---|---|---|---|---|---|
| **Revenue** | | | | | |
| Gross revenue | $75,000 | $90,000 | $105,000 | $150,000 | $180,000 |
| Cost of goods sold | $22,500 | $27,000 | $ 31,500 | $ 45,000 | $ 54,000 |
| Gross margin | 30% | 30% | 30% | 30% | 30% |
|  | $52,500 | $63,000 | $ 73,500 | $105,000 | $126,000 |
| **Expenses** | | | | | |
| Advertising & marketing | $ 7,500 | $ 8,500 | $ 9,500 | $ 12,000 | $ 12,000 |
| General/administrative | $ 800 | $ 800 | $ 800 | $ 800 | $ 800 |
| Accounting & legal | $ 1,500 | $ 1,100 | $ 1,100 | $ 1,100 | $ 1,100 |
| Office supplies | $ 750 | $ 500 | $ 500 | $ 500 | $ 500 |
| Computers/peripherals | $ 2,500 | $ 500 | $ 500 | $ 500 | $ 500 |
| Business insurance | $ 1,500 | $ 1,575 | $ 1,654 | $ 1,736 | $ 1,823 |
| Payroll | $25,000 | $30,000 | $ 35,000 | $ 55,000 | $ 60,000 |
| Payroll taxes | $ 3,750 | $ 4,500 | $ 5,250 | $ 7,500 | $ 8,250 |
| Postage | $ 500 | $ 500 | $ 500 | $ 500 | $ 500 |
| Startup loan | $ 5,148 | $ 5,148 | $ 5,148 | $ 0 | $ 0 |
| Equipment | $ 1,000 | $ 1,000 | $ 1,000 | $ 1,000 | $ 1,000 |
| Maintenance | $ 500 | $ 500 | $ 500 | $ 500 | $ 500 |
| **Total expenses** | **$50,448** | **$54,623** | **$ 61,452** | **$ 81,136** | **$ 86,973** |
| **Net income** | **$ 2,052** | **$ 8,377** | **$ 12,048** | **$ 23,864** | **$ 39,027** |

Brian Nelson is seeking a three-year, $15,000 business loan to cover the cost of the portable mini putt putt course. He will invest $10,000 of his own funds, which will be used to purchase a 6 x 12 cargo trailer ($5,000) and provide initial funds for operations.

# Personal Chef Service

Angela's Personal Chef Service

1920 Cary St.
Buffalo, NY 14208

*Brenda Kubiac*

*Angela's Personal Chef Service designs and executes menus for clients on a regular basis.*

## 1.0 EXECUTIVE SUMMARY

### 1.1 Business Overview

Angela's Personal Chef Service is a New York-based sole proprietorship located in Buffalo. As two incomes have become prevalent among American families, so has the need for personal chefs. In fact, some industry watchers predict the industry will continue to evolve at a rapid pace.

By joining a network of professionals, the United States Personal Chef Association (USPCA), Angela Preston was guided through the process of opening up Angela's Personal Chef Service, especially as it related to certification and insurance needs. The American Personal & Private Chef Association (http://www.personalchefmedia.com/wcr.php) reported that "The largest demographic for clients are homes with two incomes where the incomes totals $70,000 or more. Those homes fall within two distinct categories: those without children who want an alternative to the fine restaurant dining they've been accustomed, and those with children who are concerned that the family gets good nutritious food and can find a way to fit mealtime into busy schedules."

According to the United States Personal Chef Association (USPCA) (https://www.uspca.com), "a personal chef service specializes in making great meals ideal for family meals or casual entertaining. The service is designed so clients eat healthier meals, have more free time, and enjoy their favorite foods, all prepared at their home." "A common misconception is that a personal chef service is only for the wealthy. Anyone who has a need to solve the 'what's for dinner?' problem can hire a personal chef," according to the United States Personal Chef Association (USPCA).

Angela's Personal Chef Service will target the estimated 259,384 consumers that reside in Buffalo, New York. Angela like her competition has her own specialties to tempt potential clients.

### 1.2 Mission Statement

The mission of Angela's Personal Chef Service is to provide families with delicious, but healthy meals in a professional manner while delivering excellent customer service.

# 2.0 STRATEGIC AND MARKET ANALYSIS

## 2.1 Industry Analysis

According to the American Personal & Private Chef Association (APCA) (www.personalchef.com), the current number of personal chefs is estimated at 9,000 serving 72,000 customers. Industry observers predict the number will double over the next 5 years. On average, personal chefs generate between $200 and $500 per day.

According to the Bureau of Labor Statistics chefs in the New York City metropolitan area lead all other U.S. cities, with annual earnings averaging $79,820, or $38.38 per hour.

## 2.2 Market Analysis

Angela hired 3 personal chefs within her target market, which gave her a better idea of what to expect in terms of time spent preparing meals, prices, menus, which local wholesalers they used and were satisfied with, competition and so on.

As the number of families with two working parents expands, so too will the need for personal chefs. As family time spent together continues to decline, the need for personal chefs will be on the upswing.

## 2.3 Target Market

- Two-income couples with or without children
- Busy professionals
- Those with special dietary or health needs
- Those recovering from surgery
- Seniors
- Those who enjoy fine dining
- Companies hosting small parties
- Parents throwing birthday parties
- New mothers
- Those looking for a unique gift idea

## 2.4 Competition

Both direct and indirect competition is definitely a risk factor; however, Angela feels that her experience and services will speak for themselves and guarantee her clients. For an added bonus, she is also a pro when it comes to tasty confections in which her clients will benefit.

# 3.0 PERSONNEL

## 3.1 Management Summary

Angela's Personal Chef Service is owned and operated by Angela Preston who gained her experience while working in restaurants and banquet halls. Rather than being confined in a restaurant setting or banquet menu Angela decided to become a personal chef where she would have a greater say in what she cooks. Angela successfully completed training from the American Personal Chef Institute and also carries a current State of New York Food Handler's Card and has been trained and certified in the nationally recognizable ServSafe food and safety program.

Angela is an active member of the American Personal & Private Chef Association and the United States Personal Chef Association (USPCA). As a member of the USPCA, Angela is able to mingle among her peers and gain insight from long time personal chefs. More importantly, the association has assisted in finding clients.

# 4.0 PROFESSIONAL AND ADVISORY SUPPORT

Day-to-day bookkeeping will be done in-house. For added accounting and financial functions, Angela has retained the services of Simmons Accounting Services, Inc. For all legal aspects relating the business, the company has retained the services of Simon & Blake, LLP who will provide a universal personal chef service agreement. For all of its insurance needs, Angela has retained the services of Delaney Insurance Group. Angela's Personal Chef Service acquired necessary insurance from APPCA that covers law suits filed by clients, medical expenses as a result of injuries that may occur on the job, and damage to cooking equipment. A business account along with a line of credit was set up at Cornerstone Commercial Bank, including a merchant account and processing equipment for accepting credit card payments from clients. For added convenience Angela's Personal Chef Service will accept PayPal payment for services via her website.

In the event the company experiences a growth spurt, Angela will hire an assistant to help with preparation and clean-up while she focuses on cooking by offering an internship to local culinary students from the academy.

# 5.0 GROWTH STRATEGY

Angela's Personal Chef Service plans to maintain and grow the brand equity that the company creates.

# 6.0 PRODUCTS AND SERVICES

## 6.1 Products

Products include:

- Basic personal chef services start at $65 per hour (minimum 3.5 hours) plus the cost of food.
- Weekly service with lunch and dinner for $35 per hour plus the cost of food.

## 6.2 Services

Service fee covers menu planning, grocery shopping, food preparation, pantry items (spices, oils, vinegars, condiments) and food packaging required for meals. Service packages include:

- Initial client consultation
- Customized menu planning
- Grocery shopping
- Pantry items such as herbs, spices, and oils
- Meal preparation
- Packaging and labeling of food with reheating instructions

Standard services and fees are listed below:

**Biweekly Service for One**
- Five entrees plus one side dish per entree
- Two servings each
- 10 dinners total for two weeks
- $300 plus groceries

**Weekly Service for Two**
- Five entrees plus one side dish per entree
- Two servings each
- 10 dinners total for one week
- $300 plus groceries

**Weekly Service for Four**
- Five entrees plus one side dish per entree
- Four servings each
- 20 dinners total for one week
- $350 plus groceries

**Entree Only Service**
- Five entries
- Four servings
- $300 plus groceries

**Note:** Extra fee for special diets that take extra time to prepare.

**Other services**
- Wine tasting parties
- Romantic meals
- In-home cooking classes for small groups
- Tasting events
- Volunteering

Angela's Personal Chef Service accepts MasterCard, Visa, Dinner Club and Discover, cash or money orders. No checks.

# 7.0 MARKETING PLAN

Angela's Personal Chef Service plans to maintain an extensive marketing campaign that reaches its targeted market. An overview of both marketing objectives and strategies are listed below.

## 7.1 Marketing Objectives
- Have enough clients to guarantee full-time employment
- Hear from satisfied clients sharing positive experiences about my prepared dishes
- Word-of-mouth referrals
- Keep up with new trends
- Utilize social media as a major marketing tool

### 7.2 Marketing Strategies

1. Develop a professional website describing chef services and fees along with sample menus and photographs

2. Build a portfolio with pictures of menu items including menu samples and certification; continue to maintain portfolio by expanding with letters of recommendation and awards, as well as any media attention or newspaper or magazine clippings

3. Listed on USPCAs Hire-a-Chef database (www.hireachef.com)

4. Leave flyers at day-care centers, health food stores, doctor offices, health clubs, etc.

5. Wear chef jacket with company name and logo printed on it when shopping for clients

6. Create promotional kit that includes resume, biography, articles written about Angela's Personal Chef Service, menus Angela's Personal Chef Service has created, special events Angela's Personal Chef Service has cooked for, and client list

7. Google ads

8. Write a press release about new business

9. Join the Chamber of Commerce

10. Tweeting about services

11. Cooking at philanthropic events

12. Updates on Facebook pages

13. Leave business cards with satisfied clients to pass along

14. Advertise on local cable TV, *The Buffalo News*, or industry magazine

15. Food blog sharing menus, cooking tips and recipes with potential clients

16. Teach classes at local health food store

17. Donate a meal to a charity auction

18. Cater an event to advertise my service

19. Use car as a mobile advertising with signage

## 8.0 OPERATIONS

### 8.1 Customers

Typical clients don't have the time to cook while others lack the ability and others are tired of eating out and want some nutritious meals and better quality ingredients. Some clients are placed on a restrictive diet and need someone to prepare the food for them. Another group that needs the services of a personal chef who need a healthy diet and the help are the convalescing.

### 8.2 Equipment

- Two non-stick skillets (one with lid)
- One 4-quart saucepan with lid
- One cast-iron grill pan
- One Dutch oven with lid
- Two or more plastic cutting boards

- Disposable cutting mats to use over the top of cutting boards
- Stainless-steel or plastic mixing bowls
- Plastic colander
- Fine mesh strainer
- Four nonstick baking sheets with sides
- Wire cooling rack
- Roasting pan
- Hand mixer
- Immersion mixer
- Mini size food processor

**Disposables to leave at client's home**
- Aluminum foil
- Plastic wrap
- Gallon- and quart-size freezer bags
- Disposables for finished meals

## 8.3 Toolbox
- Knives with knife guards
- Spatulas for turning and scraping
- Tongs
- Spoons
- Instant-read thermometer
- Scissors
- Whisk
- Measuring cups and spoons
- Can opener
- Wine opener
- Vegetable peeler
- Zester
- Potato masher
- Microplane grater and regular grater
- Two kitchen timers
- Kitchen twine

## 8.4 Cleaning kit
- Liquid dish soap
- Dishwasher soap packets
- Rubber gloves

- Scrub brush or sponge

- Grease-cutting kitchen cleaner

- Glass cleaner

- Antibacterial cleaner

- Paper towels

- Garbage bags

## 8.5 Hours

Mon–Fri: 9 a.m.–5 p.m.

Sat: 10 a.m.–5 p.m.

Sun: Closed

## 8.6 Production

Below is a list of services offered by Angela's Personal Chef Service before during and after meal preparation:

1. Meet with client to discuss likes, dislikes, food allergies, health needs, and any other dietary concerns, such as diabetes, gluten free, high blood pressure, high cholesterol or cardiac diets, and customizes menus to select from.

2. A food questionnaire will be used to help establish client preferences to better plan their menu.

3. Email menu choices weekly for client to review.

4. Once the menu is decided, Angela's Personal Chef Service will do all the grocery shopping while staying within the clients' budget on the scheduled day of choice.

5. On the day decided, Angela will go to a variety of stores to purchase only the freshest items before going to the client's home to prepare meals.

6. Angela will prepare a week's worth of meals that the customer requested that will take about six hours.

7. Label and reheating instructions are provided.

8. Clean kitchen before leaving.

## 8.7 Facility and Location

Angela's Personal Chef Service will be a home-based business located at 1920 Cary St., Buffalo, New York. There is ample space set aside to store extra items or supplies if needed.

## 9.0 FINANCIAL ANALYSIS

### Startup expenses

| | |
|---|---|
| Gas | $ 2,000 |
| Other auto (insurance, repair) | $ 1,500 |
| Business books and cookbooks | $ 240 |
| Magazines | $ 35 |
| Uniform purchase and cleaning | $ 75 |
| Equipment purchase: knives, pots and pans, kit boxes, etc. | $ 2,500 |
| Pantry items & supplies | $ 400 |
| Equipment repair and knife sharpening | $ 175 |
| Office supplies: business cards, mailings, flyers, etc. | $ 600 |
| Phone/cell service | $ 100 |
| Internet service | $ 100 |
| MenuMagic software (leased annually) | $ 189 |
| Insurance/license fees | $ 500 |
| Advertising/website costs | $ 1,500 |
| Membership fees | $ 250 |
| Accounting software (QuickBooks) | $ 99 |
| Accounting fees | $ 100 |
| **Total expenses** | **$10,363** |

### 9.1 2014 Balance Sheet

**Revenue**

| | |
|---|---|
| Personal chef services | $40,000 |
| Cooking lessons | $ 9,000 |
| **Total revenue** | **$49,000** |
| **Expenses** | **$10,363** |
| **Net income** | **$38,637** |

# Pet Aftercare Products, Services, and Gifts

Heavenly Pet Memorials, LLC

2080 Fountain Plaza, Suite 500
Asheville, NC 28704

*Fran Fletcher*

*Heavenly Pet Memorials, LLC is a pet aftercare company providing customers with a variety of options to memorialize their furry family members. The company will set itself apart by providing great customer service, offering hand crafted urns that can be painted to match the customer's home decor, and by offering online pet tributes.*

## BUSINESS SUMMARY

Heavenly Pet Memorials, LLC is a pet aftercare company providing customers with a variety of options to memorialize their furry family members. Heavenly Pet Memorials will make aftercare arrangements based on the client's wishes, including scheduling individual cremation at an offsite facility, arranging burial in a pet cemetery, and planning memorial services. Heavenly Pet Memorials will stock a vast collection of urns, caskets, grave markers, and statues in order to give customers the opportunity to choose the item that best memorializes their pet. The company will set itself apart by providing great customer service, offering hand crafted urns that can be painted to match the customer's home decor, and by offering online pet tributes.

The idea for Heavenly Pet Memorials was born when Darla Doberman lost her beloved dachshund named Buddy a couple of years ago. At that time, there were no local businesses offering pet memorial products and services. She felt that Buddy did not get the special treatment he deserved after being her loving companion for ten years. Heavenly Pet Memorials' number one goal is to help ease the pain of its customers when that dreaded day occurs by offering compassion and great aftercare products, services, and gifts.

Pet aftercare is a growing segment of the billion-dollar pet care industry, which is expected to increase by 4 percent each year over the next several years. Asheville was recently listed as number 7 in *Live Out Loud Magazine's* "Top 10 Pet Cities" for its pet parks, pet boutiques, and pet-friendly restaurants. Approximately 18,000 Asheville households include pets. This large number of pet owners and the special treatment pets receive will provide a large customer base for the business. Heavenly Pet Memorials has one local competitor specializing in pet memorial gifts; therefore, Heavenly Pet Memorials will be the only pet aftercare company in the area offering a full selection of cremation and burial products. The store will be located on the perimeter of Asheville's shopping district in the Fountain Plaza and will be easily accessible to local residents and customers from surrounding communities.

Marketing will include a grand opening celebration, advertising in local newspapers, social media, advertising at local veterinarian clinics, and classes where pet owners can create their own unique urn, plaque, or stepping stones.

Ms. Doberman has secured a location to lease and is currently seeking financing for this venture in the form of a business loan or line of credit in the amount of $20,000 to cover start-up costs.

# COMPANY DESCRIPTION

## Location

Heavenly Pet Memorials is located in the Fountain Plaza in Asheville's shopping district. The Fountain Plaza is also home to several popular retail outlets. The retail space perfectly suits the owner's needs and will not need modifying. There is plenty of space to display the company's aftercare products and gifts.

## Hours of Operation

Heavenly Pet Memorials will operate as follows:

Monday-Friday 9 AM–6 PM

Saturday 10 AM–2 PM

Sunday by appointment only

## Personnel

### Darla Doberman

Ms. Doberman will be the office manager and will provide and arrange services for clients. She will be responsible for the daily activities of the business.

### Assistant

A part time assistant will be hired to assist with daily operations.

## Products and Services

### Memorial Products

- Grave markers
- Urns
- Caskets
- Statues
- Headstones
- Crosses
- Garden stones
- Plaques
- Burial Blankets

### Memorial Gifts

- Necklaces
- Bracelets
- Keychains
- Photo frames
- Figurines
- Blankets

### Services

- Memorial services
- Cremation arrangements
- Burial arrangements
- Pet tributes

## MARKET ANALYSIS

### Industry Overview

Pet aftercare is a growing but relatively untracked segment of the billion-dollar pet care industry. In 2012, there were only about 700 facilities in the United States providing services including funeral homes, crematories, and cemeteries. According to Research Firm, pet ownership has been on the rise for the last ten years. According to the 2013-2014 pet survey, 82.5 million or 68 percent of American households are pet owners. Pet ownership is expected to continue to increase especially in single-person and retiree households. Since there is an increasing trend in the humanization of pets, there is also increased demand for specialty products and services. The pet care industry is projected to grow 4 percent each year for the next five years.

### Target Market

Pet owners who treat their pets like family members are the target market for Heavenly Pet Memorials. This type of pet owner will wish to memorialize their pets with aftercare products and services.

According to demographics.com, Asheville's pet population was 36,000 in 2010. An estimated 18,000 Asheville households contain pets (11,800 households include dogs and 9,880 households include cats). Asheville ranked number 7 in *Live Out Loud Magazine's* "Top 10 Pet Cities" for its special treatment of pets including pet parks, pet boutiques, and restaurants that allow pets to dine alongside their masters. This special treatment of pets should ensure a large customer base for the company's specialized aftercare products.

### Competition

The idea for Heavenly Pet Memorials was born when Darla Doberman lost her beloved dachshund named Buddy a couple of years ago. The Doberman family was devastated when there were no businesses in the area offering pet memorial products and services. Ms. Doberman felt that Buddy did not get the special treatment he deserved after being her loving companion for ten years. The Dobermans want to share their passion for memorializing special pets so that others will have options when that dreaded day happens.

Beloved Pet Keepsakes is currently the only other pet aftercare business in Asheville. However, the majority of its store inventory is pet memorial gifts.

## GROWTH STRATEGY

The overall growth strategy of Heavenly Pet Memorials is to corner the market in Asheville's pet aftercare niche. The company will offer many products and services in a wide range of price levels in order to fit the needs of its clients. Heavenly Pet Memorials hopes to achieve financial independence during the first two years of operation. After funding is repaid and the owners have saved additional cash, Heavenly Pet Memorials would consider opening additional locations and possibly franchise the business.

## Sales and Marketing

The company has identified key tactics to support the company's growth strategy.

Heavenly Pet Memorials will hold a grand opening to showcase its products and services to the community.

Initial advertising will include the following:

- Advertising in the Asheville Times

- Advertising through local veterinarian clinics

- Advertising through local pet stores and breeders

- Offering discounted pet portrait sessions with a local photographer

Ongoing marketing strategies include the following:

- Social media

- Heavenly Pet Memorials website (including pet tributes page)

- Offer workshops (urn painting, paw print stepping stones, pet jewelry)

- Co-sponsor pet shelter initiatives

# FINANCIAL ANALYSIS

## Start-up Costs

The Dobermans have secured a space to lease that is ready to occupy. Miscellaneous start-up costs are estimated at $20,300.

### Estimated Start-up Costs

| | |
|---|---|
| Legal fees | $ 5,000 |
| Store inventory | $10,000 |
| Office furniture | $ 4,000 |
| Business license | $ 250 |
| Website | $ 50 |
| Initial advertising | $ 500 |
| Insurance | $ 500 |
| **Total** | **$20,300** |

## Estimated Monthly Expenses

Monthly expenses are expected to remain constant each month.

### Monthly Expenses

| | |
|---|---|
| Lease | $ 800 |
| Phone/internet | $ 150 |
| Advertising | $ 100 |
| Loan repayment | $ 340 |
| Insurance | $ 100 |
| Wages owner | $2,000 |
| Wages part time personnel | $ 800 |
| Inventory | $ 400 |
| **Total** | **$4,690** |

## Estimated Monthly Income

Based on conservative estimates, the company projects monthly sales to start at $4,000 per month, which is approximately $150 in sales per day, for the first several months, and then gradually increase as the business becomes established in the community.

### Aftercare Products/Prices

**Urns**

| | |
|---|---|
| Ceramic | $ 85 |
| Hand painted | $125 |
| Large (up to 90 lbs live wt) | $130 |
| Black granite photo outdoor | $200 |

**Cremains bags**

| | |
|---|---|
| Satin small | $ 10 |
| Satin medium | $ 12 |
| Satin large | $ 15 |
| Bag tags (personalized) | $ 20 |

**Caskets**

| | |
|---|---|
| Extra small | $100 |
| Small | $150 |
| Medium | $175 |
| Large | $200 |
| Octagonal | $175 |
| Burial container | $150 |

**Burial blankets**

| | |
|---|---|
| Small | $ 50 |
| Large | $ 75 |

**Headstones**

| | |
|---|---|
| Black granite photo | $175 |

**Grave markers**

| | |
|---|---|
| Black granite photo | $125 |

**Statues**

| | |
|---|---|
| Dog | $250 |
| Cat | $250 |
| Angel | $250 |
| Cross | $200 |
| Custom | $500 |
| Garden stones | $ 20 |
| Plaques | $200 |

### Aftercare Services/Prices

| Service | Price |
|---|---|
| Private cremation arrangements | $300 |
| Burial arrangements—pet cemetery | $400 |
| Burial arrangements—home | $150 |
| Memorial service | $300 |
| Online tribute (5 pictures) | $200 |

### Aftercare Packages/Prices

| Cherub cremation package $500 | Cherub burial package $750 | Angel cremation package $1,000 | Angel burial package $1,200 |
|---|---|---|---|
| Private cremation | Casket | Private cremation | Casket and blanket |
| Urn | Cemetery plot | Urn | Cemetery plot |
| 1 Pet keepsake | 1 Pet keepsake | Memorial service | Memorial service |
| Pet tribute 5 pictures | Pet tribute 5 pictures | 2 Pet keepsakes | 2 Pet keepsakes |
| | | Pet tribute 10 pictures | Pet tribute 10 pictures |
| | | | Black granite headstone |

## Profit/Loss

Heavenly Pet Memorials is prepared for profit loss until the business becomes established. According to estimated expenses and income data, the first three months show some profit loss. In Month 4, a small profit is made and steadily increases in Months 5 through 7. Conservative estimates show profits staying steady from Month 7 through Month 12. The estimated profits in Months 5 through 12 are enough to make up for the initial losses as shown in the "Annual Profit/Loss" chart.

**Monthly profit/loss**

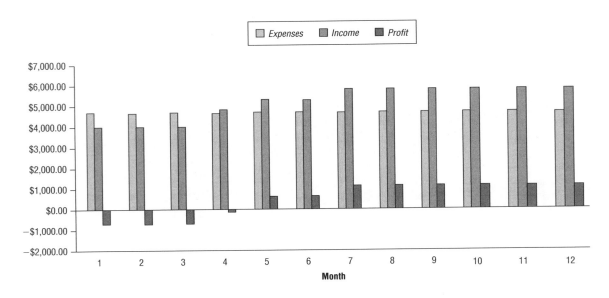

**Annual profit/loss**

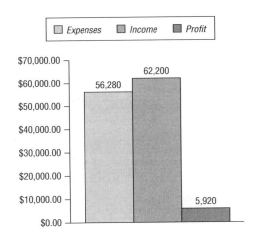

## Financing

Heavenly Pet Memorials is currently seeking financing for start-up expenses in the amount of $20,000. Ms. Doberman has placed the loan payment in her monthly expenses and is confident that she will be able to repay this loan within five years as illustrated in the "Repayment Plan" chart. Ms. Doberman is prepared to personally absorb profit losses that may occur in the first months of operation.

**Repayment plan**

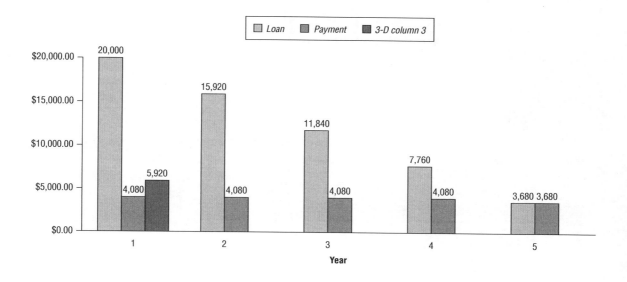

# Photo Retouching Service

BestImage Photo Editing, Inc.

2073 Langford Dr.
Sunnyvale, TN 37000

*Paul Greenland*

*BestImage Photo Editing Inc. is a photo editing and restoration business.*

## EXECUTIVE SUMMARY

### Business Overview

The advent of digital cameras and mobile devices equipped with high-quality cameras has produced a skyrocketing number of digital images. According to a May 27, 2013, article in *Popular Photography*, the largest photography magazine in the world, an estimated 880 billion photos will be taken in 2014 alone. The beauty of digital photography is that retouching and enhancements can be done quite easily. However, many consumers don't have the technical skill or the time to edit their photos. Demand also exists within the commercial market, where photographers, book publishers, magazines, and manufacturers require the services of highly skilled photo editors.

BestImage Photo Editing Inc. is a photo editing and restoration business established by Crystal Matthews, a recent graduate of Sunnyvale Technical College. In addition to earning her associate's degree, Matthews took courses in Photoshop and advanced Photoshop, giving her the technical skills required for working with digital images. In addition, she also completed several small business management courses, providing her with the fundamental knowledge needed to own and operate a small business.

Matthews decided to establish BestImage Photo Editing after performing photo editing for friends and family. In addition to earning a part-time income, this also allowed her to slowly build a portfolio of impressive "before" and "after" pictures for showcasing her abilities. Matthews also has performed some photo editing work for a local photographer. She is now ready to apply her technical skill and small-business management knowledge on a full-time basis in a market with strong potential.

## MARKET ANALYSIS

### Target Markets

Because BestImage Photo Editing will conduct its business online, it has no geographic restrictions. Matthews will focus the business' marketing efforts on the following target markets:

- Advertising Agencies
- Art Galleries
- Book Publishers

- Commercial Photographers
- Historical Societies
- Hospitals/Healthcare Systems
- Individual Consumers
- Manufacturers
- Museums
- Photo Laboratories
- Portrait Photographers
- Printers
- Professional/Trade Magazines

## Market Growth

According to a May 27, 2013, article in *Popular Photography,* the largest photography magazine in the world, an estimated 880 billion photos will be taken in 2014 alone, according to a presentation by Yahoo! Social media platforms provide insight into the number of digital photos taken on a daily basis. For example, the publication referenced data from the social news and entertainment website, Buzzfeed (www.buzzfeed), indicating that 208,300 photos are uploaded every minute to Facebook, and 27,800 photos are uploaded every minute to Instagram.

By 2014 a growing number of tablet computers, cell phones, and other mobile devices were equipped with cameras capable of producing high-resolution digital images. In addition, these devices were becoming more prolific in the United States and worldwide. These trends should result in an increase in the number of digital photos requiring editing and retouching.

Beyond the growing volume of digital images produced by individual consumers, growth also is expected within the commercial market. Professional photographers are but one example. According to data from the U.S. Department of Labor, Bureau of Labor Statistics, there were approximately 139,500 professional photographers in 2010. By 2020 this number was expected to increase approximately 13 percent, resulting in the addition of 17,500 additional photographers.

## Competitive Analysis

BestImage Photo Editing will face competition from the very beginning. There already are many photo editing/retouching services online, and new ones enter the market on a regular basis. Although demand for routine photo editing is strong, Matthews will differentiate BestImage Photo Editing by gradually pursuing more challenging (and higher paying) work from book publishers, magazines, historical societies, and professional photographers. As outlined in the Growth Strategy section of this plan, specialized markets (and more advanced photo editing work) are expected to account for most of BestImage Photo Editing's volume by its fifth year of operation.

# PERSONNEL

### Crystal Matthews (Owner)

BestImage Photo Editing is being established by Crystal Matthews. From an early age, Matthews exhibited a strong eye for detail. When looking at photographs or magazines, or even watching movies, she had a knack for noticing things overlooked by most people. While pursuing the courses needed to complete her associate's degree at Sunnyvale Technical College, Matthews was still contemplating her career path. This changed when she took courses in Photoshop and advanced Photoshop. In addition to gaining new technical skills, Matthews discovered that she had a real passion for working with digital images.

In her Photoshop training, Matthews also completed several small business management courses, providing her with the fundamental knowledge needed to own and operate a small business. By establishing BestImage Photo Editing, Matthews will be in a position to apply her technical skill and small-business management knowledge in a market with strong potential.

### Professional & Advisory Support

BestImage Photo Editing has established a business banking account with Sunnyvale Bank, including a merchant account for accepting credit card payments. Tax advisement is provided by Accurate Accounting LLC.

## GROWTH STRATEGY

BestImage Photo Editing expects to edit a total of 7,000 images during its first year of business, generating gross revenues of $31,250. Based on a 250-day work year, Matthews initially expects to devote about five hours per workday to photo restoration activities, resulting in capacity of 3,750 hours (based on a 40-hour workweek). Realizing that some hours will need to be devoted to administrative and marketing-related tasks, but also considering the significant productivity gains that will result from additional experience, Matthews has established a goal of increasing her volume steadily each year.

Matthews has established four price points/categories (Standard, Plus, Advanced, and Premium) for customers, depending on how extensive their photo retouching/enhancement needs are. During the first year, she anticipates that 50 percent of the photo restoration/enhancement projects handled by her business will fall within the Standard category, 29 percent will fall within the Plus category, 14 percent will fall within the Advanced category, and 7 percent will fall within the Premium category.

Matthews anticipates that individual consumers and portrait photographers will account for the majority of BestImage Photo Editing's business during its first several years of operation. Her goal is to gradually transition the business away from providing consumers and photographers with routine photo retouching and to begin providing more technically advanced photo editing and retouching services for more specialized markets. This will help to differentiate the business from the competition, and also result in higher paying work.

Following is a summary of BestImage Photo Editing's growth targets during its first five years of operations:

*Year One:* Focus heavily on marketing and new business development, especially the acquisition of clients with ongoing needs (e.g., photographers, printers, etc.). Achieve annual volume of 7,000 images.

### Year 1 Project volume projections

| | | |
|---|---|---|
| Standard | 3,500 | 50% |
| Plus | 2,000 | 29% |
| Advanced | 1,000 | 14% |
| Premium | 500 | 7% |
| **Total** | **7,000** | **100%** |

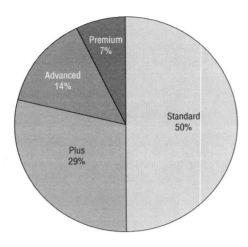

*Year Two:* Continue to focus heavily on marketing and new business development. Achieve annual volume of 8,855 images.

*Year Three:* Concentrate on maintaining existing customers/steady business growth. Achieve annual volume of 9,741 images.

**Year 3  Project volume projections**

| | | |
|---|---|---|
| Standard | 3,000 | 31% |
| Plus | 3,000 | 31% |
| Advanced | 2,500 | 25% |
| Premium | 1,250 | 13% |
| **Total** | **9,750** | **100%** |

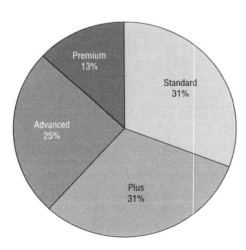

*Year Four:* Continue to concentrate on maintaining existing customers/steady new business growth. Achieve annual volume of 10,715 images.

*Year Five:* By this time, Matthews anticipates that her business will be at full capacity, editing approximately 47 images per workday. Annual volume is projected to reach 11,780 images.

**Year 5 Project volume projections**

| | | |
|---|---|---|
| Standard | 1,000 | 8% |
| Plus | 3,780 | 32% |
| Advanced | 4,500 | 38% |
| Premium | 2,500 | 22% |
| **Total** | **11,780** | **100%** |

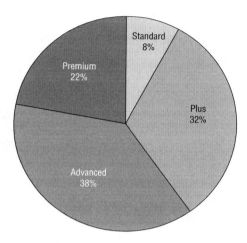

## SERVICES

Photo editing and restoration often involves routine corrections, such as removing red eye or improving image color or sharpness. However, customers may want to remove an individual from an image, open someone's closed eyes, change someone's eye color or hair color, remove skin blemishes, whiten teeth, or add a different background. Requests for changes are limited only by one's imagination (and budget).

Matthews has established four price points/categories (Standard, Plus, Advanced, and Premium) for customers, depending on the extent of their photo retouching needs.

### Service Package Descriptions

The Standard package provides simple corrections that are easy to do (e.g., red eye removal, teeth whitening, simple spot removal, color enhancement, etc.).

### Plus

The Plus package provides everything included in the Standard package, plus image background replacement with a solid color of the customer's choice. Additionally, more advanced, but routine, corrections are included, such as opening closed eyes, fixing crooked teeth, removing orthodontia, etc.

### Advanced

The Advanced package includes everything available with lower-level packages, plus more substantial changes to image subjects and backgrounds. Unlike the Plus package, which offers background replacement with a solid color, the Advanced package offers customers the ability to put photo subjects in an entirely different background or landscape. Additionally, objects or individuals within a photograph can be removed or altered in appearance (e.g., size, color, shape, orientation, etc.).

### Premium

The Premium package includes all services offered in lower-level packages, and more. Premium services are required for the restoration of digitized photos that are very old or extensively damaged (e.g., portions of image missing, very blurry, scratches, cracks, etc.). Additionally, this package includes the application of a wide range of special effects, or the creation of custom collages/images based on the customer's specification.

### Pricing

The following rate structure has been established for each service package:

**Service packages/per-unit fees**

| Package | Gross charge |
| --- | --- |
| Standard | $ 2.50 |
| Plus | $ 5.00 |
| Advanced | $ 7.50 |
| Premium | $15.00 |

Customers are required to designate the level of service requested for the images they submit to BestImage Photo Editing. Matthews will contact the customer if they have selected a service level that she feels is inappropriate (e.g., too extensive or not extensive enough). Pricing also can be designated for large batches of photos, especially from commercial customers who simply want to ensure a certain level of quality for all photos submitted.

BestImage Photo Editing's Web site will feature a simple tool for uploading photos and submitting online payment using a major credit card or PayPal. BestImage Photo Editing guarantees that images will be corrected within 10 business days (although turnaround typically will be two to three business days). Customer images will be retained for 60 days, and then deleted; BestImage Photo Editing does not provide long-term archival services for digital images.

## MARKETING & SALES

BestImage Photo Editing has developed a marketing plan that includes the following primary tactics:

1.  Because BestImage Photo Editing will operate mainly as an online business, significant effort will be applied to the establishment of a high-quality Web site. The site will showcase a wide range of "before" and "after" photos in different service-level packages, in order to demonstrate Crystal Matthews' skills. To convey an image of trust, Matthews will prominently feature testimonials from customers and pursue membership in the Better Business Bureau. The site will include an image upload tool, as well as e-commerce functionality, enabling customers to pay for their orders online using major credit cards or PayPal.

2.  BestImage Photo Editing will develop a series of high-quality, four-color glossy postcards, show-casing Matthews' best work. These will be used for a regularly scheduled direct mail campaign targeting commercial prospects, including photographers, printers, and book publishers. Mailing lists will be purchased from a reputable list broker, and Matthews will utilize the services of a mail house located in Georgia.

3.  An e-mail marketing campaign will be developed, targeting key prospects. As with direct mail, e-mail lists will be purchased from a reputable list broker, and Matthews will take advantage of a popular e-mail marketing service, which will send messages on behalf of BestImage Photo Editing.

4.  A social media strategy involving Twitter, Facebook, and LinkedIn. These social media platforms will be integrated with BestImage Photo Editing's Web site.

5. A new customer discount program will be developed, providing new clients with one free photo edit (in any category), as well as a 10 percent discount off of the first order (discount applies to 25 images or less).

6. A customer loyalty program, providing five free photo edits (in any category) for every 50 purchased.

## OPERATIONS

One main advantage to this business is that there is virtually no overhead. All work is performed in Crystal Matthews' home office and delivered to customers digitally, via e-mail, CD/DVD, or FTP. Beyond a computer and photo editing software, there is no need to purchase supplies or maintain inventory.

### Location

BestImage Photo Editing will operate from a home office in Crystal Matthews' residence, located at 2073 Langford Dr. in Sunnyvale, Tennessee.

### Telecommunications/Internet

Matthews has contracted for broadband Internet service from a local service provider. In addition, she also has added a business telephone line from the same provider, in the event that customers need to speak to her by phone. However, she anticipates that the majority of communications will take place via e-mail.

### Back-up

Matthews has established arrangements with two independent contractors who are able to provide her with assistance on a work-for-hire basis during periods of extremely high volume, or in the event of illness/vacation.

### Insurance

A liability insurance policy has been obtained to cover the scope of services provided. However, Matthews does not anticipate substantial business-related risks, since her business will only handle digital images, and not original photographs or artwork.

### Equipment

BestImage Photo Editing will require the following equipment and computer software prior to start-up ($2,100):

- Dell XPS 8700 Desktop Computer, Intel i5-4440 3.1GHz, 8GB RAM, 1TB HDD, Windows 8 ($700)

- Dell - 27" Widescreen Flat-Panel IPS LED HD Monitor ($300)

- Adobe Photoshop CS6 ($600)

- Office Furniture ($500)

### Hours of Operation

Matthews generally will answer customer service-related requests between the hours of 9 AM and 5 PM, Monday through Friday. She has chosen not to work on the following major holidays:

- Christmas Day

- Christmas Eve

- July 4

- Labor Day
- Memorial Day
- New Year's Day
- Thanksgiving Day

## FINANCIAL ANALYSIS

Crystal Matthews will cover the aforementioned startup costs of $2,100 from her own personal savings.

Following are revenue projections for BestImage Photo Editing's first five years of operations:

**Revenue projections: 2014–2018**

| Year | Annual volume | Annual revenue |
|------|---------------|----------------|
| 2014 | 7,000 | $31,250 |
| 2015 | 8,855 | $39,848 |
| 2016 | 9,750 | $60,000 |
| 2017 | 10,715 | $74,580 |
| 2018 | 11,780 | $92,650 |

**Annual revenue**

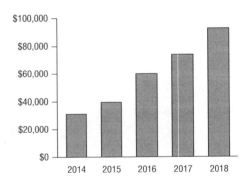

# Residential Cleaning Service

Simply Clean

16152 Landview
Macomb, MI 48041

*Brenda Kubiac*

*Simply Clean is a diversified cleaning service specializing in not only basic residential housecleaning but also deep cleaning, new construction clean up, real estate cleaning, and window washing.*

## 1.0 EXECUTIVE SUMMARY

### 1.1 Business Overview

Simply Clean is a Michigan-based sole proprietorship that provides residential plus additional cleaning services throughout Macomb and the surrounding areas. Jacklyn Jackson, founder of Simply Clean, left corporate America to pursue a business where she intends to determine her own wealth through hard work and strong values.

Simply Clean will provide quality cleaning services performed by a bonded company, at competitive prices, and will generate sales of $100,000 or more by the second year of operation with a 40 percent net profit return. Our clients are the estimated 5,000 homeowners in the area who have a disposable income and the need for a cleaning service.

According to the SBDC Clearinghouse (http://www.sbdcnet.org/small-business-research-reports/janitorial-services-2012), "[t]he primary users of household cleaning services are households in the upper income brackets. The number of households with annual incomes exceeding $100,000 is expected to rise at an average annual rate of 1.6 percent between 2011 and 2016, which will result in greater demand for residential cleaning services."

Simply Clean plans to use all natural, non-toxic cleaning supplies and is fully insured and bonded for their clients' protection. The company offers weekly, bi-weekly, monthly, and deep cleaning services. A team of two cleaning specialists, owner Jacklyn and her assistant Jennifer, will treat homes with the same expertise.

Jacklyn Jackson is a member of the Association for the Residential Cleaning Services International (ARCSI), and as a member, Simply Clean is located in their searchable database where potential clients are able to view her services.

### 1.2 Mission

Simply Clean is committed to providing professional, affordable, and customized house cleaning services in Macomb, and surrounding cities. Jacklyn promises to treat every home she cleans as if it were her own.

### 1.3 Goals and Objectives

- Establish credibility
- Build strong relationship with clients by delivering exceptional customer service
- Continue to foster relationships with clients
- Develop a client base of who use Simply Clean on a regular weekly, biweekly, or monthly schedule
- Become an expert on product usage
- Generate sales of $100,000 by the second year with a 40 percent net profit return
- Keep informed about technological advances that affect the equipment used or how safety issues affect chemical uses

### 1.4 Organizational Structure

Simply Clean is a sole proprietorship owned and operated by Jacklyn Jackson.

## 2.0 STRATEGIC & MARKET ANALYSIS

### 2.1 Industry Analysis

According to American Demographics, about 10 percent of Americans hire someone else to clean their home. The overall demand for household cleaning services is expected to grow at a rate of 7 percent annually, according to the U.S. Bureau of Labor Statistics. In addition, the U.S. Department of Commerce expects 80 percent of two-income households to use an outside housecleaning service within the next few years.

### 2.2 Market Analysis

According to a report by American Demographics, "[w]e have found that typical clients are dual-income households, professional single adults, high income single parent families, and affluent empty nesters and retirees. They will typically be between 35 and 65 years of age, with a household income over $75,000 annually. However, virtually EVERY household earning over $100,000 a year, regardless of other demographics, is a prime candidate for a weekly, biweekly or monthly cleaning service. Even households with high six- or seven-figure incomes who have part- or fulltime domestics often hire outside professional cleaners to assist their live-in help"(http://www.housecleaningbiz101.com/Clean ingIndustryFacts.htm).

## 3.0 COMPETITION

Jacklyn conducted research by reviewing websites, newspapers, Yellow Pages, business cards from bulletin boards, and flyers posted at grocery stores in order to locate competition within the target market. Then, by posing as a potential customer via phone inquiry, she was able to find out how they might affect her business. For example, some questions included how long had they been in business and if they were insured and bonded, if they served the target area and how soon she could obtain an estimate for housecleaning, if they charged by the hour or by the job, and how routine visits were scheduled. In addition, Jacklyn reviewed the national chains pricing structures. She had five different cleaning companies clean her home in an effort to compare their charges and the specifics of the tasks involved.

Unlike a number of cleaning companies that are cleaning the old fashioned way and have not kept up on the latest trends when it comes to green cleaning products and procedures, Simply Clean offers alternate eco-friendly cleaning products for those clients that prefer green cleaning.

## 4.0 PROFESSIONAL AND ADVISORY SUPPORT

Day-to-day bookkeeping will be done in-house. For added accounting and financial functions, Jacklyn Jackson has retained the services of Schultz Accounting Services. For all legal aspects relating the business, the company has retained the services of Foster law, LLP, & address. For all of its insurance needs, Simply Clean has retained the services of Miller Insurance Group, who put a liability insurance policy in place, as well as a surety bond. A business account able to accept credit and debit cards along with a line of credit was set up at Macomb Commercial Bank, including a merchant account and processing equipment for accepting credit card payments from clients. For added convenience Simply Clean will accept PayPal payment for services via the website.

## 5.0 GROWTH STRATEGY

Jacklyn plans to grow her company by hiring additional employees when the number of clients exceeds the number she can accommodate efficiently.

## 6.0 PRODUCTS AND SERVICES

Below is a list of standard services including additional and other services upon request:

- Dust entire house, including furniture and blinds
- Vacuum entire home, including carpet and furniture
- Scrub bathtubs and showers
- Clean toilets
- Scrub sinks and faucets
- Clean kitchen and bathroom countertops
- Clean outside of appliances
- Wipe down inside of microwave oven
- Wipe down outside of kitchen cupboards
- Make beds
- Polish furniture
- Collect and dispose of trash
- Clean mirrors
- Wipe TV screens

### 6.1 Additional ad-on services

- Change bed and bath linens
- Clean inside of refrigerator
- Defrost freezer
- Clean oven and underneath stovetop
- Wash walls

- Clean out fireplace

- Strip, wax, and buff floors

- Oil woodwork

- Clean carpets

- Wash windows

- Wipe windowsills, baseboards, doors, and door frames

### 6.2 Other services

- Deep cleaning

- New construction clean up

- Real estate cleaning & window washing

- Moving in or out cleaning

### 6.3 Fees

- Initial consultations are free of charge

- Each two-hour weekday visit to a house or an apartment is $70

- Each four-hour weekday visit to an apartment or house is $140

- Each additional weekday hour beyond a four-hour visit is $35

- Clean stove or refrigerator for $25 each (add-on)

- Weekend visits are billed at the rate of $85 per two-hour visit

- Seniors and veterans receive a 10 percent discount

- Offers a 50 percent discount on a single four-hour visit for all completed referrals

## 7.0 MARKETING PLAN

After searching the Yellow Pages and the Chamber of Commerce for cleaning services within target market, Jacklyn narrowed it down to what she viewed as key competitors. Of these, Jacklyn approached 15 competitors and had her home cleaned by 7 of them. This allowed Jacklyn to acquire the marketing materials these competitors use, including price structure. Other marketing efforts are listed below:

- Website that includes company name, mission statement, geographic area served, services and brief description, contact number, email, opportunity to request Guide to Services manual or a form to request a quote, and discount coupon valued at $30 off your first and second house cleanings

- Advertise in Macomb County Newspapers, Advisor and Source Newspapers

- Advertise in Yellow Pages

- Newspaper

- Promote business at trade shows

- Direct mail

- Distribute literature through a mail pack with other advertisers

# 8.0 OPERATIONS

## 8.1 Customers

Typical housecleaning clients will be single working people who would prefer a social life outside of work instead of cleaning on Saturday. Simply Clean plans to target families with both spouses working whose incomes are $60,000 and up, households with income levels surpassing $100,000, singles who don't have the time, and seniors who are physically unable.

Macomb Township, Michigan, reported a population of 56,571 residents 16 years and over who were employed. According to the U.S. Census statistics, the median household income (in dollars) was $82,626. Of these residents, 4,909 residents had an income of $50,000 to $74,999; 4,710 residents earned $75,000 to $99,999; 6,438 had incomes between $100,000 to $149,999; 2,086 with an income of $150,000 to $199,000; and 924 residents that earned $200,000 or more.

Simply Clean will also serve Rochester, Rochester Hills, Washington Twp., Richmond, Utica, Sterling Heights, Roseville, Centerline, Chesterfield, New Baltimore, Clinton Twp., Fraser, and Madison Heights. The company plans to schedule clients in a way that minimizes travel time to about 15 to 20 minutes apart.

## 8.2 Equipment

### Basic Equipment

| | |
|---|---|
| Separate phone line with voice mail | $25 per month |
| Large table $100 or computer armoire | $ 400–3,000 |
| Comfortable chair | $ 125 |
| 1 or 2 locking file cabinets | $ 150 |
| Fireproof safe | $ 120 |
| Computer | $ 300–1,500 |
| Multifunction printer, scanner, copy, and fax machine | $ 100–200 |
| **Total** | **$ 1,720** |

### Additional supplies

*   Stapler

*   Pens and pencils

*   CD-ROMS and storage case

*   Dry erase board to use as calendar

*   Copy paper

*   Paper-recycling bin

*   Index cards and storage box

*   Rolodex

*   *Total = $250*

## 8.3 Hours of Operation

Simply Clean generally provides services between 7:00 a.m. and 6:00 p.m., Monday through Friday. Business hours for voice mail are between 9:00 a.m. and 8:00 p.m., Monday through Friday. Email may be sent at any time.

# 9.0 FINANCIAL ANALYSIS

## 9.1 Startup Costs

| Item | Cost |
|---|---|
| **Advertising** | |
| Business cards (500) | $ 100.00 |
| Advertising literature | $ 550.00 |
| Advertising campaigns | $ 185.00 |
| Telephone (one business line) and Yellow Pages ad | $ 480.00 |
| Answering machine or service | $ 250.00 |
| **Administration** | |
| Register business at local County Clerk's Office | $ 25.00 |
| Invoices/receipt book | $ 15.00 |
| Receipts and disbursements journal | $ 25.00 |
| Liability Insurance | $ 600.00 |
| Legal/accounting (includes business license) | $ 500.00 |
| **Total supplies** | **$ 2,730.00** |

| Item | Quantity | Cost |
|---|---|---|
| Degreaser | 4 | $ 85.00 |
| Furniture polish | 4 | $ 98.00 |
| Industrial glass cleaner | 4 | $ 20.00 |
| Bleach | 4 | $ 16.00 |
| Spray bottles | 12 | $ 24.00 |
| Buckets | 4 | $ 26.00 |
| Scrub pads | 24 | $ 12.00 |
| Wall-wash rag mops | 8 | $ 52.00 |
| Cotton washing sleeve | 2 | $ 25.00 |
| Swivel-headed wall-wash attachment | 2 | $ 15.00 |
| 8" rubber squeegee | 2 | $ 26.00 |
| 12" rubber squeegee | 2 | $ 30.00 |
| Lightweight extension pole | 1 | $ 63.00 |
| Horsehair brush | 1 | $ 18.00 |
| Chamois | 6 | $ 30.00 |
| Oven cleaner | 1 | $ 5.00 |
| 100% cotton cloths | 60 | $ 90.00 |
| Carryalls or cadies for supplies | 2 | $ 75.00 |
| Vacuum equipment (optional) | | $1,000.00 |
| **Total** | | **$1,710.00** |

## 9.2 2014 balance sheet

| Revenue | |
|---|---|
| Regular cleaning | $45,000 |
| Deep cleaning | $ 3,500 |
| New construction cleaning service | $12,000 |
| Window washing | $14,000 |
| Moving in or out | $ 2,400 |
| Real estate cleaning | $ 2,100 |
| **Total revenue** | **$79,000** |
| **Total expenses** | **$ 6,410** |
| **Net income** | **$72,590** |

# Senior Errand Service

Alexis's Errand Services

67349 Delray St.
Warren, MI 48093

*Brenda Kubiac*

*Alexis's Errand Services is an errand running company that caters to senior citizens.*

## 1.0 EXECUTIVE SUMMARY

### 1.1 Business Overview

Alexis's Errand Services is a Michigan-based sole proprietorship that provides errand services for senior citizens located in Warren. Warren is listed as one of the cities with the highest number of senior residents that are 65 years of age and older, and it ranks fourth when it comes to seniors 85 years of age and older living in the U.S.

A senior errand service business requires little overhead cost and can be operated from the comfort of a home-based office. The only supplies needed are a cell phone, a reliable vehicle, and a computer. Insured and bonded, Alexis's Errand Services was founded by Alexis Davis. Alexis sold her gas guzzling sport utility to buy a fuel-efficient car so gas wouldn't cut into profits. Since the car was a few years old she took it to a reputable mechanic for a full inspection to ensure the reliability of the car prior to purchase.

With the population aging, this is the perfect time to open up an errand running service. According to *The State of Aging & Health in America 2013*, "[t]he growth in the number and proportion of older adults is unprecedented in the history of the United States. Two factors—longer life spans and aging baby boomers—will combine to double the population of Americans aged 65 years or older during the next 25 years to about 72 million. By 2030, older adults will account for roughly 20 percent of the U.S. population."

### 1.2 Mission Statement

Alexis's Errand Services is committed to providing seniors nothing less than the service they deserve and expect.

### 1.3 Business Philosophy

Alexis's Errand Services will operate a compassionate business with focus on helping seniors remain in their homes.

## 2.0 STRATEGIC AND MARKET ANALYSIS

### 2.1 Industry Analysis

Employment opportunities for personal care and service occupations are expected to increase by 20.4 percent in the 2008-2018 decade, which is nearly twice as fast as most occupations, according to a report by the U.S. Bureau of Labor Statistics (BLS). According to the Administration on Aging, there were 41.4 million Americans aged 65 and up in 2011. The population 65 and over has increased from 35 million in 2000 to 41.4 million in 2011 (an 18 percent increase) and is projected to increase to 79.7 million in 2040.

### 2.2 Market Analysis

Alexis's Errand Services concluded Warren is a prime market for a senior errand service with a population of 134,056 residents, of which 21,644 of them (16.1 percent) are age 65 and older. The city of Warren also has the fourth-highest percentage of individuals age 85 and older.

Alexis approached the seniors themselves in her target market to ask what errand services would they be interested in, how much they will be willing to pay, and what locations they thought would be a good place to advertise.

### 2.3 Competition

Alexis researched her competition by reviewing websites and online directory listings to learn more about the various types of errand services provided and found home care services such as home care aids, companions, personal shoppers, personal chefs, pet services, transportation service, and franchises that provide similar services for seniors and were considered her indirect competition. For example, being available on weekends will help stay ahead of competition since some clients will prefer weekends.

While there is lots of competition, no two errand services are identical. Alexis plans to focus on services not being met by these errand services to distinguish Alexis's Errand Services from her competition. To accomplish this, Alexis searched other senior errand services and general errand service firms within her area to determine the services they offer, how much they charge, and the tactics used to target the senior market. This information will also be useful in an effort to further differentiate her business from her competition.

## 3.0 MANAGEMENT SUMMARY

Alexis Davis founded Alexis's Errand Services after she began running errands for her grandmother following a hip replacement. Even after her grandmothers' recovery she was unable to get around like she did prior to the surgery and continued to require help, especially with errands. Alexis quickly discovered that not only within her immediate family but seniors in general could use the help of an errand service.

Both marketing and maintaining reliable transportation is vital to running a successful errand service business, as is fuel efficiency. Therefore, Alexis sold her gas guzzling sport utility to buy a used fuel-efficient car and took it to a reputable mechanic for a full inspection to ensure the reliability of the car prior to purchase and errand running.

## 4.0 PROFESSIONAL AND ADVISORY SUPPORT

Day-to-day bookkeeping will be done in-house. For added accounting and financial functions, Alexis's Errand Services has retained the services of Schultz Accounting Services. For all legal aspects relating the business, Alexis's Errand Services has retained the services of Foster law, LLP, & address. For all of its insurance needs, Alexis's Errand Services has retained the services of Miller Insurance Group. A business account along with a line of credit was set up at Warren Commercial Bank, including a merchant account and processing equipment for accepting credit card payments from clients. For added convenience Alexis's Errand Services will accept PayPal payment for services via her website. In addition, Alexis is prepared to hire a virtual assistant to take care of phone, manage all correspondence, take care of bookkeeping, and schedule clients on an as needed basis.

## 5.0 GROWTH STRATEGY

The company will keep track of all business expenses and re-evaluate the cost of doing business regularly to keep up with inflation. For example, if the price of gas increases so must Alexis's Errand Services fees to reflect that increase. Marketing and maintaining reliable transportation is vital to running a successful errand service business for the long haul.

## 6.0 PRODUCTS AND SERVICES

Below is a list of services provided by Alexis's Errand Services with possible additional errand services available upon request:

- House and pet sitting
- Stopping at post office
- Shop for grocery items and other household supplies
- Perform house checks while a customer is out of town
- Transport
- Go to library
- Computer help
- Hair salon
- Doctors appointment
- Hospital test
- Shop for clothing, personal items, and gifts
- Dog walking, transporting pets to veterinarian or groomer
- Pick up prescriptions at pharmacy
- Banking needs
- Drop-off and pick-up dry-cleaning or laundry
- Take clients' car for service or repair
- Pick-up and deliver library books, video, and DVD rentals
- Pick-up meal from favorite area restaurants

### 6.1 Other Products
Gift certificates are also available.

### 6.2 Pricing
Based on market research Alexis found senior errand runners rates were typically between $18 and $35 per hour, depending on what part of the country they live in with the national average at $25 per hour.

Alexis's Errand Services plans to offer a competitive rate of $25 per hour with a five or ten hour service package for one month of errands.

## 6.3 Fees and payment schedule

1. Fees for services can be charged either hourly or at a flat rate depending on preference or errand

2. Membership packages will be available for frequent clients either per month or per year

3. 5 percent discount on hourly rates for customers 65 years or older

4. Payment is due at the conclusion of service unless prior arrangements were discussed

5. New clients receive $5 off first errand

6. Payment for monthly packages must be paid in advance

7. Payment is due when services are completed unless other arrangements were agreed upon prior

8. Additional charges apply if running errands outside of normal business hours or on holidays

9. Cancellation fee of $25 will apply if errand is not cancelled within 24 hours of the scheduled time

10. A small per-hour fuel surcharge will be added to invoice

11. Parking fees per client will also be included in invoice

12. Alexis's Errand Services accepts cash, check, Visa, MasterCard and Discover as payment for services

## 7.0 MARKETING PLAN

Alexis's Errand Services plans to not only target seniors but also the children who are caregivers (i.e. decision makers) of their aging parents. Others who could benefit from getting assistance with errands are disabled or physically challenged individuals.

There will be flyers posted on bulletin boards at local grocery stores, senior centers, senior community centers, senior housing complexes, local dry cleaners, garden shops, elderly care homes, retirement residences, day care centers, etc. In addition, Alexis placed an ad in every senior center monthly newsletter within her target market, as well as joined the Chamber of Commerce.

### 7.1 Marketing Objectives

- Maintain client base

- Grow business by delivering excellent customer service

- Generate a minimum of $200 per day

### 7.2 Marketing Strategies

1. Locate other errand running companies in my target market to obtain quotes for a fictitious errand and found most charge by the hour

2. Monitor websites such as Yelp where consumers voice their opinions and post reviews

3. Get the word out of the new business venture to family, friends, neighbors, church members, co-workers, business associates etc.

4. Created a Website with the help of a web designer to point potential clients to my listing that includes contact information, prices, hours of operation, and testimonials

5. Place ad in every senior center monthly newsletter

6. Created marketing materials (i.e. business cards, post cards, fliers, and brochures)

7. Network, network, network

## 8.0 OPERATIONS

### 8.1 Customers

Alexis Errand Services plans to target senior citizens in Warren, Michigan, who are having difficulty running their own errands for one reason or another. Alexis's Errand Services will operate out of a home-based office already equipped with computer equipment, Internet, and phone, requiring less startup cost and overhead expense.

### 8.2 Hours

Monday-Thursday 7:a.m.-10p.m.

Friday and Saturday 7:a.m.-midnight

Sunday 7:a.m.-10p.m.

### 8.3 Facility and location

Alexis's Errand Services will be a home-based business located at 67349 Delray Street in Warren, Michigan.

## 9.0 FINANCIAL ANALYSIS

### 9.1 2014 Balance Sheet

| | |
|---|---|
| **Total revenue** | **$50,000** |
| **Expenses** | |
| A reliable fuel efficient car | $ 8,500 |
| Cell phone | $ 100 |
| iPad | $ 499 |
| Computer equipment | $ 1,500 |
| Desk & chair | $ 300 |
| Internet | $ 100 |
| Business license | $ 25 |
| Business Insurance | $ 250 |
| Professional services (lawyer, accountant, etc.) | $ 500 |
| Bookkeeping & invoicing software | $ 65 |
| Office supplies | $ 150 |
| Marketing materials | $ 1,000 |
| Website | $ 100 |
| GPS unit | $ 100 |
| **Total expenses** | **$13,189** |
| **Net income** | **$36,811** |

# Senior Transportation Service

GoldenWheels Inc.

2183 Robbins Way
Franklin Grove, PA 15100

*Paul Greenland*

*GoldenWheels Inc. is a transportation service for senior citizens.*

## EXECUTIVE SUMMARY

### Business Overview

According to figures from the Administration on Aging, about 13 percent of the U.S. population was over the age of 65 in 2009 (39.6 million people). By 2030 this age group will account for 19 percent of the population (72.1 million people). As the senior citizen community grows in size, all communities will face a growing demand for a variety of services. Because mobility is essential to quality of life, transportation services are essential for this population.

A report by *The State of Aging & Health in America 2013*, published by the National Center for Chronic Disease Prevention and Health Promotion, Division of Population Health, has shown that the majority of individuals will outlive their ability to drive, typically by 6 to 10 years. At the same time, population dynamics are such that many older individuals live with, or are cared for, by their adult children. As a transportation service for senior citizens, GoldenWheels Inc., will provide a solution to older adults who are unable to drive, and the family members responsible for coordinating their care and life activities.

GoldenWheels is being established by Franklin Grove, Pennsylvania, native Parker McMurry, who previously owned and operated A1 Limousine Service. McMurry experienced the need for senior transportation services firsthand, while trying to coordinate transportation for his father to an adult daycare program. After conducting additional research into the growing need for senior services, McMurry decided to apply his business experience in the transportation sector to a new market. GoldenWheels has the potential to generate strong profits while meeting an important community need at the same time.

## MARKET ANALYSIS

The population of Franklin Grove, Pennsylvania, included 129,599 people in 2013. Individuals over the age of 55 accounted for 34.3 percent of the population (much higher than the national average of 25.4 percent). By 2018 the population is projected to reach 132,712, at which time individuals over 55 will account for 34.5 percent of the population (compared to 27.3 percent nationally). The following table shows a detailed breakdown of Franklin Grove's population, with comparisons to the U.S. population for both 2013 and 2018.

| | Franklin Ridge | United States |
|---|---|---|
| **2013** | | |
| Age 55–64 | 12.70% | 12.20% |
| Age 65–74 | 11.10% | 7.20% |
| Age 75–84 | 7.70% | 4.20% |
| Age 85+ | 2.80% | 1.80% |
| | **34.30%** | **25.40%** |
| **2018** | | |
| Age 55–64 | 12.90% | 12.70% |
| Age 65–74 | 11.20% | 8.40% |
| Age 75–84 | 7.60% | 4.30% |
| Age 85+ | 2.80% | 1.90% |
| | **34.50%** | **27.30%** |

Beyond Franklin Grove, significant senior populations also exist in the nearby communities of Rogersville, Shotton, and Lexington Park, providing opportunities for future geographic expansion.

Parker McMurry estimates that 85 percent of GoldenWheels' business will come from regular routes between private homes or apartments and adult day care centers. In 2013 there were seven adult day programs located within the Franklin Grove market, including:

- Franklin Grove Multipurpose Center

- Northwest Senior Center

- Sunlight Senior Center

- Midtown Adult Day Support Center

- Pathways Adult Day Center

- Southwest Valley Adult Day Support Center

- Bethany Penton Adult Day Program

As the population ages, the number of adult day programs is projected to increase, resulting in growing demand for transportation solutions.

The remaining 15 percent of GoldenWheels' business will come from "specials" or individual/variable trips between private homes or apartments and locations such as shopping malls, grocery stores, doctors' offices, and hospitals. Most of these locations are located on a convenient route, which can be serviced by a dedicated driver. These include locations such as: Franklin Grove Community Hospital, Doctors Park I, Doctors Park II, Rockland Mall, and Schnapps Supermarket.

## Competitive Analysis

Parker McMurry has the advantage of establishing GoldenWheels at a time when there are no dedicated senior-focused transportation providers in the Franklin Grove market. Some competition is provided by the Franklin Grove Mass Transit District, which operates a fleet of city buses, including a limited number of paratransit vehicles equipped with wheelchair lifts. Based on trends in communities with similar demographics, GoldenWheels expects at least one competitor to enter the local market within the company's first two years of operations. Within five years, GoldenWheels will likely have at least two competitors.

## INDUSTRY ANALYSIS

GoldenWheels falls within two different industry segments: senior care services and taxi and shuttle services. According to figures from the Administration on Aging, the portion of the U.S. population over the age of 65 will increase from 39.6 million people in 2009 to 72.1 million people by 2030. As the senior citizen community grows in size, all communities will face a growing demand for a variety of services, including housing, home care, safety/security, medical equipment, and mobility. Because mobility is essential to quality of life, transportation services are an essential service for this population.

Taxi and shuttle services are part of the larger contracted transportation industry. Services such as these employee taxi drivers, chauffeurs, para-transit drivers, and bus drivers. Non-bus transportation services specific to older adults are becoming more commonplace in many markets as a result of households in which senior citizens live with their adult children or other relatives.

Although no specific data is available for senior transportation services, the U.S. Bureau of Labor and Statistics (BLS) projects that the number of taxi driver and chauffeur jobs will increase 20 percent between 2010 and 2020, resulting in the creation of 47,000 new jobs. Specifically, the BLS projects that paratransit services will experience rapid growth, driven by an increasing number of elderly people who wish to remain independent. Additionally, federal legislation requiring agencies to provide disabled and elderly individuals with paratransit services also is expected to contribute to the growth of services provided by GoldenWheels.

## PERSONNEL

### Parker McMurry (Owner)

GoldenWheels is owned and operated by Parker McMurry. A native of Franklin Grove, Pennsylvania, McMurry previously owned and operated A1 Limousine Service. He has experienced the need for senior transportation services firsthand, while trying to coordinate transportation for his father to and from an adult daycare program. After conducting additional research into the growing need for senior services, McMurry decided to apply his business experience in the transportation sector to the senior services market and establish GoldenWheels.

### Staff

In addition to the owner, GoldenWheels will begin operations with the following positions:

- 1 Full-Time Driver

- 1 Part-Time Driver

- 1 Full-Time Dispatch Coordinator

- 1 Full-Time Administrative Assistant/Backup Dispatch Coordinator

Job descriptions for each position are available upon request.

### Professional & Advisory Support

GoldenWheels has established a business banking account with Franklin Grove Community Bank, including a merchant account for accepting credit card payments. Tax advisement is provided by Stevenson & Lewis LLC. In addition, legal services are provided by Bridgeton, Peterson & Moore LP.

## GROWTH STRATEGY

Strong revenue growth is projected for GoldenWheels during its first five years of operations. The business is projected to become profitable during the early part of its third year:

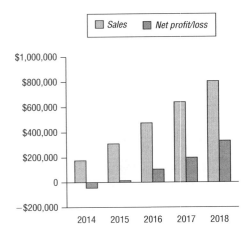

GoldenWheels anticipates strong growth in the number of service miles provided during its first five years:

**Service miles**

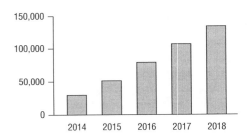

GoldenWheels has outlined the following growth strategy:

**Years One and Two:** Focus on establishing GoldenWheels in the Franklin Grove market, beginning operations with two 16-passenger vans. Become a member of the Better Business Bureau and focus on establishing a relationship of trust with senior citizens and their families throughout the community. Provide 33,176 service miles during the first year, and 55,328 service miles during the second year.

**Year Three:** Add an additional 16-passenger van and hire one additional full-time and one additional part-time driver. Provide 82,992 service miles. After breaking even, end the year with profits of approximately $119,000.

**Year Four:** Add an additional 16-passenger van and hire one additional full-time and one additional part-time driver. Provide 110,396 service miles. Generate net profits of $217,235. Conduct research regarding the potential geographic expansion of GoldenWheels, to make the business a regional player.

**Year Five:** Provide 137,956 service miles and generate net profits of $348,344. Based on the results of research during year four, began making preparations for geographic expansion during year six, including a larger facility, two additional vans, and additional drivers.

The following table provides a snapshot of GoldenWheels' projected weekly transportation volume from 2014 to 2018:

**Projected weekly transportation volume**

| Year | Weekly trip totals | Weekly revenue |
| --- | --- | --- |
| 2014 | 67 | $ 3,766 |
| 2015 | 111 | $ 6,277 |
| 2016 | 167 | $ 9,415 |
| 2017 | 222 | $12,554 |
| 2018 | 278 | $15,692 |

## SERVICES

The majority of GoldenWheels' services involve contracted transportation (one- or two-way trips) between private residences or apartments and adult day care facilities and senior centers. Customers requiring regularly scheduled transportation services are asked to commit to monthly contracts. However, the business also provides transportation on a periodic/as-needed basis to appointments, doctor visits, Franklin Grove Regional Airport, Franklin Grove Bus Terminal, grocery stores, and other locations.

### Pricing

GoldenWheels will provide services based on the following fee structure:

| Miles | Single trip | Daily round-trip | One way weekly | Round-trip weekly |
| --- | --- | --- | --- | --- |
| 0–1 | $ 9.78 | $18.40 | $48.88 | $ 86.25 |
| 2–5 | $11.50 | $20.70 | $57.50 | $ 97.75 |
| 6–8 | $13.80 | $23.00 | $69.00 | $103.50 |
| 9–10 | $17.25 | $28.75 | $86.25 | $138.00 |

GoldenWheels' regular rates apply for both contracted and as-needed services. Customers are required to guarantee payment with a major credit card, although GoldenWheels will accept personal checks. Our business does not accept cash, and drivers do not carry more than $25 in cash for security reasons.

Customers are required to provide GoldenWheels with both desired drop-off and pick-up times 24 hours in advance. Customers who exceed pick-up/drop-off times may be subject to a charge of $25 per hour (billed in quarter-hour increments). There is no additional charge for a second passenger (e.g., when assistance from a friend or loved one is needed with grocery shopping, etc.), or for the transportation of items such as wheelchairs, walkers, or luggage. GoldenWheels' drivers are instructed to not accept gratuities.

## MARKETING & SALES

GoldenWheels has developed a marketing plan that includes the following primary tactics:

1. A four-color brochure with lifestyle photos depicting senior citizens with family members and a GoldenWheels vehicle/staff member. In addition to the description of the business and

services provided, the brochure also will feature the Better Business Bureau logo, a profile of owner Parker McMurry, and information about the fact that GoldenWheels is fully bonded and insured. The objective will be to convey an image of trust. Brochures will be distributed via direct mail (see below) and to area adult day care programs, senior apartment complexes, and senior centers.

2. A radio advertising campaign, featuring a 60-second spot. The station mix will include a popular light rock station, as well as an AM talk station.

3. Regular direct mailings to households with residents over the age of 65 and reported household income of at least $50,000.

4. Monthly lunch meetings with area adult day care program managers, in an effort to build relationships with them.

5. A Web site with complete details about GoldenWheels and the services we offer.

6. A Facebook page.

7. A regular quarter-page print advertisement in *The Senior Courier*, a free local newspaper serving older adults in Franklin Grove and surrounding communities.

8. Submission of periodic "success stories" featuring GoldenWheels and its customers to local TV network affiliates and newspapers.

9. Expert interview pitches to local news media, positioning Parker McMurry and GoldenWheels as local "aging in place" experts.

*This marketing plan will be adjusted/expanded annually as the business grows and faces rising competition.

## OPERATIONS

### Facility & Location
GoldenWheels has identified a heated garage at 2183 Robbins Way in Franklin Grove that is available for lease. The facility should accommodate operations for the business' first five years, as it includes space for up to 5 vehicles. The building includes convenient overhead door access, along with office space and a conference room for meetings with customers.

### Vehicles
GoldenWheels initially will lease two 2013 Ford E-Series 16-passenger vans, at a cost of $9,600 annually. By leasing, the business will be able to effectively manage its maintenance and repair costs.

### Equipment
GoldenWheels will need to purchase several items prior to start-up:

- First Aid Kit ($150)
- Automated External Defibrillators ($1,500)
- Wheelchair Lift ($2,500)
- Computer ($1,300)
- GPS Navigation System ($200)
- Used VoIP 18-Channel Radio Dispatch Counsel with Five Radios ($650)

### Hours of Operation

GoldenWheels will provide transportation services between the hours of 7:00 AM and 7:00 PM Monday through Friday. After hours, customer voicemail messages regarding schedule changes will be routed to the administrative person on call (e.g., Parker McMurry, dispatch coordinator, and/or administrative assistant). Calls will be returned promptly after 6:30 AM the following business day when appropriate.

GoldenWheels will not provide transportation services on these major holidays:

- Christmas Day

- Christmas Eve

- July 4

- Labor Day

- Memorial Day

- New Year's Day

- Thanksgiving Day

## LEGAL

GoldenWheels will adhere to all local, state, and federal transportation and vehicle safety regulations. The Pennsylvania Department of Transportation does not require drivers to obtain a chauffeurs license. Our business will maintain appropriate liability and automotive insurance policies (available upon request). In addition, criminal background checks, drug and alcohol testing, and CPR/first aid certification will be required for all part- and full-time drivers.

## FINANCIAL ANALYSIS

GoldenWheels is expected to sustain a net loss of approximately $42,000 during its first year of operation. After generating a net profit of nearly $36,000 in year two, the business is expected to break even during the early part of its third year. After breaking even, the business is projected to end its third year with a profit of $119,156, and is projected to generate collective profits of $565,579 during years four and five.

Parker McMurry will cover the nominal startup costs referenced in the Operations section of this plan, which total $6,300. In addition, he will invest $20,000 of his own funds in the business. McMurry is seeking an additional $50,000 commitment from a private investor.

GoldenWheels has prepared a complete set of pro forma financial statements in partnership with our accountants, which are available upon request. The following table provides an overview of key projections during the first five years of operations:

**2014–18 Pro forma profit and loss statement**

| | 2014 | 2015 | 2016 | 2017 | 2018 |
|---|---|---|---|---|---|
| **Sales** | $195,832 | $326,404 | $489,580 | $652,808 | $815,984 |
| **Expenses** | | | | | |
| Payroll | $134,200 | $140,910 | $188,400 | $229,336 | $242,600 |
| Facility lease | $ 12,800 | $ 12,800 | $ 12,800 | $ 12,800 | $ 12,800 |
| Vehicle leases | $ 9,600 | $ 9,600 | $ 14,400 | $ 19,200 | $ 19,200 |
| Marketing | $ 35,000 | $ 40,000 | $ 45,000 | $ 50,000 | $ 55,000 |
| Licenses & fees | $ 950 | $ 950 | $ 1,325 | $ 1,550 | $ 1,550 |
| Consulting & legal | $ 5,500 | $ 2,500 | $ 2,500 | $ 2,500 | $ 2,500 |
| Training | $ 2,500 | $ 1,250 | $ 1,250 | $ 1,250 | $ 1,250 |
| Business insurance | $ 2,750 | $ 2,750 | $ 2,750 | $ 2,750 | $ 2,750 |
| Fuel | $ 7,298 | $ 12,172 | $ 18,258 | $ 24,287 | $ 30,350 |
| Software | $ 1,200 | $ 250 | $ 250 | $ 250 | $ 250 |
| Telecommunications | $ 3,500 | $ 3,500 | $ 4,000 | $ 4,000 | $ 4,500 |
| Utilities | $ 1,500 | $ 1,750 | $ 2,000 | $ 2,250 | $ 2,500 |
| Employee benefits | $ 0 | $ 40,000 | $ 45,000 | $ 50,000 | $ 55,000 |
| Payroll taxes | $ 20,100 | $ 21,137 | $ 25,260 | $ 34,400 | $ 36,390 |
| Miscellaneous | $ 1,000 | $ 1,000 | $ 1,000 | $ 1,000 | $ 1,000 |
| **Total operating costs** | $237,898 | $290,569 | $364,193 | $435,573 | $467,640 |
| **Net profit/loss** | −$ 42,066 | $ 35,835 | $125,387 | $217,235 | $348,344 |

# Specialty Retail

Professional Wear by Casandra

8786 S. Madison Blvd.
Dallas, TX 77006

*Brenda Kubiac*

*Professional Wear by Casandra is a specialty boutique that specializes in women's business suits.*

## 1.0 EXECUTIVE SUMMARY

### 1.1 Business Overview

Professional Wear by Casandra is a Texas-based limited liability retail specialty boutique that plans to cater to the 12,000 women business professionals located in Dallas, Texas, a place where women-owned businesses have grown significantly over the last few years.

The company was founded by Casandra Cado, who took over the leased space at a silk scarf boutique that was going out-of-business. Located in the downtown Dallas business district, it was an ideal location for her boutique, and since the silk scarves complemented her suit sets, Casandra purchased the remaining scarf inventory.

Casandra plans to concentrate on developing a clientele consisting primarily of professional working women, who need stylish tailored suit sets ranging in size from 2 to 32, including tall sizes. Casandra will offer a unique mix and match format with a wide selection of colors and styles from which to choose. The boutique will also carry blouses, slacks, and dresses.

### 1.2 Mission Statement

Professional Wear by Casandra promises to deliver nothing less than exceptional personalized service to every woman that walks through the door of the boutique.

## 2.0 STRATEGIC AND MARKET ANALYSIS

### 2.1 Industry Analysis

Professional Wear by Casandra competes with the larger clothing industry, which is expected to generate sales of $2.53 trillion in 2014, according to the National Retail Federation; however, Casandra believes there is a place for her specialty services within the booming women business clothing retail market.

According to the *2013 Women-Owned Business Report,* (http://www.womenable.com/userfiles/down loads/2013_State_of_Women-Owned_Businesses_Report_FINAL.pdf), "Between 1997 and 2013, the number of women-owned businesses increased by 59 percent—1.5 times the rate of U.S. businesses overall. What's more, over the past 16 years, employment by companies owned by female entrepreneurs was up by 10% and their revenues grew by 63%. Both of those increases exceed those of all but the largest, publicly traded firms," The report also notes that "As of 2013, it is estimated that there are over 8.6 million women-owned businesses in the United States, generating over $1.3 trillion in revenues and employing nearly 7.8 million people."

### 2.2 Market Analysis

The U.S. Census Bureau reported that of the 1,241,162 Dallas, Texas residents, 50 percent were women in 2012 of which 27.5 percent were business owners. Upon review of industry magazines, Casandra became familiar with upcoming fashion trends prior to making her final purchases for the boutique. During the market analysis Casandra found a real need for women's business suits, especially for professional plus-size and tall women. Further research concluded the target demographic area and competition lacked business clothing in general.

### 2.3 Competition

Professional Wear by Casandra incorporated the Yellow Pages and Local Chamber of Commerce to research competition and found no other specialty stores that sell women's suits. Although there are other retailers within the target market that sell business suit sets, there are none that do so exclusively or that offer the services Professional Wear by Casandra plans to offer.

## 3.0 MANAGEMENT SUMMARY

The boutique will be run by Casandra Cado, who brings 12 years of purchasing experience to her boutique. Before deciding to open her own specialty boutique Casandra was employed by Hamilton Group, a company that sells high-end fashion and luxury brands at highly discounted prices.

Upon opening, Casandra will run the business by herself, but is prepared to hire two part-time sales clerks if necessary. She has enough financial backing to pay bills and buy enough merchandise for two years.

## 4.0 PROFESSIONAL AND ADVISORY SUPPORT

Day-to-day bookkeeping will be done in-house. For added accounting and financial functions, Casandra has retained the services of Barnes Financial. For all legal aspects relating to the business, Casandra has retained the services of Stanton Law, LLP. Stanton Law was instrumental negotiating favorable lease terms. Sanford Insurance Group will provide all insurance needs, such as commercial property insurance, general insurance, and product liability insurance. The company has also applied for a federal tax identification number from Internal Revenue Service, as well as set up business structure. Casandra secured a line of credit from the Prospect Commercial Bank at the same time she opened a business account. She also obtained a merchant processing account so clients can pay via credit card.

## 5.0 STRATEGIES

### 5.1 Business strategies

1. Stay on top of trends and brands by daily visits to blogs and online stores such as fashionweekdaily.com and girlshop.com among others, as well as attend frequent trade shows.

2. Keep costs down by purchasing shelves and clothing racks at discount prices from retailers going out-of-business.

3. Encourage word-of-mouth advertising by delivering excellent customer service, quality merchandise at affordable prices, and abundant inventory.

4. Nurture customer relationships by sending hand written thank-you cards to customers.

5. Hire a design firm to create an eye-catching storefront prior to the grand opening.

6. Tailor suits to fit right in the store and have the alterations completed within 24 hours.

7. Remove non-selling items off the shelves after 3 months by lowering the price of the item by 30 percent or more.

8. Travel to New York, Los Angeles, Paris, or Milan to buy specialty items for the boutique.

## 5.2 Growth strategy

Professional Wear by Casandra plans to grow the business over its first five years of operations by staying on top of trends and brands and by nurturing customer relationships. Future growth depends on ease of shopping, cleanliness of the boutique, and where things are placed in the store. At the close of the first year Casandra will determine whether the initial concept was viable and tweak if necessary. Focusing on the customer will provide a solid foundation going into the second year of operation. By the third year Casandra will continue to nurture good customers and in return increase gross sales by 20 percent.

# 6.0 PRODUCTS AND SERVICES

The boutique plans to sell business suits that come in a variety of mix and match colors, paired with either a skirt or pants, in a wide selection of styles and fabrics. Other products to complement the suits include blouses, sweaters, cardigans, and decorative scarfs made by local artisans. Casandra will also retail designer one-of-a-kind garments made by a private tailor. Casandra hopes to expand her offerings by entering into consignment arrangements with local artisan's to make custom-made jewelry to add to the overall shopping experience and entice new customers.

## 6.1 Services Include the following:

- In-house seamstress who will handle alterations and pressing, free of charge and with a 24-hour turnaround time, for as long as the customer owns the suit

- Gift wrapping

- $25 to $1,000 Gift cards for use online or in-store

- Liberal return policy: If you are not completely satisfied, you may exchange or return your purchase within 90 days from the original date of purchase; returns after 90 days are eligible to receive a gift card for the returned amount

- Online store

- Seasonal print catalog

# 7.0 MARKETING & SALES

## 7.1 Advertising and Promotion

1. Advertise in local newspapers, the *North Dallas Gazette* and the *Dallas Business Journal*

2. Advertise online, in print magazines and papers, flyers, and direct mail

3. Place posters and signs in the windows and on the door announcing grand opening

4. For shopping pleasure a pianist will play at grand opening wine and cheeses will be served

5. Two-for-one or buy 3 get 1 free type of promotion

6. Percentage-off sales

7. Email promotions

8. Website

# 8.0 OPERATIONS

## 8.1 Customers

Professional Wear by Casandra's primary target customers are the working women who currently shop at area department stores for their business attire.

The specialty boutique will cater to local businesswomen, professionals, government employees, college professors, etc.

## 8.2 Suppliers

Professional Wear by Casandra chose to continue the established relationship with local artisans for silk scarves put in place by the previous owner. The company has negotiated a net of 60 days and secured two months inventory with an additional six suppliers. Professional Wear by Casandra has the following provisions for suppliers:

- Ethical in their business dealings and in sound financial shape

- Reasonable prices and terms and conditions fit company's needs

- Stocks are ample to fill repeat orders along with price guarantees on reorders

- Deliveries are made promptly

The six suppliers that met Professional Wear by Casandra's specifications include the following:

- Custom Fashions by Carly

- Fashion Wholesale

- Kristen's Collection

- Finest Apparel

- Textured Garments Unlimited

- Wool Co.

## 8.3 Equipment

Professional Wear by Casandra store equipment/fixture expenditures are listed below:

- Checkout counter

- Cash registers

- Store phone

- Sewing machines

- Garment steamer

- Mannequins

- Tables

- Hangers

- Clothing racks

- Lighting

- Ticketing machines
- Computer
- Business/marketing software
- Security alarms
- Miscellaneous fixtures
- Miscellaneous office supplies (point-of-purchase software)

## 8.4 Hours

Professional Wear by Casandra decided to coordinate hours of operation with area businesses. The boutique will conduct business seven days a week from 10.a.m. to 6 p.m. Monday through Thursday, from 10.a.m. to 8 p.m. Friday and Saturday, and 12 p.m. to 6 p.m. on Sunday.

Casandra intends to monitor when the majority of sales transpire throughout the day for the first year and adjust hours of operation accordingly if necessary.

## 8.5 Production

Casandra implemented a stock control system to monitor store inventory via a manual tag system. By examining inventory ratios the right items will be purchased in the right amounts.

## 8.6 Facility and Location

The 1,200-square-foot boutique is located at 8786 S Madison Blvd. in Dallas, Texas. Casandra chose this specific location not only because of the ideal customer demographics, but also because there is lots of foot traffic from neighboring restaurants and cafes, hotels, businesses, a tourist information center, and the University of Texas. It also has ample parking that is well lit at night.

The boutique is equipped with three fitting rooms that have flattering full-length mirrors, and soft lighting. There is enough space in back of boutique to accommodate inventory storage as well as the seamstress who will be taking care of alterations.

# 9.0 FINANCIAL ANALYSIS

### 9.1 Startup Expenses

| | |
|---|---|
| Rent on lease (security deposit/first month) | $ 2,500 |
| Initial inventory | $15,000 |
| Equipment/fixtures | $ 5,620 |
| Leasehold improvements | $11,000 |
| License/tax deposits | $ 50 |
| Grand opening advertising | $ 1,350 |
| Utilities/phone deposits | $ 150 |
| Accounting/legal | $ 550 |
| Owner/operator salary | $ 1,500 |
| Payroll | $ 2,000 |
| Supplies | $ 500 |
| Insurance (first quarter) | $ 750 |
| Miscellaneous | $ 300 |
| **Total startup costs** | **$41,270** |

### 9.2 Projected Three-Year Income Statement Summary

| | Year 1: 2013 | Year 2: 2014 | Year 3: 2015 |
|---|---|---|---|
| Revenues | $92,400 | $144,790 | $230,000 |
| Operating expenses | $41,270 | $ 58,334 | $ 71,200 |
| Net income operations | $51,130 | $ 86,456 | $158,800 |

# BUSINESS PLAN TEMPLATE

## USING THIS TEMPLATE

A business plan carefully spells out a company's projected course of action over a period of time, usually the first two to three years after the start-up. In addition, banks, lenders, and other investors examine the information and financial documentation before deciding whether or not to finance a new business venture. Therefore, a business plan is an essential tool in obtaining financing and should describe the business itself in detail as well as all important factors influencing the company, including the market, industry, competition, operations and management policies, problem solving strategies, financial resources and needs, and other vital information. The plan enables the business owner to anticipate costs, plan for difficulties, and take advantage of opportunities, as well as design and implement strategies that keep the company running as smoothly as possible.

This template has been provided as a model to help you construct your own business plan. Please keep in mind that there is no single acceptable format for a business plan, and that this template is in no way comprehensive, but serves as an example.

The business plans provided in this section are fictional and have been used by small business agencies as models for clients to use in compiling their own business plans.

## GENERIC BUSINESS PLAN

Main headings included below are topics that should be covered in a comprehensive business plan. They include:

### Business Summary

**Purpose**
Provides a brief overview of your business, succinctly highlighting the main ideas of your plan.

**Includes**

- Name and Type of Business
- Description of Product/Service
- Business History and Development
- Location
- Market

- Competition
- Management
- Financial Information
- Business Strengths and Weaknesses
- Business Growth

### Table of Contents

**Purpose**
Organized in an Outline Format, the Table of Contents illustrates the selection and arrangement of information contained in your plan.

Includes

- Topic Headings and Subheadings
- Page Number References

## Business History and Industry Outlook

**Purpose**

Examines the conception and subsequent development of your business within an industry specific context.

**Includes**

- Start-up Information
- Owner/Key Personnel Experience
- Location
- Development Problems and Solutions
- Investment/Funding Information
- Future Plans and Goals
- Market Trends and Statistics
- Major Competitors
- Product/Service Advantages
- National, Regional, and Local Economic Impact

## Product/Service

**Purpose**

Introduces, defines, and details the product and/or service that inspired the information of your business.

**Includes**

- Unique Features
- Niche Served
- Market Comparison
- Stage of Product/Service Development
- Production
- Facilities, Equipment, and Labor
- Financial Requirements
- Product/Service Life Cycle
- Future Growth

## Market Examination

**Purpose**

Assessment of product/service applications in relation to consumer buying cycles.

**Includes**

- Target Market
- Consumer Buying Habits
- Product/Service Applications
- Consumer Reactions
- Market Factors and Trends
- Penetration of the Market
- Market Share
- Research and Studies
- Cost
- Sales Volume and Goals

## Competition

**Purpose**

Analysis of Competitors in the Marketplace.

**Includes**

- Competitor Information
- Product/Service Comparison
- Market Niche
- Product/Service Strengths and Weaknesses
- Future Product/Service Development

## Marketing

**Purpose**

Identifies promotion and sales strategies for your product/service.

**Includes**

- Product/Service Sales Appeal
- Special and Unique Features
- Identification of Customers
- Sales and Marketing Staff
- Sales Cycles
- Type of Advertising/Promotion
- Pricing
- Competition
- Customer Services

## Operations

**Purpose**

Traces product/service development from production/inception to the market environment.

**Includes**

- Cost Effective Production Methods
- Facility
- Location
- Equipment
- Labor
- Future Expansion

## Administration and Management

**Purpose**

Offers a statement of your management philosophy with an in-depth focus on processes and procedures.

**Includes**

- Management Philosophy
- Structure of Organization
- Reporting System
- Methods of Communication
- Employee Skills and Training
- Employee Needs and Compensation
- Work Environment
- Management Policies and Procedures
- Roles and Responsibilities

## Key Personnel

**Purpose**

Describes the unique backgrounds of principle employees involved in business.

**Includes**

- Owner(s)/Employee Education and Experience
- Positions and Roles
- Benefits and Salary
- Duties and Responsibilities
- Objectives and Goals

## Potential Problems and Solutions

**Purpose**

Discussion of problem solving strategies that change issues into opportunities.

**Includes**

- Risks
- Litigation
- Future Competition
- Economic Impact
- Problem Solving Skills

## Financial Information

**Purpose**

Secures needed funding and assistance through worksheets and projections detailing financial plans, methods of repayment, and future growth opportunities.

**Includes**

- Financial Statements
- Bank Loans
- Methods of Repayment
- Tax Returns
- Start-up Costs
- Projected Income (3 years)
- Projected Cash Flow (3 Years)
- Projected Balance Statements (3 years)

## Appendices

**Purpose**

Supporting documents used to enhance your business proposal.

**Includes**

- Photographs of product, equipment, facilities, etc.
- Copyright/Trademark Documents
- Legal Agreements
- Marketing Materials
- Research and or Studies
- Operation Schedules
- Organizational Charts
- Job Descriptions
- Resumes
- Additional Financial Documentation

# Fictional Food Distributor

Commercial Foods, Inc.

3003 Avondale Ave.
Knoxville, TN 37920

*This plan demonstrates how a partnership can have a positive impact on a new business. It demonstrates how two individuals can carve a niche in the specialty foods market by offering gourmet foods to upscale restaurants and fine hotels. This plan is fictional and has not been used to gain funding from a bank or other lending institution.*

## STATEMENT OF PURPOSE

Commercial Foods, Inc. seeks a loan of $75,000 to establish a new business. This sum, together with $5,000 equity investment by the principals, will be used as follows:

- Merchandise inventory $25,000
- Office fixture/equipment $12,000
- Warehouse equipment $14,000
- One delivery truck $10,000
- Working capital $39,000
- Total $100,000

## DESCRIPTION OF THE BUSINESS

Commercial Foods, Inc. will be a distributor of specialty food service products to hotels and upscale restaurants in the geographical area of a 50 mile radius of Knoxville. Richard Roberts will direct the sales effort and John Williams will manage the warehouse operation and the office. One delivery truck will be used initially with a second truck added in the third year. We expect to begin operation of the business within 30 days after securing the requested financing.

## MANAGEMENT

A. Richard Roberts is a native of Memphis, Tennessee. He is a graduate of Memphis State University with a Bachelor's degree from the School of Business. After graduation, he worked for a major manufacturer of specialty food service products as a detail sales person for five years, and, for the past three years, he has served as a product sales manager for this firm.

B. John Williams is a native of Nashville, Tennessee. He holds a B.S. Degree in Food Technology from the University of Tennessee. His career includes five years as a product development chemist in gourmet food products and five years as operations manager for a food service distributor.

Both men are healthy and energetic. Their backgrounds complement each other, which will ensure the success of Commercial Foods, Inc. They will set policies together and personnel decisions will be made jointly. Initial salaries for the owners will be $1,000 per month for the first few years. The spouses of both principals are successful in the business world and earn enough to support the families.

They have engaged the services of Foster Jones, CPA, and William Hale, Attorney, to assist them in an advisory capacity.

## PERSONNEL

The firm will employ one delivery truck driver at a wage of $8.00 per hour. One office worker will be employed at $7.50 per hour. One part-time employee will be used in the office at $5.00 per hour. The driver will load and unload his own trucks. Mr. Williams will assist in the warehouse operation as needed to assist one stock person at $7.00 per hour. An additional delivery truck and driver will be added the third year.

## LOCATION

The firm will lease a 20,000 square foot building at 3003 Avondale Ave., in Knoxville, which contains warehouse and office areas equipped with two-door truck docks. The annual rental is $9,000. The building was previously used as a food service warehouse and very little modification to the building will be required.

## PRODUCTS AND SERVICES

The firm will offer specialty food service products such as soup bases, dessert mixes, sauce bases, pastry mixes, spices, and flavors, normally used by upscale restaurants and nice hotels. We are going after a niche in the market with high quality gourmet products. There is much less competition in this market than in standard run of the mill food service products. Through their work experiences, the principals have contacts with supply sources and with local chefs.

## THE MARKET

We know from our market survey that there are over 200 hotels and upscale restaurants in the area we plan to serve. Customers will be attracted by a direct sales approach. We will offer samples of our products and product application data on use of our products in the finished prepared foods. We will cultivate the chefs in these establishments. The technical background of John Williams will be especially useful here.

## COMPETITION

We find that we will be only distributor in the area offering a full line of gourmet food service products. Other foodservice distributors offer only a few such items in conjunction with their standard product line. Our survey shows that many of the chefs are ordering products from Atlanta and Memphis because of a lack of adequate local supply.

## SUMMARY

Commercial Foods, Inc. will be established as a foodservice distributor of specialty food in Knoxville. The principals, with excellent experience in the industry, are seeking a $75,000 loan to establish the business. The principals are investing $25,000 as equity capital.

The business will be set up as an S Corporation with each principal owning 50% of the common stock in the corporation.

# FICTIONAL HARDWARE STORE

OSHKOSH HARDWARE, INC.

123 Main St.
Oshkosh, WI 54901

*The following plan outlines how a small hardware store can survive competition from large discount chains by offering products and providing expert advice in the use of any product it sells. This plan is fictional and has not been used to gain funding from a bank or other lending institution.*

## EXECUTIVE SUMMARY

Oshkosh Hardware, Inc. is a new corporation that is going to establish a retail hardware store in a strip mall in Oshkosh, Wisconsin. The store will sell hardware of all kinds, quality tools, paint, and housewares. The business will make revenue and a profit by servicing its customers not only with needed hardware but also with expert advice in the use of any product it sells.

Oshkosh Hardware, Inc. will be operated by its sole shareholder, James Smith. The company will have a total of four employees. It will sell its products in the local market. Customers will buy our products because we will provide free advice on the use of all of our products and will also furnish a full refund warranty.

Oshkosh Hardware, Inc. will sell its products in the Oshkosh store staffed by three sales representatives. No additional employees will be needed to achieve its short and long range goals. The primary short range goal is to open the store by October 1, 1994. In order to achieve this goal a lease must be signed by July 1, 1994 and the complete inventory ordered by August 1, 1994.

Mr. James Smith will invest $30,000 in the business. In addition, the company will have to borrow $150,000 during the first year to cover the investment in inventory, accounts receivable, and furniture and equipment. The company will be profitable after six months of operation and should be able to start repayment of the loan in the second year.

## THE BUSINESS

The business will sell hardware of all kinds, quality tools, paint, and housewares. We will purchase our products from three large wholesale buying groups.

In general our customers are homeowners who do their own repair and maintenance, hobbyists, and housewives. Our business is unique in that we will have a complete line of all hardware items and will be able to get special orders by overnight delivery. The business makes revenue and profits by servicing our customers not only with needed hardware but also with expert advice in the use of any product we sell. Our major costs for bringing our products to market are cost of merchandise of 36%, salaries of $45,000, and occupancy costs of $60,000.

Oshkosh Hardware, Inc.'s retail outlet will be located at 1524 Frontage Road, which is in a newly developed retail center of Oshkosh. Our location helps facilitate accessibility from all parts of town and reduces our delivery costs. The store will occupy 7500 square feet of space. The major equipment involved in our business is counters and shelving, a computer, a paint mixing machine, and a truck.

## THE MARKET

Oshkosh Hardware, Inc. will operate in the local market. There are 15,000 potential customers in this market area. We have three competitors who control approximately 98% of the market at present. We feel we can capture 25% of the market within the next four years. Our major reason for believing this is that our staff is technically competent to advise our customers in the correct use of all products we sell.

After a careful market analysis, we have determined that approximately 60% of our customers are men and 40% are women. The percentage of customers that fall into the following age categories are:

Under 16: 0%
17-21: 5%
22-30: 30%
31-40: 30%
41-50: 20%
51-60: 10%
61-70: 5%
Over 70: 0%

The reasons our customers prefer our products is our complete knowledge of their use and our full refund warranty.

We get our information about what products our customers want by talking to existing customers. There seems to be an increasing demand for our product. The demand for our product is increasing in size based on the change in population characteristics.

## SALES

At Oshkosh Hardware, Inc. we will employ three sales people and will not need any additional personnel to achieve our sales goals. These salespeople will need several years experience in home repair and power tool usage. We expect to attract 30% of our customers from newspaper ads, 5% of our customers from local directories, 5% of our customers from the yellow pages, 10% of our customers from family and friends, and 50% of our customers from current customers. The most cost effect source will be current customers. In general our industry is growing.

## MANAGEMENT

We would evaluate the quality of our management staff as being excellent. Our manager is experienced and very motivated to achieve the various sales and quality assurance objectives we have set. We will use a management information system that produces key inventory, quality assurance, and sales data on a weekly basis. All data is compared to previously established goals for that week, and deviations are the primary focus of the management staff.

## GOALS IMPLEMENTATION

The short term goals of our business are:

1.  Open the store by October 1, 1994
2.  Reach our breakeven point in two months
3.  Have sales of $100,000 in the first six months

In order to achieve our first short term goal we must:

1.  Sign the lease by July 1, 1994
2.  Order a complete inventory by August 1, 1994

In order to achieve our second short term goal we must:

1.  Advertise extensively in Sept. and Oct.
2.  Keep expenses to a minimum

In order to achieve our third short term goal we must:

1.  Promote power tool sales for the Christmas season
2.  Keep good customer traffic in Jan. and Feb.

The long term goals for our business are:

1.  Obtain sales volume of $600,000 in three years
2.  Become the largest hardware dealer in the city
3.  Open a second store in Fond du Lac

The most important thing we must do in order to achieve the long term goals for our business is to develop a highly profitable business with excellent cash flow.

## FINANCE

Oshkosh Hardware, Inc. Faces some potential threats or risks to our business. They are discount house competition. We believe we can avoid or compensate for this by providing quality products complimented by quality advice on the use of every product we sell. The financial projections we have prepared are located at the end of this document.

## JOB DESCRIPTION-GENERAL MANAGER

The General Manager of the business of the corporation will be the president of the corporation. He will be responsible for the complete operation of the retail hardware store which is owned by the corporation. A detailed description of his duties and responsibilities is as follows.

### Sales

Train and supervise the three sales people. Develop programs to motivate and compensate these employees. Coordinate advertising and sales promotion effects to achieve sales totals as outlined in budget. Oversee purchasing function and inventory control procedures to insure adequate merchandise at all times at a reasonable cost.

## Finance

Prepare monthly and annual budgets. Secure adequate line of credit from local banks. Supervise office personnel to insure timely preparation of records, statements, all government reports, control of receivables and payables, and monthly financial statements.

### Administration

Perform duties as required in the areas of personnel, building leasing and maintenance, licenses and permits, and public relations.

# Organizations, Agencies, & Consultants

*A listing of Associations and Consultants of interest to entrepreneurs, followed by the ten Small Business Administration Regional Offices, Small Business Development Centers, Service Corps of Retired Executives offices, and Venture Capital and Finance Companies.*

## Associations

*This section contains a listing of associations and other agencies of interest to the small business owner. Entries are listed alphabetically by organization name.*

**American Business Women's Association**
9100 Ward Pkwy.
PO Box 8728
Kansas City, MO 64114-0728
(800)228-0007
E-mail: abwa@abwa.org
Website: http://www.abwa.org
Jeanne Banks, National President

**American Franchisee Association**
53 W Jackson Blvd., Ste. 1157
Chicago, IL 60604
(312)431-0545
E-mail: info@franchisee.org
Website: http://www.franchisee.org
Susan P. Kezios, President

**American Independent Business Alliance**
222 S Black Ave.
Bozeman, MT 59715
(406)582-1255
E-mail: info@amiba.net
Website: http://www.amiba.net
Jennifer Rockne, Director

**American Small Businesses Association**
206 E College St., Ste. 201
Grapevine, TX 76051
800-942-2722
E-mail: info@asbaonline.org
Website: http://www.asbaonline.org/

**American Women's Economic Development Corporation**
216 East 45th St., 10th Floor
New York, NY 10017
(917)368-6100

Fax: (212)986-7114
E-mail: info@awed.org
Website: http://www.awed.org
Roseanne Antonucci, Exec. Dir.

**Association for Enterprise Opportunity**
1601 N Kent St., Ste. 1101
Arlington, VA 22209
(703)841-7760
Fax: (703)841-7748
E-mail: aeo@assoceo.org
Website: http://www.micro
enterpriseworks.org
Bill Edwards, Exec.Dir.

**Association of Small Business Development Centers**
c/o Don Wilson
8990 Burke Lake Rd.
Burke, VA 22015
(703)764-9850
Fax: (703)764-1234
E-mail: info@asbdc-us.org
Website: http://www.asbdc-us.org
Don Wilson, Pres./CEO

**BEST Employers Association**
2505 McCabe Way
Irvine, CA 92614
(949)253-4080
800-433-0088
Fax: (714)553-0883
E-mail: info@bestlife.com
Website: http://www.bestlife.com
Donald R. Lawrenz, CEO

**Center for Family Business**
PO Box 24219
Cleveland, OH 44124
(440)460-5409
E-mail: grummi@aol.com
Dr. Leon A. Danco, Chm.

**Coalition for Government Procurement**
1990 M St. NW, Ste. 400
Washington, DC 20036
(202)331-0975
E-mail: info@thecgp.org
Website: http://www.coalgovpro.org
Paul Caggiano, Pres.

**Employers of America**
PO Box 1874
Mason City, IA 50402-1874
(641)424-3187
800-728-3187
Fax: (641)424-1673
E-mail: employer@employerhelp.org
Website: http://www.employerhelp.org
Jim Collison, Pres.

**Family Firm Institute**
200 Lincoln St., Ste. 201
Boston, MA 02111
(617)482-3045
Fax: (617)482-3049
E-mail: ffi@ffi.org
Website: http://www.ffi.org
Judy L. Green, Ph.D., Exec.Dir.

**Independent Visually Impaired Enterprisers**
500 S 3rd St., Apt. H
Burbank, CA 91502
(818)238-9321
E-mail: abazyn@bazyn
communications.com
http://www.acb.org/affiliates
Adris Bazyn, Pres.

**International Association for Business Organizations**
3 Woodthorn Ct., Ste. 12
Owings Mills, MD 21117
(410)581-1373
E-mail: nahbb@msn.com
Rudolph Lewis, Exec. Officer

**International Council for Small Business**
The George Washington University
School of Business and Public
Management
2115 G St. NW, Ste. 403
Washington, DC 20052
(202)994-0704
Fax: (202)994-4930
E-mail: icsb@gwu.edu
Website: http://www.icsb.org
Susan G. Duffy. Admin.

**International Small Business Consortium**
3309 Windjammer St.
Norman, OK 73072
E-mail: sb@isbc.com
Website: http://www.isbc.com

**Kauffman Center for Entrepreneurial Leadership**
4801 Rockhill Rd.
Kansas City, MO 64110-2046
(816)932-1000
E-mail: info@kauffman.org
Website: http://www.entreworld.org

**National Alliance for Fair Competition**
3 Bethesda Metro Center, Ste. 1100
Bethesda, MD 20814
(410)235-7116
Fax: (410)235-7116
E-mail: ampesq@aol.com
Tony Ponticelli, Exec.Dir.

**National Association for the Self-Employed**
PO Box 612067
DFW Airport
Dallas, TX 75261-2067
(800)232-6273
E-mail: mpetron@nase.org
Website: http://www.nase.org
Robert Hughes, Pres.

**National Association of Business Leaders**
4132 Shoreline Dr., Ste. J & H
Earth City, MO 63045
Fax: (314)298-9110
E-mail: nabl@nabl.com
Website: http://www.nabl.com/
Gene Blumenthal, Contact

**National Association of Private Enterprise**
PO Box 15550
Long Beach, CA 90815
888-224-0953

Fax: (714)844-4942
Website: http://www.napeonline.net
Laura Squiers, Exec.Dir.

**National Association of Small Business Investment Companies**
666 11th St. NW, Ste. 750
Washington, DC 20001
(202)628-5055
Fax: (202)628-5080
E-mail: nasbic@nasbic.org
Website: http://www.nasbic.org
Lee W. Mercer, Pres.

**National Business Association**
PO Box 700728
5151 Beltline Rd., Ste. 1150
Dallas, TX 75370
(972)458-0900
800-456-0440
Fax: (972)960-9149
E-mail: info@nationalbusiness.org
Website: http://www.national
business.org
Raj Nisankarao, Pres.

**National Business Owners Association**
PO Box 111
Stuart, VA 24171
(276)251-7500
(866)251-7505
Fax: (276)251-2217
E-mail: membershipservices@nboa.org
Website: http://www.rvmdb.com.nboa
Paul LaBarr, Pres.

**National Center for Fair Competition**
PO Box 220
Annandale, VA 22003
(703)280-4622
Fax: (703)280-0942
E-mail: kentonp1@aol.com
Kenton Pattie, Pres.

**National Family Business Council**
1640 W. Kennedy Rd.
Lake Forest, IL 60045
(847)295-1040
Fax: (847)295-1898
E-mail: lmsnfbc@email.msn.com
Jogn E. Messervey, Pres.

**National Federation of Independent Business**
53 Century Blvd., Ste. 250
Nashville, TN 37214
(615)872-5800
800-NFIBNOW
Fax: (615)872-5353
Website: http://www.nfib.org
Jack Faris, Pres. and CEO

**National Small Business Association**
1156 15th St. NW, Ste. 1100
Washington, DC 20005
(202)293-8830
800-345-6728
Fax: (202)872-8543
E-mail: press@nsba.biz
Website: http://www.nsba.biz
Rob Yunich, Dir. of Communications

**PUSH Commercial Division**
930 E 50th St.
Chicago, IL 60615-2702
(773)373-3366
Fax: (773)373-3571
E-mail: info@rainbowpush.org
Website: http://www.rainbowpush.org
Rev. Willie T. Barrow, Co-Chm.

**Research Institute for Small and Emerging Business**
722 12th St. NW
Washington, DC 20005
(202)628-8382
Fax: (202)628-8392
E-mail: info@riseb.org
Website: http://www.riseb.org
Allan Neece, Jr., Chm.

**Sales Professionals USA**
PO Box 149
Arvada, CO 80001
(303)534-4937
888-736-7767
E-mail: salespro@salesprofessionals-usa.com
Website: http://www.salesprofessionals-usa.com
Sharon Herbert, Natl. Pres.

**Score Association - Service Corps of Retired Executives**
409 3rd St. SW, 6th Fl.
Washington, DC 20024
(202)205-6762
800-634-0245
Fax: (202)205-7636
E-mail: media@score.org
Website: http://www.score.org
W. Kenneth Yancey, Jr., CEO

**Small Business and Entrepreneurship Council**
1920 L St. NW, Ste. 200
Washington, DC 20036
(202)785-0238
Fax: (202)822-8118
E-mail: membership@sbec.org
Website: http://www.sbecouncil.org
Karen Kerrigan, Pres./CEO

**Small Business in Telecommunications**
1331 H St. NW, Ste. 500
Washington, DC 20005
(202)347-4511
Fax: (202)347-8607
E-mail: sbt@sbthome.org
Website: http://www.sbthome.org
Lonnie Danchik, Chm.

**Small Business Legislative Council**
1010 Massachusetts Ave. NW, Ste. 540
Washington, DC 20005
(202)639-8500
Fax: (202)296-5333
E-mail: email@sblc.org
Website: http://www.sblc.org
John Satagaj, Pres.

**Small Business Service Bureau**
554 Main St.
PO Box 15014
Worcester, MA 01615-0014
(508)756-3513
800-343-0939
Fax: (508)770-0528
E-mail: membership@sbsb.com
Website: http://www.sbsb.com
Francis R. Carroll, Pres.

**Small Publishers Association
of North America**
1618 W Colorado Ave.
Colorado Springs, CO 80904
(719)475-1726
Fax: (719)471-2182
E-mail: span@spannet.org
Website: http://www.spannet.org
Scott Flora, Exec. Dir.

**SOHO America**
PO Box 941
Hurst, TX 76053-0941
800-495-SOHO
E-mail: soho@1sas.com
Website: http://www.soho.org

**Structured Employment Economic
Development Corporation**
915 Broadway, 17th Fl.
New York, NY 10010
(212)473-0255
Fax: (212)473-0357
E-mail: info@seedco.org
Website: http://www.seedco.org
William Grinker, CEO

**Support Services Alliance**
107 Prospect St.
Schoharie, NY 12157
800-836-4772

E-mail: info@ssamembers.com
Website: http://www.ssainfo.com
Steve COle, Pres.

**United States Association for Small
Business and Entrepreneurship**
975 University Ave., No. 3260
Madison, WI 53706
(608)262-9982
Fax: (608)263-0818
E-mail: jgillman@wisc.edu
Website: http://www.ususbe.org
Joan Gillman, Exec. Dir.

## Consultants

*This section contains a listing of consultants specializing in small business development. It is arranged alphabetically by country, then by state or province, then by city, then by firm name.*

## Canada

### Alberta

**Common Sense Solutions**
3405 16A Ave.
Edmonton, AB, Canada
(403)465-7330
Fax: (403)465-7380
E-mail: gcoulson@comsense
solutions.com
Website: http://www.comsense
solutions.com

**Varsity Consulting Group**
School of Business
University of Alberta
Edmonton, AB, Canada T6G 2R6
(780)492-2994
Fax: (780)492-5400
Website: http://www.bus.ualberta.ca/vcg

**Viro Hospital Consulting**
42 Commonwealth Bldg., 9912-106
St. NW
Edmonton, AB, Canada T5K 1C5
(403)425-3871
Fax: (403)425-3871
E-mail: rpb@freenet.edmonton.ab.ca

### British Columbia

**SRI Strategic Resources Inc.**
4330 Kingsway, Ste. 1600
Burnaby, BC, Canada V5H 4G7
(604)435-0627
Fax: (604)435-2782

E-mail: inquiry@sri.bc.ca
Website: http://www.sri.com

**Andrew R. De Boda Consulting**
1523 Milford Ave.
Coquitlam, BC, Canada V3J 2V9
(604)936-4527
Fax: (604)936-4527
E-mail: deboda@intergate.bc.ca
Website: http://www.ourworld.
compuserve.com/homepages/deboda

**The Sage Group Ltd.**
980 - 355 Burrard St.
744 W Haistings, Ste. 410
Vancouver, BC, Canada V6C 1A5
(604)669-9269
Fax: (604)669-6622

**Tikkanen-Bradley**
1345 Nelson St., Ste. 202
Vancouver, BC, Canada V6E 1J8
(604)669-0583
E-mail: webmaster@tikkanen
bradley.com
Website: http://www.tikkanenbradley.com

### Ontario

**The Cynton Co.**
17 Massey St.
Brampton, ON, Canada L6S 2V6
(905)792-7769
Fax: (905)792-8116
E-mail: cynton@home.com
Website: http://www.cynton.com

**Begley & Associates**
RR 6
Cambridge, ON, Canada N1R 5S7
(519)740-3629
Fax: (519)740-3629
E-mail: begley@in.on.ca
Website: http://www.in.on.ca/~begley/
index.htm

**CRO Engineering Ltd.**
1895 William Hodgins Ln.
Carp, ON, Canada K0A 1L0
(613)839-1108
Fax: (613)839-1406
E-mail: J.Grefford@ieee.ca
Website: http://www.geocities.com/
WallStreet/District/7401/

**Task Enterprises**
Box 69, RR 2 Hamilton
Flamborough, ON, Canada L8N 2Z7
(905)659-0153
Fax: (905)659-0861

## HST Group Ltd.
430 Gilmour St.
Ottawa, ON, Canada K2P 0R8
(613)236-7303
Fax: (613)236-9893

## Harrison Associates
BCE Pl.
181 Bay St., Ste. 3740
PO Box 798
Toronto, ON, Canada M5J 2T3
(416)364-5441
Fax: (416)364-2875

## TCI Convergence Ltd. Management Consultants
99 Crown's Ln.
Toronto, ON, Canada M5R 3P4
(416)515-4146
Fax: (416)515-2097
E-mail: tci@inforamp.net
Website: http://tciconverge.com/index.1.html

## Ken Wyman & Associates Inc.
64B Shuter St., Ste. 200
Toronto, ON, Canada M5B 1B1
(416)362-2926
Fax: (416)362-3039
E-mail: kenwyman@compuserve.com

## JPL Business Consultants
82705 Metter Rd.
Wellandport, ON, Canada L0R 2J0
(905)386-7450
Fax: (905)386-7450
E-mail: plamarch@freenet.npiec.on.ca

## Quebec

### The Zimmar Consulting Partnership Inc.
Westmount
PO Box 98
Montreal, QC, Canada H3Z 2T1
(514)484-1459
Fax: (514)484-3063

## Saskatchewan

### Trimension Group
No. 104-110 Research Dr.
Innovation Place, SK, Canada S7N 3R3
(306)668-2560
Fax: (306)975-1156
E-mail: trimension@trimension.ca
Website: http://www.trimension.ca

### Corporate Management Consultants
40 Government Road - PO Box 185
Prud Homme, SK, Canada, S0K 3K0
(306)654-4569
Fax: (650)618-2742

E-mail: cmccorporatemanagement@shaw.ca
Website: http://www.Corporate managementconsultants.com
Gerald Rekve

# United States

## Alabama

### Business Planning Inc.
300 Office Park Dr.
Birmingham, AL 35223-2474
(205)870-7090
Fax: (205)870-7103

### Tradebank of Eastern Alabama
546 Broad St., Ste. 3
Gadsden, AL 35901
(205)547-8700
Fax: (205)547-8718
E-mail: mansion@webex.com
Website: http://www.webex.com/~tea

## Alaska

### AK Business Development Center
3335 Arctic Blvd., Ste. 203
Anchorage, AK 99503
(907)562-0335
Free: 800-478-3474
Fax: (907)562-6988
E-mail: abdc@gci.net
Website: http://www.abdc.org

### Business Matters
PO Box 287
Fairbanks, AK 99707
(907)452-5650

## Arizona

### Carefree Direct Marketing Corp.
8001 E Serene St.
PO Box 3737
Carefree, AZ 85377-3737
(480)488-4227
Fax: (480)488-2841

### Trans Energy Corp.
1739 W 7th Ave.
Mesa, AZ 85202
(480)827-7915
Fax: (480)967-6601
E-mail: aha@clean-air.org
Website: http://www.clean-air.org

### CMAS
5125 N 16th St.
Phoenix, AZ 85016

(602)395-1001
Fax: (602)604-8180

### Comgate Telemanagement Ltd.
706 E Bell Rd., Ste. 105
Phoenix, AZ 85022
(602)485-5708
Fax: (602)485-5709
E-mail: comgate@netzone.com
Website: http://www.comgate.com

### Moneysoft Inc.
1 E Camelback Rd. #550
Phoenix, AZ 85012
Free: 800-966-7797
E-mail: mbray@moneysoft.com

### Harvey C. Skoog
PO Box 26439
Prescott Valley, AZ 86312
(520)772-1714
Fax: (520)772-2814

### LMC Services
8711 E Pinnacle Peak Rd., No. 340
Scottsdale, AZ 85255-3555
(602)585-7177
Fax: (602)585-5880
E-mail: louws@earthlink.com

### Sauerbrun Technology Group Ltd.
7979 E Princess Dr., Ste. 5
Scottsdale, AZ 85255-5878
(602)502-4950
Fax: (602)502-4292
E-mail: info@sauerbrun.com
Website: http://www.sauerbrun.com

### Gary L. McLeod
PO Box 230
Sonoita, AZ 85637
Fax: (602)455-5661

### Van Cleve Associates
6932 E 2nd St.
Tucson, AZ 85710
(520)296-2587
Fax: (520)296-3358

## California

### Acumen Group Inc.
(650)949-9349
Fax: (650)949-4845
E-mail: acumen-g@ix.netcom.com
Website: http://pw2.netcom.com/~janed/acumen.html

### On-line Career and Management Consulting
420 Central Ave., No. 314
Alameda, CA 94501

(510)864-0336
Fax: (510)864-0336
E-mail: career@dnai.com
Website: http://www.dnai.com/~career

**Career Paths-Thomas E. Church
& Associates Inc.**
PO Box 2439
Aptos, CA 95001
(408)662-7950
Fax: (408)662-7955
E-mail: church@ix.netcom.com
Website: http://www.careerpaths-tom.com

**Keck & Co. Business Consultants**
410 Walsh Rd.
Atherton, CA 94027
(650)854-9588
Fax: (650)854-7240
E-mail: info@keckco.com
Website: http://www.keckco.com

**Ben W. Laverty III, PhD, REA, CEI**
4909 Stockdale Hwy., Ste. 132
Bakersfield, CA 93309
(661)283-8300
Free: 800-833-0373
Fax: (661)283-8313
E-mail: cstc@cstcsafety.com
Website: http://www.cstcsafety.com/cstc

**Lindquist Consultants-Venture
Planning**
225 Arlington Ave.
Berkeley, CA 94707
(510)524-6685
Fax: (510)527-6604

**Larson Associates**
PO Box 9005
Brea, CA 92822
(714)529-4121
Fax: (714)572-3606
E-mail: ray@consultlarson.com
Website: http://www.consultlarson.com

**Kremer Management Consulting**
PO Box 500
Carmel, CA 93921
(408)626-8311
Fax: (408)624-2663
E-mail: ddkremer@aol.com

**W and J PARTNERSHIP**
PO Box 2499
18876 Edwin Markham Dr.
Castro Valley, CA 94546
(510)583-7751
Fax: (510)583-7645
E-mail: wamorgan@wjpartnership.com
Website: http://www.wjpartnership.com

**JB Associates**
21118 Gardena Dr.
Cupertino, CA 95014
(408)257-0214
Fax: (408)257-0216
E-mail: semarang@sirius.com

**House Agricultural Consultants**
PO Box 1615
Davis, CA 95617-1615
(916)753-3361
Fax: (916)753-0464
E-mail: infoag@houseag.com
Website: http://www.houseag.com/

**3C Systems Co.**
16161 Ventura Blvd., Ste. 815
Encino, CA 91436
(818)907-1302
Fax: (818)907-1357
E-mail: mark@3CSysCo.com
Website: http://www.3CSysCo.com

**Technical Management
Consultants**
3624 Westfall Dr.
Encino, CA 91436-4154
(818)784-0626
Fax: (818)501-5575
E-mail: tmcrs@aol.com

**RAINWATER-GISH & Associates,
Business Finance & Development**
317 3rd St., Ste. 3
Eureka, CA 95501
(707)443-0030
Fax: (707)443-5683

**Global Tradelinks**
451 Pebble Beach Pl.
Fullerton, CA 92835
(714)441-2280
Fax: (714)441-2281
E-mail: info@globaltradelinks.com
Website: http://www.globaltradelinks.com

**Strategic Business Group**
800 Cienaga Dr.
Fullerton, CA 92835-1248
(714)449-1040
Fax: (714)525-1631

**Burnes Consulting**
20537 Wolf Creek Rd.
Grass Valley, CA 95949
(530)346-8188
Free: 800-949-9021
Fax: (530)346-7704
E-mail: kent@burnesconsulting.com
Website: http://www.burnesconsulting.com

**Pioneer Business Consultants**
9042 Garfield Ave., Ste. 312
Huntington Beach, CA 92646
(714)964-7600

**Beblie, Brandt & Jacobs Inc.**
16 Technology, Ste. 164
Irvine, CA 92618
(714)450-8790
Fax: (714)450-8799
E-mail: darcy@bbjinc.com
Website: http://198.147.90.26

**Fluor Daniel Inc.**
3353 Michelson Dr.
Irvine, CA 92612-0650
(949)975-2000
Fax: (949)975-5271
E-mail: sales.consulting@fluordaniel.com
Website: http://www.fluordaniel
consulting.com

**MCS Associates**
18300 Von Karman, Ste. 710
Irvine, CA 92612
(949)263-8700
Fax: (949)263-0770
E-mail: info@mcsassociates.com
Website: http://www.mcsassociates.com

**Inspired Arts Inc.**
4225 Executive Sq., Ste. 1160
La Jolla, CA 92037
(619)623-3525
Free: 800-851-4394
Fax: (619)623-3534
E-mail: info@inspiredarts.com
Website: http://www.inspiredarts.com

**The Laresis Companies**
PO Box 3284
La Jolla, CA 92038
(619)452-2720
Fax: (619)452-8744

**RCL & Co.**
PO Box 1143
737 Pearl St., Ste. 201
La Jolla, CA 92038
(619)454-8883
Fax: (619)454-8880

**Comprehensive Business Services**
3201 Lucas Cir.
Lafayette, CA 94549
(925)283-8272
Fax: (925)283-8272

**The Ribble Group**
27601 Forbes Rd., Ste. 52
Laguna Niguel, CA 92677

(714)582-1085
Fax: (714)582-6420
E-mail: ribble@deltanet.com

**Norris Bernstein, CMC**
9309 Marina Pacifica Dr. N
Long Beach, CA 90803
(562)493-5458
Fax: (562)493-5459
E-mail: norris@ctecomputer.com
Website: http://foodconsultants.com/
bernstein/

**Horizon Consulting Services**
1315 Garthwick Dr.
Los Altos, CA 94024
(415)967-0906
Fax: (415)967-0906

**Brincko Associates Inc.**
1801 Avenue of the Stars, Ste. 1054
Los Angeles, CA 90067
(310)553-4523
Fax: (310)553-6782

**Rubenstein/Justman Management
Consultants**
2049 Century Park E, 24th Fl.
Los Angeles, CA 90067
(310)282-0800
Fax: (310)282-0400
E-mail: info@rjmc.net
Website: http://www.rjmc.net

**F.J. Schroeder & Associates**
1926 Westholme Ave.
Los Angeles, CA 90025
(310)470-2655
Fax: (310)470-6378
E-mail: fjsacons@aol.com
Website: http://www.mcninet.com/
GlobalLook/Fjschroe.html

**Western Management Associates**
5959 W Century Blvd., Ste. 565
Los Angeles, CA 90045-6506
(310)645-1091
Free: (888)788-6534
Fax: (310)645-1092
E-mail: gene@cfoforrent.com
Website: http://www.cfoforrent.com

**Darrell Sell and Associates**
Los Gatos, CA 95030
(408)354-7794
E-mail: darrell@netcom.com

**Leslie J. Zambo**
3355 Michael Dr.
Marina, CA 93933
(408)384-7086

Fax: (408)647-4199
E-mail: 104776.1552@compuserve.com

**Marketing Services Management**
PO Box 1377
Martinez, CA 94553
(510)370-8527
Fax: (510)370-8527
E-mail: markserve@biotechnet.com

**William M. Shine Consulting Service**
PO Box 127
Moraga, CA 94556-0127
(510)376-6516

**Palo Alto Management Group Inc.**
2672 Bayshore Pky., Ste. 701
Mountain View, CA 94043
(415)968-4374
Fax: (415)968-4245
E-mail: mburwen@pamg.com

**BizplanSource**
1048 Irvine Ave., Ste. 621
Newport Beach, CA 92660
Free: 888-253-0974
Fax: 800-859-8254
E-mail: info@bizplansource.com
Website: http://www.bizplansource.com
Adam Greengrass, President

**The Market Connection**
4020 Birch St., Ste. 203
Newport Beach, CA 92660
(714)731-6273
Fax: (714)833-0253

**Muller Associates**
PO Box 7264
Newport Beach, CA 92658
(714)646-1169
Fax: (714)646-1169

**International Health Resources**
PO Box 329
North San Juan, CA 95960-0329
(530)292-1266
Fax: (530)292-1243
Website: http://www.futureof
healthcare.com

**NEXUS - Consultants to Management**
PO Box 1531
Novato, CA 94948
(415)897-4400
Fax: (415)898-2252
E-mail: jimnexus@aol.com

**Aerospcace.Org**
PO Box 28831
Oakland, CA 94604-8831

(510)530-9169
Fax: (510)530-3411
Website: http://www.aerospace.org

**Intelequest Corp.**
722 Gailen Ave.
Palo Alto, CA 94303
(415)968-3443
Fax: (415)493-6954
E-mail: frits@iqix.com

**McLaughlin & Associates**
66 San Marino Cir.
Rancho Mirage, CA 92270
(760)321-2932
Fax: (760)328-2474
E-mail: jackmcla@msn.com

**Carrera Consulting Group, a division
of Maximus**
2110 21st St., Ste. 400
Sacramento, CA 95818
(916)456-3300
Fax: (916)456-3306
E-mail: central@carreraconsulting.com
Website: http://www.carreraconsulting.com

**Bay Area Tax Consultants and Bayhill
Financial Consultants**
1150 Bayhill Dr., Ste. 1150
San Bruno, CA 94066-3004
(415)952-8786
Fax: (415)588-4524
E-mail: baytax@compuserve.com
Website: http://www.baytax.com/

**AdCon Services, LLC**
8871 Hillery Dr.
Dan Diego, CA 92126
(858)433-1411
E-mail: adam@adconservices.com
Website: http://www.adconservices.com
Adam Greengrass

**California Business Incubation Network**
101 W Broadway, No. 480
San Diego, CA 92101
(619)237-0559
Fax: (619)237-0521

**G.R. Gordetsky Consultants Inc.**
11414 Windy Summit Pl.
San Diego, CA 92127
(619)487-4939
Fax: (619)487-5587
E-mail: gordet@pacbell.net

**Freeman, Sullivan & Co.**
131 Steuart St., Ste. 500
San Francisco, CA 94105
(415)777-0707

Free: 800-777-0737
Fax: (415)777-2420
Website: http://www.fsc-research.com

**Ideas Unlimited**
2151 California St., Ste. 7
San Francisco, CA 94115
(415)931-0641
Fax: (415)931-0880

**Russell Miller Inc.**
300 Montgomery St., Ste. 900
San Francisco, CA 94104
(415)956-7474
Fax: (415)398-0620
E-mail: rmi@pacbell.net
Website: http://www.rmisf.com

**PKF Consulting**
425 California St., Ste. 1650
San Francisco, CA 94104
(415)421-5378
Fax: (415)956-7708
E-mail: callahan@pkfc.com
Website: http://www.pkfonline.com

**Welling & Woodard Inc.**
1067 Broadway
San Francisco, CA 94133
(415)776-4500
Fax: (415)776-5067

**Highland Associates**
16174 Highland Dr.
San Jose, CA 95127
(408)272-7008
Fax: (408)272-4040

**ORDIS Inc.**
6815 Trinidad Dr.
San Jose, CA 95120-2056
(408)268-3321
Free: 800-446-7347
Fax: (408)268-3582
E-mail: ordis@ordis.com
Website: http://www.ordis.com

**Stanford Resources Inc.**
20 Great Oaks Blvd., Ste. 200
San Jose, CA 95119
(408)360-8400
Fax: (408)360-8410
E-mail: sales@stanfordsources.com
Website: http://www.stanfordresources.com

**Technology Properties Ltd. Inc.**
PO Box 20250
San Jose, CA 95160
(408)243-9898
Fax: (408)296-6637
E-mail: sanjose@tplnet.com

**Helfert Associates**
1777 Borel Pl., Ste. 508
San Mateo, CA 94402-3514
(650)377-0540
Fax: (650)377-0472

**Mykytyn Consulting Group Inc.**
185 N Redwood Dr., Ste. 200
San Rafael, CA 94903
(415)491-1770
Fax: (415)491-1251
E-mail: info@mcgi.com
Website: http://www.mcgi.com

**Omega Management Systems Inc.**
3 Mount Darwin Ct.
San Rafael, CA 94903-1109
(415)499-1300
Fax: (415)492-9490
E-mail: omegamgt@ix.netcom.com

**The Information Group Inc.**
4675 Stevens Creek Blvd., Ste. 100
Santa Clara, CA 95051
(408)985-7877
Fax: (408)985-2945
E-mail: dvincent@tig-usa.com
Website: http://www.tig-usa.com

**Cast Management Consultants**
1620 26th St., Ste. 2040N
Santa Monica, CA 90404
(310)828-7511
Fax: (310)453-6831

**Cuma Consulting Management**
Box 724
Santa Rosa, CA 95402
(707)785-2477
Fax: (707)785-2478

**The E-Myth Academy**
131B Stony Cir., Ste. 2000
Santa Rosa, CA 95401
(707)569-5600
Free: 800-221-0266
Fax: (707)569-5700
E-mail: info@e-myth.com
Website: http://www.e-myth.com

**Reilly, Connors & Ray**
1743 Canyon Rd.
Spring Valley, CA 91977
(619)698-4808
Fax: (619)460-3892
E-mail: davidray@adnc.com

**Management Consultants**
Sunnyvale, CA 94087-4700
(408)773-0321

**RJR Associates**
1639 Lewiston Dr.
Sunnyvale, CA 94087
(408)737-7720
E-mail: bobroy@rjrassoc.com
Website: http://www.rjrassoc.com

**Schwafel Associates**
333 Cobalt Way, Ste. 21
Sunnyvale, CA 94085
(408)720-0649
Fax: (408)720-1796
E-mail: schwafel@ricochet.net
Website: http://www.patca.org

**Staubs Business Services**
23320 S Vermont Ave.
Torrance, CA 90502-2940
(310)830-9128
Fax: (310)830-9128
E-mail: Harry_L_Staubs@Lamg.com

**Out of Your Mind...and Into the Marketplace**
13381 White Sands Dr.
Tustin, CA 92780-4565
(714)544-0248
Free: 800-419-1513
Fax: (714)730-1414
E-mail: lpinson@aol.com
Website: http://www.business-plan.com

**Independent Research Services**
PO Box 2426
Van Nuys, CA 91404-2426
(818)993-3622

**Ingman Company Inc.**
7949 Woodley Ave., Ste. 120
Van Nuys, CA 91406-1232
(818)375-5027
Fax: (818)894-5001

**Innovative Technology Associates**
3639 E Harbor Blvd., Ste. 203E
Ventura, CA 93001
(805)650-9353

**Grid Technology Associates**
20404 Tufts Cir.
Walnut, CA 91789
(909)444-0922
Fax: (909)444-0922
E-mail: grid_technology@msn.com

**Ridge Consultants Inc.**
100 Pringle Ave., Ste. 580
Walnut Creek, CA 94596
(925)274-1990
Fax: (510)274-1956
E-mail: info@ridgecon.com
Website: http://www.ridgecon.com

**Bell Springs Publishing**
PO Box 1240
Willits, CA 95490
(707)459-6372
E-mail: bellsprings@sabernet
Website: http://www.bellsprings.com

**Hutchinson Consulting and Appraisal**
23245 Sylvan St., Ste. 103
Woodland Hills, CA 91367
(818)888-8175
Free: 800-977-7548
Fax: (818)888-8220
E-mail: r.f.hutchinson-cpa@worldnet.
att.net

## Colorado

**Sam Boyer & Associates**
4255 S Buckley Rd., No. 136
Aurora, CO 80013
Free: 800-785-0485
Fax: (303)766-8740
E-mail: samboyer@samboyer.com
Website: http://www.samboyer.com/

**Ameriwest Business Consultants Inc.**
PO Box 26266
Colorado Springs, CO 80936
(719)380-7096
Fax: (719)380-7096
E-mail: email@abchelp.com
Website: http://www.abchelp.com

**GVNW Consulting Inc.**
2270 La Montana Way
Colorado Springs, CO 80936
(719)594-5800
Fax: (719)594-5803
Website: http://www.gvnw.com

**M-Squared Inc.**
755 San Gabriel Pl.
Colorado Springs, CO 80906
(719)576-2554
Fax: (719)576-2554

**Thornton Financial FNIC**
1024 Centre Ave., Bldg. E
Fort Collins, CO 80526-1849
(970)221-2089
Fax: (970)484-5206

**TenEyck Associates**
1760 Cherryville Rd.
Greenwood Village, CO 80121-1503
(303)758-6129
Fax: (303)761-8286

**Associated Enterprises Ltd.**
13050 W Ceder Dr., Unit 11
Lakewood, CO 80228

(303)988-6695
Fax: (303)988-6739
E-mail: ael1@classic.msn.com

**The Vincent Company Inc.**
200 Union Blvd., Ste. 210
Lakewood, CO 80228
(303)989-7271
Free: 800-274-0733
Fax: (303)989-7570
E-mail: vincent@vincentco.com
Website: http://www.vincentco.com

**Johnson & West Management Consultants Inc.**
7612 S Logan Dr.
Littleton, CO 80122
(303)730-2810
Fax: (303)730-3219

**Western Capital Holdings Inc.**
10050 E Applwood Dr.
Parker, CO 80138
(303)841-1022
Fax: (303)770-1945

## Connecticut

**Stratman Group Inc.**
40 Tower Ln.
Avon, CT 06001-4222
(860)677-2898
Free: 800-551-0499
Fax: (860)677-8210

**Cowherd Consulting Group Inc.**
106 Stephen Mather Rd.
Darien, CT 06820
(203)655-2150
Fax: (203)655-6427

**Greenwich Associates**
8 Greenwich Office Park
Greenwich, CT 06831-5149
(203)629-1200
Fax: (203)629-1229
E-mail: lisa@greenwich.com
Website: http://www.greenwich.com

**Follow-up News**
185 Pine St., Ste. 818
Manchester, CT 06040
(860)647-7542
Free: 800-708-0696
Fax: (860)646-6544
E-mail: Followupnews@aol.com

**Lovins & Associates Consulting**
309 Edwards St.
New Haven, CT 06511
(203)787-3367

Fax: (203)624-7599
E-mail: Alovinsphd@aol.com
Website: http://www.lovinsgroup.com

**JC Ventures Inc.**
4 Arnold St.
Old Greenwich, CT 06870-1203
(203)698-1990
Free: 800-698-1997
Fax: (203)698-2638

**Charles L. Hornung Associates**
52 Ned's Mountain Rd.
Ridgefield, CT 06877
(203)431-0297

**Manus**
100 Prospect St., S Tower
Stamford, CT 06901
(203)326-3880
Free: 800-445-0942
Fax: (203)326-3890
E-mail: manus1@aol.com
Website: http://www.RightManus.com

**RealBusinessPlans.com**
156 Westport Rd.
Wilton, CT 06897
(914)837-2886
E-mail: ct@realbusinessplans.com
Website: http://www.RealBusinessPlans.com
Tony Tecce

## Delaware

**Focus Marketing**
61-7 Habor Dr.
Claymont, DE 19703
(302)793-3064

**Daedalus Ventures Ltd.**
PO Box 1474
Hockessin, DE 19707
(302)239-6758
Fax: (302)239-9991
E-mail: daedalus@mail.del.net

**The Formula Group**
PO Box 866
Hockessin, DE 19707
(302)456-0952
Fax: (302)456-1354
E-mail: formula@netaxs.com

**Selden Enterprises Inc.**
2502 Silverside Rd., Ste. 1
Wilmington, DE 19810-3740
(302)529-7113
Fax: (302)529-7442
E-mail: selden2@bellatlantic.net
Website: http://www.seldenenterprises.com

## District of Columbia

**Bruce W. McGee and Associates**
7826 Eastern Ave. NW, Ste. 30
Washington, DC 20012
(202)726-7272
Fax: (202)726-2946

**McManis Associates Inc.**
1900 K St. NW, Ste. 700
Washington, DC 20006
(202)466-7680
Fax: (202)872-1898
Website: http://www.mcmanis-mmi.com

**Smith, Dawson & Andrews Inc.**
1000 Connecticut Ave., Ste. 302
Washington, DC 20036
(202)835-0740
Fax: (202)775-8526
E-mail: webmaster@sda-inc.com
Website: http://www.sda-inc.com

## Florida

**BackBone, Inc.**
20404 Hacienda Court
Boca Raton, FL 33498
(561)470-0965
Fax: 516-908-4038
E-mail: BPlans@backboneinc.com
Website: http://www.backboneinc.com
Charles Epstein, President

**Whalen & Associates Inc.**
4255 Northwest 26 Ct.
Boca Raton, FL 33434
(561)241-5950
Fax: (561)241-7414
E-mail: drwhalen@ix.netcom.com

**E.N. Rysso & Associates**
180 Bermuda Petrel Ct.
Daytona Beach, FL 32119
(386)760-3028
E-mail: erysso@aol.com

**Virtual Technocrats LLC**
560 Lavers Circle, #146
Delray Beach, FL 33444
(561)265-3509
E-mail: josh@virtualtechnocrats.com;
info@virtualtechnocrats.com
Website: http://www.virtualtechno
crats.com
Josh Eikov, Managing Director

**Eric Sands Consulting Services**
6193 Rock Island Rd., Ste. 412
Fort Lauderdale, FL 33319
(954)721-4767

Fax: (954)720-2815
E-mail: easands@aol.com
Website: http://www.ericsandsconsultig.com

**Professional Planning Associates, Inc.**
1975 E. Sunrise Blvd. Suite 607
Fort Lauderdale, FL 33304
(954)764-5204
Fax: 954-463-4172
E-mail: Mgoldstein@proplana.com
Website: http://proplana.com
Michael Goldstein, President

**Host Media Corp.**
3948 S 3rd St., Ste. 191
Jacksonville Beach, FL 32250
(904)285-3239
Fax: (904)285-5618
E-mail: msconsulting@compuserve.com
Website: http://www.media
servicesgroup.com

**William V. Hall**
1925 Brickell, Ste. D-701
Miami, FL 33129
(305)856-9622
Fax: (305)856-4113
E-mail: williamvhall@compuserve.com

**F.A. McGee Inc.**
800 Claughton Island Dr., Ste. 401
Miami, FL 33131
(305)377-9123

**Taxplan Inc.**
Mirasol International Ctr.
2699 Collins Ave.
Miami Beach, FL 33140
(305)538-3303

**T.C. Brown & Associates**
8415 Excalibur Cir., Apt. B1
Naples, FL 34108
(941)594-1949
Fax: (941)594-0611
E-mail: tcater@naples.net.com

**RLA International Consulting**
713 Lagoon Dr.
North Palm Beach, FL 33408
(407)626-4258
Fax: (407)626-5772

**Comprehensive Franchising Inc.**
2465 Ridgecrest Ave.
Orange Park, FL 32065
(904)272-6567
Free: 800-321-6567
Fax: (904)272-6750
E-mail: theimp@cris.com
Website: http://www.franchise411.com

**Hunter G. Jackson Jr. - Consulting Environmental Physicist**
PO Box 618272
Orlando, FL 32861-8272
(407)295-4188
E-mail: hunterjackson@juno.com

**F. Newton Parks**
210 El Brillo Way
Palm Beach, FL 33480
(561)833-1727
Fax: (561)833-4541

**Avery Business Development Services**
2506 St. Michel Ct.
Ponte Vedra Beach, FL 32082
(904)285-6033
Fax: (904)285-6033

**Strategic Business Planning Co.**
PO Box 821006
South Florida, FL 33082-1006
(954)704-9100
Fax: (954)438-7333
E-mail: info@bizplan.com
Website: http://www.bizplan.com

**Dufresne Consulting Group Inc.**
10014 N Dale Mabry, Ste. 101
Tampa, FL 33618-4426
(813)264-4775
Fax: (813)264-9300
Website: http://www.dcgconsult.com

**Agrippa Enterprises Inc.**
PO Box 175
Venice, FL 34284-0175
(941)355-7876
E-mail: webservices@agrippa.com
Website: http://www.agrippa.com

**Center for Simplified Strategic Planning Inc.**
PO Box 3324
Vero Beach, FL 32964-3324
(561)231-3636
Fax: (561)231-1099
Website: http://www.cssp.com

## Georgia

**Marketing Spectrum Inc.**
115 Perimeter Pl., Ste. 440
Atlanta, GA 30346
(770)395-7244
Fax: (770)393-4071

**Business Ventures Corp.**
1650 Oakbrook Dr., Ste. 405
Norcross, GA 30093
(770)729-8000
Fax: (770)729-8028

**Informed Decisions Inc.**
100 Falling Cheek
Sautee Nacoochee, GA 30571
(706)878-1905
Fax: (706)878-1802
E-mail: skylake@compuserve.com

**Tom C. Davis & Associates, P.C.**
3189 Perimeter Rd.
Valdosta, GA 31602
(912)247-9801
Fax: (912)244-7704
E-mail: mail@tcdcpa.com
Website: http://www.tcdcpa.com/

## Illinois

**TWD and Associates**
431 S Patton
Arlington Heights, IL 60005
(847)398-6410
Fax: (847)255-5095
E-mail: tdoo@aol.com

**Management Planning Associates Inc.**
2275 Half Day Rd., Ste. 350
Bannockburn, IL 60015-1277
(847)945-2421
Fax: (847)945-2425

**Phil Faris Associates**
86 Old Mill Ct.
Barrington, IL 60010
(847)382-4888
Fax: (847)382-4890
E-mail: pfaris@meginsnet.net

**Seven Continents Technology**
787 Stonebridge
Buffalo Grove, IL 60089
(708)577-9653
Fax: (708)870-1220

**Grubb & Blue Inc.**
2404 Windsor Pl.
Champaign, IL 61820
(217)366-0052
Fax: (217)356-0117

**ACE Accounting Service Inc.**
3128 N Bernard St.
Chicago, IL 60618
(773)463-7854
Fax: (773)463-7854

**AON Consulting Worldwide**
200 E Randolph St., 10th Fl.
Chicago, IL 60601
(312)381-4800
Free: 800-438-6487
Fax: (312)381-0240
Website: http://www.aon.com

**FMS Consultants**
5801 N Sheridan Rd., Ste. 3D
Chicago, IL 60660
(773)561-7362
Fax: (773)561-6274

**Grant Thornton**
800 1 Prudential Plz.
130 E Randolph St.
Chicago, IL 60601
(312)856-0001
Fax: (312)861-1340
E-mail: gtinfo@gt.com
Website: http://www.grantthornton.com

**Kingsbury International Ltd.**
5341 N Glenwood Ave.
Chicago, IL 60640
(773)271-3030
Fax: (773)728-7080
E-mail: jetlag@mcs.com
Website: http://www.kingbiz.com

**MacDougall & Blake Inc.**
1414 N Wells St., Ste. 311
Chicago, IL 60610-1306
(312)587-3330
Fax: (312)587-3699
E-mail: jblake@compuserve.com

**James C. Osburn Ltd.**
6445 N. Western Ave., Ste. 304
Chicago, IL 60645
(773)262-4428
Fax: (773)262-6755
E-mail: osburnltd@aol.com

**Tarifero & Tazewell Inc.**
211 S Clark
Chicago, IL 60690
(312)665-9714
Fax: (312)665-9716

**Human Energy Design Systems**
620 Roosevelt Dr.
Edwardsville, IL 62025
(618)692-0258
Fax: (618)692-0819

**China Business Consultants Group**
931 Dakota Cir.
Naperville, IL 60563
(630)778-7992
Fax: (630)778-7915
E-mail: cbcq@aol.com

**Center for Workforce Effectiveness**
500 Skokie Blvd., Ste. 222
Northbrook, IL 60062
(847)559-8777
Fax: (847)559-8778

E-mail: office@cwelink.com
Website: http://www.cwelink.com

**Smith Associates**
1320 White Mountain Dr.
Northbrook, IL 60062
(847)480-7200
Fax: (847)480-9828

**Francorp Inc.**
20200 Governors Dr.
Olympia Fields, IL 60461
(708)481-2900
Free: 800-372-6244
Fax: (708)481-5885
E-mail: francorp@aol.com
Website: http://www.francorpinc.com

**Camber Business Strategy Consultants**
1010 S Plum Tree Ct
Palatine, IL 60078-0986
(847)202-0101
Fax: (847)705-7510
E-mail: camber@ameritech.net

**Partec Enterprise Group**
5202 Keith Dr.
Richton Park, IL 60471
(708)503-4047
Fax: (708)503-9468

**Rockford Consulting Group Ltd.**
Century Plz., Ste. 206
7210 E State St.
Rockford, IL 61108
(815)229-2900
Free: 800-667-7495
Fax: (815)229-2612
E-mail: rligus@RockfordConsulting.com
Website: http://www.Rockford
Consulting.com

**RSM McGladrey Inc.**
1699 E Woodfield Rd., Ste. 300
Schaumburg, IL 60173-4969
(847)413-6900
Fax: (847)517-7067
Website: http://www.rsmmcgladrey.com

**A.D. Star Consulting**
320 Euclid
Winnetka, IL 60093
(847)446-7827
Fax: (847)446-7827
E-mail: startwo@worldnet.att.net

## Indiana

**Modular Consultants Inc.**
3109 Crabtree Ln.
Elkhart, IN 46514

(219)264-5761
Fax: (219)264-5761
E-mail: sasabo5313@aol.com

**Midwest Marketing Research**
PO Box 1077
Goshen, IN 46527
(219)533-0548
Fax: (219)533-0540
E-mail: 103365.654@compuserve

**Ketchum Consulting Group**
8021 Knue Rd., Ste. 112
Indianapolis, IN 46250
(317)845-5411
Fax: (317)842-9941

**MDI Management
Consulting**
1519 Park Dr.
Munster, IN 46321
(219)838-7909
Fax: (219)838-7909

## Iowa

**McCord Consulting Group Inc.**
4533 Pine View Dr. NE
PO Box 11024
Cedar Rapids, IA 52410
(319)378-0077
Fax: (319)378-1577
E-mail: smmccord@hom.com
Website: http://www.mccordgroup.com

**Management Solutions L.C.**
3815 Lincoln Pl. Dr.
Des Moines, IA 50312
(515)277-6408
Fax: (515)277-3506
E-mail: wasunimers@uswest.net

**Grandview Marketing**
15 Red Bridge Dr.
Sioux City, IA 51104
(712)239-3122
Fax: (712)258-7578
E-mail: eandrews@pionet.net

## Kansas

**Assessments in Action**
513A N Mur-Len
Olathe, KS 66062
(913)764-6270
Free: (888)548-1504
Fax: (913)764-6495
E-mail: lowdene@qni.com
Website: http://www.assessments-
in-action.com

## Maine

**Edgemont Enterprises**
PO Box 8354
Portland, ME 04104
(207)871-8964
Fax: (207)871-8964

**Pan Atlantic Consultants**
5 Milk St.
Portland, ME 04101
(207)871-8622
Fax: (207)772-4842
E-mail: pmurphy@maine.rr.com
Website: http://www.panatlantic.net

## Maryland

**Clemons & Associates Inc.**
5024-R Campbell Blvd.
Baltimore, MD 21236
(410)931-8100
Fax: (410)931-8111
E-mail: info@clemonsmgmt.com
Website: http://www.clemonsmgmt.com

**Imperial Group Ltd.**
305 Washington Ave., Ste. 204
Baltimore, MD 21204-6009
(410)337-8500
Fax: (410)337-7641

**Leadership Institute**
3831 Yolando Rd.
Baltimore, MD 21218
(410)366-9111
Fax: (410)243-8478
E-mail: behconsult@aol.com

**Burdeshaw Associates Ltd.**
4701 Sangamore Rd.
Bethesda, MD 20816-2508
(301)229-5800
Fax: (301)229-5045
E-mail: jstacy@burdeshaw.com
Website: http://www.burdeshaw.com

**Michael E. Cohen**
5225 Pooks Hill Rd., Ste. 1119 S
Bethesda, MD 20814
(301)530-5738
Fax: (301)530-2988
E-mail: mecohen@crosslink.net

**World Development Group Inc.**
5272 River Rd., Ste. 650
Bethesda, MD 20816-1405
(301)652-1818
Fax: (301)652-1250
E-mail: wdg@has.com
Website: http://www.worlddg.com

**Swartz Consulting**
PO Box 4301
Crofton, MD 21114-4301
(301)262-6728

**Software Solutions International Inc.**
9633 Duffer Way
Gaithersburg, MD 20886
(301)330-4136
Fax: (301)330-4136

**Strategies Inc.**
8 Park Center Ct., Ste. 200
Owings Mills, MD 21117
(410)363-6669
Fax: (410)363-1231
E-mail: strategies@strat1.com
Website: http://www.strat1.com

**Hammer Marketing Resources**
179 Inverness Rd.
Severna Park, MD 21146
(410)544-9191
Fax: (305)675-3277
E-mail: info@gohammer.com
Website: http://www.gohammer.com

**Andrew Sussman & Associates**
13731 Kretsinger
Smithsburg, MD 21783
(301)824-2943
Fax: (301)824-2943

## Massachusetts

**Geibel Marketing and Public Relations**
PO Box 611
Belmont, MA 02478-0005
(617)484-8285
Fax: (617)489-3567
E-mail: jgeibel@geibelpr.com
Website: http://www.geibelpr.com

**Bain & Co.**
2 Copley Pl.
Boston, MA 02116
(617)572-2000
Fax: (617)572-2427
E-mail: corporate.inquiries@bain.com
Website: http://www.bain.com

**Mehr & Co.**
62 Kinnaird St.
Cambridge, MA 02139
(617)876-3311
Fax: (617)876-3023
E-mail: mehrco@aol.com

**Monitor Company Inc.**
2 Canal Park
Cambridge, MA 02141

Organizations, Agencies, & Consultants

(617)252-2000
Fax: (617)252-2100
Website: http://www.monitor.com

**Information & Research Associates**
PO Box 3121
Framingham, MA 01701
(508)788-0784

**Walden Consultants Ltd.**
252 Pond St.
Hopkinton, MA 01748
(508)435-4882
Fax: (508)435-3971
Website: http://www.waldencon
sultants.com

**Jeffrey D. Marshall**
102 Mitchell Rd.
Ipswich, MA 01938-1219
(508)356-1113
Fax: (508)356-2989

**Consulting Resources Corp.**
6 Northbrook Park
Lexington, MA 02420
(781)863-1222
Fax: (781)863-1441
E-mail: res@consultingresources.net
Website: http://www.consulting
resources.net

**Planning Technologies Group L.L.C.**
92 Hayden Ave.
Lexington, MA 02421
(781)778-4678
Fax: (781)861-1099
E-mail: ptg@plantech.com
Website: http://www.plantech.com

**Kalba International Inc.**
23 Sandy Pond Rd.
Lincoln, MA 01773
(781)259-9589
Fax: (781)259-1460
E-mail: info@kalbainternational.com
Website: http://www.kalbainter
national.com

**VMB Associates Inc.**
115 Ashland St.
Melrose, MA 02176
(781)665-0623
Fax: (425)732-7142
E-mail: vmbinc@aol.com

**The Company Doctor**
14 Pudding Stone Ln.
Mendon, MA 01756
(508)478-1747
Fax: (508)478-0520

**Data and Strategies Group Inc.**
190 N Main St.
Natick, MA 01760
(508)653-9990
Fax: (508)653-7799
E-mail: dsginc@dsggroup.com
Website: http://www.dsggroup.com

**The Enterprise Group**
73 Parker Rd.
Needham, MA 02494
(617)444-6631
Fax: (617)433-9991
E-mail: lsacco@world.std.com
Website: http://www.enterprise-group.com

**PSMJ Resources Inc.**
10 Midland Ave.
Newton, MA 02458
(617)965-0055
Free: 800-537-7765
Fax: (617)965-5152
E-mail: psmj@tiac.net
Website: http://www.psmj.com

**Scheur Management Group Inc.**
255 Washington St., Ste. 100
Newton, MA 02458-1611
(617)969-7500
Fax: (617)969-7508
E-mail: smgnow@scheur.com
Website: http://www.scheur.com

**I.E.E.E., Boston Section**
240 Bear Hill Rd., 202B
Waltham, MA 02451-1017
(781)890-5294
Fax: (781)890-5290

**Business Planning and Consulting Services**
20 Beechwood Ter.
Wellesley, MA 02482
(617)237-9151
Fax: (617)237-9151

## Michigan

**Walter Frederick Consulting**
1719 South Blvd.
Ann Arbor, MI 48104
(313)662-4336
Fax: (313)769-7505

**Fox Enterprises**
6220 W Freeland Rd.
Freeland, MI 48623
(517)695-9170
Fax: (517)695-9174
E-mail: foxjw@concentric.net
Website: http://www.cris.com/~foxjw

**G.G.W. and Associates**
1213 Hampton
Jackson, MI 49203
(517)782-2255
Fax: (517)782-2255

**Altamar Group Ltd.**
6810 S Cedar, Ste. 2-B
Lansing, MI 48911
(517)694-0910
Free: 800-443-2627
Fax: (517)694-1377

**Sheffieck Consultants Inc.**
23610 Greening Dr.
Novi, MI 48375-3130
(248)347-3545
Fax: (248)347-3530
E-mail: cfsheff@concentric.net

**Rehmann, Robson PC**
5800 Gratiot
Saginaw, MI 48605
(517)799-9580
Fax: (517)799-0227
Website: http://www.rrpc.com

**Francis & Co.**
17200 W 10 Mile Rd., Ste. 207
Southfield, MI 48075
(248)559-7600
Fax: (248)559-5249

**Private Ventures Inc.**
16000 W 9 Mile Rd., Ste. 504
Southfield, MI 48075
(248)569-1977
Free: 800-448-7614
Fax: (248)569-1838
E-mail: pventuresi@aol.com

**JGK Associates**
14464 Kerner Dr.
Sterling Heights, MI 48313
(810)247-9055
Fax: (248)822-4977
E-mail: kozlowski@home.com

## Minnesota

**Health Fitness Corp.**
3500 W 80th St., Ste. 130
Bloomington, MN 55431
(612)831-6830
Fax: (612)831-7264

**Consatech Inc.**
PO Box 1047
Burnsville, MN 55337
(612)953-1088
Fax: (612)435-2966

**Robert F. Knotek**
14960 Ironwood Ct.
Eden Prairie, MN 55346
(612)949-2875

**DRI Consulting**
7715 Stonewood Ct.
Edina, MN 55439
(612)941-9656
Fax: (612)941-2693
E-mail: dric@dric.com
Website: http://www.dric.com

**Markin Consulting**
12072 87th Pl. N
Maple Grove, MN 55369
(612)493-3568
Fax: (612)493-5744
E-mail: markin@markinconsulting.com
Website: http://www.markin
consulting.com

**Minnesota Cooperation Office for
Small Business & Job Creation Inc.**
5001 W 80th St., Ste. 825
Minneapolis, MN 55437
(612)830-1230
Fax: (612)830-1232
E-mail: mncoop@msn.com
Website: http://www.mnco.org

**Enterprise Consulting Inc.**
PO Box 1111
Minnetonka, MN 55345
(612)949-5909
Fax: (612)906-3965

**Amdahl International**
724 1st Ave. SW
Rochester, MN 55902
(507)252-0402
Fax: (507)252-0402
E-mail: amdahl@best-service.com
Website: http://www.wp.com/amdahl_int

**Power Systems Research**
1365 Corporate Center Curve, 2nd Fl.
St. Paul, MN 55121
(612)905-8400
Free: (888)625-8612
Fax: (612)454-0760
E-mail: Barb@Powersys.com
Website: http://www.powersys.com

## Missouri

**Business Planning and Development
Corp.**
4030 Charlotte St.
Kansas City, MO 64110
(816)753-0495

E-mail: humph@bpdev.demon.co.uk
Website: http://www.bpdev.demon.co.uk

**CFO Service**
10336 Donoho
St. Louis, MO 63131
(314)750-2940
E-mail: jskae@cfoservice.com
Website: http://www.cfoservice.com

## Nebraska

**International Management Consulting
Group Inc.**
1309 Harlan Dr., Ste. 205
Bellevue, NE 68005
(402)291-4545
Free: 800-665-IMCG
Fax: (402)291-4343
E-mail: imcg@neonramp.com
Website: http://www.mgtcon
sulting.com

**Heartland Management Consulting
Group**
1904 Barrington Pky.
Papillion, NE 68046
(402)339-2387
Fax: (402)339-1319

## Nevada

**The DuBois Group**
865 Tahoe Blvd., Ste. 108
Incline Village, NV 89451
(775)832-0550
Free: 800-375-2935
Fax: (775)832-0556
E-mail: DuBoisGrp@aol.com

## New Hampshire

**Wolff Consultants**
10 Buck Rd.
Hanover, NH 03755
(603)643-6015

**BPT Consulting Associates Ltd.**
12 Parmenter Rd., Ste. B-6
Londonderry, NH 03053
(603)437-8484
Free: (888)278-0030
Fax: (603)434-5388
E-mail: bptcons@tiac.net
Website: http://www.bptconsulting.com

## New Jersey

**Bedminster Group Inc.**
1170 Rte. 22 E
Bridgewater, NJ 08807

(908)500-4155
Fax: (908)766-0780
E-mail: info@bedminstergroup.com
Website: http://www.bedminster
group.com
Fax: (202)806-1777
Terry Strong, Acting Regional Dir.

**Delta Planning Inc.**
PO Box 425
Denville, NJ 07834
(913)625-1742
Free: 800-672-0762
Fax: (973)625-3531
E-mail: DeltaP@worldnet.att.net
Website: http://deltaplanning.com

**Kumar Associates Inc.**
1004 Cumbermeade Rd.
Fort Lee, NJ 07024
(201)224-9480
Fax: (201)585-2343
E-mail: mail@kumarassociates.com
Website: http://kumarassociates.com

**John Hall & Company Inc.**
PO Box 187
Glen Ridge, NJ 07028
(973)680-4449
Fax: (973)680-4581
E-mail: jhcompany@aol.com

**Market Focus**
PO Box 402
Maplewood, NJ 07040
(973)378-2470
Fax: (973)378-2470
E-mail: mcss66@marketfocus.com

**Vanguard Communications Corp.**
100 American Rd.
Morris Plains, NJ 07950
(973)605-8000
Fax: (973)605-8329
Website: http://www.vanguard.net/

**ConMar International Ltd.**
1901 US Hwy. 130
North Brunswick, NJ 08902
(732)940-8347
Fax: (732)274-1199

**KLW New Products**
156 Cedar Dr.
Old Tappan, NJ 07675
(201)358-1300
Fax: (201)664-2594
E-mail: lrlarsen@usa.net
Website: http://www.klwnew
products.com

## PA Consulting Group
315A Enterprise Dr.
Plainsboro, NJ 08536
(609)936-8300
Fax: (609)936-8811
E-mail: info@paconsulting.com
Website: http://www.pa-consulting.com

## Aurora Marketing Management Inc.
66 Witherspoon St., Ste. 600
Princeton, NJ 08542
(908)904-1125
Fax: (908)359-1108
E-mail: aurora2@voicenet.com
Website: http://www.auroramarketing.net

## Smart Business Supersite
88 Orchard Rd., CN-5219
Princeton, NJ 08543
(908)321-1924
Fax: (908)321-5156
E-mail: irv@smartbiz.com
Website: http://www.smartbiz.com

## Tracelin Associates
1171 Main St., Ste. 6K
Rahway, NJ 07065
(732)381-3288

## Schkeeper Inc.
130-6 Bodman Pl.
Red Bank, NJ 07701
(732)219-1965
Fax: (732)530-3703

## Henry Branch Associates
2502 Harmon Cove Twr.
Secaucus, NJ 07094
(201)866-2008
Fax: (201)601-0101
E-mail: hbranch161@home.com

## Robert Gibbons & Company Inc.
46 Knoll Rd.
Tenafly, NJ 07670-1050
(201)871-3933
Fax: (201)871-2173
E-mail: crisisbob@aol.com

## PMC Management Consultants Inc.
6 Thistle Ln.
Three Bridges, NJ 08887-0332
(908)788-1014
Free: 800-PMC-0250
Fax: (908)806-7287
E-mail: int@pmc-management.com
Website: http://www.pmc-management.com

## R.W. Bankart & Associates
20 Valley Ave., Ste. D-2

Westwood, NJ 07675-3607
(201)664-7672

# New Mexico

## Vondle & Associates Inc.
4926 Calle de Tierra, NE
Albuquerque, NM 87111
(505)292-8961
Fax: (505)296-2790
E-mail: vondle@aol.com

## InfoNewMexico
2207 Black Hills Rd., NE
Rio Rancho, NM 87124
(505)891-2462
Fax: (505)896-8971

# New York

## Powers Research and Training Institute
PO Box 78
Bayville, NY 11709
(516)628-2250
Fax: (516)628-2252
E-mail: powercocch@compuserve.com
Website: http://www.nancypowers.com

## Consortium House
296 Wittenberg Rd.
Bearsville, NY 12409
(845)679-8867
Fax: (845)679-9248
E-mail: eugenegs@aol.com
Website: http://www.chpub.com

## Progressive Finance Corp.
3549 Tiemann Ave.
Bronx, NY 10469
(718)405-9029
Free: 800-225-8381
Fax: (718)405-1170

## Wave Hill Associates Inc.
2621 Palisade Ave., Ste. 15-C
Bronx, NY 10463
(718)549-7368
Fax: (718)601-9670
E-mail: pepper@compuserve.com

## Management Insight
96 Arlington Rd.
Buffalo, NY 14221
(716)631-3319
Fax: (716)631-0203
E-mail: michalski@foodserviceinsight.com
Website: http://www.foodserviceinsight.com

## Samani International Enterprises, Marions Panyaught Consultancy
2028 Parsons
Flushing, NY 11357-3436
(917)287-8087
Fax: 800-873-8939
E-mail: vjp2@biostrategist.com
Website: http://www.biostrategist.com

## Marketing Resources Group
71-58 Austin St.
Forest Hills, NY 11375
(718)261-8882

## Mangabay Business Plans & Development Subsidiary of Innis Asset Allocation
125-10 Queens Blvd., Ste. 2202
Kew Gardens, NY 11415
(905)527-1947
Fax: 509-472-1935
E-mail: mangabay@mangabay.com
Website: http://www.mangabay.com
Lee Toh, Managing Partner

## ComputerEase Co.
1301 Monmouth Ave.
Lakewood, NY 08701
(212)406-9464
Fax: (914)277-5317
E-mail: crawfordc@juno.com

## Boice Dunham Group
30 W 13th St.
New York, NY 10011
(212)924-2200
Fax: (212)924-1108

## Elizabeth Capen
27 E 95th St.
New York, NY 10128
(212)427-7654
Fax: (212)876-3190

## Haver Analytics
60 E 42nd St., Ste. 2424
New York, NY 10017
(212)986-9300
Fax: (212)986-5857
E-mail: data@haver.com
Website: http://www.haver.com

## The Jordan, Edmiston Group Inc.
150 E 52nd Ave., 18th Fl.
New York, NY 10022
(212)754-0710
Fax: (212)754-0337

## KPMG International
345 Park Ave.
New York, NY 10154-0102
(212)758-9700

Fax: (212)758-9819
Website: http://www.kpmg.com

**Mahoney Cohen Consulting Corp.**
111 W 40th St., 12th Fl.
New York, NY 10018
(212)490-8000
Fax: (212)790-5913

**Management Practice Inc.**
342 Madison Ave.
New York, NY 10173-1230
(212)867-7948
Fax: (212)972-5188
Website: http://www.mpiweb.com

**Moseley Associates Inc.**
342 Madison Ave., Ste. 1414
New York, NY 10016
(212)213-6673
Fax: (212)687-1520

**Practice Development Counsel**
60 Sutton Pl. S
New York, NY 10022
(212)593-1549
Fax: (212)980-7940
E-mail: pwhaserot@pdcounsel.com
Website: http://www.pdcounsel.com

**Unique Value International Inc.**
575 Madison Ave., 10th Fl.
New York, NY 10022-1304
(212)605-0590
Fax: (212)605-0589

**The Van Tulleken Co.**
126 E 56th St.
New York, NY 10022
(212)355-1390
Fax: (212)755-3061
E-mail: newyork@vantulleken.com

**Vencon Management Inc.**
301 W 53rd St.
New York, NY 10019
(212)581-8787
Fax: (212)397-4126
Website: http://www.venconinc.com

**Werner International Inc.**
55 E 52nd, 29th Fl.
New York, NY 10055
(212)909-1260
Fax: (212)909-1273
E-mail: richard.downing@rgh.com
Website: http://www.wernertex.com

**Zimmerman Business Consulting Inc.**
44 E 92nd St., Ste. 5-B
New York, NY 10128

(212)860-3107
Fax: (212)860-7730
E-mail: ljzzbci@aol.com
Website: http://www.zbcinc.com

**Overton Financial**
7 Allen Rd.
Peekskill, NY 10566
(914)737-4649
Fax: (914)737-4696

**Stromberg Consulting**
2500 Westchester Ave.
Purchase, NY 10577
(914)251-1515
Fax: (914)251-1562
E-mail: strategy@stromberg_consulting.com
Website: http://www.stromberg_consulting.com

**Innovation Management Consulting Inc.**
209 Dewitt Rd.
Syracuse, NY 13214-2006
(315)425-5144
Fax: (315)445-8989
E-mail: missonneb@axess.net

**M. Clifford Agress**
891 Fulton St.
Valley Stream, NY 11580
(516)825-8955
Fax: (516)825-8955

**Destiny Kinal Marketing Consultancy**
105 Chemung St.
Waverly, NY 14892
(607)565-8317
Fax: (607)565-4083

**Valutis Consulting Inc.**
5350 Main St., Ste. 7
Williamsville, NY 14221-5338
(716)634-2553
Fax: (716)634-2554
E-mail: valutis@localnet.com
Website: http://www.valutisconsulting.com

## North Carolina

**Best Practices L.L.C.**
6320 Quadrangle Dr., Ste. 200
Chapel Hill, NC 27514
(919)403-0251
Fax: (919)403-0144
E-mail: best@best:in/class
Website: http://www.best-in-class.com

**Norelli & Co.**
Bank of America Corporate Ctr.
100 N Tyron St., Ste. 5160

Charlotte, NC 28202-4000
(704)376-5484
Fax: (704)376-5485
E-mail: consult@norelli.com
Website: http://www.norelli.com

## North Dakota

**Center for Innovation**
4300 Dartmouth Dr.
PO Box 8372
Grand Forks, ND 58202
(701)777-3132
Fax: (701)777-2339
E-mail: bruce@innovators.net
Website: http://www.innovators.net

## Ohio

**Transportation Technology Services**
208 Harmon Rd.
Aurora, OH 44202
(330)562-3596

**Empro Systems Inc.**
4777 Red Bank Expy., Ste. 1
Cincinnati, OH 45227-1542
(513)271-2042
Fax: (513)271-2042

**Alliance Management International Ltd.**
1440 Windrow Ln.
Cleveland, OH 44147-3200
(440)838-1922
Fax: (440)838-0979
E-mail: bgruss@amiltd.com
Website: http://www.amiltd.com

**Bozell Kamstra Public Relations**
1301 E 9th St., Ste. 3400
Cleveland, OH 44114
(216)623-1511
Fax: (216)623-1501
E-mail: jfeniger@cleveland.bozellkamstra.com
Website: http://www.bozellkamstra.com

**Cory Dillon Associates**
111 Schreyer Pl. E
Columbus, OH 43214
(614)262-8211
Fax: (614)262-3806

**Holcomb Gallagher Adams**
300 Marconi, Ste. 303
Columbus, OH 43215
(614)221-3343
Fax: (614)221-3367
E-mail: riadams@acme.freenet.oh.us

**Young & Associates**
PO Box 711
Kent, OH 44240
(330)678-0524
Free: 800-525-9775
Fax: (330)678-6219
E-mail: online@younginc.com
Website: http://www.younginc.com

**Robert A. Westman & Associates**
8981 Inversary Dr. SE
Warren, OH 44484-2551
(330)856-4149
Fax: (330)856-2564

## Oklahoma

**Innovative Partners L.L.C.**
4900 Richmond Sq., Ste. 100
Oklahoma City, OK 73118
(405)840-0033
Fax: (405)843-8359
E-mail: ipartners@juno.com

## Oregon

**INTERCON - The International Converting Institute**
5200 Badger Rd.
Crooked River Ranch, OR 97760
(541)548-1447
Fax: (541)548-1618
E-mail: johnbowler@
crookedriverranch.com

**Talbott ARM**
HC 60, Box 5620
Lakeview, OR 97630
(541)635-8587
Fax: (503)947-3482

**Management Technology Associates Ltd.**
2768 SW Sherwood Dr, Ste. 105
Portland, OR 97201-2251
(503)224-5220
Fax: (503)224-5334
E-mail: lcuster@mta-ltd.com
Website: http://www.mgmt-tech.com

## Pennsylvania

**Healthscope Inc.**
400 Lancaster Ave.
Devon, PA 19333
(610)687-6199
Fax: (610)687-6376
E-mail: health@voicenet.com
Website: http://www.healthscope.net/

**Elayne Howard & Associates Inc.**
3501 Masons Mill Rd., Ste. 501

Huntingdon Valley, PA 19006-3509
(215)657-9550

**GRA Inc.**
115 West Ave., Ste. 201
Jenkintown, PA 19046
(215)884-7500
Fax: (215)884-1385
E-mail: gramail@gra-inc.com
Website: http://www.gra-inc.com

**Mifflin County Industrial Development Corp.**
Mifflin County Industrial Plz.
6395 SR 103 N
Bldg. 50
Lewistown, PA 17044
(717)242-0393
Fax: (717)242-1842
E-mail: mcide@acsworld.net

**Autech Products**
1289 Revere Rd.
Morrisville, PA 19067
(215)493-3759
Fax: (215)493-9791
E-mail: autech4@yahoo.com

**Advantage Associates**
434 Avon Dr.
Pittsburgh, PA 15228
(412)343-1558
Fax: (412)362-1684
E-mail: ecocba1@aol.com

**Regis J. Sheehan & Associates**
Pittsburgh, PA 15220
(412)279-1207

**James W. Davidson Company Inc.**
23 Forest View Rd.
Wallingford, PA 19086
(610)566-1462

## Puerto Rico

**Diego Chevere & Co.**
Metro Parque 7, Ste. 204
Metro Office
Caparra Heights, PR 00920
(787)774-9595
Fax: (787)774-9566
E-mail: dcco@coqui.net

**Manuel L. Porrata and Associates**
898 Munoz Rivera Ave., Ste. 201
San Juan, PR 00927
(787)765-2140
Fax: (787)754-3285
E-mail: m_porrata@manuelporrata.com
Website: http://manualporrata.com

## South Carolina

**Aquafood Business Associates**
PO Box 13267
Charleston, SC 29422
(843)795-9506
Fax: (843)795-9477
E-mail: rraba@aol.com

**Profit Associates Inc.**
PO Box 38026
Charleston, SC 29414
(803)763-5718
Fax: (803)763-5719
E-mail: bobrog@awod.com
Website: http://www.awod.com/gallery/
business/proasc

**Strategic Innovations International**
12 Executive Ct.
Lake Wylie, SC 29710
(803)831-1225
Fax: (803)831-1177
E-mail: stratinnov@aol.com
Website: http://www.
strategicinnovations.com

**Minus Stage**
Box 4436
Rock Hill, SC 29731
(803)328-0705
Fax: (803)329-9948

## Tennessee

**Daniel Petchers & Associates**
8820 Fernwood CV
Germantown, TN 38138
(901)755-9896

**Business Choices**
1114 Forest Harbor, Ste. 300
Hendersonville, TN 37075-9646
(615)822-8692
Free: 800-737-8382
Fax: (615)822-8692
E-mail: bz-ch@juno.com

**RCFA Healthcare Management Services L.L.C.**
9648 Kingston Pke., Ste. 8
Knoxville, TN 37922
(865)531-0176
Free: 800-635-4040
Fax: (865)531-0722
E-mail: info@rcfa.com
Website: http://www.rcfa.com

**Growth Consultants of America**
3917 Trimble Rd.
Nashville, TN 37215

(615)383-0550
Fax: (615)269-8940
E-mail: 70244.451@compuserve.com

## Texas

**Integrated Cost Management Systems Inc.**
2261 Brookhollow Plz. Dr., Ste. 104
Arlington, TX 76006
(817)633-2873
Fax: (817)633-3781
E-mail: abm@icms.net
Website: http://www.icms.net

**Lori Williams**
1000 Leslie Ct.
Arlington, TX 76012
(817)459-3934
Fax: (817)459-3934

**Business Resource Software Inc.**
2013 Wells Branch Pky., Ste. 305
Austin, TX 78728
Free: 800-423-1228
Fax: (512)251-4401
E-mail: info@brs-inc.com
Website: http://www.brs-inc.com

**Erisa Adminstrative Services Inc.**
12325 Hymeadow Dr., Bldg. 4
Austin, TX 78750-1847
(512)250-9020
Fax: (512)250-9487
Website: http://www.cserisa.com

**R. Miller Hicks & Co.**
1011 W 11th St.
Austin, TX 78703
(512)477-7000
Fax: (512)477-9697
E-mail: millerhicks@rmhicks.com
Website: http://www.rmhicks.com

**Pragmatic Tactics Inc.**
3303 Westchester Ave.
College Station, TX 77845
(409)696-5294
Free: 800-570-5294
Fax: (409)696-4994
E-mail: ptactics@aol.com
Website: http://www.ptatics.com

**Perot Systems**
12404 Park Central Dr.
Dallas, TX 75251
(972)340-5000
Free: 800-688-4333
Fax: (972)455-4100
E-mail: corp.comm@ps.net
Website: http://www.perotsystems.com

**ReGENERATION Partners**
3838 Oak Lawn Ave.
Dallas, TX 75219
(214)559-3999
Free: 800-406-1112
E-mail: info@regeneration-partner.com
Website: http://www.regeneration-partners.com

**High Technology Associates - Division of Global Technologies Inc.**
1775 St. James Pl., Ste. 105
Houston, TX 77056
(713)963-9300
Fax: (713)963-8341
E-mail: hta@infohwy.com

**MasterCOM**
103 Thunder Rd.
Kerrville, TX 78028
(830)895-7990
Fax: (830)443-3428
E-mail: jmstubblefield@master training.com
Website: http://www.mastertraining.com

**PROTEC**
4607 Linden Pl.
Pearland, TX 77584
(281)997-9872
Fax: (281)997-9895
E-mail: p.oman@ix.netcom.com

**Alpha Quadrant Inc.**
10618 Auldine
San Antonio, TX 78230
(210)344-3330
Fax: (210)344-8151
E-mail: mbussone@sbcglobal.net
Website:http://www.a-quadrant.com
Michele Bussone

**Bastian Public Relations**
614 San Dizier
San Antonio, TX 78232
(210)404-1839
E-mail: lisa@bastianpr.com
Website: http://www.bastianpr.com
Lisa Bastian CBC

**Business Strategy Development Consultants**
PO Box 690365
San Antonio, TX 78269
(210)696-8000
Free: 800-927-BSDC
Fax: (210)696-8000

**Tom Welch, CPC**
6900 San Pedro Ave., Ste. 147
San Antonio, TX 78216-6207

(210)737-7022
Fax: (210)737-7022
E-mail: bplan@iamerica.net
Website: http://www.moneywords.com

## Utah

**Business Management Resource**
PO Box 521125
Salt Lake City, UT 84152-1125
(801)272-4668
Fax: (801)277-3290
E-mail: pingfong@worldnet.att.net

## Virginia

**Tindell Associates**
209 Oxford Ave.
Alexandria, VA 22301
(703)683-0109
Fax: 703-783-0219
E-mail: scott@tindell.net
Website: http://www.tindell.net
Scott Lockett, President

**Elliott B. Jaffa**
2530-B S Walter Reed Dr.
Arlington, VA 22206
(703)931-0040
E-mail: thetrainingdoctor@excite.com
Website: http://www.tregistry.com/jaffa.htm

**Koach Enterprises - USA**
5529 N 18th St.
Arlington, VA 22205
(703)241-8361
Fax: (703)241-8623

**Federal Market Development**
5650 Chapel Run Ct.
Centreville, VA 20120-3601
(703)502-8930
Free: 800-821-5003
Fax: (703)502-8929

**Huff, Stuart & Carlton**
2107 Graves Mills Rd., Ste. C
Forest, VA 24551
(804)316-9356
Free: (888)316-9356
Fax: (804)316-9357
Website: http://www.wealthmgt.net

**AMX International Inc.**
1420 Spring Hill Rd. , Ste. 600
McLean, VA 22102-3006
(703)690-4100
Fax: (703)643-1279
E-mail: amxmail@amxi.com
Website: http://www.amxi.com

**Charles Scott Pugh (Investor)**
4101 Pittaway Dr.
Richmond, VA 23235-1022
(804)560-0979
Fax: (804)560-4670

**John C. Randall and Associates Inc.**
PO Box 15127
Richmond, VA 23227
(804)746-4450
Fax: (804)730-8933
E-mail: randalljcx@aol.com
Website: http://www.johncrandall.com

**McLeod & Co.**
410 1st St.
Roanoke, VA 24011
(540)342-6911
Fax: (540)344-6367
Website: http://www.mcleodco.com/

**Salzinger & Company Inc.**
8000 Towers Crescent Dr., Ste. 1350
Vienna, VA 22182
(703)442-5200
Fax: (703)442-5205
E-mail: info@salzinger.com
Website: http://www.salzinger.com

**The Small Business Counselor**
12423 Hedges Run Dr., Ste. 153
Woodbridge, VA 22192
(703)490-6755
Fax: (703)490-1356

## Washington

**Burlington Consultants**
10900 NE 8th St., Ste. 900
Bellevue, WA 98004
(425)688-3060
Fax: (425)454-4383
E-mail: partners@burlington
consultants.com
Website: http://www.burlington
consultants.com

**Perry L. Smith Consulting**
800 Bellevue Way NE, Ste. 400
Bellevue, WA 98004-4208
(425)462-2072
Fax: (425)462-5638

**St. Charles Consulting Group**
1420 NW Gilman Blvd.
Issaquah, WA 98027
(425)557-8708
Fax: (425)557-8731
E-mail: info@stcharlesconsulting.com
Website: http://www.stcharlescon
sulting.com

**Independent Automotive Training Services**
PO Box 334
Kirkland, WA 98083
(425)822-5715
E-mail: ltunney@autosvccon.com
Website: http://www.autosvccon.com

**Kahle Associate Inc.**
6203 204th Dr. NE
Redmond, WA 98053
(425)836-8763
Fax: (425)868-3770
E-mail: randykahle@kahleassociates.com
Website: http://www.kahleassociates.com

**Dan Collin**
3419 Wallingord Ave N, No. 2
Seattle, WA 98103
(206)634-9469
E-mail: dc@dancollin.com
Website: http://members.home.net/
dcollin/

**ECG Management Consultants Inc.**
1111 3rd Ave., Ste. 2700
Seattle, WA 98101-3201
(206)689-2200
Fax: (206)689-2209
E-mail: ecg@ecgmc.com
Website: http://www.ecgmc.com

**Northwest Trade Adjustment Assistance Center**
900 4th Ave., Ste. 2430
Seattle, WA 98164-1001
(206)622-2730
Free: 800-667-8087
Fax: (206)622-1105
E-mail: matchingfunds@nwtaac.org
Website: http://www.taacenters.org

**Business Planning Consultants**
S 3510 Ridgeview Dr.
Spokane, WA 99206
(509)928-0332
Fax: (509)921-0842
E-mail: bpci@nextdim.com

## West Virginia

**Stanley & Associates Inc./
BusinessandMarketingPlans.com**
1687 Robert C. Byrd Dr.
Beckley, WV 25801
(304)252-0324
Free: 888-752-6720
Fax: (304)252-0470
E-mail: cclay@charterinternet.com

Website: http://www.Businessand
MarketingPlans.com
Christopher Clay

## Wisconsin

**White & Associates Inc.**
5349 Somerset Ln. S
Greenfield, WI 53221
(414)281-7373
Fax: (414)281-7006
E-mail: wnaconsult@aol.com

## Small business administration regional offices

*This section contains a listing of Small Business Administration offices arranged numerically by region. Service areas are provided. Contact the appropriate office for a referral to the nearest field office, or visit the Small Business Administration online at www.sba.gov.*

## Region 1

**U.S. Small Business Administration**
Region I Office
10 Causeway St., Ste. 812
Boston, MA 02222-1093
Phone: (617)565-8415
Fax: (617)565-8420
Serves Connecticut, Maine, Massachusetts, New Hampshire, Rhode Island, and Vermont.

## Region 2

**U.S. Small Business Administration**
Region II Office
26 Federal Plaza, Ste. 3108
New York, NY 10278
Phone: (212)264-1450
Fax: (212)264-0038
Serves New Jersey, New York, Puerto Rico, and the Virgin Islands.

## Region 3

**U.S. Small Business Administration**
Region III Office
Robert N C Nix Sr. Federal Building
900 Market St., 5th Fl.
Philadelphia, PA 19107
(215)580-2807
Serves Delaware, the District of Columbia, Maryland, Pennsylvania, Virginia, and West Virginia.

### Region 4

**U.S. Small Business Administration**
Region IV Office
233 Peachtree St. NE
Harris Tower 1800
Atlanta, GA 30303
Phone: (404)331-4999
Fax: (404)331-2354
Serves Alabama, Florida, Georgia, Kentucky, Mississippi, North Carolina, South Carolina, and Tennessee.

### Region 5

**U.S. Small Business Administration**
Region V Office
500 W. Madison St.
Citicorp Center, Ste. 1240
Chicago, IL 60661-2511
Phone: (312)353-0357
Fax: (312)353-3426
Serves Illinois, Indiana, Michigan, Minnesota, Ohio, and Wisconsin.

### Region 6

**U.S. Small Business Administration**
Region VI Office
4300 Amon Carter Blvd., Ste. 108
Fort Worth, TX 76155
Phone: (817)684-5581
Fax: (817)684-5588
Serves Arkansas, Louisiana, New Mexico, Oklahoma, and Texas.

### Region 7

**U.S. Small Business Administration**
Region VII Office
323 W. 8th St., Ste. 307
Kansas City, MO 64105-1500
Phone: (816)374-6380
Fax: (816)374-6339
Serves Iowa, Kansas, Missouri, and Nebraska.

### Region 8

**U.S. Small Business Administration**
Region VIII Office
721 19th St., Ste. 400
Denver, CO 80202
Phone: (303)844-0500
Fax: (303)844-0506
Serves Colorado, Montana, North Dakota, South Dakota, Utah, and Wyoming.

### Region 9

**U.S. Small Business Administration**
Region IX Office
330 N Brand Blvd., Ste. 1270
Glendale, CA 91203-2304
Phone: (818)552-3434
Fax: (818)552-3440
Serves American Samoa, Arizona, California, Guam, Hawaii, Nevada, and the Trust Territory of the Pacific Islands.

### Region 10

**U.S. Small Business Administration**
Region X Office
2401 Fourth Ave., Ste. 400
Seattle, WA 98121
Phone: (206)553-5676
Fax: (206)553-4155
Serves Alaska, Idaho, Oregon, and Washington.

## Small business development centers

*This section contains a listing of all Small Business Development Centers, organized alphabetically by state/U.S. territory, then by city, then by agency name.*

### Alabama

**Alabama SBDC**
**UNIVERSITY OF ALABAMA**
2800 Milan Court Suite 124
Birmingham, AL 35211-6908
Phone: 205-943-6750
Fax: 205-943-6752
E-Mail: wcampbell@provost.uab.edu
Website: http://www.asbdc.org
Mr. William Campbell Jr, State Director

### Alaska

**Alaska SBDC**
**UNIVERSITY OF ALASKA - ANCHORAGE**
430 West Seventh Avenue, Suite 110
Anchorage, AK 99501
Phone: 907-274 -7232
Fax: 907-274-9524
E-Mail: anerw@uaa.alaska.edu
Website: http://www.aksbdc.org
Ms. Jean R. Wall, State Director

### American Samoa

**American Samoa SBDC**
**AMERICAN SAMOA COMMUNITY COLLEGE**
P.O. Box 2609
Pago Pago, American Samoa 96799
Phone: 011-684-699-4830
Fax: 011-684-699-6132
E-Mail: htalex@att.net
Mr. Herbert Thweatt, Director

### Arizona

**Arizona SBDC**
**MARICOPA COUNTY COMMUNITY COLLEGE**
2411 West 14th Street, Suite 132
Tempe, AZ 85281
Phone: 480-731-8720
Fax: 480-731-8729
E-Mail: mike.york@domail.maricopa.edu
Website: http://www.dist.maricopa.edu.sbdc
Mr. Michael York, State Director

### Arkansas

**Arkansas SBDC**
**UNIVERSITY OF ARKANSAS**
2801 South University Avenue
Little Rock, AR 72204
Phone: 501-324-9043
Fax: 501-324-9049
E-Mail: jmroderick@ualr.edu
Website: http://asbdc.ualr.edu
Ms. Janet M. Roderick, State Director

### California

**California - San Francisco SBDC**
**Northern California SBDC Lead Center**
**HUMBOLDT STATE UNIVERSITY**
Office of Economic Development
1 Harpst Street 2006A, Siemens Hall
Arcata, CA, 95521
Phone: 707-826-3922
Fax: 707-826-3206
E-Mail: gainer@humboldt.edu
Ms. Margaret A. Gainer, Regional Director

**California - Sacramento SBDC**
**CALIFORNIA STATE UNIVERSITY - CHICO**
Chico, CA 95929-0765
Phone: 530-898-4598
Fax: 530-898-4734

E-Mail: dripke@csuchico.edu
Website: http://gsbdc.csuchico.edu
Mr. Dan Ripke, Interim Regional Director

**California - San Diego SBDC**
**SOUTHWESTERN COMMUNITY**
**COLLEGE DISTRICT**
900 Otey Lakes Road
Chula Vista, CA 91910
Phone: 619-482-6388
Fax: 619-482-6402
E-Mail: dtrujillo@swc.cc.ca.us
Website: http://www.sbditc.org
Ms. Debbie P. Trujillo, Regional Director

**California - Fresno SBDC**
**UC Merced Lead Center**
**UNIVERSITY OF CALIFORNIA -**
**MERCED**
550 East Shaw, Suite 105A
Fresno, CA 93710
Phone: 559-241-6590
Fax: 559-241-7422
E-Mail: crosander@ucmerced.edu
Website: http://sbdc.ucmerced.edu
Mr. Chris Rosander, State Director

**California - Santa Ana SBDC**
**Tri-County Lead SBDC**
**CALIFORNIA STATE UNIVERSITY -**
**FULLERTON**
800 North State College Boulevard, LH640
Fullerton, CA 92834
Phone: 714-278-2719
Fax: 714-278-7858
E-Mail: vpham@fullerton.edu
Website: http://www.leadsbdc.org
Ms. Vi Pham, Lead Center Director

**California - Los Angeles Region SBDC**
**LONG BEACH COMMUNITY**
**COLLEGE DISTRICT**
3950 Paramount Boulevard, Ste 101
Lakewood, CA 90712
Phone: 562-938-5004
Fax: 562-938-5030
E-Mail: ssloan@lbcc.edu
Ms. Sheneui Sloan, Interim Lead Center
Director

## Colorado

**Colorado SBDC**
**OFFICE OF ECONOMIC**
**DEVELOPMENT**
1625 Broadway, Suite 170
Denver, CO 80202
Phone: 303-892-3864
Fax: 303-892-3848
E-Mail: Kelly.Manning@state.co.us

Website: http://www.state.co.us/oed/sbdc
Ms. Kelly Manning, State Director

## Connecticut

**Connecticut SBDC**
**UNIVERSITY OF CONNECTICUT**
1376 Storrs Road, Unit 4094
Storrs, CT 06269-1094
Phone: 860-870-6370
Fax: 860-870-6374
E-Mail: richard.cheney@uconn.edu
Website: http://www.sbdc.uconn.edu
Mr. Richard Cheney, Interim State Director

## Delaware

**Delaware SBDC**
**DELAWARE TECHNOLOGY PARK**
1 Innovation Way, Suite 301
Newark, DE 19711
Phone: 302-831-2747
Fax: 302-831-1423
E-Mail: Clinton.tymes@mvs.udel.edu
Website: http://www.delawaresbdc.org
Mr. Clinton Tymes, State Director

## District of Columbia

**District of Columbia SBDC**
**HOWARD UNIVERSITY**
2600 6th Street, NW Room 128
Washington, DC 20059
Phone: 202-806-1550
Fax: 202-806-1777
E-Mail: hturner@howard.edu
Website: http://www.dcsbdc.com/
Mr. Henry Turner, Executive Director

## Florida

**Florida SBDC**
**UNIVERSITY OF WEST FLORIDA**
401 East Chase Street, Suite 100
Pensacola, FL 32502
Phone: 850-473-7800
Fax: 850-473-7813
E-Mail: jcartwri@uwf.edu
Website: http://www.floridasbdc.com
Mr. Jerry Cartwright, State Director

## Georgia

**Georgia SBDC**
**UNIVERSITY OF GEORGIA**
1180 East Broad Street
Athens, GA 30602
Phone: 706-542-6762
Fax: 706-542-6776
E-mail: aadams@sbdc.uga.edu

Website: http://www.sbdc.uga.edu
Mr. Allan Adams, Interim State Director

## Guam

**Guam Small Business Development**
**Center**
**UNIVERSITY OF GUAM**
Pacific Islands SBDC
P.O. Box 5014 - U.O.G. Station
Mangilao, GU 96923
Phone: 671-735-2590
Fax: 671-734-2002
E-mail: casey@pacificsbdc.com
Website: http://www.uog.edu/sbdc
Mr. Casey Jeszenka, Director

## Hawaii

**Hawaii SBDC**
**UNIVERSITY OF HAWAII - HILO**
308 Kamehameha Avenue, Suite 201
Hilo, HI 96720
Phone: 808-974-7515
Fax: 808-974-7683
E-Mail: darrylm@interpac.net
Website: http://www.hawaii-sbdc.org
Mr. Darryl Mleynek, State Director

## Idaho

**Idaho SBDC**
**BOISE STATE UNIVERSITY**
1910 University Drive
Boise, ID 83725
Phone: 208-426-3799
Fax: 208-426-3877
E-mail: jhogge@boisestate.edu
Website: http://www.idahosbdc.org
Mr. Jim Hogge, State Director

## Illinois

**Illinois SBDC**
**DEPARTMENT OF COMMERCE**
**AND ECONOMIC OPPORTUNITY**
620 E. Adams, S-4
Springfield, IL 62701
Phone: 217-524-5700
Fax: 217-524-0171
E-mail: mpatrilli@ildceo.net
Website: http://www.ilsbdc.biz
Mr. Mark Petrilli, State Director

## Indiana

**Indiana SBDC**
**INDIANA ECONOMIC**
**DEVELOPMENT CORPORATION**
One North Capitol, Suite 900
Indianapolis, IN 46204

Phone: 317-234-8872
Fax: 317-232-8874
E-mail: dtrocha@isbdc.org
Website: http://www.isbdc.org
Ms. Debbie Bishop Trocha, State
Director

## Iowa

### Iowa SBDC
**IOWA STATE UNIVERSITY**
340 Gerdin Business Bldg.
Ames, IA 50011-1350
Phone: 515-294-2037
Fax: 515-294-6522
E-mail: jonryan@iastate.edu
Website: http://www.iabusnet.org
Mr. Jon Ryan, State Director

## Kansas

### Kansas SBDC
**FORT HAYS STATE UNIVERSITY**
214 SW Sixth Street, Suite 301
Topeka, KS 66603
Phone: 785-296-6514
Fax: 785-291-3261
E-mail: ksbdc.wkearns@fhsu.edu
Website: http://www.fhsu.edu/ksbdc
Mr. Wally Kearns, State Director

## Kentucky

### Kentucky SBDC
**UNIVERSITY OF KENTUCKY**
225 Gatton College of Business
Economics Building
Lexington, KY 40506-0034
Phone: 859-257-7668
Fax: 859-323-1907
E-mail: lrnaug0@pop.uky.edu
Website: http://www.ksbdc.org
Ms. Becky Naugle, State Director

## Louisiana

### Louisiana SBDC
**UNIVERSITY OF LOUISIANA -
MONROE**
**College of Business Administration**
700 University Avenue
Monroe, LA 71209
Phone: 318-342-5506
Fax: 318-342-5510
E-mail: wilkerson@ulm.edu
Website: http://www.lsbdc.org
Ms. Mary Lynn Wilkerson, State
Director

## Maine

### Maine SBDC
**UNIVERSITY OF SOUTHERN
MAINE**
96 Falmouth Street P.O. Box 9300
Portland, ME 04103
Phone: 207-780-4420
Fax: 207-780-4810
E-mail: jrmassaua@maine.edu
Website: http://www.mainesbdc.org
Mr. John Massaua, State Director

## Maryland

### Maryland SBDC
**UNIVERSITY OF MARYLAND**
7100 Baltimore Avenue, Suite 401
College Park, MD 20742
Phone: 301-403-8300
Fax: 301-403-8303
E-mail: rsprow@mdsbdc.umd.edu
Website: http://www.mdsbdc.umd.edu
Ms. Renee Sprow, State Director

## Massachusetts

### Massachusetts SBDC
**UNIVERSITY OF MASSACHUSETTS**
School of Management, Room 205
Amherst, MA 01003-4935
Phone: 413-545-6301
Fax: 413-545-1273
E-mail: gep@msbdc.umass.edu
Website: http://msbdc.som.umass.edu
Ms. Georgianna Parkin, State Director

## Michigan

### Michigan SBTDC
**GRAND VALLEY STATE
UNIVERSITY**
510 West Fulton Avenue
Grand Rapids, MI 49504
Phone: 616-331-7485
Fax: 616-331-7389
E-mail: lopuckic@gvsu.edu
Website: http://www.misbtdc.org
Ms. Carol Lopucki, State Director

## Minnesota

### Minnesota SBDC
**MINNESOTA SMALL BUSINESS
DEVELOPMENT CENTER**
1st National Bank Building
332 Minnesota Street, Suite E200
St. Paul, MN 55101-1351
Phone: 651-297-5773
Fax: 651-296-5287

E-mail: michael.myhre@state.mn.us
Website: http://www.mnsbdc.com
Mr. Michael Myhre, State Director

## Mississippi

### Mississippi SBDC
**UNIVERSITY OF MISSISSIPPI**
B-19 Jeanette Phillips Drive
P.O. Box 1848
University, MS 38677
Phone: 662-915-5001
Fax: 662-915-5650
E-mail: wgurley@olemiss.edu
Website: http://www.olemiss.edu/depts/
mssbdc
Mr. Doug Gurley, Jr., State Director

## Missouri

### Missouri SBDC
**UNIVERSITY OF MISSOURI**
1205 University Avenue, Suite 300
Columbia, MO 65211
Phone: 573-882-1348
Fax: 573-884-4297
E-mail: summersm@missouri.edu
Website: http://www.mo-sbdc.org/
index.shtml
Mr. Max Summers, State Director

## Montana

### Montana SBDC
**DEPARTMENT OF COMMERCE**
301 South Park Avenue, Room 114 /
P.O. Box 200505
Helena, MT 59620
Phone: 406-841-2746
Fax: 406-444-1872
E-mail: adesch@state.mt.us
Website: http://commerce.state.mt.us/
brd/BRD_SBDC.html
Ms. Ann Desch, State Director

## Nebraska

### Nebraska SBDC
**UNIVERSITY OF NEBRASKA -
OMAHA**
60th & Dodge Street, CBA Room 407
Omaha, NE 68182
Phone: 402-554-2521
Fax: 402-554-3473
E-mail: rbernier@unomaha.edu
Website: http://nbdc.unomaha.edu
Mr. Robert Bernier, State Director

## Nevada

**Nevada SBDC**
**UNIVERSITY OF NEVADA - RENO**
Reno College of Business
Administration, Room 411
Reno, NV 89557-0100
Phone: 775-784-1717
Fax: 775-784-4337
E-mail: males@unr.edu
Website: http://www.nsbdc.org
Mr. Sam Males, State Director

## New Hampshire

**New Hampshire SBDC**
**UNIVERSITY OF NEW HAMPSHIRE**
108 McConnell Hall
Durham, NH 03824-3593
Phone: 603-862-4879
Fax: 603-862-4876
E-mail: Mary.Collins@unh.edu
Website: http://www.nhsbdc.org
Ms. Mary Collins, State Director

## New Jersey

**New Jersey SBDC**
**RUTGERS UNIVERSITY**
49 Bleeker Street
Newark, NJ 07102-1993
Phone: 973-353-5950
Fax: 973-353-1110
E-mail: bhopper@njsbdc.com
Website: http://www.njsbdc.com/home
Ms. Brenda Hopper, State Director

## New Mexico

**New Mexico SBDC**
**SANTA FE COMMUNITY COLLEGE**
6401 Richards Avenue
Santa Fe, NM 87505
Phone: 505-428-1362
Fax: 505-471-9469
E-mail: rmiller@santa-fe.cc.nm.us
Website: http://www.nmsbdc.org
Mr. Roy Miller, State Director

## New York

**New York SBDC**
**STATE UNIVERSITY OF NEW YORK**
SUNY Plaza, S-523
Albany, NY 12246
Phone: 518-443-5398
Fax: 518-443-5275
E-mail: j.king@nyssbdc.org
Website: http://www.nyssbdc.org
Mr. Jim King, State Director

## North Carolina

**North Carolina SBDTC**
**UNIVERSITY OF NORTH CAROLINA**
5 West Hargett Street, Suite 600
Raleigh, NC 27601
Phone: 919-715-7272
Fax: 919-715-7777
E-mail: sdaugherty@sbtdc.org
Website: http://www.sbtdc.org
Mr. Scott Daugherty, State Director

## North Dakota

**North Dakota SBDC**
**UNIVERSITY OF NORTH DAKOTA**
1600 E. Century Avenue, Suite 2
Bismarck, ND 58503
Phone: 701-328-5375
Fax: 701-328-5320
E-mail: christine.martin@und.nodak.edu
Website: http://www.ndsbdc.org
Ms. Christine Martin-Goldman, State
Director

## Ohio

**Ohio SBDC**
**OHIO DEPARTMENT
OF DEVELOPMENT**
77 South High Street
Columbus, OH 43216
Phone: 614-466-5102
Fax: 614-466-0829
E-mail: mabraham@odod.state.oh.us
Website: http://www.ohiosbdc.org
Ms. Michele Abraham, State Director

## Oklahoma

**Oklahoma SBDC**
**SOUTHEAST OKLAHOMA STATE
UNIVERSITY**
517 University, Box 2584, Station A
Durant, OK 74701
Phone: 580-745-7577
Fax: 580-745-7471
E-mail: gpennington@sosu.edu
Website: http://www.osbdc.org
Mr. Grady Pennington, State Director

## Oregon

**Oregon SBDC**
**LANE COMMUNITY COLLEGE**
99 West Tenth Avenue, Suite 390
Eugene, OR 97401-3021
Phone: 541-463-5250
Fax: 541-345-6006
E-mail: carterb@lanecc.edu

Website: http://www.bizcenter.org
Mr. William Carter, State Director

## Pennsylvania

**Pennsylvania SBDC**
**UNIVERSITY OF PENNSYLVANIA**
**The Wharton School**
3733 Spruce Street
Philadelphia, PA 19104-6374
Phone: 215-898-1219
Fax: 215-573-2135
E-mail: ghiggins@wharton.upenn.edu
Website: http://pasbdc.org
Mr. Gregory Higgins, State Director

## Puerto Rico

**Puerto Rico SBDC**
**INTER-AMERICAN UNIVERSITY
OF PUERTO RICO**
416 Ponce de Leon Avenue, Union Plaza,
Seventh Floor
Hato Rey, PR 00918
Phone: 787-763-6811
Fax: 787-763-4629
E-mail: cmarti@prsbdc.org
Website: http://www.prsbdc.org
Ms. Carmen Marti, Executive Director

## Rhode Island

**Rhode Island SBDC**
**BRYANT UNIVERSITY**
1150 Douglas Pike
Smithfield, RI 02917
Phone: 401-232-6923
Fax: 401-232-6933
E-mail: adawson@bryant.edu
Website: http://www.risbdc.org
Ms. Diane Fournaris, Interim State Director

## South Carolina

**South Carolina SBDC**
**UNIVERSITY OF SOUTH CAROLINA**
**College of Business Administration**
1710 College Street
Columbia, SC 29208
Phone: 803-777-4907
Fax: 803-777-4403
E-mail: lenti@moore.sc.edu
Website: http://scsbdc.moore.sc.edu
Mr. John Lenti, State Director

## South Dakota

**South Dakota SBDC**
**UNIVERSITY OF SOUTH DAKOTA**
414 East Clark Street, Patterson Hall
Vermillion, SD 57069

Phone: 605-677-6256
Fax: 605-677-5427
E-mail: jshemmin@usd.edu
Website: http://www.sdsbdc.org
Mr. John S. Hemmingstad, State Director

## Tennessee

**Tennessee SBDC**
**TENNESSEE BOARD OF REGENTS**
1415 Murfressboro Road, Suite 540
Nashville, TN 37217-2833
Phone: 615-898-2745
Fax: 615-893-7089
E-mail: pgeho@mail.tsbdc.org
Website: http://www.tsbdc.org
Mr. Patrick Geho, State Director

## Texas

**Texas-North SBDC**
**DALLAS COUNTY COMMUNITY COLLEGE**
1402 Corinth Street
Dallas, TX 75215
Phone: 214-860-5835
Fax: 214-860-5813
E-mail: emk9402@dcccd.edu
Website: http://www.ntsbdc.org
Ms. Liz Klimback, Region Director

**Texas-Houston SBDC**
**UNIVERSITY OF HOUSTON**
2302 Fannin, Suite 200
Houston, TX 77002
Phone: 713-752-8425
Fax: 713-756-1500
E-mail: fyoung@uh.edu
Website: http://sbdcnetwork.uh.edu
Mr. Mike Young, Executive Director

**Texas-NW SBDC**
**TEXAS TECH UNIVERSITY**
2579 South Loop 289, Suite 114
Lubbock, TX 79423
Phone: 806-745-3973
Fax: 806-745-6207
E-mail: c.bean@nwtsbdc.org
Website: http://www.nwtsbdc.org
Mr. Craig Bean, Executive Director

**Texas-South-West Texas Border Region SBDC**
**UNIVERSITY OF TEXAS - SAN ANTONIO**
501 West Durango Boulevard
San Antonio, TX 78207-4415
Phone: 210-458-2742
Fax: 210-458-2464

E-mail: albert.salgado@utsa.edu
Website: http://www.iedtexas.org
Mr. Alberto Salgado, Region Director

## Utah

**Utah SBDC**
**SALT LAKE COMMUNITY COLLEGE**
9750 South 300 West
Sandy, UT 84070
Phone: 801-957-3493
Fax: 801-957-3488
E-mail: Greg.Panichello@slcc.edu
Website: http://www.slcc.edu/sbdc
Mr. Greg Panichello, State Director

## Vermont

**Vermont SBDC**
**VERMONT TECHNICAL COLLEGE**
PO Box 188, 1 Main Street
Randolph Center, VT 05061-0188
Phone: 802-728-9101
Fax: 802-728-3026
E-mail: lquillen@vtc.edu
Website: http://www.vtsbdc.org
Ms. Lenae Quillen-Blume, State Director

## Virgin Islands

**Virgin Islands SBDC**
**UNIVERSITY OF THE VIRGIN ISLANDS**
8000 Nisky Center, Suite 720
St. Thomas, VI 00802-5804
Phone: 340-776-3206
Fax: 340-775-3756
E-mail: wbush@webmail.uvi.edu
Website: http://rps.uvi.edu/SBDC
Mr. Warren Bush, State Director

## Virginia

**Virginia SBDC**
**GEORGE MASON UNIVERSITY**
4031 University Drive, Suite 200
Fairfax, VA 22030-3409
Phone: 703-277-7727
Fax: 703-352-8515
E-mail: jkeenan@gmu.edu
Website: http://www.virginiasbdc.org
Ms. Jody Keenan, Director

## Washington

**Washington SBDC**
**WASHINGTON STATE UNIVERSITY**
534 E. Trent Avenue
P.O. Box 1495
Spokane, WA 99210-1495

Phone: 509-358-7765
Fax: 509-358-7764
E-mail: barogers@wsu.edu
Website: http://www.wsbdc.org
Mr. Brett Rogers, State Director

## West Virginia

**West Virginia SBDC**
**WEST VIRGINIA DEVELOPMENT OFFICE**
Capital Complex, Building 6, Room 652
Charleston, WV 25301
Phone: 304-558-2960
Fax: 304-558-0127
E-mail: csalyer@wvsbdc.org
Website: http://www.wvsbdc.org
Mr. Conley Salyor, State Director

## Wisconsin

**Wisconsin SBDC**
**UNIVERSITY OF WISCONSIN**
432 North Lake Street, Room 423
Madison, WI 53706
Phone: 608-263-7794
Fax: 608-263-7830
E-mail: erica.kauten@uwex.edu
Website: http://www.wisconsinsbdc.org
Ms. Erica Kauten, State Director

## Wyoming

**Wyoming SBDC**
**UNIVERSITY OF WYOMING**
P.O. Box 3922
Laramie, WY 82071-3922
Phone: 307-766-3505
Fax: 307-766-3406
E-mail: DDW@uwyo.edu
Website: http://www.uwyo.edu/sbdc
Ms. Debbie Popp, Acting State Director

## Service corps of retired executives (score) offices

*This section contains a listing of all SCORE offices organized alphabetically by state/U.S. territory, then by city, then by agency name.*

## Alabama

**SCORE Office (Northeast Alabama)**
1330 Quintard Ave.
Anniston, AL 36202
(256)237-3536

**SCORE Office (North Alabama)**
901 South 15th St, Rm. 201
Birmingham, AL 35294-2060
(205)934-6868
Fax: (205)934-0538

**SCORE Office (Baldwin County)**
29750 Larry Dee Cawyer Dr.
Daphne, AL 36526
(334)928-5838

**SCORE Office (Shoals)**
612 S. COurt
Florence, AL 35630
(256)764-4661
Fax: (256)766-9017
E-mail: shoals@shoalschamber.com

**SCORE Office (Mobile)**
600 S Court St.
Mobile, AL 36104
(334)240-6868
Fax: (334)240-6869

**SCORE Office (Alabama Capitol City)**
600 S. Court St.
Montgomery, AL 36104
(334)240-6868
Fax: (334)240-6869

**SCORE Office (East Alabama)**
601 Ave. A
Opelika, AL 36801
(334)745-4861
E-mail: score636@hotmail.com
Website: http://www.angelfire.com/sc/
score636/

**SCORE Office (Tuscaloosa)**
2200 University Blvd.
Tuscaloosa, AL 35402
(205)758-7588

## Alaska

**SCORE Office (Anchorage)**
510 L St., Ste. 310
Anchorage, AK 99501
(907)271-4022
Fax: (907)271-4545

## Arizona

**SCORE Office (Lake Havasu)**
10 S. Acoma Blvd.
Lake Havasu City, AZ 86403
(520)453-5951
E-mail: SCORE@ctaz.com
Website: http://www.scorearizona.org/
lake_havasu/

**SCORE Office (East Valley)**
Federal Bldg., Rm. 104
26 N. MacDonald St.
Mesa, AZ 85201
(602)379-3100
Fax: (602)379-3143
E-mail: 402@aol.com
Website: http://www.scorearizona.
org/mesa/

**SCORE Office (Phoenix)**
2828 N. Central Ave., Ste. 800
Central & One Thomas
Phoenix, AZ 85004
(602)640-2329
Fax: (602)640-2360
E-mail: e-mail@SCORE-phoenix.org
Website: http://www.score-phoenix.org/

**SCORE Office (Prescott Arizona)**
1228 Willow Creek Rd., Ste. 2
Prescott, AZ 86301
(520)778-7438
Fax: (520)778-0812
E-mail: score@northlink.com
Website: http://www.scorearizona.org/
prescott/

**SCORE Office (Tucson)**
110 E. Pennington St.
Tucson, AZ 85702
(520)670-5008
Fax: (520)670-5011
E-mail: score@azstarnet.com
Website: http://www.scorearizona.org/
tucson/

**SCORE Office (Yuma)**
281 W. 24th St., Ste. 116
Yuma, AZ 85364
(520)314-0480
E-mail: score@C2i2.com
Website: http://www.scorearizona.org/
yuma

## Arkansas

**SCORE Office (South Central)**
201 N. Jackson Ave.
El Dorado, AR 71730-5803
(870)863-6113
Fax: (870)863-6115

**SCORE Office (Ozark)**
Fayetteville, AR 72701
(501)442-7619

**SCORE Office (Northwest Arkansas)**
Glenn Haven Dr., No. 4
Ft. Smith, AR 72901
(501)783-3556

**SCORE Office (Garland County)**
Grand & Ouachita
PO Box 6012
Hot Springs Village, AR 71902
(501)321-1700

**SCORE Office (Little Rock)**
2120 Riverfront Dr., Rm. 100
Little Rock, AR 72202-1747
(501)324-5893
Fax: (501)324-5199

**SCORE Office (Southeast Arkansas)**
121 W. 6th
Pine Bluff, AR 71601
(870)535-7189
Fax: (870)535-1643

## California

**SCORE Office (Golden Empire)**
1706 Chester Ave., No. 200
Bakersfield, CA 93301
(805)322-5881
Fax: (805)322-5663

**SCORE Office (Greater Chico Area)**
1324 Mangrove St., Ste. 114
Chico, CA 95926
(916)342-8932
Fax: (916)342-8932

**SCORE Office (Concord)**
2151-A Salvio St., Ste. B
Concord, CA 94520
(510)685-1181
Fax: (510)685-5623

**SCORE Office (Covina)**
935 W. Badillo St.
Covina, CA 91723
(818)967-4191
Fax: (818)966-9660

**SCORE Office (Rancho Cucamonga)**
8280 Utica, Ste. 160
Cucamonga, CA 91730
(909)987-1012
Fax: (909)987-5917

**SCORE Office (Culver City)**
PO Box 707
Culver City, CA 90232-0707
(310)287-3850
Fax: (310)287-1350

**SCORE Office (Danville)**
380 Diablo Rd., Ste. 103
Danville, CA 94526
(510)837-4400

**SCORE Office (Downey)**
11131 Brookshire Ave.
Downey, CA 90241
(310)923-2191
Fax: (310)864-0461

**SCORE Office (El Cajon)**
109 Rea Ave.
El Cajon, CA 92020
(619)444-1327
Fax: (619)440-6164

**SCORE Office (El Centro)**
1100 Main St.
El Centro, CA 92243
(619)352-3681
Fax: (619)352-3246

**SCORE Office (Escondido)**
720 N. Broadway
Escondido, CA 92025
(619)745-2125
Fax: (619)745-1183

**SCORE Office (Fairfield)**
1111 Webster St.
Fairfield, CA 94533
(707)425-4625
Fax: (707)425-0826

**SCORE Office (Fontana)**
17009 Valley Blvd., Ste. B
Fontana, CA 92335
(909)822-4433
Fax: (909)822-6238

**SCORE Office (Foster City)**
1125 E. Hillsdale Blvd.
Foster City, CA 94404
(415)573-7600
Fax: (415)573-5201

**SCORE Office (Fremont)**
2201 Walnut Ave., Ste. 110
Fremont, CA 94538
(510)795-2244
Fax: (510)795-2240

**SCORE Office (Central California)**
2719 N. Air Fresno Dr., Ste. 200
Fresno, CA 93727-1547
(559)487-5605
Fax: (559)487-5636

**SCORE Office (Gardena)**
1204 W. Gardena Blvd.
Gardena, CA 90247
(310)532-9905
Fax: (310)515-4893

**SCORE Office (Lompoc)**
330 N. Brand Blvd., Ste. 190
Glendale, CA 91203-2304

(818)552-3206
Fax: (818)552-3323

**SCORE Office (Los Angeles)**
330 N. Brand Blvd., Ste. 190
Glendale, CA 91203-2304
(818)552-3206
Fax: (818)552-3323

**SCORE Office (Glendora)**
131 E. Foothill Blvd.
Glendora, CA 91740
(818)963-4128
Fax: (818)914-4822

**SCORE Office (Grover Beach)**
177 S. 8th St.
Grover Beach, CA 93433
(805)489-9091
Fax: (805)489-9091

**SCORE Office (Hawthorne)**
12477 Hawthorne Blvd.
Hawthorne, CA 90250
(310)676-1163
Fax: (310)676-7661

**SCORE Office (Hayward)**
22300 Foothill Blvd., Ste. 303
Hayward, CA 94541
(510)537-2424

**SCORE Office (Hemet)**
1700 E. Florida Ave.
Hemet, CA 92544-4679
(909)652-4390
Fax: (909)929-8543

**SCORE Office (Hesperia)**
16367 Main St.
PO Box 403656
Hesperia, CA 92340
(619)244-2135

**SCORE Office (Holloster)**
321 San Felipe Rd., No. 11
Hollister, CA 95023

**SCORE Office (Hollywood)**
7018 Hollywood Blvd.
Hollywood, CA 90028
(213)469-8311
Fax: (213)469-2805

**SCORE Office (Indio)**
82503 Hwy. 111
PO Drawer TTT
Indio, CA 92202
(619)347-0676

**SCORE Office (Inglewood)**
330 Queen St.

Inglewood, CA 90301
(818)552-3206

**SCORE Office (La Puente)**
218 N. Grendanda St. D.
La Puente, CA 91744
(818)330-3216
Fax: (818)330-9524

**SCORE Office (La Verne)**
2078 Bonita Ave.
La Verne, CA 91750
(909)593-5265
Fax: (714)929-8475

**SCORE Office (Lake Elsinore)**
132 W. Graham Ave.
Lake Elsinore, CA 92530
(909)674-2577

**SCORE Office (Lakeport)**
PO Box 295
Lakeport, CA 95453
(707)263-5092

**SCORE Office (Lakewood)**
5445 E. Del Amo Blvd., Ste. 2
Lakewood, CA 90714
(213)920-7737

**SCORE Office (Long Beach)**
1 World Trade Center
Long Beach, CA 90831

**SCORE Office (Los Alamitos)**
901 W. Civic Center Dr., Ste. 160
Los Alamitos, CA 90720

**SCORE Office (Los Altos)**
321 University Ave.
Los Altos, CA 94022
(415)948-1455

**SCORE Office (Manhattan Beach)**
PO Box 3007
Manhattan Beach, CA 90266
(310)545-5313
Fax: (310)545-7203

**SCORE Office (Merced)**
1632 N. St.
Merced, CA 95340
(209)725-3800
Fax: (209)383-4959

**SCORE Office (Milpitas)**
75 S. Milpitas Blvd., Ste. 205
Milpitas, CA 95035
(408)262-2613
Fax: (408)262-2823

**SCORE Office (Yosemite)**
1012 11th St., Ste. 300
Modesto, CA 95354
(209)521-9333

**SCORE Office (Montclair)**
5220 Benito Ave.
Montclair, CA 91763

**SCORE Office (Monterey Bay)**
380 Alvarado St.
PO Box 1770
Monterey, CA 93940-1770
(408)649-1770

**SCORE Office (Moreno Valley)**
25480 Alessandro
Moreno Valley, CA 92553

**SCORE Office (Morgan Hill)**
25 W. 1st St.
PO Box 786
Morgan Hill, CA 95038
(408)779-9444
Fax: (408)778-1786

**SCORE Office (Morro Bay)**
880 Main St.
Morro Bay, CA 93442
(805)772-4467

**SCORE Office (Mountain View)**
580 Castro St.
Mountain View, CA 94041
(415)968-8378
Fax: (415)968-5668

**SCORE Office (Napa)**
1556 1st St.
Napa, CA 94559
(707)226-7455
Fax: (707)226-1171

**SCORE Office (North Hollywood)**
5019 Lankershim Blvd.
North Hollywood, CA 91601
(818)552-3206

**SCORE Office (Northridge)**
8801 Reseda Blvd.
Northridge, CA 91324
(818)349-5676

**SCORE Office (Novato)**
807 De Long Ave.
Novato, CA 94945
(415)897-1164
Fax: (415)898-9097

**SCORE Office (East Bay)**
519 17th St.
Oakland, CA 94612

(510)273-6611
Fax: (510)273-6015
E-mail: webmaster@eastbayscore.org
Website: http://www.eastbayscore.org

**SCORE Office (Oceanside)**
928 N. Coast Hwy.
Oceanside, CA 92054
(619)722-1534

**SCORE Office (Ontario)**
121 West B. St.
Ontario, CA 91762
Fax: (714)984-6439

**SCORE Office (Oxnard)**
PO Box 867
Oxnard, CA 93032
(805)385-8860
Fax: (805)487-1763

**SCORE Office (Pacifica)**
450 Dundee Way, Ste. 2
Pacifica, CA 94044
(415)355-4122

**SCORE Office (Palm Desert)**
72990 Hwy. 111
Palm Desert, CA 92260
(619)346-6111
Fax: (619)346-3463

**SCORE Office (Palm Springs)**
650 E. Tahquitz Canyon Way Ste. D
Palm Springs, CA 92262-6706
(760)320-6682
Fax: (760)323-9426

**SCORE Office (Lakeside)**
2150 Low Tree
Palmdale, CA 93551
(805)948-4518
Fax: (805)949-1212

**SCORE Office (Palo Alto)**
325 Forest Ave.
Palo Alto, CA 94301
(415)324-3121
Fax: (415)324-1215

**SCORE Office (Pasadena)**
117 E. Colorado Blvd., Ste. 100
Pasadena, CA 91105
(818)795-3355
Fax: (818)795-5663

**SCORE Office (Paso Robles)**
1225 Park St.
Paso Robles, CA 93446-2234
(805)238-0506
Fax: (805)238-0527

**SCORE Office (Petaluma)**
799 Baywood Dr., Ste. 3
Petaluma, CA 94954
(707)762-2785
Fax: (707)762-4721

**SCORE Office (Pico Rivera)**
9122 E. Washington Blvd.
Pico Rivera, CA 90660

**SCORE Office (Pittsburg)**
2700 E. Leland Rd.
Pittsburg, CA 94565
(510)439-2181
Fax: (510)427-1599

**SCORE Office (Pleasanton)**
777 Peters Ave.
Pleasanton, CA 94566
(510)846-9697

**SCORE Office (Monterey Park)**
485 N. Garey
Pomona, CA 91769

**SCORE Office (Pomona)**
485 N. Garey Ave.
Pomona, CA 91766
(909)622-1256

**SCORE Office (Antelope Valley)**
4511 West Ave. M-4
Quartz Hill, CA 93536
(805)272-0087
E-mail: avscore@ptw.com
Website: http://www.score.av.org/

**SCORE Office (Shasta)**
737 Auditorium Dr.
Redding, CA 96099
(916)225-2770

**SCORE Office (Redwood City)**
1675 Broadway
Redwood City, CA 94063
(415)364-1722
Fax: (415)364-1729

**SCORE Office (Richmond)**
3925 MacDonald Ave.
Richmond, CA 94805

**SCORE Office (Ridgecrest)**
PO Box 771
Ridgecrest, CA 93555
(619)375-8331
Fax: (619)375-0365

**SCORE Office (Riverside)**
3685 Main St., Ste. 350
Riverside, CA 92501
(909)683-7100

**SCORE Office (Sacramento)**
9845 Horn Rd., 260-B
Sacramento, CA 95827
(916)361-2322
Fax: (916)361-2164
E-mail: sacchapter@directcon.net

**SCORE Office (Salinas)**
PO Box 1170
Salinas, CA 93902
(408)424-7611
Fax: (408)424-8639

**SCORE Office (Inland Empire)**
777 E. Rialto Ave.
Purchasing
San Bernardino, CA 92415-0760
(909)386-8278

**SCORE Office (San Carlos)**
San Carlos Chamber of Commerce
PO Box 1086
San Carlos, CA 94070
(415)593-1068
Fax: (415)593-9108

**SCORE Office (Encinitas)**
550 W. C St., Ste. 550
San Diego, CA 92101-3540
(619)557-7272
Fax: (619)557-5894

**SCORE Office (San Diego)**
550 West C. St., Ste. 550
San Diego, CA 92101-3540
(619)557-7272
Fax: (619)557-5894
Website: http://www.score-sandiego.org

**SCORE Office (Menlo Park)**
1100 Merrill St.
San Francisco, CA 94105
(415)325-2818
Fax: (415)325-0920

**SCORE Office (San Francisco)**
455 Market St., 6th Fl.
San Francisco, CA 94105
(415)744-6827
Fax: (415)744-6750
E-mail: sfscore@sfscore.
Website: http://www.sfscore.com

**SCORE Office (San Gabriel)**
401 W. Las Tunas Dr.
San Gabriel, CA 91776
(818)576-2525
Fax: (818)289-2901

**SCORE Office (San Jose)**
Deanza College
208 S. 1st St., Ste. 137
San Jose, CA 95113
(408)288-8479
Fax: (408)535-5541

**SCORE Office (Silicon Valley)**
84 W. Santa Clara St., Ste. 100
San Jose, CA 95113
(408)288-8479
Fax: (408)535-5541
E-mail: info@svscore.org
Website: http://www.svscore.org

**SCORE Office (San Luis Obispo)**
3566 S. Hiquera, No. 104
San Luis Obispo, CA 93401
(805)547-0779

**SCORE Office (San Mateo)**
1021 S. El Camino, 2nd Fl.
San Mateo, CA 94402
(415)341-5679

**SCORE Office (San Pedro)**
390 W. 7th St.
San Pedro, CA 90731
(310)832-7272

**SCORE Office (Orange County)**
200 W. Santa Anna Blvd., Ste. 700
Santa Ana, CA 92701
(714)550-7369
Fax: (714)550-0191
Website: http://www.score114.org

**SCORE Office (Santa Barbara)**
3227 State St.
Santa Barbara, CA 93130
(805)563-0084

**SCORE Office (Central Coast)**
509 W. Morrison Ave.
Santa Maria, CA 93454
(805)347-7755

**SCORE Office (Santa Maria)**
614 S. Broadway
Santa Maria, CA 93454-5111
(805)925-2403
Fax: (805)928-7559

**SCORE Office (Santa Monica)**
501 Colorado, Ste. 150
Santa Monica, CA 90401
(310)393-9825
Fax: (310)394-1868

**SCORE Office (Santa Rosa)**
777 Sonoma Ave., Rm. 115E
Santa Rosa, CA 95404

(707)571-8342
Fax: (707)541-0331
Website: http://www.pressdemo.com/community/score/score.html

**SCORE Office (Scotts Valley)**
4 Camp Evers Ln.
Scotts Valley, CA 95066
(408)438-1010
Fax: (408)438-6544

**SCORE Office (Simi Valley)**
40 W. Cochran St., Ste. 100
Simi Valley, CA 93065
(805)526-3900
Fax: (805)526-6234

**SCORE Office (Sonoma)**
453 1st St. E
Sonoma, CA 95476
(707)996-1033

**SCORE Office (Los Banos)**
222 S. Shepard St.
Sonora, CA 95370
(209)532-4212

**SCORE Office (Tuolumne County)**
39 North Washington St.
Sonora, CA 95370
(209)588-0128
E-mail: score@mlode.com

**SCORE Office (South San Francisco)**
445 Market St., Ste. 6th Fl.
South San Francisco, CA 94105
(415)744-6827
Fax: (415)744-6812

**SCORE Office (Stockton)**
401 N. San Joaquin St., Rm. 215
Stockton, CA 95202
(209)946-6293

**SCORE Office (Taft)**
314 4th St.
Taft, CA 93268
(805)765-2165
Fax: (805)765-6639

**SCORE Office (Conejo Valley)**
625 W. Hillcrest Dr.
Thousand Oaks, CA 91360
(805)499-1993
Fax: (805)498-7264

**SCORE Office (Torrance)**
3400 Torrance Blvd., Ste. 100
Torrance, CA 90503
(310)540-5858
Fax: (310)540-7662

**SCORE Office (Truckee)**
PO Box 2757
Truckee, CA 96160
(916)587-2757
Fax: (916)587-2439

**SCORE Office (Visalia)**
113 S. M St,
Tulare, CA 93274
(209)627-0766
Fax: (209)627-8149

**SCORE Office (Upland)**
433 N. 2nd Ave.
Upland, CA 91786
(909)931-4108

**SCORE Office (Vallejo)**
2 Florida St.
Vallejo, CA 94590
(707)644-5551
Fax: (707)644-5590

**SCORE Office (Van Nuys)**
14540 Victory Blvd.
Van Nuys, CA 91411
(818)989-0300
Fax: (818)989-3836

**SCORE Office (Ventura)**
5700 Ralston St., Ste. 310
Ventura, CA 93001
(805)658-2688
Fax: (805)658-2252
E-mail: scoreven@jps.net
Website: http://www.jps.net/scoreven

**SCORE Office (Vista)**
201 E. Washington St.
Vista, CA 92084
(619)726-1122
Fax: (619)226-8654

**SCORE Office (Watsonville)**
PO Box 1748
Watsonville, CA 95077
(408)724-3849
Fax: (408)728-5300

**SCORE Office (West Covina)**
811 S. Sunset Ave.
West Covina, CA 91790
(818)338-8496
Fax: (818)960-0511

**SCORE Office (Westlake)**
30893 Thousand Oaks Blvd.
Westlake Village, CA 91362
(805)496-5630
Fax: (818)991-1754

## Colorado

**SCORE Office (Colorado Springs)**
2 N. Cascade Ave., Ste. 110
Colorado Springs, CO 80903
(719)636-3074
Website: http://www.cscc.org/score02/
index.html

**SCORE Office (Denver)**
US Custom's House, 4th Fl.
721 19th St.
Denver, CO 80201-0660
(303)844-3985
Fax: (303)844-6490
E-mail: score62@csn.net
Website: http://www.sni.net/score62

**SCORE Office (Tri-River)**
1102 Grand Ave.
Glenwood Springs, CO 81601
(970)945-6589

**SCORE Office (Grand Junction)**
2591 B & 3/4 Rd.
Grand Junction, CO 81503
(970)243-5242

**SCORE Office (Gunnison)**
608 N. 11th
Gunnison, CO 81230
(303)641-4422

**SCORE Office (Montrose)**
1214 Peppertree Dr.
Montrose, CO 81401
(970)249-6080

**SCORE Office (Pagosa Springs)**
PO Box 4381
Pagosa Springs, CO 81157
(970)731-4890

**SCORE Office (Rifle)**
0854 W. Battlement Pky., Apt. C106
Parachute, CO 81635
(970)285-9390

**SCORE Office (Pueblo)**
302 N. Santa Fe
Pueblo, CO 81003
(719)542-1704
Fax: (719)542-1624
E-mail: mackey@iex.net
Website: http://www.pueblo.org/score

**SCORE Office (Ridgway)**
143 Poplar Pl.
Ridgway, CO 81432

**SCORE Office (Silverton)**
PO Box 480

Silverton, CO 81433
(303)387-5430

**SCORE Office (Minturn)**
PO Box 2066
Vail, CO 81658
(970)476-1224

## Connecticut

**SCORE Office (Greater Bridgeport)**
230 Park Ave.
Bridgeport, CT 06601-0999
(203)576-4369
Fax: (203)576-4388

**SCORE Office (Bristol)**
10 Main St. 1st. Fl.
Bristol, CT 06010
(203)584-4718
Fax: (203)584-4722

**SCORE office (Greater Danbury)**
246 Federal Rd.
Unit LL2, Ste. 7
Brookfield, CT 06804
(203)775-1151

**SCORE Office (Greater Danbury)**
246 Federal Rd., Unit LL2, Ste. 7
Brookfield, CT 06804
(203)775-1151

**SCORE Office (Eastern Connecticut)**
Administration Bldg., Rm. 313
PO 625
61 Main St. (Chapter 579)
Groton, CT 06475
(203)388-9508

**SCORE Office (Greater Hartford County)**
330 Main St.
Hartford, CT 06106
(860)548-1749
Fax: (860)240-4659
Website: http://www.score56.org

**SCORE Office (Manchester)**
20 Hartford Rd.
Manchester, CT 06040
(203)646-2223
Fax: (203)646-5871

**SCORE Office (New Britain)**
185 Main St., Ste. 431
New Britain, CT 06051
(203)827-4492
Fax: (203)827-4480

**SCORE Office (New Haven)**
25 Science Pk., Bldg. 25, Rm. 366

New Haven, CT 06511
(203)865-7645

**SCORE Office (Fairfield County)**
24 Beldon Ave., 5th Fl.
Norwalk, CT 06850
(203)847-7348
Fax: (203)849-9308

**SCORE Office (Old Saybrook)**
146 Main St.
Old Saybrook, CT 06475
(860)388-9508

**SCORE Office (Simsbury)**
Box 244
Simsbury, CT 06070
(203)651-7307
Fax: (203)651-1933

**SCORE Office (Torrington)**
23 North Rd.
Torrington, CT 06791
(203)482-6586

## Delaware

**SCORE Office (Dover)**
Treadway Towers
PO Box 576
Dover, DE 19903
(302)678-0892
Fax: (302)678-0189

**SCORE Office (Lewes)**
PO Box 1
Lewes, DE 19958
(302)645-8073
Fax: (302)645-8412

**SCORE Office (Milford)**
204 NE Front St.
Milford, DE 19963
(302)422-3301

**SCORE Office (Wilmington)**
824 Market St., Ste. 610
Wilmington, DE 19801
(302)573-6652
Fax: (302)573-6092
Website: http://www.scoredelaware.com

## District of Columbia

**SCORE Office (George Mason University)**
409 3rd St. SW, 4th Fl.
Washington, DC 20024
800-634-0245

**SCORE Office (Washington DC)**
1110 Vermont Ave. NW, 9th Fl.

Washington, DC 20043
(202)606-4000
Fax: (202)606-4225
E-mail: dcscore@hotmail.com
Website: http://www.scoredc.org/

## Florida

**SCORE Office (Desota County Chamber of Commerce)**
16 South Velucia Ave.
Arcadia, FL 34266
(941)494-4033

**SCORE Office (Suncoast/Pinellas)**
Airport Business Ctr.
4707 - 140th Ave. N, No. 311
Clearwater, FL 33755
(813)532-6800
Fax: (813)532-6800

**SCORE Office (DeLand)**
336 N. Woodland Blvd.
DeLand, FL 32720
(904)734-4331
Fax: (904)734-4333

**SCORE Office (South Palm Beach)**
1050 S. Federal Hwy., Ste. 132
Delray Beach, FL 33483
(561)278-7752
Fax: (561)278-0288

**SCORE Office (Ft. Lauderdale)**
Federal Bldg., Ste. 123
299 E. Broward Blvd.
Ft. Lauderdale, FL 33301
(954)356-7263
Fax: (954)356-7145

**SCORE Office (Southwest Florida)**
The Renaissance
8695 College Pky., Ste. 345 & 346
Ft. Myers, FL 33919
(941)489-2935
Fax: (941)489-1170

**SCORE Office (Treasure Coast)**
Professional Center, Ste. 2
3220 S. US, No. 1
Ft. Pierce, FL 34982
(561)489-0548

**SCORE Office (Gainesville)**
101 SE 2nd Pl., Ste. 104
Gainesville, FL 32601
(904)375-8278

**SCORE Office (Hialeah Dade Chamber)**
59 W. 5th St.
Hialeah, FL 33010

(305)887-1515
Fax: (305)887-2453

**SCORE Office (Daytona Beach)**
921 Nova Rd., Ste. A
Holly Hills, FL 32117
(904)255-6889
Fax: (904)255-0229
E-mail: score87@dbeach.com

**SCORE Office (South Broward)**
3475 Sheridian St., Ste. 203
Hollywood, FL 33021
(305)966-8415

**SCORE Office (Citrus County)**
5 Poplar Ct.
Homosassa, FL 34446
(352)382-1037

**SCORE Office (Jacksonville)**
7825 Baymeadows Way, Ste. 100-B
Jacksonville, FL 32256
(904)443-1911
Fax: (904)443-1980
E-mail: scorejax@juno.com
Website: http://www.scorejax.org/

**SCORE Office (Jacksonville Satellite)**
3 Independent Dr.
Jacksonville, FL 32256
(904)366-6600
Fax: (904)632-0617

**SCORE Office (Central Florida)**
5410 S. Florida Ave., No. 3
Lakeland, FL 33801
(941)687-5783
Fax: (941)687-6225

**SCORE Office (Lakeland)**
100 Lake Morton Dr.
Lakeland, FL 33801
(941)686-2168

**SCORE Office (St. Petersburg)**
800 W. Bay Dr., Ste. 505
Largo, FL 33712
(813)585-4571

**SCORE Office (Leesburg)**
9501 US Hwy. 441
Leesburg, FL 34788-8751
(352)365-3556
Fax: (352)365-3501

**SCORE Office (Cocoa)**
1600 Farno Rd., Unit 205
Melbourne, FL 32935
(407)254-2288

**SCORE Office (Melbourne)**
Melbourne Professional Complex
1600 Sarno, Ste. 205
Melbourne, FL 32935
(407)254-2288
Fax: (407)245-2288

**SCORE Office (Merritt Island)**
1600 Sarno Rd., Ste. 205
Melbourne, FL 32935
(407)254-2288
Fax: (407)254-2288

**SCORE Office (Space Coast)**
Melbourn Professional Complex
1600 Sarno, Ste. 205
Melbourne, FL 32935
(407)254-2288
Fax: (407)254-2288

**SCORE Office (Dade)**
49 NW 5th St.
Miami, FL 33128
(305)371-6889
Fax: (305)374-1882
E-mail: score@netrox.net
Website: http://www.netrox.net/~score/

**SCORE Office (Naples of Collier)**
International College
2654 Tamiami Trl. E
Naples, FL 34112
(941)417-1280
Fax: (941)417-1281
E-mail: score@naples.net
Website: http://www.naples.net/clubs/
score/index.htm

**SCORE Office (Pasco County)**
6014 US Hwy. 19, Ste. 302
New Port Richey, FL 34652
(813)842-4638

**SCORE Office (Southeast Volusia)**
115 Canal St.
New Smyrna Beach, FL 32168
(904)428-2449
Fax: (904)423-3512

**SCORE Office (Ocala)**
110 E. Silver Springs Blvd.
Ocala, FL 34470
(352)629-5959

**Clay County SCORE Office**
Clay County Chamber of Commerce
1734 Kingsdey Ave.
PO Box 1441
Orange Park, FL 32073
(904)264-2651
Fax: (904)269-0363

**SCORE Office (Orlando)**
80 N. Hughey Ave.
Rm. 445 Federal Bldg.
Orlando, FL 32801
(407)648-6476
Fax: (407)648-6425

**SCORE Office (Emerald Coast)**
19 W. Garden St., No. 325
Pensacola, FL 32501
(904)444-2060
Fax: (904)444-2070

**SCORE Office (Charlotte County)**
201 W. Marion Ave., Ste. 211
Punta Gorda, FL 33950
(941)575-1818
E-mail: score@gls3c.com
Website: http://www.charlotte-
florida.com/business/scorepg01.htm

**SCORE Office (St. Augustine)**
1 Riberia St.
St. Augustine, FL 32084
(904)829-5681
Fax: (904)829-6477

**SCORE Office (Bradenton)**
2801 Fruitville, Ste. 280
Sarasota, FL 34237
(813)955-1029

**SCORE Office (Manasota)**
2801 Fruitville Rd., Ste. 280
Sarasota, FL 34237
(941)955-1029
Fax: (941)955-5581
E-mail: score116@gte.net
Website: http://www.score-suncoast.org/

**SCORE Office (Tallahassee)**
200 W. Park Ave.
Tallahassee, FL 32302
(850)487-2665

**SCORE Office (Hillsborough)**
4732 Dale Mabry Hwy. N, Ste. 400
Tampa, FL 33614-6509
(813)870-0125

**SCORE Office (Lake Sumter)**
122 E. Main St.
Tavares, FL 32778-3810
(352)365-3556

**SCORE Office (Titusville)**
2000 S. Washington Ave.
Titusville, FL 32780
(407)267-3036
Fax: (407)264-0127

**SCORE Office (Venice)**
257 N. Tamiami Trl.
Venice, FL 34285
(941)488-2236
Fax: (941)484-5903

**SCORE Office (Palm Beach)**
500 Australian Ave. S, Ste. 100
West Palm Beach, FL 33401
(561)833-1672
Fax: (561)833-1712

**SCORE Office (Wildwood)**
103 N. Webster St.
Wildwood, FL 34785

## Georgia

**SCORE Office (Atlanta)**
Harris Tower, Suite 1900
233 Peachtree Rd., NE
Atlanta, GA 30309
(404)347-2442
Fax: (404)347-1227

**SCORE Office (Augusta)**
3126 Oxford Rd.
Augusta, GA 30909
(706)869-9100

**SCORE Office (Columbus)**
School Bldg.
PO Box 40
Columbus, GA 31901
(706)327-3654

**SCORE Office (Dalton-Whitfield)**
305 S. Thorton Ave.
Dalton, GA 30720
(706)279-3383

**SCORE Office (Gainesville)**
PO Box 374
Gainesville, GA 30503
(770)532-6206
Fax: (770)535-8419

**SCORE Office (Macon)**
711 Grand Bldg.
Macon, GA 31201
(912)751-6160

**SCORE Office (Brunswick)**
4 Glen Ave.
St. Simons Island, GA 31520
(912)265-0620
Fax: (912)265-0629

**SCORE Office (Savannah)**
111 E. Liberty St., Ste. 103
Savannah, GA 31401
(912)652-4335

Fax: (912)652-4184
E-mail: info@scoresav.org
Website: http://www.coastalempire.com/score/index.htm

## Guam

**SCORE Office (Guam)**
Pacific News Bldg., Rm. 103
238 Archbishop Flores St.
Agana, GU 96910-5100
(671)472-7308

## Hawaii

**SCORE Office (Hawaii, Inc.)**
1111 Bishop St., Ste. 204
PO Box 50207
Honolulu, HI 96813
(808)522-8132
Fax: (808)522-8135
E-mail: hnlscore@juno.com

**SCORE Office (Kahului)**
250 Alamaha, Unit N16A
Kahului, HI 96732
(808)871-7711

**SCORE Office (Maui, Inc.)**
590 E. Lipoa Pkwy., Ste. 227
Kihei, HI 96753
(808)875-2380

## Idaho

**SCORE Office (Treasure Valley)**
1020 Main St., No. 290
Boise, ID 83702
(208)334-1696
Fax: (208)334-9353

**SCORE Office (Eastern Idaho)**
2300 N. Yellowstone, Ste. 119
Idaho Falls, ID 83401
(208)523-1022
Fax: (208)528-7127

## Illinois

**SCORE Office (Fox Valley)**
40 W. Downer Pl.
PO Box 277
Aurora, IL 60506
(630)897-9214
Fax: (630)897-7002

**SCORE Office (Greater Belvidere)**
419 S. State St.
Belvidere, IL 61008
(815)544-4357
Fax: (815)547-7654

**SCORE Office (Bensenville)**
1050 Busse Hwy. Suite 100
Bensenville, IL 60106
(708)350-2944
Fax: (708)350-2979

**SCORE Office (Central Illinois)**
402 N. Hershey Rd.
Bloomington, IL 61704
(309)644-0549
Fax: (309)663-8270
E-mail: webmaster@central-illinois-score.org
Website: http://www.central-illinois-score.org/

**SCORE Office (Southern Illinois)**
150 E. Pleasant Hill Rd.
Box 1
Carbondale, IL 62901
(618)453-6654
Fax: (618)453-5040

**SCORE Office (Chicago)**
Northwest Atrium Ctr.
500 W. Madison St., No. 1250
Chicago, IL 60661
(312)353-7724
Fax: (312)886-5688
Website: http://www.mcs.net/~bic/

**SCORE Office (Chicago–Oliver Harvey College)**
Pullman Bldg.
1000 E. 11th St., 7th Fl.
Chicago, IL 60628
Fax: (312)468-8086

**SCORE Office (Danville)**
28 W. N. Street
Danville, IL 61832
(217)442-7232
Fax: (217)442-6228

**SCORE Office (Decatur)**
Milliken University
1184 W. Main St.
Decatur, IL 62522
(217)424-6297
Fax: (217)424-3993
E-mail: charding@mail.millikin.edu
Website: http://www.millikin.edu/academics/Tabor/score.html

**SCORE Office (Downers Grove)**
925 Curtis
Downers Grove, IL 60515
(708)968-4050
Fax: (708)968-8368

**SCORE Office (Elgin)**
24 E. Chicago, 3rd Fl.
PO Box 648
Elgin, IL 60120
(847)741-5660
Fax: (847)741-5677

**SCORE Office (Freeport Area)**
26 S. Galena Ave.
Freeport, IL 61032
(815)233-1350
Fax: (815)235-4038

**SCORE Office (Galesburg)**
292 E. Simmons St.
PO Box 749
Galesburg, IL 61401
(309)343-1194
Fax: (309)343-1195

**SCORE Office (Glen Ellyn)**
500 Pennsylvania
Glen Ellyn, IL 60137
(708)469-0907
Fax: (708)469-0426

**SCORE Office (Greater Alton)**
Alden Hall
5800 Godfrey Rd.
Godfrey, IL 62035-2466
(618)467-2280
Fax: (618)466-8289
Website: http://www.altonweb.com/score/

**SCORE Office (Grayslake)**
19351 W. Washington St.
Grayslake, IL 60030
(708)223-3633
Fax: (708)223-9371

**SCORE Office (Harrisburg)**
303 S. Commercial
Harrisburg, IL 62946-1528
(618)252-8528
Fax: (618)252-0210

**SCORE Office (Joliet)**
100 N. Chicago
Joliet, IL 60432
(815)727-5371
Fax: (815)727-5374

**SCORE Office (Kankakee)**
101 S. Schuyler Ave.
Kankakee, IL 60901
(815)933-0376
Fax: (815)933-0380

**SCORE Office (Macomb)**
216 Seal Hall, Rm. 214

Macomb, IL 61455
(309)298-1128
Fax: (309)298-2520

**SCORE Office (Matteson)**
210 Lincoln Mall
Matteson, IL 60443
(708)709-3750
Fax: (708)503-9322

**SCORE Office (Mattoon)**
1701 Wabash Ave.
Mattoon, IL 61938
(217)235-5661
Fax: (217)234-6544

**SCORE Office (Quad Cities)**
622 19th St.
Moline, IL 61265
(309)797-0082
Fax: (309)757-5435
E-mail: score@qconline.com
Website: http://www.qconline.com/
business/score/

**SCORE Office (Naperville)**
131 W. Jefferson Ave.
Naperville, IL 60540
(708)355-4141
Fax: (708)355-8355

**SCORE Office (Northbrook)**
2002 Walters Ave.
Northbrook, IL 60062
(847)498-5555
Fax: (847)498-5510

**SCORE Office (Palos Hills)**
10900 S. 88th Ave.
Palos Hills, IL 60465
(847)974-5468
Fax: (847)974-0078

**SCORE Office (Peoria)**
124 SW Adams, Ste. 300
Peoria, IL 61602
(309)676-0755
Fax: (309)676-7534

**SCORE Office (Prospect Heights)**
1375 Wolf Rd.
Prospect Heights, IL 60070
(847)537-8660
Fax: (847)537-7138

**SCORE Office (Quincy Tri-State)**
300 Civic Center Plz., Ste. 245
Quincy, IL 62301
(217)222-8093
Fax: (217)222-3033

**SCORE Office (River Grove)**
2000 5th Ave.
River Grove, IL 60171
(708)456-0300
Fax: (708)583-3121

**SCORE Office (Northern Illinois)**
515 N. Court St.
Rockford, IL 61103
(815)962-0122
Fax: (815)962-0122

**SCORE Office (St. Charles)**
103 N. 1st Ave.
St. Charles, IL 60174-1982
(847)584-8384
Fax: (847)584-6065

**SCORE Office (Springfield)**
511 W. Capitol Ave., Ste. 302
Springfield, IL 62704
(217)492-4416
Fax: (217)492-4867

**SCORE Office (Sycamore)**
112 Somunak St.
Sycamore, IL 60178
(815)895-3456
Fax: (815)895-0125

**SCORE Office (University)**
Hwy. 50 & Stuenkel Rd. Ste. C3305
University Park, IL 60466
(708)534-5000
Fax: (708)534-8457

## Indiana

**SCORE Office (Anderson)**
205 W. 11th St.
Anderson, IN 46015
(317)642-0264

**SCORE Office (Bloomington)**
Star Center
216 W. Allen
Bloomington, IN 47403
(812)335-7334
E-mail: wtfische@indiana.edu
Website: http://www.brainfreezemedia.
com/score527/

**SCORE Office (South East Indiana)**
500 Franklin St.
Box 29
Columbus, IN 47201
(812)379-4457

**SCORE Office (Corydon)**
310 N. Elm St.
Corydon, IN 47112

(812)738-2137
Fax: (812)738-6438

**SCORE Office (Crown Point)**
Old Courthouse Sq. Ste. 206
PO Box 43
Crown Point, IN 46307
(219)663-1800

**SCORE Office (Elkhart)**
418 S. Main St.
Elkhart, IN 46515
(219)293-1531
Fax: (219)294-1859

**SCORE Office (Evansville)**
1100 W. Lloyd Expy., Ste. 105
Evansville, IN 47708
(812)426-6144

**SCORE Office (Fort Wayne)**
1300 S. Harrison St.
Ft. Wayne, IN 46802
(219)422-2601
Fax: (219)422-2601

**SCORE Office (Gary)**
973 W. 6th Ave., Rm. 326
Gary, IN 46402
(219)882-3918

**SCORE Office (Hammond)**
7034 Indianapolis Blvd.
Hammond, IN 46324
(219)931-1000
Fax: (219)845-9548

**SCORE Office (Indianapolis)**
429 N. Pennsylvania St., Ste. 100
Indianapolis, IN 46204-1873
(317)226-7264
Fax: (317)226-7259
E-mail: inscore@indy.net
Website: http://www.score-
indianapolis.org/

**SCORE Office (Jasper)**
PO Box 307
Jasper, IN 47547-0307
(812)482-6866

**SCORE Office (Kokomo/Howard
Counties)**
106 N. Washington St.
Kokomo, IN 46901
(765)457-5301
Fax: (765)452-4564

**SCORE Office (Logansport)**
300 E. Broadway, Ste. 103
Logansport, IN 46947
(219)753-6388

**SCORE Office (Madison)**
301 E. Main St.
Madison, IN 47250
(812)265-3135
Fax: (812)265-2923

**SCORE Office (Marengo)**
Rt. 1 Box 224D
Marengo, IN 47140
Fax: (812)365-2793

**SCORE Office (Marion/Grant Counties)**
215 S. Adams
Marion, IN 46952
(765)664-5107

**SCORE Office (Merrillville)**
255 W. 80th Pl.
Merrillville, IN 46410
(219)769-8180
Fax: (219)736-6223

**SCORE Office (Michigan City)**
200 E. Michigan Blvd.
Michigan City, IN 46360
(219)874-6221
Fax: (219)873-1204

**SCORE Office (South Central Indiana)**
4100 Charleston Rd.
New Albany, IN 47150-9538
(812)945-0066

**SCORE Office (Rensselaer)**
104 W. Washington
Rensselaer, IN 47978

**SCORE Office (Salem)**
210 N. Main St.
Salem, IN 47167
(812)883-4303
Fax: (812)883-1467

**SCORE Office (South Bend)**
300 N. Michigan St.
South Bend, IN 46601
(219)282-4350
E-mail: chair@southbend-score.org
Website: http://www.southbend-score.org/

**SCORE Office (Valparaiso)**
150 Lincolnway
Valparaiso, IN 46383
(219)462-1105
Fax: (219)469-5710

**SCORE Office (Vincennes)**
27 N. 3rd
PO Box 553
Vincennes, IN 47591
(812)882-6440
Fax: (812)882-6441

**SCORE Office (Wabash)**
PO Box 371
Wabash, IN 46992
(219)563-1168
Fax: (219)563-6920

## Iowa

**SCORE Office (Burlington)**
Federal Bldg.
300 N. Main St.
Burlington, IA 52601
(319)752-2967

**SCORE Office (Cedar Rapids)**
2750 1st Ave. NE, Ste 350
Cedar Rapids, IA 52401-1806
(319)362-6405
Fax: (319)362-7861
E:mail: score@scorecr.org
Website: http://www.scorecr.org

**SCORE Office (Illowa)**
333 4th Ave. S
Clinton, IA 52732
(319)242-5702

**SCORE Office (Council Bluffs)**
7 N. 6th St.
Council Bluffs, IA 51502
(712)325-1000

**SCORE Office (Northeast Iowa)**
3404 285th St.
Cresco, IA 52136
(319)547-3377

**SCORE Office (Des Moines)**
Federal Bldg., Rm. 749
210 Walnut St.
Des Moines, IA 50309-2186
(515)284-4760

**SCORE Office (Ft. Dodge)**
Federal Bldg., Rm. 436
205 S. 8th St.
Ft. Dodge, IA 50501
(515)955-2622

**SCORE Office (Independence)**
110 1st. St. east
Independence, IA 50644
(319)334-7178
Fax: (319)334-7179

**SCORE Office (Iowa City)**
210 Federal Bldg.
PO Box 1853
Iowa City, IA 52240-1853
(319)338-1662

**SCORE Office (Keokuk)**
401 Main St.
Pierce Bldg., No. 1
Keokuk, IA 52632
(319)524-5055

**SCORE Office (Central Iowa)**
Fisher Community College
709 S. Center
Marshalltown, IA 50158
(515)753-6645

**SCORE Office (River City)**
15 West State St.
Mason City, IA 50401
(515)423-5724

**SCORE Office (South Central)**
SBDC, Indian Hills Community College
525 Grandview Ave.
Ottumwa, IA 52501
(515)683-5127
Fax: (515)683-5263

**SCORE Office (Dubuque)**
10250 Sundown Rd.
Peosta, IA 52068
(319)556-5110

**SCORE Office (Southwest Iowa)**
614 W. Sheridan
Shenandoah, IA 51601
(712)246-3260

**SCORE Office (Sioux City)**
Federal Bldg.
320 6th St.
Sioux City, IA 51101
(712)277-2324
Fax: (712)277-2325

**SCORE Office (Iowa Lakes)**
122 W. 5th St.
Spencer, IA 51301
(712)262-3059

**SCORE Office (Vista)**
119 W. 6th St.
Storm Lake, IA 50588
(712)732-3780

**SCORE Office (Waterloo)**
215 E. 4th
Waterloo, IA 50703
(319)233-8431

## Kansas

**SCORE Office (Southwest Kansas)**
501 W. Spruce
Dodge City, KS 67801
(316)227-3119

**SCORE Office (Emporia)**
811 Homewood
Emporia, KS 66801
(316)342-1600

**SCORE Office (Golden Belt)**
1307 Williams
Great Bend, KS 67530
(316)792-2401

**SCORE Office (Hays)**
PO Box 400
Hays, KS 67601
(913)625-6595

**SCORE Office (Hutchinson)**
1 E. 9th St.
Hutchinson, KS 67501
(316)665-8468
Fax: (316)665-7619

**SCORE Office (Southeast Kansas)**
404 Westminster Pl.
PO Box 886
Independence, KS 67301
(316)331-4741

**SCORE Office (McPherson)**
306 N. Main
PO Box 616
McPherson, KS 67460
(316)241-3303

**SCORE Office (Salina)**
120 Ash St.
Salina, KS 67401
(785)243-4290
Fax: (785)243-1833

**SCORE Office (Topeka)**
1700 College
Topeka, KS 66621
(785)231-1010

**SCORE Office (Wichita)**
100 E. English, Ste. 510
Wichita, KS 67202
(316)269-6273
Fax: (316)269-6499

**SCORE Office (Ark Valley)**
205 E. 9th St.
Winfield, KS 67156
(316)221-1617

## Kentucky

**SCORE Office (Ashland)**
PO Box 830
Ashland, KY 41105
(606)329-8011
Fax: (606)325-4607

**SCORE Office (Bowling Green)**
812 State St.
PO Box 51
Bowling Green, KY 42101
(502)781-3200
Fax: (502)843-0458

**SCORE Office (Tri-Lakes)**
508 Barbee Way
Danville, KY 40422-1548
(606)231-9902

**SCORE Office (Glasgow)**
301 W. Main St.
Glasgow, KY 42141
(502)651-3161
Fax: (502)651-3122

**SCORE Office (Hazard)**
B & I Technical Center
100 Airport Gardens Rd.
Hazard, KY 41701
(606)439-5856
Fax: (606)439-1808

**SCORE Office (Lexington)**
410 W. Vine St., Ste. 290, Civic C
Lexington, KY 40507
(606)231-9902
Fax: (606)253-3190
E-mail: scorelex@uky.campus.mci.net

**SCORE Office (Louisville)**
188 Federal Office Bldg.
600 Dr. Martin L. King Jr. Pl.
Louisville, KY 40202
(502)582-5976

**SCORE Office (Madisonville)**
257 N. Main
Madisonville, KY 42431
(502)825-1399
Fax: (502)825-1396

**SCORE Office (Paducah)**
Federal Office Bldg.
501 Broadway, Rm. B-36
Paducah, KY 42001
(502)442-5685

## Louisiana

**SCORE Office (Central Louisiana)**
802 3rd St.
Alexandria, LA 71309
(318)442-6671

**SCORE Office (Baton Rouge)**
564 Laurel St.
PO Box 3217
Baton Rouge, LA 70801

(504)381-7130
Fax: (504)336-4306

**SCORE Office (North Shore)**
2 W. Thomas
Hammond, LA 70401
(504)345-4457
Fax: (504)345-4749

**SCORE Office (Lafayette)**
804 St. Mary Blvd.
Lafayette, LA 70505-1307
(318)233-2705
Fax: (318)234-8671
E-mail: score302@aol.com

**SCORE Office (Lake Charles)**
120 W. Pujo St.
Lake Charles, LA 70601
(318)433-3632

**SCORE Office (New Orleans)**
365 Canal St., Ste. 3100
New Orleans, LA 70130
(504)589-2356
Fax: (504)589-2339

**SCORE Office (Shreveport)**
400 Edwards St.
Shreveport, LA 71101
(318)677-2536
Fax: (318)677-2541

## Maine

**SCORE Office (Augusta)**
40 Western Ave.
Augusta, ME 04330
(207)622-8509

**SCORE Office (Bangor)**
Peabody Hall, Rm. 229
One College Cir.
Bangor, ME 04401
(207)941-9707

**SCORE Office (Central & Northern Arroostock)**
111 High St.
Caribou, ME 04736
(207)492-8010
Fax: (207)492-8010

**SCORE Office (Penquis)**
South St.
Dover Foxcroft, ME 04426
(207)564-7021

**SCORE Office (Maine Coastal)**
Mill Mall
Box 1105
Ellsworth, ME 04605-1105

(207)667-5800
E-mail: score@arcadia.net

**SCORE Office (Lewiston-Auburn)**
BIC of Maine-Bates Mill Complex
35 Canal St.
Lewiston, ME 04240-7764
(207)782-3708
Fax: (207)783-7745

**SCORE Office (Portland)**
66 Pearl St., Rm. 210
Portland, ME 04101
(207)772-1147
Fax: (207)772-5581
E-mail: Score53@score.maine.org
Website: http://www.score.maine.org/
chapter53/

**SCORE Office (Western Mountains)**
255 River St.
PO Box 252
Rumford, ME 04257-0252
(207)369-9976

**SCORE Office (Oxford Hills)**
166 Main St.
South Paris, ME 04281
(207)743-0499

## Maryland

**SCORE Office (Southern Maryland)**
2525 Riva Rd., Ste. 110
Annapolis, MD 21401
(410)266-9553
Fax: (410)573-0981
E-mail: score390@aol.com
Website: http://members.aol.com/
score390/index.htm

**SCORE Office (Baltimore)**
The City Crescent Bldg., 6th Fl.
10 S. Howard St.
Baltimore, MD 21201
(410)962-2233
Fax: (410)962-1805

**SCORE Office (Bel Air)**
108 S. Bond St.
Bel Air, MD 21014
(410)838-2020
Fax: (410)893-4715

**SCORE Office (Bethesda)**
7910 Woodmont Ave., Ste. 1204
Bethesda, MD 20814
(301)652-4900
Fax: (301)657-1973

**SCORE Office (Bowie)**
6670 Race Track Rd.
Bowie, MD 20715
(301)262-0920
Fax: (301)262-0921

**SCORE Office (Dorchester County)**
203 Sunburst Hwy.
Cambridge, MD 21613
(410)228-3575

**SCORE Office (Upper Shore)**
210 Marlboro Ave.
Easton, MD 21601
(410)822-4606
Fax: (410)822-7922

**SCORE Office (Frederick County)**
43A S. Market St.
Frederick, MD 21701
(301)662-8723
Fax: (301)846-4427

**SCORE Office (Gaithersburg)**
9 Park Ave.
Gaithersburg, MD 20877
(301)840-1400
Fax: (301)963-3918

**SCORE Office (Glen Burnie)**
103 Crain Hwy. SE
Glen Burnie, MD 21061
(410)766-8282
Fax: (410)766-9722

**SCORE Office (Hagerstown)**
111 W. Washington St.
Hagerstown, MD 21740
(301)739-2015
Fax: (301)739-1278

**SCORE Office (Laurel)**
7901 Sandy Spring Rd. Ste. 501
Laurel, MD 20707
(301)725-4000
Fax: (301)725-0776

**SCORE Office (Salisbury)**
300 E. Main St.
Salisbury, MD 21801
(410)749-0185
Fax: (410)860-9925

## Massachusetts

**SCORE Office (NE Massachusetts)**
100 Cummings Ctr., Ste. 101 K
Beverly, MA 01923
(978)922-9441
Website: http://www1.shore.net/~score/

**SCORE Office (Boston)**
10 Causeway St., Rm. 265
Boston, MA 02222-1093
(617)565-5591
Fax: (617)565-5598
E-mail: boston-score-20@worldnet.att.net
Website: http://www.scoreboston.org/

**SCORE office (Bristol/Plymouth County)**
53 N. 6th St., Federal Bldg.
Bristol, MA 02740
(508)994-5093

**SCORE Office (SE Massachusetts)**
60 School St.
Brockton, MA 02401
(508)587-2673
Fax: (508)587-1340
Website: http://www.metrosouth
chamber.com/score.html

**SCORE Office (North Adams)**
820 N. State Rd.
Cheshire, MA 01225
(413)743-5100

**SCORE Office (Clinton Satellite)**
1 Green St.
Clinton, MA 01510
Fax: (508)368-7689

**SCORE Office (Greenfield)**
PO Box 898
Greenfield, MA 01302
(413)773-5463
Fax: (413)773-7008

**SCORE Office (Haverhill)**
87 Winter St.
Haverhill, MA 01830
(508)373-5663
Fax: (508)373-8060

**SCORE Office (Hudson Satellite)**
PO Box 578
Hudson, MA 01749
(508)568-0360
Fax: (508)568-0360

**SCORE Office (Cape Cod)**
Independence Pk., Ste. 5B
270 Communications Way
Hyannis, MA 02601
(508)775-4884
Fax: (508)790-2540

**SCORE Office (Lawrence)**
264 Essex St.
Lawrence, MA 01840
(508)686-0900
Fax: (508)794-9953

**SCORE Office (Leominster Satellite)**
110 Erdman Way
Leominster, MA 01453
(508)840-4300
Fax: (508)840-4896

**SCORE Office (Bristol/Plymouth Counties)**
53 N. 6th St., Federal Bldg.
New Bedford, MA 02740
(508)994-5093

**SCORE Office (Newburyport)**
29 State St.
Newburyport, MA 01950
(617)462-6680

**SCORE Office (Pittsfield)**
66 West St.
Pittsfield, MA 01201
(413)499-2485

**SCORE Office (Haverhill-Salem)**
32 Derby Sq.
Salem, MA 01970
(508)745-0330
Fax: (508)745-3855

**SCORE Office (Springfield)**
1350 Main St.
Federal Bldg.
Springfield, MA 01103
(413)785-0314

**SCORE Office (Carver)**
12 Taunton Green, Ste. 201
Taunton, MA 02780
(508)824-4068
Fax: (508)824-4069

**SCORE Office (Worcester)**
33 Waldo St.
Worcester, MA 01608
(508)753-2929
Fax: (508)754-8560

## Michigan

**SCORE Office (Allegan)**
PO Box 338
Allegan, MI 49010
(616)673-2479

**SCORE Office (Ann Arbor)**
425 S. Main St., Ste. 103
Ann Arbor, MI 48104
(313)665-4433

**SCORE Office (Battle Creek)**
34 W. Jackson Ste. 4A
Battle Creek, MI 49017-3505

(616)962-4076
Fax: (616)962-6309

**SCORE Office (Cadillac)**
222 Lake St.
Cadillac, MI 49601
(616)775-9776
Fax: (616)768-4255

**SCORE Office (Detroit)**
477 Michigan Ave., Rm. 515
Detroit, MI 48226
(313)226-7947
Fax: (313)226-3448

**SCORE Office (Flint)**
708 Root Rd., Rm. 308
Flint, MI 48503
(810)233-6846

**SCORE Office (Grand Rapids)**
111 Pearl St. NW
Grand Rapids, MI 49503-2831
(616)771-0305
Fax: (616)771-0328
E-mail: scoreone@iserv.net
Website: http://www.iserv.net/
~scoreone/

**SCORE Office (Holland)**
480 State St.
Holland, MI 49423
(616)396-9472

**SCORE Office (Jackson)**
209 East Washington
PO Box 80
Jackson, MI 49204
(517)782-8221
Fax: (517)782-0061

**SCORE Office (Kalamazoo)**
345 W. Michigan Ave.
Kalamazoo, MI 49007
(616)381-5382
Fax: (616)384-0096
E-mail: score@nucleus.net

**SCORE Office (Lansing)**
117 E. Allegan
PO Box 14030
Lansing, MI 48901
(517)487-6340
Fax: (517)484-6910

**SCORE Office (Livonia)**
15401 Farmington Rd.
Livonia, MI 48154
(313)427-2122
Fax: (313)427-6055

**SCORE Office (Madison Heights)**
26345 John R
Madison Heights, MI 48071
(810)542-5010
Fax: (810)542-6821

**SCORE Office (Monroe)**
111 E. 1st
Monroe, MI 48161
(313)242-3366
Fax: (313)242-7253

**SCORE Office (Mt. Clemens)**
58 S/B Gratiot
Mt. Clemens, MI 48043
(810)463-1528
Fax: (810)463-6541

**SCORE Office (Muskegon)**
PO Box 1087
230 Terrace Plz.
Muskegon, MI 49443
(616)722-3751
Fax: (616)728-7251

**SCORE Office (Petoskey)**
401 E. Mitchell St.
Petoskey, MI 49770
(616)347-4150

**SCORE Office (Pontiac)**
Executive Office Bldg.
1200 N. Telegraph Rd.
Pontiac, MI 48341
(810)975-9555

**SCORE Office (Pontiac)**
PO Box 430025
Pontiac, MI 48343
(810)335-9600

**SCORE Office (Port Huron)**
920 Pinegrove Ave.
Port Huron, MI 48060
(810)985-7101

**SCORE Office (Rochester)**
71 Walnut Ste. 110
Rochester, MI 48307
(810)651-6700
Fax: (810)651-5270

**SCORE Office (Saginaw)**
901 S. Washington Ave.
Saginaw, MI 48601
(517)752-7161
Fax: (517)752-9055

**SCORE Office (Upper Peninsula)**
2581 I-75 Business Spur
Sault Ste. Marie, MI 49783
(906)632-3301

**SCORE Office (Southfield)**
21000 W. 10 Mile Rd.
Southfield, MI 48075
(810)204-3050
Fax: (810)204-3099

**SCORE Office (Traverse City)**
202 E. Grandview Pkwy.
PO Box 387
Traverse City, MI 49685
(616)947-5075
Fax: (616)946-2565

**SCORE Office (Warren)**
30500 Van Dyke, Ste. 118
Warren, MI 48093
(810)751-3939

## Minnesota

**SCORE Office (Aitkin)**
Aitkin, MN 56431
(218)741-3906

**SCORE Office (Albert Lea)**
202 N. Broadway Ave.
Albert Lea, MN 56007
(507)373-7487

**SCORE Office (Austin)**
PO Box 864
Austin, MN 55912
(507)437-4561
Fax: (507)437-4869

**SCORE Office (South Metro)**
Ames Business Ctr.
2500 W. County Rd., No. 42
Burnsville, MN 55337
(612)898-5645
Fax: (612)435-6972
E-mail: southmetro@scoreminn.org
Website: http://www.scoreminn.org/
southmetro/

**SCORE Office (Duluth)**
1717 Minnesota Ave.
Duluth, MN 55802
(218)727-8286
Fax: (218)727-3113
E-mail: duluth@scoreminn.org
Website: http://www.scoreminn.org

**SCORE Office (Fairmont)**
PO Box 826
Fairmont, MN 56031
(507)235-5547
Fax: (507)235-8411

**SCORE Office (Southwest Minnesota)**
112 Riverfront St.

Box 999
Mankato, MN 56001
(507)345-4519
Fax: (507)345-4451
Website: http://www.scoreminn.org/

**SCORE Office (Minneapolis)**
North Plaza Bldg., Ste. 51
5217 Wayzata Blvd.
Minneapolis, MN 55416
(612)591-0539
Fax: (612)544-0436
Website: http://www.scoreminn.org/

**SCORE Office (Owatonna)**
PO Box 331
Owatonna, MN 55060
(507)451-7970
Fax: (507)451-7972

**SCORE Office (Red Wing)**
2000 W. Main St., Ste. 324
Red Wing, MN 55066
(612)388-4079

**SCORE Office (Southeastern Minnesota)**
220 S. Broadway, Ste. 100
Rochester, MN 55901
(507)288-1122
Fax: (507)282-8960
Website: http://www.scoreminn.org/

**SCORE Office (Brainerd)**
St. Cloud, MN 56301

**SCORE Office (Central Area)**
1527 Northway Dr.
St. Cloud, MN 56301
(320)240-1332
Fax: (320)255-9050
Website: http://www.scoreminn.org/

**SCORE Office (St. Paul)**
350 St. Peter St., No. 295
Lowry Professional Bldg.
St. Paul, MN 55102
(651)223-5010
Fax: (651)223-5048
Website: http://www.scoreminn.org/

**SCORE Office (Winona)**
Box 870
Winona, MN 55987
(507)452-2272
Fax: (507)454-8814

**SCORE Office (Worthington)**
1121 3rd Ave.
Worthington, MN 56187
(507)372-2919
Fax: (507)372-2827

## Mississippi

**SCORE Office (Delta)**
915 Washington Ave.
PO Box 933
Greenville, MS 38701
(601)378-3141

**SCORE Office (Gulfcoast)**
1 Government Plaza
2909 13th St., Ste. 203
Gulfport, MS 39501
(228)863-0054

**SCORE Office (Jackson)**
1st Jackson Center, Ste. 400
101 W. Capitol St.
Jackson, MS 39201
(601)965-5533

**SCORE Office (Meridian)**
5220 16th Ave.
Meridian, MS 39305
(601)482-4412

## Missouri

**SCORE Office (Lake of the Ozark)**
University Extension
113 Kansas St.
PO Box 1405
Camdenton, MO 65020
(573)346-2644
Fax: (573)346-2694
E-mail: score@cdoc.net
Website: http://sites.cdoc.net/score/

**Chamber of Commerce (Cape Girardeau)**
PO Box 98
Cape Girardeau, MO 63702-0098
(314)335-3312

**SCORE Office (Mid-Missouri)**
1705 Halstead Ct.
Columbia, MO 65203
(573)874-1132

**SCORE Office (Ozark-Gateway)**
1486 Glassy Rd.
Cuba, MO 65453-1640
(573)885-4954

**SCORE Office (Kansas City)**
323 W. 8th St., Ste. 104
Kansas City, MO 64105
(816)374-6675
Fax: (816)374-6692
E-mail: SCOREBIC@AOL.COM
Website: http://www.crn.org/score/

**SCORE Office (Sedalia)**
Lucas Place
323 W. 8th St., Ste.104
Kansas City, MO 64105
(816)374-6675

**SCORE office (Tri-Lakes)**
PO Box 1148
Kimberling, MO 65686
(417)739-3041

**SCORE Office (Tri-Lakes)**
HCRI Box 85
Lampe, MO 65681
(417)858-6798

**SCORE Office (Mexico)**
111 N. Washington St.
Mexico, MO 65265
(314)581-2765

**SCORE Office (Southeast Missouri)**
Rte. 1, Box 280
Neelyville, MO 63954
(573)989-3577

**SCORE office (Poplar Bluff Area)**
806 Emma St.
Poplar Bluff, MO 63901
(573)686-8892

**SCORE Office (St. Joseph)**
3003 Frederick Ave.
St. Joseph, MO 64506
(816)232-4461

**SCORE Office (St. Louis)**
815 Olive St., Rm. 242
St. Louis, MO 63101-1569
(314)539-6970
Fax: (314)539-3785
E-mail: info@stlscore.org
Website: http://www.stlscore.org/

**SCORE Office (Lewis & Clark)**
425 Spencer Rd.
St. Peters, MO 63376
(314)928-2900
Fax: (314)928-2900
E-mail: score01@mail.win.org

**SCORE Office (Springfield)**
620 S. Glenstone, Ste. 110
Springfield, MO 65802-3200
(417)864-7670
Fax: (417)864-4108

**SCORE office (Southeast Kansas)**
1206 W. First St.
Webb City, MO 64870
(417)673-3984

## Montana

**SCORE Office (Billings)**
815 S. 27th St.
Billings, MT 59101
(406)245-4111

**SCORE Office (Bozeman)**
1205 E. Main St.
Bozeman, MT 59715
(406)586-5421

**SCORE Office (Butte)**
1000 George St.
Butte, MT 59701
(406)723-3177

**SCORE Office (Great Falls)**
710 First Ave. N
Great Falls, MT 59401
(406)761-4434
E-mail: scoregtf@in.tch.com

**SCORE Office (Havre, Montana)**
518 First St.
Havre, MT 59501
(406)265-4383

**SCORE Office (Helena)**
Federal Bldg.
301 S. Park
Helena, MT 59626-0054
(406)441-1081

**SCORE Office (Kalispell)**
2 Main St.
Kalispell, MT 59901
(406)756-5271
Fax: (406)752-6665

**SCORE Office (Missoula)**
723 Ronan
Missoula, MT 59806
(406)327-8806
E-mail: score@safeshop.com
Website: http://missoula.bigsky.net/
score/

## Nebraska

**SCORE Office (Columbus)**
Columbus, NE 68601
(402)564-2769

**SCORE Office (Fremont)**
92 W. 5th St.
Fremont, NE 68025
(402)721-2641

**SCORE Office (Hastings)**
Hastings, NE 68901
(402)463-3447

**SCORE Office (Lincoln)**
8800 O St.
Lincoln, NE 68520
(402)437-2409

**SCORE Office (Panhandle)**
150549 CR 30
Minatare, NE 69356
(308)632-2133
Website: http://www.tandt.com/
SCORE

**SCORE Office (Norfolk)**
3209 S. 48th Ave.
Norfolk, NE 68106
(402)564-2769

**SCORE Office (North Platte)**
3301 W. 2nd St.
North Platte, NE 69101
(308)532-4466

**SCORE Office (Omaha)**
11145 Mill Valley Rd.
Omaha, NE 68154
(402)221-3606
Fax: (402)221-3680
E-mail: infoctr@ne.uswest.net
Website: http://www.tandt.com/score/

## Nevada

**SCORE Office (Incline Village)**
969 Tahoe Blvd.
Incline Village, NV 89451
(702)831-7327
Fax: (702)832-1605

**SCORE Office (Carson City)**
301 E. Stewart
PO Box 7527
Las Vegas, NV 89125
(702)388-6104

**SCORE Office (Las Vegas)**
300 Las Vegas Blvd. S, Ste. 1100
Las Vegas, NV 89101
(702)388-6104

**SCORE Office (Northern Nevada)**
SBDC, College of Business
Administration
Univ. of Nevada
Reno, NV 89557-0100
(702)784-4436
Fax: (702)784-4337

## New Hampshire

**SCORE Office (North Country)**
PO Box 34

Berlin, NH 03570
(603)752-1090

**SCORE Office (Concord)**
143 N. Main St., Rm. 202A
PO Box 1258
Concord, NH 03301
(603)225-1400
Fax: (603)225-1409

**SCORE Office (Dover)**
299 Central Ave.
Dover, NH 03820
(603)742-2218
Fax: (603)749-6317

**SCORE Office (Monadnock)**
34 Mechanic St.
Keene, NH 03431-3421
(603)352-0320

**SCORE Office (Lakes Region)**
67 Water St., Ste. 105
Laconia, NH 03246
(603)524-9168

**SCORE Office (Upper Valley)**
Citizens Bank Bldg., Rm. 310
20 W. Park St.
Lebanon, NH 03766
(603)448-3491
Fax: (603)448-1908
E-mail: billt@valley.net
Website: http://www.valley.net/~score/

**SCORE Office (Merrimack Valley)**
275 Chestnut St., Rm. 618
Manchester, NH 03103
(603)666-7561
Fax: (603)666-7925

**SCORE Office (Mt. Washington Valley)**
PO Box 1066
North Conway, NH 03818
(603)383-0800

**SCORE Office (Seacoast)**
195 Commerce Way, Unit-A
Portsmouth, NH 03801-3251
(603)433-0575

## New Jersey

**SCORE Office (Somerset)**
Paritan Valley Community College,
Rte. 28
Branchburg, NJ 08807
(908)218-8874
E-mail: nj-score@grizbiz.com.
Website: http://www.nj-score.org/

**SCORE Office (Chester)**
5 Old Mill Rd.
Chester, NJ 07930
(908)879-7080

**SCORE Office
(Greater Princeton)**
4 A George Washington Dr.
Cranbury, NJ 08512
(609)520-1776

**SCORE Office (Freehold)**
36 W. Main St.
Freehold, NJ 07728
(908)462-3030
Fax: (908)462-2123

**SCORE Office (North West)**
Picantinny Innovation Ctr.
3159 Schrader Rd.
Hamburg, NJ 07419
(973)209-8525
Fax: (973)209-7252
E-mail: nj-score@grizbiz.com
Website: http://www.nj-score.org/

**SCORE Office (Monmouth)**
765 Newman Springs Rd.
Lincroft, NJ 07738
(908)224-2573
E-mail: nj-score@grizbiz.com
Website: http://www.nj-score.org/

**SCORE Office (Manalapan)**
125 Symmes Dr.
Manalapan, NJ 07726
(908)431-7220

**SCORE Office (Jersey City)**
2 Gateway Ctr., 4th Fl.
Newark, NJ 07102
(973)645-3982
Fax: (973)645-2375

**SCORE Office (Newark)**
2 Gateway Center, 15th Fl.
Newark, NJ 07102-5553
(973)645-3982
Fax: (973)645-2375
E-mail: nj-score@grizbiz.com
Website: http://www.nj-score.org

**SCORE Office (Bergen County)**
327 E. Ridgewood Ave.
Paramus, NJ 07652
(201)599-6090
E-mail: nj-score@grizbiz.com
Website: http://www.nj-score.org/

**SCORE Office (Pennsauken)**
4900 Rte. 70

Pennsauken, NJ 08109
(609)486-3421

**SCORE Office (Southern New Jersey)**
4900 Rte. 70
Pennsauken, NJ 08109
(609)486-3421
E-mail: nj-score@grizbiz.com
Website: http://www.nj-score.org/

**SCORE Office (Greater Princeton)**
216 Rockingham Row
Princeton Forrestal Village
Princeton, NJ 08540
(609)520-1776
Fax: (609)520-9107
E-mail: nj-score@grizbiz.com
Website: http://www.nj-score.org/

**SCORE Office (Shrewsbury)**
Hwy. 35
Shrewsbury, NJ 07702
(908)842-5995
Fax: (908)219-6140

**SCORE Office (Ocean County)**
33 Washington St.
Toms River, NJ 08754
(732)505-6033
E-mail: nj-score@grizbiz.com
Website: http://www.nj-score.org/

**SCORE Office (Wall)**
2700 Allaire Rd.
Wall, NJ 07719
(908)449-8877

**SCORE Office (Wayne)**
2055 Hamburg Tpke.
Wayne, NJ 07470
(201)831-7788
Fax: (201)831-9112

## New Mexico

**SCORE Office (Albuquerque)**
525 Buena Vista, SE
Albuquerque, NM 87106
(505)272-7999
Fax: (505)272-7963

**SCORE Office (Las Cruces)**
Loretto Towne Center
505 S. Main St., Ste. 125
Las Cruces, NM 88001
(505)523-5627
Fax: (505)524-2101
E-mail: score.397@zianet.com

**SCORE Office (Roswell)**
Federal Bldg., Rm. 237

Roswell, NM 88201
(505)625-2112
Fax: (505)623-2545

**SCORE Office (Santa Fe)**
Montoya Federal Bldg.
120 Federal Place, Rm. 307
Santa Fe, NM 87501
(505)988-6302
Fax: (505)988-6300

## New York

**SCORE Office (Northeast)**
1 Computer Dr. S
Albany, NY 12205
(518)446-1118
Fax: (518)446-1228

**SCORE Office (Auburn)**
30 South St.
PO Box 675
Auburn, NY 13021
(315)252-7291

**SCORE Office (South Tier Binghamton)**
Metro Center, 2nd Fl.
49 Court St.
PO Box 995
Binghamton, NY 13902
(607)772-8860

**SCORE Office (Queens County City)**
12055 Queens Blvd., Rm. 333
Borough Hall, NY 11424
(718)263-8961

**SCORE Office (Buffalo)**
Federal Bldg., Rm. 1311
111 W. Huron St.
Buffalo, NY 14202
(716)551-4301
Website: http://www2.pcom.net/score/
buf45.html

**SCORE Office (Canandaigua)**
Chamber of Commerce Bldg.
113 S. Main St.
Canandaigua, NY 14424
(716)394-4400
Fax: (716)394-4546

**SCORE Office (Chemung)**
333 E. Water St., 4th Fl.
Elmira, NY 14901
(607)734-3358

**SCORE Office (Geneva)**
Chamber of Commerce Bldg.
PO Box 587

Geneva, NY 14456
(315)789-1776
Fax: (315)789-3993

**SCORE Office (Glens Falls)**
84 Broad St.
Glens Falls, NY 12801
(518)798-8463
Fax: (518)745-1433

**SCORE Office (Orange County)**
40 Matthews St.
Goshen, NY 10924
(914)294-8080
Fax: (914)294-6121

**SCORE Office (Huntington Area)**
151 W. Carver St.
Huntington, NY 11743
(516)423-6100

**SCORE Office (Tompkins County)**
904 E. Shore Dr.
Ithaca, NY 14850
(607)273-7080

**SCORE Office (Long Island City)**
120-55 Queens Blvd.
Jamaica, NY 11424
(718)263-8961
Fax: (718)263-9032

**SCORE Office (Chatauqua)**
101 W. 5th St.
Jamestown, NY 14701
(716)484-1103

**SCORE Office (Westchester)**
2 Caradon Ln.
Katonah, NY 10536
(914)948-3907
Fax: (914)948-4645
E-mail: score@w-w-w.com
Website: http://w-w-w.com/score/

**SCORE Office (Queens County)**
Queens Borough Hall
120-55 Queens Blvd. Rm. 333
Kew Gardens, NY 11424
(718)263-8961
Fax: (718)263-9032

**SCORE Office (Brookhaven)**
3233 Rte. 112
Medford, NY 11763
(516)451-6563
Fax: (516)451-6925

**SCORE Office (Melville)**
35 Pinelawn Rd., Rm. 207-W
Melville, NY 11747
(516)454-0771

**SCORE Office (Nassau County)**
400 County Seat Dr., No. 140
Mineola, NY 11501
(516)571-3303
E-mail: Counse1998@aol.com
Website: http://members.aol.com/
Counse1998/Default.htm

**SCORE Office (Mt. Vernon)**
4 N. 7th Ave.
Mt. Vernon, NY 10550
(914)667-7500

**SCORE Office (New York)**
26 Federal Plz., Rm. 3100
New York, NY 10278
(212)264-4507
Fax: (212)264-4963
E-mail: score1000@erols.com
Website: http://users.erols.com/
score-nyc/

**SCORE Office (Newburgh)**
47 Grand St.
Newburgh, NY 12550
(914)562-5100

**SCORE Office (Owego)**
188 Front St.
Owego, NY 13827
(607)687-2020

**SCORE Office (Peekskill)**
1 S. Division St.
Peekskill, NY 10566
(914)737-3600
Fax: (914)737-0541

**SCORE Office (Penn Yan)**
2375 Rte. 14A
Penn Yan, NY 14527
(315)536-3111

**SCORE Office (Dutchess)**
110 Main St.
Poughkeepsie, NY 12601
(914)454-1700

**SCORE Office (Rochester)**
601 Keating Federal Bldg., Rm. 410
100 State St.
Rochester, NY 14614
(716)263-6473
Fax: (716)263-3146
Website: http://www.ggw.org/score/

**SCORE Office (Saranac Lake)**
30 Main St.
Saranac Lake, NY 12983
(315)448-0415

**SCORE Office (Suffolk)**
286 Main St.
Setauket, NY 11733
(516)751-3886

**SCORE Office (Staten Island)**
130 Bay St.
Staten Island, NY 10301
(718)727-1221

**SCORE Office (Ulster)**
Clinton Bldg., Rm. 107
Stone Ridge, NY 12484
(914)687-5035
Fax: (914)687-5015
Website: http://www.scoreulster.org/

**SCORE Office (Syracuse)**
401 S. Salina, 5th Fl.
Syracuse, NY 13202
(315)471-9393

**SCORE Office (Utica)**
SUNY Institute of Technology, Route 12
Utica, NY 13504-3050
(315)792-7553

**SCORE Office (Watertown)**
518 Davidson St.
Watertown, NY 13601
(315)788-1200
Fax: (315)788-8251

## North Carolina

**SCORE office (Asheboro)**
317 E. Dixie Dr.
Asheboro, NC 27203
(336)626-2626
Fax: (336)626-7077

**SCORE Office (Asheville)**
Federal Bldg., Rm. 259
151 Patton
Asheville, NC 28801-5770
(828)271-4786
Fax: (828)271-4009

**SCORE Office (Chapel Hill)**
104 S. Estes Dr.
PO Box 2897
Chapel Hill, NC 27514
(919)967-7075

**SCORE Office (Coastal Plains)**
PO Box 2897
Chapel Hill, NC 27515
(919)967-7075
Fax: (919)968-6874

**SCORE Office (Charlotte)**
200 N. College St., Ste. A-2015

Charlotte, NC 28202
(704)344-6576
Fax: (704)344-6769
E-mail: CharlotteSCORE47@AOL.com
Website: http://www.charweb.org/
business/score/

**SCORE Office (Durham)**
411 W. Chapel Hill St.
Durham, NC 27707
(919)541-2171

**SCORE Office (Gastonia)**
PO Box 2168
Gastonia, NC 28053
(704)864-2621
Fax: (704)854-8723

**SCORE Office (Greensboro)**
400 W. Market St., Ste. 103
Greensboro, NC 27401-2241
(910)333-5399

**SCORE Office (Henderson)**
PO Box 917
Henderson, NC 27536
(919)492-2061
Fax: (919)430-0460

**SCORE Office (Hendersonville)**
Federal Bldg., Rm. 108
W. 4th Ave. & Church St.
Hendersonville, NC 28792
(828)693-8702
E-mail: score@circle.net
Website: http://www.wncguide.com/
score/Welcome.html

**SCORE Office (Unifour)**
PO Box 1828
Hickory, NC 28603
(704)328-6111

**SCORE Office (High Point)**
1101 N. Main St.
High Point, NC 27262
(336)882-8625
Fax: (336)889-9499

**SCORE Office (Outer Banks)**
Collington Rd. and Mustain
Kill Devil Hills, NC 27948
(252)441-8144

**SCORE Office (Down East)**
312 S. Front St., Ste. 6
New Bern, NC 28560
(252)633-6688
Fax: (252)633-9608

**SCORE Office (Kinston)**
PO Box 95

New Bern, NC 28561
(919)633-6688

**SCORE Office (Raleigh)**
Century Post Office Bldg., Ste. 306
300 Federal St. Mall
Raleigh, NC 27601
(919)856-4739
E-mail: jendres@ibm.net
Website: http://www.intrex.net/score96/
score96.htm

**SCORE Office (Sanford)**
1801 Nash St.
Sanford, NC 27330
(919)774-6442
Fax: (919)776-8739

**SCORE Office (Sandhills Area)**
1480 Hwy. 15-501
PO Box 458
Southern Pines, NC 28387
(910)692-3926

**SCORE Office (Wilmington)**
Corps of Engineers Bldg.
96 Darlington Ave., Ste. 207
Wilmington, NC 28403
(910)815-4576
Fax: (910)815-4658

## North Dakota

**SCORE Office
(Bismarck-Mandan)**
700 E. Main Ave., 2nd Fl.
PO Box 5509
Bismarck, ND 58506-5509
(701)250-4303

**SCORE Office (Fargo)**
657 2nd Ave., Rm. 225
Fargo, ND 58108-3083
(701)239-5677

**SCORE Office (Upper Red River)**
4275 Technology Dr., Rm. 156
Grand Forks, ND 58202-8372
(701)777-3051

**SCORE Office (Minot)**
100 1st St. SW
Minot, ND 58701-3846
(701)852-6883
Fax: (701)852-6905

## Ohio

**SCORE Office (Akron)**
1 Cascade Plz., 7th Fl.
Akron, OH 44308

(330)379-3163
Fax: (330)379-3164

**SCORE Office (Ashland)**
Gill Center
47 W. Main St.
Ashland, OH 44805
(419)281-4584

**SCORE Office (Canton)**
116 Cleveland Ave. NW, Ste. 601
Canton, OH 44702-1720
(330)453-6047

**SCORE Office (Chillicothe)**
165 S. Paint St.
Chillicothe, OH 45601
(614)772-4530

**SCORE Office (Cincinnati)**
Ameritrust Bldg., Rm. 850
525 Vine St.
Cincinnati, OH 45202
(513)684-2812
Fax: (513)684-3251
Website: http://www.score.
chapter34.org/

**SCORE Office (Cleveland)**
Eaton Center, Ste. 620
1100 Superior Ave.
Cleveland, OH 44114-2507
(216)522-4194
Fax: (216)522-4844

**SCORE Office (Columbus)**
2 Nationwide Plz., Ste. 1400
Columbus, OH 43215-2542
(614)469-2357
Fax: (614)469-2391
E-mail: info@scorecolumbus.org
Website: http://www.scorecolumbus.org/

**SCORE Office (Dayton)**
Dayton Federal Bldg., Rm. 505
200 W. Second St.
Dayton, OH 45402-1430
(513)225-2887
Fax: (513)225-7667

**SCORE Office (Defiance)**
615 W. 3rd St.
PO Box 130
Defiance, OH 43512
(419)782-7946

**SCORE Office (Findlay)**
123 E. Main Cross St.
PO Box 923
Findlay, OH 45840
(419)422-3314

**SCORE Office (Lima)**
147 N. Main St.
Lima, OH 45801
(419)222-6045
Fax: (419)229-0266

**SCORE Office (Mansfield)**
55 N. Mulberry St.
Mansfield, OH 44902
(419)522-3211

**SCORE Office (Marietta)**
Thomas Hall
Marietta, OH 45750
(614)373-0268

**SCORE Office (Medina)**
County Administrative Bldg.
144 N. Broadway
Medina, OH 44256
(216)764-8650

**SCORE Office (Licking County)**
50 W. Locust St.
Newark, OH 43055
(614)345-7458

**SCORE Office (Salem)**
2491 State Rte. 45 S
Salem, OH 44460
(216)332-0361

**SCORE Office (Tiffin)**
62 S. Washington St.
Tiffin, OH 44883
(419)447-4141
Fax: (419)447-5141

**SCORE Office (Toledo)**
608 Madison Ave, Ste. 910
Toledo, OH 43624
(419)259-7598
Fax: (419)259-6460

**SCORE Office (Heart of Ohio)**
377 W. Liberty St.
Wooster, OH 44691
(330)262-5735
Fax: (330)262-5745

**SCORE Office (Youngstown)**
306 Williamson Hall
Youngstown, OH 44555
(330)746-2687

## Oklahoma

**SCORE Office (Anadarko)**
PO Box 366
Anadarko, OK 73005
(405)247-6651

**SCORE Office (Ardmore)**
410 W. Main
Ardmore, OK 73401
(580)226-2620

**SCORE Office (Northeast Oklahoma)**
210 S. Main
Grove, OK 74344
(918)787-2796
Fax: (918)787-2796
E-mail: Score595@greencis.net

**SCORE Office (Lawton)**
4500 W. Lee Blvd., Bldg. 100, Ste. 107
Lawton, OK 73505
(580)353-8727
Fax: (580)250-5677

**SCORE Office (Oklahoma City)**
210 Park Ave., No. 1300
Oklahoma City, OK 73102
(405)231-5163
Fax: (405)231-4876
E-mail: score212@usa.net

**SCORE Office (Stillwater)**
439 S. Main
Stillwater, OK 74074
(405)372-5573
Fax: (405)372-4316

**SCORE Office (Tulsa)**
616 S. Boston, Ste. 406
Tulsa, OK 74119
(918)581-7462
Fax: (918)581-6908
Website: http://www.ionet.net/~tulscore/

## Oregon

**SCORE Office (Bend)**
63085 N. Hwy. 97
Bend, OR 97701
(541)923-2849
Fax: (541)330-6900

**SCORE Office (Willamette)**
1401 Willamette St.
PO Box 1107
Eugene, OR 97401-4003
(541)465-6600
Fax: (541)484-4942

**SCORE Office (Florence)**
3149 Oak St.
Florence, OR 97439
(503)997-8444
Fax: (503)997-8448

**SCORE Office (Southern Oregon)**
33 N. Central Ave., Ste. 216

Medford, OR 97501
(541)776-4220
E-mail: pgr134f@prodigy.com

**SCORE Office (Portland)**
1515 SW 5th Ave., Ste. 1050
Portland, OR 97201
(503)326-3441
Fax: (503)326-2808
E-mail: gr134@prodigy.com

**SCORE Office (Salem)**
416 State St. (corner of Liberty)
Salem, OR 97301
(503)370-2896

## Pennsylvania

**SCORE Office (Altoona-Blair)**
1212 12th Ave.
Altoona, PA 16601-3493
(814)943-8151

**SCORE Office (Lehigh Valley)**
Rauch Bldg. 37
Lehigh University
621 Taylor St.
Bethlehem, PA 18015
(610)758-4496
Fax: (610)758-5205

**SCORE Office (Butler County)**
100 N. Main St.
PO Box 1082
Butler, PA 16003
(412)283-2222
Fax: (412)283-0224

**SCORE Office (Harrisburg)**
4211 Trindle Rd.
Camp Hill, PA 17011
(717)761-4304
Fax: (717)761-4315

**SCORE Office (Cumberland Valley)**
75 S. 2nd St.
Chambersburg, PA 17201
(717)264-2935

**SCORE Office (Monroe County-Stroudsburg)**
556 Main St.
East Stroudsburg, PA 18301
(717)421-4433

**SCORE Office (Erie)**
120 W. 9th St.
Erie, PA 16501
(814)871-5650
Fax: (814)871-7530

**SCORE Office (Bucks County)**
409 Hood Blvd.
Fairless Hills, PA 19030
(215)943-8850
Fax: (215)943-7404

**SCORE Office (Hanover)**
146 Broadway
Hanover, PA 17331
(717)637-6130
Fax: (717)637-9127

**SCORE Office (Harrisburg)**
100 Chestnut, Ste. 309
Harrisburg, PA 17101
(717)782-3874

**SCORE Office (East Montgomery County)**
Baederwood Shopping Center
1653 The Fairways, Ste. 204
Jenkintown, PA 19046
(215)885-3027

**SCORE Office (Kittanning)**
2 Butler Rd.
Kittanning, PA 16201
(412)543-1305
Fax: (412)543-6206

**SCORE Office (Lancaster)**
118 W. Chestnut St.
Lancaster, PA 17603
(717)397-3092

**SCORE Office (Westmoreland County)**
300 Fraser Purchase Rd.
Latrobe, PA 15650-2690
(412)539-7505
Fax: (412)539-1850

**SCORE Office (Lebanon)**
252 N. 8th St.
PO Box 899
Lebanon, PA 17042-0899
(717)273-3727
Fax: (717)273-7940

**SCORE Office (Lewistown)**
3 W. Monument Sq., Ste. 204
Lewistown, PA 17044
(717)248-6713
Fax: (717)248-6714

**SCORE Office (Delaware County)**
602 E. Baltimore Pike
Media, PA 19063
(610)565-3677
Fax: (610)565-1606

**SCORE Office (Milton Area)**
112 S. Front St.
Milton, PA 17847

(717)742-7341
Fax: (717)792-2008

**SCORE Office (Mon-Valley)**
435 Donner Ave.
Monessen, PA 15062
(412)684-4277
Fax: (412)684-7688

**SCORE Office (Monroeville)**
William Penn Plaza
2790 Mosside Blvd., Ste. 295
Monroeville, PA 15146
(412)856-0622
Fax: (412)856-1030

**SCORE Office (Airport Area)**
986 Brodhead Rd.
Moon Township, PA 15108-2398
(412)264-6270
Fax: (412)264-1575

**SCORE Office (Northeast)**
8601 E. Roosevelt Blvd.
Philadelphia, PA 19152
(215)332-3400
Fax: (215)332-6050

**SCORE Office (Philadelphia)**
1315 Walnut St., Ste. 500
Philadelphia, PA 19107
(215)790-5050
Fax: (215)790-5057
E-mail: score46@bellatlantic.net
Website: http://www.pgweb.net/score46/

**SCORE Office (Pittsburgh)**
1000 Liberty Ave., Rm. 1122
Pittsburgh, PA 15222
(412)395-6560
Fax: (412)395-6562

**SCORE Office (Tri-County)**
801 N. Charlotte St.
Pottstown, PA 19464
(610)327-2673

**SCORE Office (Reading)**
601 Penn St.
Reading, PA 19601
(610)376-3497

**SCORE Office (Scranton)**
Oppenheim Bldg.
116 N. Washington Ave., Ste. 650
Scranton, PA 18503
(717)347-4611
Fax: (717)347-4611

**SCORE Office (Central Pennsylvania)**
200 Innovation Blvd., Ste. 242-B
State College, PA 16803

(814)234-9415
Fax: (814)238-9686
Website: http://countrystore.org/
business/score.htm

**SCORE Office (Monroe-Stroudsburg)**
556 Main St.
Stroudsburg, PA 18360
(717)421-4433

**SCORE Office (Uniontown)**
Federal Bldg.
Pittsburg St.
PO Box 2065 DTS
Uniontown, PA 15401
(412)437-4222
E-mail: uniontownscore@lcsys.net

**SCORE Office (Warren County)**
315 2nd Ave.
Warren, PA 16365
(814)723-9017

**SCORE Office (Waynesboro)**
323 E. Main St.
Waynesboro, PA 17268
(717)762-7123
Fax: (717)962-7124

**SCORE Office (Chester County)**
Government Service Center, Ste. 281
601 Westtown Rd.
West Chester, PA 19382-4538
(610)344-6910
Fax: (610)344-6919
E-mail: score@locke.ccil.org

**SCORE Office (Wilkes-Barre)**
7 N. Wilkes-Barre Blvd.
Wilkes Barre, PA 18702-5241
(717)826-6502
Fax: (717)826-6287

**SCORE Office (North Central Pennsylvania)**
240 W. 3rd St., Rm. 227
PO Box 725
Williamsport, PA 17703
(717)322-3720
Fax: (717)322-1607
E-mail: score234@mail.csrlink.net
Website: http://www.lycoming.org/
score/

**SCORE Office (York)**
Cyber Center
2101 Pennsylvania Ave.
York, PA 17404
(717)845-8830
Fax: (717)854-9333

**Puerto Rico**

**SCORE Office (Puerto Rico & Virgin Islands)**
PO Box 12383-96
San Juan, PR 00914-0383
(787)726-8040
Fax: (787)726-8135

**Rhode Island**

**SCORE Office (Barrington)**
281 County Rd.
Barrington, RI 02806
(401)247-1920
Fax: (401)247-3763

**SCORE Office (Woonsocket)**
640 Washington Hwy.
Lincoln, RI 02865
(401)334-1000
Fax: (401)334-1009

**SCORE Office (Wickford)**
8045 Post Rd.
North Kingstown, RI 02852
(401)295-5566
Fax: (401)295-8987

**SCORE Office (J.G.E. Knight)**
380 Westminster St.
Providence, RI 02903
(401)528-4571
Fax: (401)528-4539
Website: http://www.riscore.org

**SCORE Office (Warwick)**
3288 Post Rd.
Warwick, RI 02886
(401)732-1100
Fax: (401)732-1101

**SCORE Office (Westerly)**
74 Post Rd.
Westerly, RI 02891
(401)596-7761
800-732-7636
Fax: (401)596-2190

**South Carolina**

**SCORE Office (Aiken)**
PO Box 892
Aiken, SC 29802
(803)641-1111
800-542-4536
Fax: (803)641-4174

**SCORE Office (Anderson)**
Anderson Mall
3130 N. Main St.

Anderson, SC 29621
(864)224-0453

**SCORE Office (Coastal)**
284 King St.
Charleston, SC 29401
(803)727-4778
Fax: (803)853-2529

**SCORE Office (Midlands)**
Strom Thurmond Bldg., Rm. 358
1835 Assembly St., Rm 358
Columbia, SC 29201
(803)765-5131
Fax: (803)765-5962
Website: http://www.scoremid
lands.org/

**SCORE Office (Piedmont)**
Federal Bldg., Rm. B-02
300 E. Washington St.
Greenville, SC 29601
(864)271-3638

**SCORE Office (Greenwood)**
PO Drawer 1467
Greenwood, SC 29648
(864)223-8357

**SCORE Office (Hilton Head Island)**
52 Savannah Trail
Hilton Head, SC 29926
(803)785-7107
Fax: (803)785-7110

**SCORE Office (Grand Strand)**
937 Broadway
Myrtle Beach, SC 29577
(803)918-1079
Fax: (803)918-1083
E-mail: score381@aol.com

**SCORE Office (Spartanburg)**
PO Box 1636
Spartanburg, SC 29304
(864)594-5000
Fax: (864)594-5055

**South Dakota**

**SCORE Office (West River)**
Rushmore Plz. Civic Ctr.
444 Mount Rushmore Rd., No. 209
Rapid City, SD 57701
(605)394-5311
E-mail: score@gwtc.net

**SCORE Office (Sioux Falls)**
First Financial Center
110 S. Phillips Ave., Ste. 200
Sioux Falls, SD 57104-6727

(605)330-4231
Fax: (605)330-4231

## Tennessee

**SCORE Office (Chattanooga)**
Federal Bldg., Rm. 26
900 Georgia Ave.
Chattanooga, TN 37402
(423)752-5190
Fax: (423)752-5335

**SCORE Office (Cleveland)**
PO Box 2275
Cleveland, TN 37320
(423)472-6587
Fax: (423)472-2019

**SCORE Office (Upper Cumberland Center)**
1225 S. Willow Ave.
Cookeville, TN 38501
(615)432-4111
Fax: (615)432-6010

**SCORE Office (Unicoi County)**
PO Box 713
Erwin, TN 37650
(423)743-3000
Fax: (423)743-0942

**SCORE Office (Greeneville)**
115 Academy St.
Greeneville, TN 37743
(423)638-4111
Fax: (423)638-5345

**SCORE Office (Jackson)**
194 Auditorium St.
Jackson, TN 38301
(901)423-2200

**SCORE Office (Northeast Tennessee)**
1st Tennessee Bank Bldg.
2710 S. Roan St., Ste. 584
Johnson City, TN 37601
(423)929-7686
Fax: (423)461-8052

**SCORE Office (Kingsport)**
151 E. Main St.
Kingsport, TN 37662
(423)392-8805

**SCORE Office (Greater Knoxville)**
Farragot Bldg., Ste. 224
530 S. Gay St.
Knoxville, TN 37902
(423)545-4203
E-mail: scoreknox@ntown.com
Website: http://www.scoreknox.org/

**SCORE Office (Maryville)**
201 S. Washington St.
Maryville, TN 37804-5728
(423)983-2241
800-525-6834
Fax: (423)984-1386

**SCORE Office (Memphis)**
Federal Bldg., Ste. 390
167 N. Main St.
Memphis, TN 38103
(901)544-3588

**SCORE Office (Nashville)**
50 Vantage Way, Ste. 201
Nashville, TN 37228-1500
(615)736-7621

## Texas

**SCORE Office (Abilene)**
2106 Federal Post Office and Court Bldg.
Abilene, TX 79601
(915)677-1857

**SCORE Office (Austin)**
2501 S. Congress
Austin, TX 78701
(512)442-7235
Fax: (512)442-7528

**SCORE Office (Golden Triangle)**
450 Boyd St.
Beaumont, TX 77704
(409)838-6581
Fax: (409)833-6718

**SCORE Office (Brownsville)**
3505 Boca Chica Blvd., Ste. 305
Brownsville, TX 78521
(210)541-4508

**SCORE Office (Brazos Valley)**
3000 Briarcrest, Ste. 302
Bryan, TX 77802
(409)776-8876
E-mail: 102633.2612@compuserve.com

**SCORE Office (Cleburne)**
Watergarden Pl., 9th Fl., Ste. 400
Cleburne, TX 76031
(817)871-6002

**SCORE Office (Corpus Christi)**
651 Upper North Broadway, Ste. 654
Corpus Christi, TX 78477
(512)888-4322
Fax: (512)888-3418

**SCORE Office (Dallas)**
6260 E. Mockingbird
Dallas, TX 75214-2619

(214)828-2471
Fax: (214)821-8033

**SCORE Office (El Paso)**
10 Civic Center Plaza
El Paso, TX 79901
(915)534-0541
Fax: (915)534-0513

**SCORE Office (Bedford)**
100 E. 15th St., Ste. 400
Ft. Worth, TX 76102
(817)871-6002

**SCORE Office (Ft. Worth)**
100 E. 15th St., No. 24
Ft. Worth, TX 76102
(817)871-6002
Fax: (817)871-6031
E-mail: fwbac@onramp.net

**SCORE Office (Garland)**
2734 W. Kingsley Rd.
Garland, TX 75041
(214)271-9224

**SCORE Office (Granbury Chamber of Commerce)**
416 S. Morgan
Granbury, TX 76048
(817)573-1622
Fax: (817)573-0805

**SCORE Office (Lower Rio Grande Valley)**
222 E. Van Buren, Ste. 500
Harlingen, TX 78550
(956)427-8533
Fax: (956)427-8537

**SCORE Office (Houston)**
9301 Southwest Fwy., Ste. 550
Houston, TX 77074
(713)773-6565
Fax: (713)773-6550

**SCORE Office (Irving)**
3333 N. MacArthur Blvd., Ste. 100
Irving, TX 75062
(214)252-8484
Fax: (214)252-6710

**SCORE Office (Lubbock)**
1205 Texas Ave., Rm. 411D
Lubbock, TX 79401
(806)472-7462
Fax: (806)472-7487

**SCORE Office (Midland)**
Post Office Annex
200 E. Wall St., Rm. P121
Midland, TX 79701
(915)687-2649

Organizations, Agencies, & Consultants

**SCORE Office (Orange)**
1012 Green Ave.
Orange, TX 77630-5620
(409)883-3536
800-528-4906
Fax: (409)886-3247

**SCORE Office (Plano)**
1200 E. 15th St.
PO Drawer 940287
Plano, TX 75094-0287
(214)424-7547
Fax: (214)422-5182

**SCORE Office (Port Arthur)**
4749 Twin City Hwy., Ste. 300
Port Arthur, TX 77642
(409)963-1107
Fax: (409)963-3322

**SCORE Office (Richardson)**
411 Belle Grove
Richardson, TX 75080
(214)234-4141
800-777-8001
Fax: (214)680-9103

**SCORE Office (San Antonio)**
Federal Bldg., Rm. A527
727 E. Durango
San Antonio, TX 78206
(210)472-5931
Fax: (210)472-5935

**SCORE Office (Texarkana State College)**
819 State Line Ave.
Texarkana, TX 75501
(903)792-7191
Fax: (903)793-4304

**SCORE Office (East Texas)**
RTDC
1530 SSW Loop 323, Ste. 100
Tyler, TX 75701
(903)510-2975
Fax: (903)510-2978

**SCORE Office (Waco)**
401 Franklin Ave.
Waco, TX 76701
(817)754-8898
Fax: (817)756-0776
Website: http://www.brc-waco.com/

**SCORE Office (Wichita Falls)**
Hamilton Bldg.
900 8th St.
Wichita Falls, TX 76307
(940)723-2741
Fax: (940)723-8773

## Utah

**SCORE Office (Northern Utah)**
160 N. Main
Logan, UT 84321
(435)746-2269

**SCORE Office (Ogden)**
1701 E. Windsor Dr.
Ogden, UT 84604
(801)629-8613
E-mail: score158@netscape.net

**SCORE Office (Central Utah)**
1071 E. Windsor Dr.
Provo, UT 84604
(801)373-8660

**SCORE Office (Southern Utah)**
225 South 700 East
St. George, UT 84770
(435)652-7751

**SCORE Office (Salt Lake)**
310 S Main St.
Salt Lake City, UT 84101
(801)746-2269
Fax: (801)746-2273

## Vermont

**SCORE Office (Champlain Valley)**
Winston Prouty Federal Bldg.
11 Lincoln St., Rm. 106
Essex Junction, VT 05452
(802)951-6762

**SCORE Office (Montpelier)**
87 State St., Rm. 205
PO Box 605
Montpelier, VT 05601
(802)828-4422
Fax: (802)828-4485

**SCORE Office (Marble Valley)**
256 N. Main St.
Rutland, VT 05701-2413
(802)773-9147

**SCORE Office (Northeast Kingdom)**
20 Main St.
PO Box 904
St. Johnsbury, VT 05819
(802)748-5101

## Virgin Islands

**SCORE Office (St. Croix)**
United Plaza Shopping Center
PO Box 4010, Christiansted
St. Croix, VI 00822
(809)778-5380

**SCORE Office (St. Thomas-St. John)**
Federal Bldg., Rm. 21
Veterans Dr.
St. Thomas, VI 00801
(809)774-8530

## Virginia

**SCORE Office (Arlington)**
2009 N. 14th St., Ste. 111
Arlington, VA 22201
(703)525-2400

**SCORE Office (Blacksburg)**
141 Jackson St.
Blacksburg, VA 24060
(540)552-4061

**SCORE Office (Bristol)**
20 Volunteer Pkwy.
Bristol, VA 24203
(540)989-4850

**SCORE Office (Central Virginia)**
1001 E. Market St., Ste. 101
Charlottesville, VA 22902
(804)295-6712
Fax: (804)295-7066

**SCORE Office (Alleghany Satellite)**
241 W. Main St.
Covington, VA 24426
(540)962-2178
Fax: (540)962-2179

**SCORE Office (Central Fairfax)**
3975 University Dr., Ste. 350
Fairfax, VA 22030
(703)591-2450

**SCORE Office (Falls Church)**
PO Box 491
Falls Church, VA 22040
(703)532-1050
Fax: (703)237-7904

**SCORE Office (Glenns)**
Glenns Campus
Box 287
Glenns, VA 23149
(804)693-9650

**SCORE Office (Peninsula)**
6 Manhattan Sq.
PO Box 7269
Hampton, VA 23666
(757)766-2000
Fax: (757)865-0339
E-mail: score100@seva.net

**SCORE Office (Tri-Cities)**
108 N. Main St.

Hopewell, VA 23860
(804)458-5536

**SCORE Office (Lynchburg)**
Federal Bldg.
1100 Main St.
Lynchburg, VA 24504-1714
(804)846-3235

**SCORE Office (Greater Prince William)**
8963 Center St
Manassas, VA 20110
(703)368-4813
Fax: (703)368-4733

**SCORE Office (Martinsville)**
115 Broad St.
Martinsville, VA 24112-0709
(540)632-6401
Fax: (540)632-5059

**SCORE Office (Hampton Roads)**
Federal Bldg., Rm. 737
200 Grandby St.
Norfolk, VA 23510
(757)441-3733
Fax: (757)441-3733
E-mail: scorehr60@juno.com

**SCORE Office (Norfolk)**
Federal Bldg., Rm. 737
200 Granby St.
Norfolk, VA 23510
(757)441-3733
Fax: (757)441-3733

**SCORE Office (Virginia Beach)**
Chamber of Commerce
200 Grandby St., Rm 737
Norfolk, VA 23510
(804)441-3733

**SCORE Office (Radford)**
1126 Norwood St.
Radford, VA 24141
(540)639-2202

**SCORE Office (Richmond)**
Federal Bldg.
400 N. 8th St., Ste. 1150
PO Box 10126
Richmond, VA 23240-0126
(804)771-2400
Fax: (804)771-8018
E-mail: scorechapter12@yahoo.com
Website: http://www.cvco.org/score/

**SCORE Office (Roanoke)**
Federal Bldg., Rm. 716
250 Franklin Rd.
Roanoke, VA 24011

(540)857-2834
Fax: (540)857-2043
E-mail: scorerva@juno.com
Website: http://hometown.aol.com/
scorerv/Index.html

**SCORE Office (Fairfax)**
8391 Old Courthouse Rd., Ste. 300
Vienna, VA 22182
(703)749-0400

**SCORE Office (Greater Vienna)**
513 Maple Ave. West
Vienna, VA 22180
(703)281-1333
Fax: (703)242-1482

**SCORE Office (Shenandoah Valley)**
301 W. Main St.
Waynesboro, VA 22980
(540)949-8203
Fax: (540)949-7740
E-mail: score427@intelos.net

**SCORE Office (Williamsburg)**
201 Penniman Rd.
Williamsburg, VA 23185
(757)229-6511
E-mail: wacc@williamsburgcc.com

**SCORE Office (Northern Virginia)**
1360 S. Pleasant Valley Rd.
Winchester, VA 22601
(540)662-4118

## Washington

**SCORE Office (Gray's Harbor)**
506 Duffy St.
Aberdeen, WA 98520
(360)532-1924
Fax: (360)533-7945

**SCORE Office (Bellingham)**
101 E. Holly St.
Bellingham, WA 98225
(360)676-3307

**SCORE Office (Everett)**
2702 Hoyt Ave.
Everett, WA 98201-3556
(206)259-8000

**SCORE Office (Gig Harbor)**
3125 Judson St.
Gig Harbor, WA 98335
(206)851-6865

**SCORE Office (Kennewick)**
PO Box 6986
Kennewick, WA 99336
(509)736-0510

**SCORE Office (Puyallup)**
322 2nd St. SW
PO Box 1298
Puyallup, WA 98371
(206)845-6755
Fax: (206)848-6164

**SCORE Office (Seattle)**
1200 6th Ave., Ste. 1700
Seattle, WA 98101
(206)553-7320
Fax: (206)553-7044
E-mail: score55@aol.com
Website: http://www.scn.org/civic/score-
online/index55.html

**SCORE Office (Spokane)**
801 W. Riverside Ave., No. 240
Spokane, WA 99201
(509)353-2820
Fax: (509)353-2600
E-mail: score@dmi.net
Website: http://www.dmi.net/score/

**SCORE Office (Clover Park)**
PO Box 1933
Tacoma, WA 98401-1933
(206)627-2175

**SCORE Office (Tacoma)**
1101 Pacific Ave.
Tacoma, WA 98402
(253)274-1288
Fax: (253)274-1289

**SCORE Office (Fort Vancouver)**
1701 Broadway, S-1
Vancouver, WA 98663
(360)699-1079

**SCORE Office (Walla Walla)**
500 Tausick Way
Walla Walla, WA 99362
(509)527-4681

**SCORE Office (Mid-Columbia)**
1113 S. 14th Ave.
Yakima, WA 98907
(509)574-4944
Fax: (509)574-2943
Website: http://www.ellensburg.com/
~score/

## West Virginia

**SCORE Office (Charleston)**
1116 Smith St.
Charleston, WV 25301
(304)347-5463
E-mail: score256@juno.com

Organizations, Agencies, & Consultants

**SCORE Office (Virginia Street)**
1116 Smith St., Ste. 302
Charleston, WV 25301
(304)347-5463

**SCORE Office (Marion County)**
PO Box 208
Fairmont, WV 26555-0208
(304)363-0486

**SCORE Office (Upper Monongahela Valley)**
1000 Technology Dr., Ste. 1111
Fairmont, WV 26555
(304)363-0486
E-mail: score537@hotmail.com

**SCORE Office (Huntington)**
1101 6th Ave., Ste. 220
Huntington, WV 25701-2309
(304)523-4092

**SCORE Office (Wheeling)**
1310 Market St.
Wheeling, WV 26003
(304)233-2575
Fax: (304)233-1320

## Wisconsin

**SCORE Office (Fox Cities)**
227 S. Walnut St.
Appleton, WI 54913
(920)734-7101
Fax: (920)734-7161

**SCORE Office (Beloit)**
136 W. Grand Ave., Ste. 100
PO Box 717
Beloit, WI 53511
(608)365-8835
Fax: (608)365-9170

**SCORE Office (Eau Claire)**
Federal Bldg., Rm. B11
510 S. Barstow St.
Eau Claire, WI 54701
(715)834-1573
E-mail: score@ecol.net
Website: http://www.ecol.net/~score/

**SCORE Office (Fond du Lac)**
207 N. Main St.
Fond du Lac, WI 54935
(414)921-9500
Fax: (414)921-9559

**SCORE Office (Green Bay)**
835 Potts Ave.
Green Bay, WI 54304
(414)496-8930
Fax: (414)496-6009

**SCORE Office (Janesville)**
20 S. Main St., Ste. 11
PO Box 8008
Janesville, WI 53547
(608)757-3160
Fax: (608)757-3170

**SCORE Office (La Crosse)**
712 Main St.
La Crosse, WI 54602-0219
(608)784-4880

**SCORE Office (Madison)**
505 S. Rosa Rd.
Madison, WI 53719
(608)441-2820

**SCORE Office (Manitowoc)**
1515 Memorial Dr.
PO Box 903
Manitowoc, WI 54221-0903
(414)684-5575
Fax: (414)684-1915

**SCORE Office (Milwaukee)**
310 W. Wisconsin Ave., Ste. 425
Milwaukee, WI 53203
(414)297-3942
Fax: (414)297-1377

**SCORE Office (Central Wisconsin)**
1224 Lindbergh Ave.
Stevens Point, WI 54481
(715)344-7729

**SCORE Office (Superior)**
Superior Business Center Inc.
1423 N. 8th St.
Superior, WI 54880
(715)394-7388
Fax: (715)393-7414

**SCORE Office (Waukesha)**
223 Wisconsin Ave.
Waukesha, WI 53186-4926
(414)542-4249

**SCORE Office (Wausau)**
300 3rd St., Ste. 200
Wausau, WI 54402-6190
(715)845-6231

**SCORE Office (Wisconsin Rapids)**
2240 Kingston Rd.
Wisconsin Rapids, WI 54494
(715)423-1830

## Wyoming

**SCORE Office (Casper)**
Federal Bldg., No. 2215
100 East B St.

Casper, WY 82602
(307)261-6529
Fax: (307)261-6530

## Venture capital & financing companies

*This section contains a listing of financing and loan companies in the United States and Canada. These listing are arranged alphabetically by country, then by state or province, then by city, then by organization name.*

## Canada

### Alberta

**Launchworks Inc.**
1902J 11th St., S.E.
Calgary, AB, Canada T2G 3G2
(403)269-1119
Fax: (403)269-1141
Website: http://www.launchworks.com

**Native Venture Capital Company, Inc.**
21 Artist View Point, Box 7
Site 25, RR 12
Calgary, AB, Canada T3E 6W3
(903)208-5380

**Miralta Capital Inc.**
4445 Calgary Trail South
888 Terrace Plaza Alberta
Edmonton, AB, Canada T6H 5R7
(780)438-3535
Fax: (780)438-3129

**Vencap Equities Alberta Ltd.**
10180-101st St., Ste. 1980
Edmonton, AB, Canada T5J 3S4
(403)420-1171
Fax: (403)429-2541

### British Columbia

**Discovery Capital**
5th Fl., 1199 West Hastings
Vancouver, BC, Canada V6E 3T5
(604)683-3000
Fax: (604)662-3457
E-mail: info@discoverycapital.com
Website: http://www.discoverycapital.com

**Greenstone Venture Partners**
1177 West Hastings St.
Ste. 400
Vancouver, BC, Canada V6E 2K3
(604)717-1977
Fax: (604)717-1976
Website: http://www.greenstonevc.com

### Growthworks Capital

2600-1055 West Georgia St.
Box 11170 Royal Centre
Vancouver, BC, Canada V6E 3R5
(604)895-7259
Fax: (604)669-7605
Website: http://www.wofund.com

### MDS Discovery Venture Management, Inc.

555 W. Eighth Ave., Ste. 305
Vancouver, BC, Canada V5Z 1C6
(604)872-8464
Fax: (604)872-2977
E-mail: info@mds-ventures.com

### Ventures West Management Inc.

1285 W. Pender St., Ste. 280
Vancouver, BC, Canada V6E 4B1
(604)688-9495
Fax: (604)687-2145
Website: http://www.ventureswest.com

## Nova Scotia

### ACF Equity Atlantic Inc.

Purdy's Wharf Tower II
Ste. 2106
Halifax, NS, Canada B3J 3R7
(902)421-1965
Fax: (902)421-1808

### Montgomerie, Huck & Co.

146 Bluenose Dr.
PO Box 538
Lunenburg, NS, Canada B0J 2C0
(902)634-7125
Fax: (902)634-7130

## Ontario

### IPS Industrial Promotion Services Ltd.

60 Columbia Way, Ste. 720
Markham, ON, Canada L3R 0C9
(905)475-9400
Fax: (905)475-5003

### Betwin Investments Inc.

Box 23110
Sault Ste. Marie, ON, Canada P6A 6W6
(705)253-0744
Fax: (705)253-0744

### Bailey & Company, Inc.

594 Spadina Ave.
Toronto, ON, Canada M5S 2H4
(416)921-6930
Fax: (416)925-4670

### BCE Capital

200 Bay St.

South Tower, Ste. 3120
Toronto, ON, Canada M5J 2J2
(416)815-0078
Fax: (416)941-1073
Website: http://www.bcecapital.com

### Castlehill Ventures

55 University Ave., Ste. 500
Toronto, ON, Canada M5J 2H7
(416)862-8574
Fax: (416)862-8875

### CCFL Mezzanine Partners of Canada

70 University Ave.
Ste. 1450
Toronto, ON, Canada M5J 2M4
(416)977-1450
Fax: (416)977-6764
E-mail: info@ccfl.com
Website: http://www.ccfl.com

### Celtic House International

100 Simcoe St., Ste. 100
Toronto, ON, Canada M5H 3G2
(416)542-2436
Fax: (416)542-2435
Website: http://www.celtic-house.com

### Clairvest Group Inc.

22 St. Clair Ave. East
Ste. 1700
Toronto, ON, Canada M4T 2S3
(416)925-9270
Fax: (416)925-5753

### Crosbie & Co., Inc.

One First Canadian Place
9th Fl.
PO Box 116
Toronto, ON, Canada M5X 1A4
(416)362-7726
Fax: (416)362-3447
E-mail: info@crosbieco.com
Website: http://www.crosbieco.com

### Drug Royalty Corp.

Eight King St. East
Ste. 202
Toronto, ON, Canada M5C 1B5
(416)863-1865
Fax: (416)863-5161

### Grieve, Horner, Brown & Asculai

8 King St. E, Ste. 1704
Toronto, ON, Canada M5C 1B5
(416)362-7668
Fax: (416)362-7660

### Jefferson Partners

77 King St. West
Ste. 4010

PO Box 136
Toronto, ON, Canada M5K 1H1
(416)367-1533
Fax: (416)367-5827
Website: http://www.jefferson.com

### J.L. Albright Venture Partners

Canada Trust Tower, 161 Bay St.
Ste. 4440
PO Box 215
Toronto, ON, Canada M5J 2S1
(416)367-2440
Fax: (416)367-4604
Website: http://www.jlaventures.com

### McLean Watson Capital Inc.

One First Canadian Place
Ste. 1410
PO Box 129
Toronto, ON, Canada M5X 1A4
(416)363-2000
Fax: (416)363-2010
Website: http://www.mcleanwatson.com

### Middlefield Capital Fund

One First Canadian Place
85th Fl.
PO Box 192
Toronto, ON, Canada M5X 1A6
(416)362-0714
Fax: (416)362-7925
Website: http://www.middlefield.com

### Mosaic Venture Partners

24 Duncan St.
Ste. 300
Toronto, ON, Canada M5V 3M6
(416)597-8889
Fax: (416)597-2345

### Onex Corp.

161 Bay St.
PO Box 700
Toronto, ON, Canada M5J 2S1
(416)362-7711
Fax: (416)362-5765

### Penfund Partners Inc.

145 King St. West
Ste. 1920
Toronto, ON, Canada M5H 1J8
(416)865-0300
Fax: (416)364-6912
Website: http://www.penfund.com

### Primaxis Technology Ventures Inc.

1 Richmond St. West, 8th Fl.
Toronto, ON, Canada M5H 3W4
(416)313-5210
Fax: (416)313-5218
Website: http://www.primaxis.com

**Priveq Capital Funds**
240 Duncan Mill Rd., Ste. 602
Toronto, ON, Canada M3B 3P1
(416)447-3330
Fax: (416)447-3331
E-mail: priveq@sympatico.ca

**Roynat Ventures**
40 King St. West, 26th Fl.
Toronto, ON, Canada M5H 1H1
(416)933-2667
Fax: (416)933-2783
Website: http://www.roynatcapital.com

**Tera Capital Corp.**
366 Adelaide St. East, Ste. 337
Toronto, ON, Canada M5A 3X9
(416)368-1024
Fax: (416)368-1427

**Working Ventures Canadian Fund Inc.**
250 Bloor St. East, Ste. 1600
Toronto, ON, Canada M4W 1E6
(416)934-7718
Fax: (416)929-0901
Website: http://www.workingventures.ca

## Quebec

**Altamira Capital Corp.**
202 University
Niveau de Maisoneuve, Bur. 201
Montreal, QC, Canada H3A 2A5
(514)499-1656
Fax: (514)499-9570

**Federal Business Development Bank**
Venture Capital Division
Five Place Ville Marie, Ste. 600
Montreal, QC, Canada H3B 5E7
(514)283-1896
Fax: (514)283-5455

**Hydro-Quebec Capitech Inc.**
75 Boul, Rene Levesque Quest
Montreal, QC, Canada H2Z 1A4
(514)289-4783
Fax: (514)289-5420
Website: http://www.hqcapitech.com

**Investissement Desjardins**
2 complexe Desjardins
C.P. 760
Montreal, QC, Canada H5B 1B8
(514)281-7131
Fax: (514)281-7808
Website: http://www.desjardins.com/id

**Marleau Lemire Inc.**
One Place Ville-Marie, Ste. 3601
Montreal, QC, Canada H3B 3P2

(514)877-3800
Fax: (514)875-6415

**Speirs Consultants Inc.**
365 Stanstead
Montreal, QC, Canada H3R 1X5
(514)342-3858
Fax: (514)342-1977

**Tecnocap Inc.**
4028 Marlowe
Montreal, QC, Canada H4A 3M2
(514)483-6009
Fax: (514)483-6045
Website: http://www.technocap.com

**Telsoft Ventures**
1000, Rue de la Gauchetiere
Quest, 25eme Etage
Montreal, QC, Canada H3B 4W5
(514)397-8450
Fax: (514)397-8451

## Saskatchewan

**Saskatchewan Government Growth Fund**
1801 Hamilton St., Ste. 1210
Canada Trust Tower
Regina, SK, Canada S4P 4B4
(306)787-2994
Fax: (306)787-2086

## United states

### Alabama

**FHL Capital Corp.**
600 20th Street North
Suite 350
Birmingham, AL 35203
(205)328-3098
Fax: (205)323-0001

**Harbert Management Corp.**
One Riverchase Pkwy. South
Birmingham, AL 35244
(205)987-5500
Fax: (205)987-5707
Website: http://www.harbert.net

**Jefferson Capital Fund**
PO Box 13129
Birmingham, AL 35213
(205)324-7709

**Private Capital Corp.**
100 Brookwood Pl., 4th Fl.
Birmingham, AL 35209
(205)879-2722
Fax: (205)879-5121

**21st Century Health Ventures**
One Health South Pkwy.
Birmingham, AL 35243
(256)268-6250
Fax: (256)970-8928

**FJC Growth Capital Corp.**
200 W. Side Sq., Ste. 340
Huntsville, AL 35801
(256)922-2918
Fax: (256)922-2909

**Hickory Venture Capital Corp.**
301 Washington St. NW
Suite 301
Huntsville, AL 35801
(256)539-1931
Fax: (256)539-5130
E-mail: hvcc@hvcc.com
Website: http://www.hvcc.com

**Southeastern Technology Fund**
7910 South Memorial Pkwy., Ste. F
Huntsville, AL 35802
(256)883-8711
Fax: (256)883-8558

**Cordova Ventures**
4121 Carmichael Rd., Ste. 301
Montgomery, AL 36106
(334)271-6011
Fax: (334)260-0120
Website: http://www.cordova
ventures.com

**Small Business Clinic of Alabama/AG
Bartholomew & Associates**
PO Box 231074
Montgomery, AL 36123-1074
(334)284-3640

### Arizona

**Miller Capital Corp.**
4909 E. McDowell Rd.
Phoenix, AZ 85008
(602)225-0504
Fax: (602)225-9024
Website: http://www.themiller
group.com

**The Columbine Venture Funds**
9449 North 90th St., Ste. 200
Scottsdale, AZ 85258
(602)661-9222
Fax: (602)661-6262

**Koch Ventures**
17767 N. Perimeter Dr., Ste. 101
Scottsdale, AZ 85255
(480)419-3600

Fax: (480)419-3606
Website: http://www.kochventures.com

**McKee & Co.**
7702 E. Doubletree Ranch Rd.
Suite 230
Scottsdale, AZ 85258
(480)368-0333
Fax: (480)607-7446

**Merita Capital Ltd.**
7350 E. Stetson Dr., Ste. 108-A
Scottsdale, AZ 85251
(480)947-8700
Fax: (480)947-8766

**Valley Ventures / Arizona Growth Partners L.P.**
6720 N. Scottsdale Rd., Ste. 208
Scottsdale, AZ 85253
(480)661-6600
Fax: (480)661-6262

**Estreetcapital.com**
660 South Mill Ave., Ste. 315
Tempe, AZ 85281
(480)968-8400
Fax: (480)968-8480
Website: http://www.estreetcapital.com

**Coronado Venture Fund**
PO Box 65420
Tucson, AZ 85728-5420
(520)577-3764
Fax: (520)299-8491

## Arkansas

**Arkansas Capital Corp.**
225 South Pulaski St.
Little Rock, AR 72201
(501)374-9247
Fax: (501)374-9425
Website: http://www.arcapital.com

## California

**Sundance Venture Partners, L.P.**
100 Clocktower Place, Ste. 130
Carmel, CA 93923
(831)625-6500
Fax: (831)625-6590

**Westar Capital (Costa Mesa)**
949 South Coast Dr., Ste. 650
Costa Mesa, CA 92626
(714)481-5160
Fax: (714)481-5166
E-mail: mailbox@westarcapital.com
Website: http://www.westarcapital.com

**Alpine Technology Ventures**
20300 Stevens Creek Boulevard, Ste. 495
Cupertino, CA 95014
(408)725-1810
Fax: (408)725-1207
Website: http://www.alpineventures.com

**Bay Partners**
10600 N. De Anza Blvd.
Cupertino, CA 95014-2031
(408)725-2444
Fax: (408)446-4502
Website: http://www.baypartners.com

**Novus Ventures**
20111 Stevens Creek Blvd., Ste. 130
Cupertino, CA 95014
(408)252-3900
Fax: (408)252-1713
Website: http://www.novusventures.com

**Triune Capital**
19925 Stevens Creek Blvd., Ste. 200
Cupertino, CA 95014
(310)284-6800
Fax: (310)284-3290

**Acorn Ventures**
268 Bush St., Ste. 2829
Daly City, CA 94014
(650)994-7801
Fax: (650)994-3305
Website: http://www.acornventures.com

**Digital Media Campus**
2221 Park Place
El Segundo, CA 90245
(310)426-8000
Fax: (310)426-8010
E-mail: info@thecampus.com
Website: http://www.digital
mediacampus.com

**BankAmerica Ventures / BA Venture Partners**
950 Tower Ln., Ste. 700
Foster City, CA 94404
(650)378-6000
Fax: (650)378-6040
Website: http://
www.baventurepartners.com

**Starting Point Partners**
666 Portofino Lane
Foster City, CA 94404
(650)722-1035
Website: http://www.startingpoint
partners.com

**Opportunity Capital Partners**
2201 Walnut Ave., Ste. 210

Fremont, CA 94538
(510)795-7000
Fax: (510)494-5439
Website: http://www.ocpcapital.com

**Imperial Ventures Inc.**
9920 S. La Cienega Boulevar, 14th Fl.
Inglewood, CA 90301
(310)417-5409
Fax: (310)338-6115

**Ventana Global (Irvine)**
18881 Von Karman Ave., Ste. 1150
Irvine, CA 92612
(949)476-2204
Fax: (949)752-0223
Website: http://www.ventanaglobal.com

**Integrated Consortium Inc.**
50 Ridgecrest Rd.
Kentfield, CA 94904
(415)925-0386
Fax: (415)461-2726

**Enterprise Partners**
979 Ivanhoe Ave., Ste. 550
La Jolla, CA 92037
(858)454-8833
Fax: (858)454-2489
Website: http://www.epvc.com

**Domain Associates**
28202 Cabot Rd., Ste. 200
Laguna Niguel, CA 92677
(949)347-2446
Fax: (949)347-9720
Website: http://www.domainvc.com

**Cascade Communications Ventures**
60 E. Sir Francis Drake Blvd., Ste. 300
Larkspur, CA 94939
(415)925-6500
Fax: (415)925-6501

**Allegis Capital**
One First St., Ste. Two
Los Altos, CA 94022
(650)917-5900
Fax: (650)917-5901
Website: http://www.allegiscapital.com

**Aspen Ventures**
1000 Fremont Ave., Ste. 200
Los Altos, CA 94024
(650)917-5670
Fax: (650)917-5677
Website: http://www.aspenventures.com

**AVI Capital L.P.**
1 First St., Ste. 2
Los Altos, CA 94022

Organizations, Agencies, & Consultants

(650)949-9862
Fax: (650)949-8510
Website: http://www.avicapital.com

**Bastion Capital Corp.**
1999 Avenue of the Stars, Ste. 2960
Los Angeles, CA 90067
(310)788-5700
Fax: (310)277-7582
E-mail: ga@bastioncapital.com
Website: http://www.bastioncapital.com

**Davis Group**
PO Box 69953
Los Angeles, CA 90069-0953
(310)659-6327
Fax: (310)659-6337

**Developers Equity Corp.**
1880 Century Park East, Ste. 211
Los Angeles, CA 90067
(213)277-0300

**Far East Capital Corp.**
350 S. Grand Ave., Ste. 4100
Los Angeles, CA 90071
(213)687-1361
Fax: (213)617-7939
E-mail: free@fareastnationalbank.com

**Kline Hawkes & Co.**
11726 San Vicente Blvd., Ste. 300
Los Angeles, CA 90049
(310)442-4700
Fax: (310)442-4707
Website: http://www.klinehawkes.com

**Lawrence Financial Group**
701 Teakwood
PO Box 491773
Los Angeles, CA 90049
(310)471-4060
Fax: (310)472-3155

**Riordan Lewis & Haden**
300 S. Grand Ave., 29th Fl.
Los Angeles, CA 90071
(213)229-8500
Fax: (213)229-8597

**Union Venture Corp.**
445 S. Figueroa St., 9th Fl.
Los Angeles, CA 90071
(213)236-4092
Fax: (213)236-6329

**Wedbush Capital Partners**
1000 Wilshire Blvd.
Los Angeles, CA 90017
(213)688-4545
Fax: (213)688-6642
Website: http://www.wedbush.com

**Advent International Corp.**
2180 Sand Hill Rd., Ste. 420
Menlo Park, CA 94025
(650)233-7500
Fax: (650)233-7515
Website: http://www.adventinter
national.com

**Altos Ventures**
2882 Sand Hill Rd., Ste. 100
Menlo Park, CA 94025
(650)234-9771
Fax: (650)233-9821
Website: http://www.altosvc.com

**Applied Technology**
1010 El Camino Real, Ste. 300
Menlo Park, CA 94025
(415)326-8622
Fax: (415)326-8163

**APV Technology Partners**
535 Middlefield, Ste. 150
Menlo Park, CA 94025
(650)327-7871
Fax: (650)327-7631
Website: http://www.apvtp.com

**August Capital Management**
2480 Sand Hill Rd., Ste. 101
Menlo Park, CA 94025
(650)234-9900
Fax: (650)234-9910
Website: http://www.augustcap.com

**Baccharis Capital Inc.**
2420 Sand Hill Rd., Ste. 100
Menlo Park, CA 94025
(650)324-6844
Fax: (650)854-3025

**Benchmark Capital**
2480 Sand Hill Rd., Ste. 200
Menlo Park, CA 94025
(650)854-8180
Fax: (650)854-8183
E-mail: info@benchmark.com
Website: http://www.benchmark.com

**Bessemer Venture Partners (Menlo Park)**
535 Middlefield Rd., Ste. 245
Menlo Park, CA 94025
(650)853-7000
Fax: (650)853-7001
Website: http://www.bvp.com

**The Cambria Group**
1600 El Camino Real Rd., Ste. 155
Menlo Park, CA 94025
(650)329-8600

Fax: (650)329-8601
Website: http://www.cambriagroup.com

**Canaan Partners**
2884 Sand Hill Rd., Ste. 115
Menlo Park, CA 94025
(650)854-8092
Fax: (650)854-8127
Website: http://www.canaan.com

**Capstone Ventures**
3000 Sand Hill Rd., Bldg. One, Ste. 290
Menlo Park, CA 94025
(650)854-2523
Fax: (650)854-9010
Website: http://www.capstonevc.com

**Comdisco Venture Group (Silicon Valley)**
3000 Sand Hill Rd., Bldg. 1, Ste. 155
Menlo Park, CA 94025
(650)854-9484
Fax: (650)854-4026

**Commtech International**
535 Middlefield Rd., Ste. 200
Menlo Park, CA 94025
(650)328-0190
Fax: (650)328-6442

**Compass Technology Partners**
1550 El Camino Real, Ste. 275
Menlo Park, CA 94025-4111
(650)322-7595
Fax: (650)322-0588
Website: http://www.compass
techpartners.com

**Convergence Partners**
3000 Sand Hill Rd., Ste. 235
Menlo Park, CA 94025
(650)854-3010
Fax: (650)854-3015
Website: http://www.conver
gencepartners.com

**The Dakota Group**
PO Box 1025
Menlo Park, CA 94025
(650)853-0600
Fax: (650)851-4899
E-mail: info@dakota.com

**Delphi Ventures**
3000 Sand Hill Rd.
Bldg. One, Ste. 135
Menlo Park, CA 94025
(650)854-9650
Fax: (650)854-2961
Website: http://www.delphiventures.com

**El Dorado Ventures**

2884 Sand Hill Rd., Ste. 121
Menlo Park, CA 94025
(650)854-1200
Fax: (650)854-1202
Website: http://www.eldorado
ventures.com

**Glynn Ventures**

3000 Sand Hill Rd., Bldg. 4, Ste. 235
Menlo Park, CA 94025
(650)854-2215

**Indosuez Ventures**

2180 Sand Hill Rd., Ste. 450
Menlo Park, CA 94025
(650)854-0587
Fax: (650)323-5561
Website: http://www.indosuez
ventures.com

**Institutional Venture Partners**

3000 Sand Hill Rd., Bldg. 2, Ste. 290
Menlo Park, CA 94025
(650)854-0132
Fax: (650)854-5762
Website: http://www.ivp.com

**Interwest Partners (Menlo Park)**

3000 Sand Hill Rd., Bldg. 3, Ste. 255
Menlo Park, CA 94025-7112
(650)854-8585
Fax: (650)854-4706
Website: http://www.interwest.com

**Kleiner Perkins Caufield & Byers (Menlo Park)**

2750 Sand Hill Rd.
Menlo Park, CA 94025
(650)233-2750
Fax: (650)233-0300
Website: http://www.kpcb.com

**Magic Venture Capital LLC**

1010 El Camino Real, Ste. 300
Menlo Park, CA 94025
(650)325-4149

**Matrix Partners**

2500 Sand Hill Rd., Ste. 113
Menlo Park, CA 94025
(650)854-3131
Fax: (650)854-3296
Website: http://www.matrixpartners.com

**Mayfield Fund**

2800 Sand Hill Rd.
Menlo Park, CA 94025
(650)854-5560
Fax: (650)854-5712
Website: http://www.mayfield.com

**McCown De Leeuw and Co. (Menlo Park)**

3000 Sand Hill Rd., Bldg. 3, Ste. 290
Menlo Park, CA 94025-7111
(650)854-6000
Fax: (650)854-0853
Website: http://www.mdcpartners.com

**Menlo Ventures**

3000 Sand Hill Rd., Bldg. 4, Ste. 100
Menlo Park, CA 94025
(650)854-8540
Fax: (650)854-7059
Website: http://www.menloventures.com

**Merrill Pickard Anderson & Eyre**

2480 Sand Hill Rd., Ste. 200
Menlo Park, CA 94025
(650)854-8600
Fax: (650)854-0345

**New Enterprise Associates (Menlo Park)**

2490 Sand Hill Rd.
Menlo Park, CA 94025
(650)854-9499
Fax: (650)854-9397
Website: http://www.nea.com

**Onset Ventures**

2400 Sand Hill Rd., Ste. 150
Menlo Park, CA 94025
(650)529-0700
Fax: (650)529-0777
Website: http://www.onset.com

**Paragon Venture Partners**

3000 Sand Hill Rd., Bldg. 1, Ste. 275
Menlo Park, CA 94025
(650)854-8000
Fax: (650)854-7260

**Pathfinder Venture Capital Funds (Menlo Park)**

3000 Sand Hill Rd., Bldg. 3, Ste. 255
Menlo Park, CA 94025
(650)854-0650
Fax: (650)854-4706

**Rocket Ventures**

3000 Sandhill Rd., Bldg. 1, Ste. 170
Menlo Park, CA 94025
(650)561-9100
Fax: (650)561-9183
Website: http://www.rocketventures.com

**Sequoia Capital**

3000 Sand Hill Rd., Bldg. 4, Ste. 280
Menlo Park, CA 94025
(650)854-3927
Fax: (650)854-2977

E-mail: sequoia@sequoiacap.com
Website: http://www.sequoiacap.com

**Sierra Ventures**

3000 Sand Hill Rd., Bldg. 4, Ste. 210
Menlo Park, CA 94025
(650)854-1000
Fax: (650)854-5593
Website: http://www.sierraventures.com

**Sigma Partners**

2884 Sand Hill Rd., Ste. 121
Menlo Park, CA 94025-7022
(650)853-1700
Fax: (650)853-1717
E-mail: info@sigmapartners.com
Website: http://www.sigmapartners.com

**Sprout Group (Menlo Park)**

3000 Sand Hill Rd.
Bldg. 3, Ste. 170
Menlo Park, CA 94025
(650)234-2700
Fax: (650)234-2779
Website: http://www.sproutgroup.com

**TA Associates (Menlo Park)**

70 Willow Rd., Ste. 100
Menlo Park, CA 94025
(650)328-1210
Fax: (650)326-4933
Website: http://www.ta.com

**Thompson Clive & Partners Ltd.**

3000 Sand Hill Rd., Bldg. 1, Ste. 185
Menlo Park, CA 94025-7102
(650)854-0314
Fax: (650)854-0670
E-mail: mail@tcvc.com
Website: http://www.tcvc.com

**Trinity Ventures Ltd.**

3000 Sand Hill Rd., Bldg. 1, Ste. 240
Menlo Park, CA 94025
(650)854-9500
Fax: (650)854-9501
Website: http://www.trinityventures.com

**U.S. Venture Partners**

2180 Sand Hill Rd., Ste. 300
Menlo Park, CA 94025
(650)854-9080
Fax: (650)854-3018
Website: http://www.usvp.com

**USVP-Schlein Marketing Fund**

2180 Sand Hill Rd., Ste. 300
Menlo Park, CA 94025
(415)854-9080
Fax: (415)854-3018
Website: http://www.usvp.com

**Venrock Associates**
2494 Sand Hill Rd., Ste. 200
Menlo Park, CA 94025
(650)561-9580
Fax: (650)561-9180
Website: http://www.venrock.com

**Brad Peery Capital Inc.**
145 Chapel Pkwy.
Mill Valley, CA 94941
(415)389-0625
Fax: (415)389-1336

**Dot Edu Ventures**
650 Castro St., Ste. 270
Mountain View, CA 94041
(650)575-5638
Fax: (650)325-5247
Website: http://www.dotedu
ventures.com

**Forrest, Binkley & Brown**
840 Newport Ctr. Dr., Ste. 480
Newport Beach, CA 92660
(949)729-3222
Fax: (949)729-3226
Website: http://www.fbbvc.com

**Marwit Capital LLC**
180 Newport Center Dr., Ste. 200
Newport Beach, CA 92660
(949)640-6234
Fax: (949)720-8077
Website: http://www.marwit.com

**Kaiser Permanente / National Venture Development**
1800 Harrison St., 22nd Fl.
Oakland, CA 94612
(510)267-4010
Fax: (510)267-4036
Website: http://www.kpventures.com

**Nu Capital Access Group, Ltd.**
7677 Oakport St., Ste. 105
Oakland, CA 94621
(510)635-7345
Fax: (510)635-7068

**Inman and Bowman**
4 Orinda Way, Bldg. D, Ste. 150
Orinda, CA 94563
(510)253-1611
Fax: (510)253-9037

**Accel Partners (San Francisco)**
428 University Ave.
Palo Alto, CA 94301
(650)614-4800
Fax: (650)614-4880
Website: http://www.accel.com

**Advanced Technology Ventures**
485 Ramona St., Ste. 200
Palo Alto, CA 94301
(650)321-8601
Fax: (650)321-0934
Website: http://www.atvcapital.com

**Anila Fund**
400 Channing Ave.
Palo Alto, CA 94301
(650)833-5790
Fax: (650)833-0590
Website: http://www.anila.com

**Asset Management Company Venture Capital**
2275 E. Bayshore, Ste. 150
Palo Alto, CA 94303
(650)494-7400
Fax: (650)856-1826
E-mail: postmaster@assetman.com
Website: http://www.assetman.com

**BancBoston Capital / BancBoston Ventures**
435 Tasso St., Ste. 250
Palo Alto, CA 94305
(650)470-4100
Fax: (650)853-1425
Website: http://www.bancboston
capital.com

**Charter Ventures**
525 University Ave., Ste. 1400
Palo Alto, CA 94301
(650)325-6953
Fax: (650)325-4762
Website: http://www.charterventures.com

**Communications Ventures**
505 Hamilton Avenue, Ste. 305
Palo Alto, CA 94301
(650)325-9600
Fax: (650)325-9608
Website: http://www.comven.com

**HMS Group**
2468 Embarcadero Way
Palo Alto, CA 94303-3313
(650)856-9862
Fax: (650)856-9864

**Jafco America Ventures, Inc.**
505 Hamilton Ste. 310
Palto Alto, CA 94301
(650)463-8800
Fax: (650)463-8801
Website: http://www.jafco.com

**New Vista Capital**
540 Cowper St., Ste. 200

Palo Alto, CA 94301
(650)329-9333
Fax: (650)328-9434
E-mail: fgreene@nvcap.com
Website: http://www.nvcap.com

**Norwest Equity Partners (Palo Alto)**
245 Lytton Ave., Ste. 250
Palo Alto, CA 94301-1426
(650)321-8000
Fax: (650)321-8010
Website: http://www.norwestvp.com

**Oak Investment Partners**
525 University Ave., Ste. 1300
Palo Alto, CA 94301
(650)614-3700
Fax: (650)328-6345
Website: http://www.oakinv.com

**Patricof & Co. Ventures, Inc. (Palo Alto)**
2100 Geng Rd., Ste. 150
Palo Alto, CA 94303
(650)494-9944
Fax: (650)494-6751
Website: http://www.patricof.com

**RWI Group**
835 Page Mill Rd.
Palo Alto, CA 94304
(650)251-1800
Fax: (650)213-8660
Website: http://www.rwigroup.com

**Summit Partners (Palo Alto)**
499 Hamilton Ave., Ste. 200
Palo Alto, CA 94301
(650)321-1166
Fax: (650)321-1188
Website: http://www.summit
partners.com

**Sutter Hill Ventures**
755 Page Mill Rd., Ste. A-200
Palo Alto, CA 94304
(650)493-5600
Fax: (650)858-1854
E-mail: shv@shv.com

**Vanguard Venture Partners**
525 University Ave., Ste. 600
Palo Alto, CA 94301
(650)321-2900
Fax: (650)321-2902
Website: http://www.vanguard
ventures.com

**Venture Growth Associates**
2479 East Bayshore St., Ste. 710
Palo Alto, CA 94303

(650)855-9100
Fax: (650)855-9104

**Worldview Technology Partners**
435 Tasso St., Ste. 120
Palo Alto, CA 94301
(650)322-3800
Fax: (650)322-3880
Website: http://www.worldview.com

**Draper, Fisher, Jurvetson / Draper Associates**
400 Seaport Ct., Ste.250
Redwood City, CA 94063
(415)599-9000
Fax: (415)599-9726
Website: http://www.dfj.com

**Gabriel Venture Partners**
350 Marine Pkwy., Ste. 200
Redwood Shores, CA 94065
(650)551-5000
Fax: (650)551-5001
Website: http://www.gabrielvp.com

**Hallador Venture Partners, L.L.C.**
740 University Ave., Ste. 110
Sacramento, CA 95825-6710
(916)920-0191
Fax: (916)920-5188
E-mail: chris@hallador.com

**Emerald Venture Group**
12396 World Trade Dr., Ste. 116
San Diego, CA 92128
(858)451-1001
Fax: (858)451-1003
Website: http://www.emerald
venture.com

**Forward Ventures**
9255 Towne Centre Dr.
San Diego, CA 92121
(858)677-6077
Fax: (858)452-8799
E-mail: info@forwardventure.com
Website: http://www.forward
venture.com

**Idanta Partners Ltd.**
4660 La Jolla Village Dr., Ste. 850
San Diego, CA 92122
(619)452-9690
Fax: (619)452-2013
Website: http://www.idanta.com

**Kingsbury Associates**
3655 Nobel Dr., Ste. 490
San Diego, CA 92122
(858)677-0600
Fax: (858)677-0800

**Kyocera International Inc.**
Corporate Development
8611 Balboa Ave.
San Diego, CA 92123
(858)576-2600
Fax: (858)492-1456

**Sorrento Associates, Inc.**
4370 LaJolla Village Dr., Ste. 1040
San Diego, CA 92122
(619)452-3100
Fax: (619)452-7607
Website: http://www.sorrento
ventures.com

**Western States Investment Group**
9191 Towne Ctr. Dr., Ste. 310
San Diego, CA 92122
(619)678-0800
Fax: (619)678-0900

**Aberdare Ventures**
One Embarcadero Center, Ste. 4000
San Francisco, CA 94111
(415)392-7442
Fax: (415)392-4264
Website: http://www.aberdare.com

**Acacia Venture Partners**
101 California St., Ste. 3160
San Francisco, CA 94111
(415)433-4200
Fax: (415)433-4250
Website: http://www.acaciavp.com

**Access Venture Partners**
319 Laidley St.
San Francisco, CA 94131
(415)586-0132
Fax: (415)392-6310
Website: http://www.access
venturepartners.com

**Alta Partners**
One Embarcadero Center, Ste. 4050
San Francisco, CA 94111
(415)362-4022
Fax: (415)362-6178
E-mail: alta@altapartners.com
Website: http://www.altapartners.com

**Bangert Dawes Reade Davis & Thom**
220 Montgomery St., Ste. 424
San Francisco, CA 94104
(415)954-9900
Fax: (415)954-9901
E-mail: bdrdt@pacbell.net

**Berkeley International Capital Corp.**
650 California St., Ste. 2800
San Francisco, CA 94108-2609

(415)249-0450
Fax: (415)392-3929
Website: http://www.berkeleyvc.com

**Blueprint Ventures LLC**
456 Montgomery St., 22nd Fl.
San Francisco, CA 94104
(415)901-4000
Fax: (415)901-4035
Website: http://www.blue
printventures.com

**Blumberg Capital Ventures**
580 Howard St., Ste. 401
San Francisco, CA 94105
(415)905-5007
Fax: (415)357-5027
Website: http://www.blumberg-
capital.com

**Burr, Egan, Deleage, and Co. (San Francisco)**
1 Embarcadero Center, Ste. 4050
San Francisco, CA 94111
(415)362-4022
Fax: (415)362-6178

**Burrill & Company**
120 Montgomery St., Ste. 1370
San Francisco, CA 94104
(415)743-3160
Fax: (415)743-3161
Website: http://www.burrillandco.com

**CMEA Ventures**
235 Montgomery St., Ste. 920
San Francisco, CA 94401
(415)352-1520
Fax: (415)352-1524
Website: http://www.cmeaventures.com

**Crocker Capital**
1 Post St., Ste. 2500
San Francisco, CA 94101
(415)956-5250
Fax: (415)959-5710

**Dominion Ventures, Inc.**
44 Montgomery St., Ste. 4200
San Francisco, CA 94104
(415)362-4890
Fax: (415)394-9245

**Dorset Capital**
Pier 1
Bay 2
San Francisco, CA 94111
(415)398-7101
Fax: (415)398-7141
Website: http://www.dorsetcapital.com

**Gatx Capital**
Four Embarcadero Center, Ste. 2200
San Francisco, CA 94904
(415)955-3200
Fax: (415)955-3449

**IMinds**
135 Main St., Ste. 1350
San Francisco, CA 94105
(415)547-0000
Fax: (415)227-0300
Website: http://www.iminds.com

**LF International Inc.**
360 Post St., Ste. 705
San Francisco, CA 94108
(415)399-0110
Fax: (415)399-9222
Website: http://www.lfvc.com

**Newbury Ventures**
535 Pacific Ave., 2nd Fl.
San Francisco, CA 94133
(415)296-7408
Fax: (415)296-7416
Website: http://www.newburyven.com

**Quest Ventures (San Francisco)**
333 Bush St., Ste. 1750
San Francisco, CA 94104
(415)782-1414
Fax: (415)782-1415

**Robertson-Stephens Co.**
555 California St., Ste. 2600
San Francisco, CA 94104
(415)781-9700
Fax: (415)781-2556
Website: http://www.omegaad
ventures.com

**Rosewood Capital, L.P.**
One Maritime Plaza, Ste. 1330
San Francisco, CA 94111-3503
(415)362-5526
Fax: (415)362-1192
Website: http://www.rosewoodvc.com

**Ticonderoga Capital Inc.**
555 California St., No. 4950
San Francisco, CA 94104
(415)296-7900
Fax: (415)296-8956

**21st Century Internet Venture Partners**
Two South Park
2nd Floor
San Francisco, CA 94107
(415)512-1221
Fax: (415)512-2650
Website: http://www.21vc.com

**VK Ventures**
600 California St., Ste.1700
San Francisco, CA 94111
(415)391-5600
Fax: (415)397-2744

**Walden Group of Venture Capital Funds**
750 Battery St., Seventh Floor
San Francisco, CA 94111
(415)391-7225
Fax: (415)391-7262

**Acer Technology Ventures**
2641 Orchard Pkwy.
San Jose, CA 95134
(408)433-4945
Fax: (408)433-5230

**Authosis**
226 Airport Pkwy., Ste. 405
San Jose, CA 95110
(650)814-3603
Website: http://www.authosis.com

**Western Technology Investment**
2010 N. First St., Ste. 310
San Jose, CA 95131
(408)436-8577
Fax: (408)436-8625
E-mail: mktg@westerntech.com

**Drysdale Enterprises**
177 Bovet Rd., Ste. 600
San Mateo, CA 94402
(650)341-6336
Fax: (650)341-1329
E-mail: drysdale@aol.com

**Greylock**
2929 Campus Dr., Ste. 400
San Mateo, CA 94401
(650)493-5525
Fax: (650)493-5575
Website: http://www.greylock.com

**Technology Funding**
2000 Alameda de las Pulgas, Ste. 250
San Mateo, CA 94403
(415)345-2200
Fax: (415)345-1797

**2M Invest Inc.**
1875 S. Grant St.
Suite 750
San Mateo, CA 94402
(650)655-3765
Fax: (650)372-9107
E-mail: 2minfo@2minvest.com
Website: http://www.2minvest.com

**Phoenix Growth Capital Corp.**
2401 Kerner Blvd.
San Rafael, CA 94901
(415)485-4569
Fax: (415)485-4663

**NextGen Partners LLC**
1705 East Valley Rd.
Santa Barbara, CA 93108
(805)969-8540
Fax: (805)969-8542
Website: http://www.nextgen
partners.com

**Denali Venture Capital**
1925 Woodland Ave.
Santa Clara, CA 95050
(408)690-4838
Fax: (408)247-6979
E-mail: wael@denaliventurecapital.com
Website: http://www.denali
venturecapital.com

**Dotcom Ventures LP**
3945 Freedom Circle, Ste. 740
Santa Clara, CA 95045
(408)919-9855
Fax: (408)919-9857
Website: http://www.dotcom
venturesatl.com

**Silicon Valley Bank**
3003 Tasman
Santa Clara, CA 95054
(408)654-7400
Fax: (408)727-8728

**Al Shugart International**
920 41st Ave.
Santa Cruz, CA 95062
(831)479-7852
Fax: (831)479-7852
Website: http://www.alshugart.com

**Leonard Mautner Associates**
1434 Sixth St.
Santa Monica, CA 90401
(213)393-9788
Fax: (310)459-9918

**Palomar Ventures**
100 Wilshire Blvd., Ste. 450
Santa Monica, CA 90401
(310)260-6050
Fax: (310)656-4150
Website: http://www.palomar
ventures.com

**Medicus Venture Partners**
12930 Saratoga Ave., Ste. D8
Saratoga, CA 95070

(408)447-8600
Fax: (408)447-8599
Website: http://www.medicusvc.com

**Redleaf Venture Management**
14395 Saratoga Ave., Ste. 130
Saratoga, CA 95070
(408)868-0800
Fax: (408)868-0810
E-mail: nancy@redleaf.com
Website: http://www.redleaf.com

**Artemis Ventures**
207 Second St., Ste. E
3rd Fl.
Sausalito, CA 94965
(415)289-2500
Fax: (415)289-1789
Website: http://www.artemisventures.com

**Deucalion Venture Partners**
19501 Brooklime
Sonoma, CA 95476
(707)938-4974
Fax: (707)938-8921

**Windward Ventures**
PO Box 7688
Thousand Oaks, CA 91359-7688
(805)497-3332
Fax: (805)497-9331

**National Investment Management, Inc.**
2601 Airport Dr., Ste.210
Torrance, CA 90505
(310)784-7600
Fax: (310)784-7605

**Southern California Ventures**
406 Amapola Ave. Ste. 125
Torrance, CA 90501
(310)787-4381
Fax: (310)787-4382

**Sandton Financial Group**
21550 Oxnard St., Ste. 300
Woodland Hills, CA 91367
(818)702-9283

**Woodside Fund**
850 Woodside Dr.
Woodside, CA 94062
(650)368-5545
Fax: (650)368-2416
Website: http://www.woodsidefund.com

## Colorado

**Colorado Venture Management**
Ste. 300
Boulder, CO 80301

(303)440-4055
Fax: (303)440-4636

**Dean & Associates**
4362 Apple Way
Boulder, CO 80301
Fax: (303)473-9900

**Roser Ventures LLC**
1105 Spruce St.
Boulder, CO 80302
(303)443-6436
Fax: (303)443-1885
Website: http://www.roserventures.com

**Sequel Venture Partners**
4430 Arapahoe Ave., Ste. 220
Boulder, CO 80303
(303)546-0400
Fax: (303)546-9728
E-mail: tom@sequelvc.com
Website: http://www.sequelvc.com

**New Venture Resources**
445C E. Cheyenne Mtn. Blvd.
Colorado Springs, CO 80906-4570
(719)598-9272
Fax: (719)598-9272

**The Centennial Funds**
1428 15th St.
Denver, CO 80202-1318
(303)405-7500
Fax: (303)405-7575
Website: http://www.centennial.com

**Rocky Mountain Capital Partners**
1125 17th St., Ste. 2260
Denver, CO 80202
(303)291-5200
Fax: (303)291-5327

**Sandlot Capital LLC**
600 South Cherry St., Ste. 525
Denver, CO 80246
(303)893-3400
Fax: (303)893-3403
Website: http://www.sandlotcapital.com

**Wolf Ventures**
50 South Steele St., Ste. 777
Denver, CO 80209
(303)321-4800
Fax: (303)321-4848
E-mail: businessplan@wolf
ventures.com
Website: http://www.wolfventures.com

**The Columbine Venture Funds**
5460 S. Quebec St., Ste. 270
Englewood, CO 80111

(303)694-3222
Fax: (303)694-9007

**Investment Securities of Colorado, Inc.**
4605 Denice Dr.
Englewood, CO 80111
(303)796-9192

**Kinship Partners**
6300 S. Syracuse Way, Ste. 484
Englewood, CO 80111
(303)694-0268
Fax: (303)694-1707
E-mail: block@vailsys.com

**Boranco Management, L.L.C.**
1528 Hillside Dr.
Fort Collins, CO 80524-1969
(970)221-2297
Fax: (970)221-4787

**Aweida Ventures**
890 West Cherry St., Ste. 220
Louisville, CO 80027
(303)664-9520
Fax: (303)664-9530
Website: http://www.aweida.com

**Access Venture Partners**
8787 Turnpike Dr., Ste. 260
Westminster, CO 80030
(303)426-8899
Fax: (303)426-8828

**Medmax Ventures LP**
1 Northwestern Dr., Ste. 203
Bloomfield, CT 06002
(860)286-2960
Fax: (860)286-9960

**James B. Kobak & Co.**
Four Mansfield Place
Darien, CT 06820
(203)656-3471
Fax: (203)655-2905

**Orien Ventures**
1 Post Rd.
Fairfield, CT 06430
(203)259-9933
Fax: (203)259-5288

**ABP Acquisition Corporation**
115 Maple Ave.
Greenwich, CT 06830
(203)625-8287
Fax: (203)447-6187

**Catterton Partners**
9 Greenwich Office Park
Greenwich, CT 06830
(203)629-4901

Fax: (203)629-4903
Website: http://www.cpequity.com

**Consumer Venture Partners**
3 Pickwick Plz.
Greenwich, CT 06830
(203)629-8800
Fax: (203)629-2019

**Insurance Venture Partners**
31 Brookside Dr., Ste. 211
Greenwich, CT 06830
(203)861-0030
Fax: (203)861-2745

**The NTC Group**
Three Pickwick Plaza
Ste. 200
Greenwich, CT 06830
(203)862-2800
Fax: (203)622-6538

**Regulus International Capital Co., Inc.**
140 Greenwich Ave.
Greenwich, CT 06830
(203)625-9700
Fax: (203)625-9706

**Axiom Venture Partners**
City Place II
185 Asylum St., 17th Fl.
Hartford, CT 06103
(860)548-7799
Fax: (860)548-7797
Website: http://www.axiomventures.com

**Conning Capital Partners**
City Place II
185 Asylum St.
Hartford, CT 06103-4105
(860)520-1289
Fax: (860)520-1299
E-mail: pe@conning.com
Website: http://www.conning.com

**First New England Capital L.P.**
100 Pearl St.
Hartford, CT 06103
(860)293-3333
Fax: (860)293-3338
E-mail: info@firstnewenglandcapital.com
Website: http://www.firstnewengland
capital.com

**Northeast Ventures**
One State St., Ste. 1720
Hartford, CT 06103
(860)547-1414
Fax: (860)246-8755

**Windward Holdings**
38 Sylvan Rd.
Madison, CT 06443
(203)245-6870
Fax: (203)245-6865

**Advanced Materials Partners, Inc.**
45 Pine St.
PO Box 1022
New Canaan, CT 06840
(203)966-6415
Fax: (203)966-8448
E-mail: wkb@amplink.com

**RFE Investment Partners**
36 Grove St.
New Canaan, CT 06840
(203)966-2800
Fax: (203)966-3109
Website: http://www.rfeip.com

**Connecticut Innovations, Inc.**
999 West St.
Rocky Hill, CT 06067
(860)563-5851
Fax: (860)563-4877
E-mail: pamela.hartley@ctin
novations.com
Website: http://www.ctinnovations.com

**Canaan Partners**
105 Rowayton Ave.
Rowayton, CT 06853
(203)855-0400
Fax: (203)854-9117
Website: http://www.canaan.com

**Landmark Partners, Inc.**
10 Mill Pond Ln.
Simsbury, CT 06070
(860)651-9760
Fax: (860)651-8890
Website: http://
www.landmarkpartners.com

**Sweeney & Company**
PO Box 567
Southport, CT 06490
(203)255-0220
Fax: (203)255-0220
E-mail: sweeney@connix.com

**Baxter Associates, Inc.**
PO Box 1333
Stamford, CT 06904
(203)323-3143
Fax: (203)348-0622

**Beacon Partners Inc.**
6 Landmark Sq., 4th Fl.
Stamford, CT 06901-2792

(203)359-5776
Fax: (203)359-5876

**Collinson, Howe, and Lennox, LLC**
1055 Washington Blvd., 5th Fl.
Stamford, CT 06901
(203)324-7700
Fax: (203)324-3636
E-mail: info@chlmedical.com
Website: http://www.chlmedical.com

**Prime Capital Management Co.**
550 West Ave.
Stamford, CT 06902
(203)964-0642
Fax: (203)964-0862

**Saugatuck Capital Co.**
1 Canterbury Green
Stamford, CT 06901
(203)348-6669
Fax: (203)324-6995
Website: http://www.sauga
tuckcapital.com

**Soundview Financial Group Inc.**
22 Gatehouse Rd.
Stamford, CT 06902
(203)462-7200
Fax: (203)462-7350
Website: http://www.sndv.com

**TSG Ventures, L.L.C.**
177 Broad St., 12th Fl.
Stamford, CT 06901
(203)406-1500
Fax: (203)406-1590

**Whitney & Company**
177 Broad St.
Stamford, CT 06901
(203)973-1400
Fax: (203)973-1422
Website: http://www.jhwhitney.com

**Cullinane & Donnelly Venture Partners L.P.**
970 Farmington Ave.
West Hartford, CT 06107
(860)521-7811

**The Crestview Investment and Financial Group**
431 Post Rd. E, Ste. 1
Westport, CT 06880-4403
(203)222-0333
Fax: (203)222-0000

**Marketcorp Venture Associates, L.P. (MCV)**
274 Riverside Ave.
Westport, CT 06880

(203)222-3030
Fax: (203)222-3033

**Oak Investment Partners (Westport)**
1 Gorham Island
Westport, CT 06880
(203)226-8346
Fax: (203)227-0372
Website: http://www.oakinv.com

**Oxford Bioscience Partners**
315 Post Rd. W
Westport, CT 06880-5200
(203)341-3300
Fax: (203)341-3309
Website: http://www.oxbio.com

**Prince Ventures (Westport)**
25 Ford Rd.
Westport, CT 06880
(203)227-8332
Fax: (203)226-5302

**LTI Venture Leasing Corp.**
221 Danbury Rd.
Wilton, CT 06897
(203)563-1100
Fax: (203)563-1111
Website: http://www.ltileasing.com

## Delaware

**Blue Rock Capital**
5803 Kennett Pike, Ste. A
Wilmington, DE 19807
(302)426-0981
Fax: (302)426-0982
Website: http://www.bluerockcapital.com

## District of Columbia

**Allied Capital Corp.**
1919 Pennsylvania Ave. NW
Washington, DC 20006-3434
(202)331-2444
Fax: (202)659-2053
Website: http://www.alliedcapital.com

**Atlantic Coastal Ventures, L.P.**
3101 South St. NW
Washington, DC 20007
(202)293-1166
Fax: (202)293-1181
Website: http://www.atlanticcv.com

**Columbia Capital Group, Inc.**
1660 L St. NW, Ste. 308
Washington, DC 20036
(202)775-8815
Fax: (202)223-0544

**Core Capital Partners**
901 15th St., NW
9th Fl.
Washington, DC 20005
(202)589-0090
Fax: (202)589-0091
Website: http://www.core-capital.com

**Next Point Partners**
701 Pennsylvania Ave. NW, Ste. 900
Washington, DC 20004
(202)661-8703
Fax: (202)434-7400
E-mail: mf@nextpoint.vc
Website: http://www.nextpointvc.com

**Telecommunications Development Fund**
2020 K. St. NW
Ste. 375
Washington, DC 20006
(202)293-8840
Fax: (202)293-8850
Website: http://www.tdfund.com

**Wachtel & Co., Inc.**
1101 4th St. NW
Washington, DC 20005-5680
(202)898-1144

**Winslow Partners LLC**
1300 Connecticut Ave. NW
Washington, DC 20036-1703
(202)530-5000
Fax: (202)530-5010
E-mail: winslow@winslowpartners.com

**Women's Growth Capital Fund**
1054 31st St., NW
Ste. 110
Washington, DC 20007
(202)342-1431
Fax: (202)341-1203
Website: http://www.wgcf.com

**Sigma Capital Corp.**
22668 Caravelle Circle
Boca Raton, FL 33433
(561)368-9783

**North American Business Development Co., L.L.C.**
111 East Las Olas Blvd.
Ft. Lauderdale, FL 33301
(305)463-0681
Fax: (305)527-0904
Website: http://
www.northamericanfund.com

**Chartwell Capital Management Co. Inc.**
1 Independent Dr., Ste. 3120

Jacksonville, FL 32202
(904)355-3519
Fax: (904)353-5833
E-mail: info@chartwellcap.com

**CEO Advisors**
1061 Maitland Center Commons
Ste. 209
Maitland, FL 32751
(407)660-9327
Fax: (407)660-2109

**Henry & Co.**
8201 Peters Rd., Ste. 1000
Plantation, FL 33324
(954)797-7400

**Avery Business Development Services**
2506 St. Michel Ct.
Ponte Vedra, FL 32082
(904)285-6033

**New South Ventures**
5053 Ocean Blvd.
Sarasota, FL 34242
(941)358-6000
Fax: (941)358-6078
Website: http://www.newsouth
ventures.com

**Venture Capital Management Corp.**
PO Box 2626
Satellite Beach, FL 32937
(407)777-1969

**Florida Capital Venture Ltd.**
325 Florida Bank Plaza
100 W. Kennedy Blvd.
Tampa, FL 33602
(813)229-2294
Fax: (813)229-2028

**Quantum Capital Partners**
339 South Plant Ave.
Tampa, FL 33606
(813)250-1999
Fax: (813)250-1998
Website: http://www.quantum
capitalpartners.com

**South Atlantic Venture Fund**
614 W. Bay St.
Tampa, FL 33606-2704
(813)253-2500
Fax: (813)253-2360
E-mail: venture@southatlantic.com
Website: http://www.southatlantic.com

**LM Capital Corp.**
120 S. Olive, Ste. 400
West Palm Beach, FL 33401

(561)833-9700
Fax: (561)655-6587
Website: http://www.lmcapital
securities.com

## Georgia

**Venture First Associates**
4811 Thornwood Dr.
Acworth, GA 30102
(770)928-3733
Fax: (770)928-6455

**Alliance Technology Ventures**
8995 Westside Pkwy., Ste. 200
Alpharetta, GA 30004
(678)336-2000
Fax: (678)336-2001
E-mail: info@atv.com
Website: http://www.atv.com

**Cordova Ventures**
2500 North Winds Pkwy., Ste. 475
Alpharetta, GA 30004
(678)942-0300
Fax: (678)942-0301
Website: http://www.cordovaventures.
com

**Advanced Technology Development
Fund**
1000 Abernathy, Ste. 1420
Atlanta, GA 30328-5614
(404)668-2333
Fax: (404)668-2333

**CGW Southeast Partners**
12 Piedmont Center, Ste. 210
Atlanta, GA 30305
(404)816-3255
Fax: (404)816-3258
Website: http://www.cgwlp.com

**Cyberstarts**
1900 Emery St., NW
3rd Fl.
Atlanta, GA 30318
(404)267-5000
Fax: (404)267-5200
Website: http://www.cyberstarts.com

**EGL Holdings, Inc.**
10 Piedmont Center, Ste. 412
Atlanta, GA 30305
(404)949-8300
Fax: (404)949-8311

**Equity South**
1790 The Lenox Bldg.
3399 Peachtree Rd. NE
Atlanta, GA 30326

(404)237-6222
Fax: (404)261-1578

**Five Paces**
3400 Peachtree Rd., Ste. 200
Atlanta, GA 30326
(404)439-8300
Fax: (404)439-8301
Website: http://www.fivepaces.com

**Frontline Capital, Inc.**
3475 Lenox Rd., Ste. 400
Atlanta, GA 30326
(404)240-7280
Fax: (404)240-7281

**Fuqua Ventures LLC**
1201 W. Peachtree St. NW, Ste. 5000
Atlanta, GA 30309
(404)815-4500
Fax: (404)815-4528
Website: http://www.fuquaventures.com

**Noro-Moseley Partners**
4200 Northside Pkwy., Bldg. 9
Atlanta, GA 30327
(404)233-1966
Fax: (404)239-9280
Website: http://www.noro-moseley.com

**Renaissance Capital Corp.**
34 Peachtree St. NW, Ste. 2230
Atlanta, GA 30303
(404)658-9061
Fax: (404)658-9064

**River Capital, Inc.**
Two Midtown Plaza
1360 Peachtree St. NE, Ste. 1430
Atlanta, GA 30309
(404)873-2166
Fax: (404)873-2158

**State Street Bank & Trust Co.**
3414 Peachtree Rd. NE, Ste. 1010
Atlanta, GA 30326
(404)364-9500
Fax: (404)261-4469

**UPS Strategic Enterprise Fund**
55 Glenlake Pkwy. NE
Atlanta, GA 30328
(404)828-8814
Fax: (404)828-8088
E-mail: jcacyce@ups.com
Website: http://www.ups.com/sef/
sef_home

**Wachovia**
191 Peachtree St. NE, 26th Fl.
Atlanta, GA 30303

(404)332-1000
Fax: (404)332-1392
Website: http://www.wachovia.com/wca

**Brainworks Ventures**
4243 Dunwoody Club Dr.
Chamblee, GA 30341
(770)239-7447

**First Growth Capital Inc.**
Best Western Plaza, Ste. 105
PO Box 815
Forsyth, GA 31029
(912)781-7131

**Financial Capital Resources, Inc.**
21 Eastbrook Bend, Ste. 116
Peachtree City, GA 30269
(404)487-6650

## Hawaii

**HMS Hawaii Management Partners**
Davies Pacific Center
841 Bishop St., Ste. 860
Honolulu, HI 96813
(808)545-3755
Fax: (808)531-2611

## Idaho

**Sun Valley Ventures**
160 Second St.
Ketchum, ID 83340
(208)726-5005
Fax: (208)726-5094

## Illinois

**Open Prairie Ventures**
115 N. Neil St., Ste. 209
Champaign, IL 61820
(217)351-7000
Fax: (217)351-7051
E-mail: inquire@openprairie.com
Website: http://www.openprairie.com

**ABN AMRO Private Equity**
208 S. La Salle St., 10th Fl.
Chicago, IL 60604
(312)855-7079
Fax: (312)553-6648
Website: http://www.abnequity.com

**Alpha Capital Partners, Ltd.**
122 S. Michigan Ave., Ste. 1700
Chicago, IL 60603
(312)322-9800
Fax: (312)322-9808
E-mail: acp@alphacapital.com

**Ameritech Development Corp.**
30 S. Wacker Dr., 37th Fl.
Chicago, IL 60606
(312)750-5083
Fax: (312)609-0244

**Apex Investment Partners**
225 W. Washington, Ste. 1450
Chicago, IL 60606
(312)857-2800
Fax: (312)857-1800
E-mail: apex@apexvc.com
Website: http://www.apexvc.com

**Arch Venture Partners**
8725 W. Higgins Rd., Ste. 290
Chicago, IL 60631
(773)380-6600
Fax: (773)380-6606
Website: http://www.archventure.com

**The Bank Funds**
208 South LaSalle St., Ste. 1680
Chicago, IL 60604
(312)855-6020
Fax: (312)855-8910

**Batterson Venture Partners**
303 W. Madison St., Ste. 1110
Chicago, IL 60606-3309
(312)269-0300
Fax: (312)269-0021
Website: http://www.battersonvp.com

**William Blair Capital Partners, L.L.C.**
222 W. Adams St., Ste. 1300
Chicago, IL 60606
(312)364-8250
Fax: (312)236-1042
E-mail: privateequity@wmblair.com
Website: http://www.wmblair.com

**Bluestar Ventures**
208 South LaSalle St., Ste. 1020
Chicago, IL 60604
(312)384-5000
Fax: (312)384-5005
Website: http://www.bluestarventures.com

**The Capital Strategy Management Co.**
233 S. Wacker Dr.
Box 06334
Chicago, IL 60606
(312)444-1170

**DN Partners**
77 West Wacker Dr., Ste. 4550
Chicago, IL 60601
(312)332-7960
Fax: (312)332-7979

**Dresner Capital Inc.**
29 South LaSalle St., Ste. 310
Chicago, IL 60603
(312)726-3600
Fax: (312)726-7448

**Eblast Ventures LLC**
11 South LaSalle St., 5th Fl.
Chicago, IL 60603
(312)372-2600
Fax: (312)372-5621
Website: http://www.eblastventures.com

**Essex Woodlands Health Ventures, L.P.**
190 S. LaSalle St., Ste. 2800
Chicago, IL 60603
(312)444-6040
Fax: (312)444-6034
Website: http://www.essexwood
lands.com

**First Analysis Venture Capital**
233 S. Wacker Dr., Ste. 9500
Chicago, IL 60606
(312)258-1400
Fax: (312)258-0334
Website: http://www.firstanalysis.com

**Frontenac Co.**
135 S. LaSalle St., Ste.3800
Chicago, IL 60603
(312)368-0044
Fax: (312)368-9520
Website: http://www.frontenac.com

**GTCR Golder Rauner, LLC**
6100 Sears Tower
Chicago, IL 60606
(312)382-2200
Fax: (312)382-2201
Website: http://www.gtcr.com

**High Street Capital LLC**
311 South Wacker Dr., Ste. 4550
Chicago, IL 60606
(312)697-4990
Fax: (312)697-4994
Website: http://www.highstr.com

**IEG Venture Management, Inc.**
70 West Madison
Chicago, IL 60602
(312)644-0890
Fax: (312)454-0369
Website: http://www.iegventure.com

**JK&B Capital**
180 North Stetson, Ste. 4500
Chicago, IL 60601
(312)946-1200
Fax: (312)946-1103

E-mail: gspencer@jkbcapital.com
Website: http://www.jkbcapital.com

**Kettle Partners L.P.**
350 W. Hubbard, Ste. 350
Chicago, IL 60610
(312)329-9300
Fax: (312)527-4519
Website: http://www.kettlevc.com

**Lake Shore Capital Partners**
20 N. Wacker Dr., Ste. 2807
Chicago, IL 60606
(312)803-3536
Fax: (312)803-3534

**LaSalle Capital Group Inc.**
70 W. Madison St., Ste. 5710
Chicago, IL 60602
(312)236-7041
Fax: (312)236-0720

**Linc Capital, Inc.**
303 E. Wacker Pkwy., Ste. 1000
Chicago, IL 60601
(312)946-2670
Fax: (312)938-4290
E-mail: bdemars@linccap.com

**Madison Dearborn Partners, Inc.**
3 First National Plz., Ste. 3800
Chicago, IL 60602
(312)895-1000
Fax: (312)895-1001
E-mail: invest@mdcp.com
Website: http://www.mdcp.com

**Mesirow Private Equity Investments Inc.**
350 N. Clark St.
Chicago, IL 60610
(312)595-6950
Fax: (312)595-6211
Website: http://www.meisrow
financial.com

**Mosaix Ventures LLC**
1822 North Mohawk
Chicago, IL 60614
(312)274-0988
Fax: (312)274-0989
Website: http://www.mosaix
ventures.com

**Nesbitt Burns**
111 West Monroe St.
Chicago, IL 60603
(312)416-3855
Fax: (312)765-8000
Website: http://www.harrisbank.com

**Polestar Capital, Inc.**
180 N. Michigan Ave., Ste. 1905
Chicago, IL 60601
(312)984-9090
Fax: (312)984-9877
E-mail: wl@polestarvc.com
Website: http://www.polestarvc.com

**Prince Ventures (Chicago)**
10 S. Wacker Dr., Ste. 2575
Chicago, IL 60606-7407
(312)454-1408
Fax: (312)454-9125

**Prism Capital**
444 N. Michigan Ave.
Chicago, IL 60611
(312)464-7900
Fax: (312)464-7915
Website: http://www.prismfund.com

**Third Coast Capital**
900 N. Franklin St., Ste. 700
Chicago, IL 60610
(312)337-3303
Fax: (312)337-2567
E-mail: manic@earthlink.com
Website: http://www.third
coastcapital.com

**Thoma Cressey Equity Partners**
4460 Sears Tower, 92nd Fl.
233 S. Wacker Dr.
Chicago, IL 60606
(312)777-4444
Fax: (312)777-4445
Website: http://www.thomacressey.com

**Tribune Ventures**
435 N. Michigan Ave., Ste. 600
Chicago, IL 60611
(312)527-8797
Fax: (312)222-5993
Website: http://www.tribuneventures.com

**Wind Point Partners (Chicago)**
676 N. Michigan Ave., Ste. 330
Chicago, IL 60611
(312)649-4000
Website: http://www.wppartners.com

**Marquette Venture Partners**
520 Lake Cook Rd., Ste. 450
Deerfield, IL 60015
(847)940-1700
Fax: (847)940-1724
Website: http://www.marquette
ventures.com

**Duchossois Investments Limited, LLC**
845 Larch Ave.
Elmhurst, IL 60126

(630)530-6105
Fax: (630)993-8644
Website: http://www.duchtec.com

**Evanston Business Investment Corp.**
1840 Oak Ave.
Evanston, IL 60201
(847)866-1840
Fax: (847)866-1808
E-mail: t-parkinson@nwu.com
Website: http://www.ebic.com

**Inroads Capital Partners L.P.**
1603 Orrington Ave., Ste. 2050
Evanston, IL 60201-3841
(847)864-2000
Fax: (847)864-9692

**The Cerulean Fund/WGC Enterprises**
1701 E. Lake Ave., Ste. 170
Glenview, IL 60025
(847)657-8002
Fax: (847)657-8168

**Ventana Financial Resources, Inc.**
249 Market Sq.
Lake Forest, IL 60045
(847)234-3434

**Beecken, Petty & Co.**
901 Warrenville Rd., Ste. 205
Lisle, IL 60532
(630)435-0300
Fax: (630)435-0370
E-mail: hep@bpcompany.com
Website: http://www.bpcompany.com

**Allstate Private Equity**
3075 Sanders Rd., Ste. G5D
Northbrook, IL 60062-7127
(847)402-8247
Fax: (847)402-0880

**KB Partners**
1101 Skokie Blvd., Ste. 260
Northbrook, IL 60062-2856
(847)714-0444
Fax: (847)714-0445
E-mail: keith@kbpartners.com
Website: http://www.kbpartners.com

**Transcap Associates Inc.**
900 Skokie Blvd., Ste. 210
Northbrook, IL 60062
(847)753-9600
Fax: (847)753-9090

**Graystone Venture Partners, L.L.C. /
Portage Venture Partners**
One Northfield Plaza, Ste. 530
Northfield, IL 60093

(847)446-9460
Fax: (847)446-9470
Website: http://www.portage
ventures.com

**Motorola Inc.**
1303 E. Algonquin Rd.
Schaumburg, IL 60196-1065
(847)576-4929
Fax: (847)538-2250
Website: http://www.mot.com/mne

## Indiana

**Irwin Ventures LLC**
500 Washington St.
Columbus, IN 47202
(812)373-1434
Fax: (812)376-1709
Website: http://www.irwinventures.com

**Cambridge Venture Partners**
4181 East 96th St., Ste. 200
Indianapolis, IN 46240
(317)814-6192
Fax: (317)944-9815

**CID Equity Partners**
One American Square, Ste. 2850
Box 82074
Indianapolis, IN 46282
(317)269-2350
Fax: (317)269-2355
Website: http://www.cidequity.com

**Gazelle Techventures**
6325 Digital Way, Ste. 460
Indianapolis, IN 46278
(317)275-6800
Fax: (317)275-1101
Website: http://www.gazellevc.com

**Monument Advisors Inc.**
Bank One Center/Circle
111 Monument Circle, Ste. 600
Indianapolis, IN 46204-5172
(317)656-5065
Fax: (317)656-5060
Website: http://www.monumentadv.com

**MWV Capital Partners**
201 N. Illinois St., Ste. 300
Indianapolis, IN 46204
(317)237-2323
Fax: (317)237-2325
Website: http://www.mwvcapital.com

**First Source Capital Corp.**
100 North Michigan St.
PO Box 1602
South Bend, IN 46601

(219)235-2180
Fax: (219)235-2227

## Iowa

**Allsop Venture Partners**
118 Third Ave. SE, Ste. 837
Cedar Rapids, IA 52401
(319)368-6675
Fax: (319)363-9515

**InvestAmerica Investment
Advisors, Inc.**
101 2nd St. SE, Ste. 800
Cedar Rapids, IA 52401
(319)363-8249
Fax: (319)363-9683

**Pappajohn Capital Resources**
2116 Financial Center
Des Moines, IA 50309
(515)244-5746
Fax: (515)244-2346
Website: http://www.pappajohn.com

**Berthel Fisher & Company Planning
Inc.**
701 Tama St.
PO Box 609
Marion, IA 52302
(319)497-5700
Fax: (319)497-4244

## Kansas

**Enterprise Merchant Bank**
7400 West 110th St., Ste. 560
Overland Park, KS 66210
(913)327-8500
Fax: (913)327-8505

**Kansas Venture Capital, Inc. (Overland
Park)**
6700 Antioch Plz., Ste. 460
Overland Park, KS 66204
(913)262-7117
Fax: (913)262-3509
E-mail: jdalton@kvci.com

**Child Health Investment Corp.**
6803 W. 64th St., Ste. 208
Shawnee Mission, KS 66202
(913)262-1436
Fax: (913)262-1575
Website: http://www.chca.com

**Kansas Technology Enterprise Corp.**
214 SW 6th, 1st Fl.
Topeka, KS 66603-3719
(785)296-5272
Fax: (785)296-1160

E-mail: ktec@ktec.com
Website: http://www.ktec.com

## Kentucky

**Kentucky Highlands Investment Corp.**
362 Old Whitley Rd.
London, KY 40741
(606)864-5175
Fax: (606)864-5194
Website: http://www.khic.org

**Chrysalis Ventures, L.L.C.**
1850 National City Tower
Louisville, KY 40202
(502)583-7644
Fax: (502)583-7648
E-mail: bobsany@chrysalisventures.com
Website: http://www.chrysalis
ventures.com

**Humana Venture Capital**
500 West Main St.
Louisville, KY 40202
(502)580-3922
Fax: (502)580-2051
E-mail: gemont@humana.com
George Emont, Director

**Summit Capital Group, Inc.**
6510 Glenridge Park Pl., Ste. 8
Louisville, KY 40222
(502)332-2700

## Louisiana

**Bank One Equity Investors, Inc.**
451 Florida St.
Baton Rouge, LA 70801
(504)332-4421
Fax: (504)332-7377

**Advantage Capital Partners**
LLE Tower
909 Poydras St., Ste. 2230
New Orleans, LA 70112
(504)522-4850
Fax: (504)522-4950
Website: http://www.advantagecap.com

## Maine

**CEI Ventures / Coastal Ventures LP**
2 Portland Fish Pier, Ste. 201
Portland, ME 04101
(207)772-5356
Fax: (207)772-5503
Website: http://www.ceiventures.com

**Commwealth Bioventures, Inc.**
4 Milk St.
Portland, ME 04101

(207)780-0904
Fax: (207)780-0913

## Maryland

**Annapolis Ventures LLC**
151 West St., Ste. 302
Annapolis, MD 21401
(443)482-9555
Fax: (443)482-9565
Website: http://www.annapolis
ventures.com

**Delmag Ventures**
220 Wardour Dr.
Annapolis, MD 21401
(410)267-8196
Fax: (410)267-8017
Website: http://www.delmag
ventures.com

**Abell Venture Fund**
111 S. Calvert St., Ste. 2300
Baltimore, MD 21202
(410)547-1300
Fax: (410)539-6579
Website: http://www.abell.org

**ABS Ventures (Baltimore)**
1 South St., Ste. 2150
Baltimore, MD 21202
(410)895-3895
Fax: (410)895-3899
Website: http://www.absventures.com

**Anthem Capital, L.P.**
16 S. Calvert St., Ste. 800
Baltimore, MD 21202-1305
(410)625-1510
Fax: (410)625-1735
Website: http://www.anthemcapital.com

**Catalyst Ventures**
1119 St. Paul St.
Baltimore, MD 21202
(410)244-0123
Fax: (410)752-7721

**Maryland Venture Capital Trust**
217 E. Redwood St., Ste. 2200
Baltimore, MD 21202
(410)767-6361
Fax: (410)333-6931

**New Enterprise Associates (Baltimore)**
1119 St. Paul St.
Baltimore, MD 21202
(410)244-0115
Fax: (410)752-7721
Website: http://www.nea.com

**T. Rowe Price Threshold Partnerships**
100 E. Pratt St., 8th Fl.
Baltimore, MD 21202
(410)345-2000
Fax: (410)345-2800

**Spring Capital Partners**
16 W. Madison St.
Baltimore, MD 21201
(410)685-8000
Fax: (410)727-1436
E-mail: mailbox@springcap.com

**Arete Corporation**
3 Bethesda Metro Ctr., Ste. 770
Bethesda, MD 20814
(301)657-6268
Fax: (301)657-6254
Website: http://www.arete-microgen.com

**Embryon Capital**
7903 Sleaford Place
Bethesda, MD 20814
(301)656-6837
Fax: (301)656-8056

**Potomac Ventures**
7920 Norfolk Ave., Ste. 1100
Bethesda, MD 20814
(301)215-9240
Website: http://www.potomac ventures.com

**Toucan Capital Corp.**
3 Bethesda Metro Center, Ste. 700
Bethesda, MD 20814
(301)961-1970
Fax: (301)961-1969
Website: http://www.toucancapital.com

**Kinetic Ventures LLC**
2 Wisconsin Cir., Ste. 620
Chevy Chase, MD 20815
(301)652-8066
Fax: (301)652-8310
Website: http://www.kineticventures.com

**Boulder Ventures Ltd.**
4750 Owings Mills Blvd.
Owings Mills, MD 21117
(410)998-3114
Fax: (410)356-5492
Website: http://www.boulderventures.com

**Grotech Capital Group**
9690 Deereco Rd., Ste. 800
Timonium, MD 21093
(410)560-2000
Fax: (410)560-1910
Website: http://www.grotech.com

## Massachusetts

**Adams, Harkness & Hill, Inc.**
60 State St.
Boston, MA 02109
(617)371-3900

**Advent International**
75 State St., 29th Fl.
Boston, MA 02109
(617)951-9400
Fax: (617)951-0566
Website: http://www.adventiner national.com

**American Research and Development**
30 Federal St.
Boston, MA 02110-2508
(617)423-7500
Fax: (617)423-9655

**Ascent Venture Partners**
255 State St., 5th Fl.
Boston, MA 02109
(617)270-9400
Fax: (617)270-9401
E-mail: info@ascentvp.com
Website: http://www.ascentvp.com

**Atlas Venture**
222 Berkeley St.
Boston, MA 02116
(617)488-2200
Fax: (617)859-9292
Website: http://www.atlasventure.com

**Axxon Capital**
28 State St., 37th Fl.
Boston, MA 02109
(617)722-0980
Fax: (617)557-6014
Website: http://www.axxoncapital.com

**BancBoston Capital/BancBoston Ventures**
175 Federal St., 10th Fl.
Boston, MA 02110
(617)434-2509
Fax: (617)434-6175
Website: http:// www.bancbostoncapital.com

**Boston Capital Ventures**
Old City Hall
45 School St.
Boston, MA 02108
(617)227-6550
Fax: (617)227-3847
E-mail: info@bcv.com
Website: http://www.bcv.com

**Boston Financial & Equity Corp.**
20 Overland St.
PO Box 15071
Boston, MA 02215
(617)267-2900
Fax: (617)437-7601
E-mail: debbie@bfec.com

**Boston Millennia Partners**
30 Rowes Wharf
Boston, MA 02110
(617)428-5150
Fax: (617)428-5160
Website: http://www.millennia partners.com

**Bristol Investment Trust**
842A Beacon St.
Boston, MA 02215-3199
(617)566-5212
Fax: (617)267-0932

**Brook Venture Management LLC**
50 Federal St., 5th Fl.
Boston, MA 02110
(617)451-8989
Fax: (617)451-2369
Website: http://www.brookventure.com

**Burr, Egan, Deleage, and Co. (Boston)**
200 Clarendon St., Ste. 3800
Boston, MA 02116
(617)262-7770
Fax: (617)262-9779

**Cambridge/Samsung Partners**
One Exeter Plaza
Ninth Fl.
Boston, MA 02116
(617)262-4440
Fax: (617)262-5562

**Chestnut Street Partners, Inc.**
75 State St., Ste. 2500
Boston, MA 02109
(617)345-7220
Fax: (617)345-7201
E-mail: chestnut@chestnutp.com

**Claflin Capital Management, Inc.**
10 Liberty Sq., Ste. 300
Boston, MA 02109
(617)426-6505
Fax: (617)482-0016
Website: http://www.claflincapital.com

**Copley Venture Partners**
99 Summer St., Ste. 1720
Boston, MA 02110
(617)737-1253
Fax: (617)439-0699

**Corning Capital / Corning Technology Ventures**
121 High Street, Ste. 400
Boston, MA 02110
(617)338-2656
Fax: (617)261-3864
Website: http://www.corningventures.com

**Downer & Co.**
211 Congress St.
Boston, MA 02110
(617)482-6200
Fax: (617)482-6201
E-mail: cdowner@downer.com
Website: http://www.downer.com

**Fidelity Ventures**
82 Devonshire St.
Boston, MA 02109
(617)563-6370
Fax: (617)476-9023
Website: http://www.fidelityventures.com

**Greylock Management Corp. (Boston)**
1 Federal St.
Boston, MA 02110-2065
(617)423-5525
Fax: (617)482-0059

**Gryphon Ventures**
222 Berkeley St., Ste.1600
Boston, MA 02116
(617)267-9191
Fax: (617)267-4293
E-mail: all@gryphoninc.com

**Halpern, Denny & Co.**
500 Boylston St.
Boston, MA 02116
(617)536-6602
Fax: (617)536-8535

**Harbourvest Partners, LLC**
1 Financial Center, 44th Fl.
Boston, MA 02111
(617)348-3707
Fax: (617)350-0305
Website: http://www.hvpllc.com

**Highland Capital Partners**
2 International Pl.
Boston, MA 02110
(617)981-1500
Fax: (617)531-1550
E-mail: info@hcp.com
Website: http://www.hcp.com

**Lee Munder Venture Partners**
John Hancock Tower T-53
200 Clarendon St.
Boston, MA 02103

(617)380-5600
Fax: (617)380-5601
Website: http://www.leemunder.com

**M/C Venture Partners**
75 State St., Ste. 2500
Boston, MA 02109
(617)345-7200
Fax: (617)345-7201
Website: http://www.mcventure
partners.com

**Massachusetts Capital Resources Co.**
420 Boylston St.
Boston, MA 02116
(617)536-3900
Fax: (617)536-7930

**Massachusetts Technology Development Corp. (MTDC)**
148 State St.
Boston, MA 02109
(617)723-4920
Fax: (617)723-5983
E-mail: jhodgman@mtdc.com
Website: http://www.mtdc.com

**New England Partners**
One Boston Place, Ste. 2100
Boston, MA 02108
(617)624-8400
Fax: (617)624-8999
Website: http://www.nepartners.com

**North Hill Ventures**
Ten Post Office Square
11th Fl.
Boston, MA 02109
(617)788-2112
Fax: (617)788-2152
Website: http://www.northhill
ventures.com

**OneLiberty Ventures**
150 Cambridge Park Dr.
Boston, MA 02140
(617)492-7280
Fax: (617)492-7290
Website: http://www.oneliberty.com

**Schroder Ventures**
Life Sciences
60 State St., Ste. 3650
Boston, MA 02109
(617)367-8100
Fax: (617)367-1590
Website: http://www.shroderventures.com

**Shawmut Capital Partners**
75 Federal St., 18th Fl.
Boston, MA 02110

(617)368-4900
Fax: (617)368-4910
Website: http://www.shawmutcapital.com

**Solstice Capital LLC**
15 Broad St., 3rd Fl.
Boston, MA 02109
(617)523-7733
Fax: (617)523-5827
E-mail: solticecapital@solcap.com

**Spectrum Equity Investors**
One International Pl., 29th Fl.
Boston, MA 02110
(617)464-4600
Fax: (617)464-4601
Website: http://www.spectrumequity.com

**Spray Venture Partners**
One Walnut St.
Boston, MA 02108
(617)305-4140
Fax: (617)305-4144
Website: http://www.sprayventure.com

**The Still River Fund**
100 Federal St., 29th Fl.
Boston, MA 02110
(617)348-2327
Fax: (617)348-2371
Website: http://www.stillriverfund.com

**Summit Partners**
600 Atlantic Ave., Ste. 2800
Boston, MA 02210-2227
(617)824-1000
Fax: (617)824-1159
Website: http://www.summitpartners.com

**TA Associates, Inc. (Boston)**
High Street Tower
125 High St., Ste. 2500
Boston, MA 02110
(617)574-6700
Fax: (617)574-6728
Website: http://www.ta.com

**TVM Techno Venture Management**
101 Arch St., Ste. 1950
Boston, MA 02110
(617)345-9320
Fax: (617)345-9377
E-mail: info@tvmvc.com
Website: http://www.tvmvc.com

**UNC Ventures**
64 Burough St.
Boston, MA 02130-4017
(617)482-7070
Fax: (617)522-2176

**Venture Investment Management Company (VIMAC)**
177 Milk St.
Boston, MA 02190-3410
(617)292-3300
Fax: (617)292-7979
E-mail: bzeisig@vimac.com
Website: http://www.vimac.com

**MDT Advisers, Inc.**
125 Cambridge Park Dr.
Cambridge, MA 02140-2314
(617)234-2200
Fax: (617)234-2210
Website: http://www.mdtai.com

**TTC Ventures**
One Main St., 6th Fl.
Cambridge, MA 02142
(617)528-3137
Fax: (617)577-1715
E-mail: info@ttcventures.com

**Zero Stage Capital Co. Inc.**
101 Main St., 17th Fl.
Cambridge, MA 02142
(617)876-5355
Fax: (617)876-1248
Website: http://www.zerostage.com

**Atlantic Capital**
164 Cushing Hwy.
Cohasset, MA 02025
(617)383-9449
Fax: (617)383-6040
E-mail: info@atlanticcap.com
Website: http://www.atlanticcap.com

**Seacoast Capital Partners**
55 Ferncroft Rd.
Danvers, MA 01923
(978)750-1300
Fax: (978)750-1301
E-mail: gdeli@seacoastcapital.com
Website: http://www.seacoast
capital.com

**Sage Management Group**
44 South Street
PO Box 2026
East Dennis, MA 02641
(508)385-7172
Fax: (508)385-7272
E-mail: sagemgt@capecod.net

**Applied Technology**
1 Cranberry Hill
Lexington, MA 02421-7397
(617)862-8622
Fax: (617)862-8367

**Royalty Capital Management**
5 Downing Rd.
Lexington, MA 02421-6918
(781)861-8490

**Argo Global Capital**
210 Broadway, Ste. 101
Lynnfield, MA 01940
(781)592-5250
Fax: (781)592-5230
Website: http://www.gsmcapital.com

**Industry Ventures**
6 Bayne Lane
Newburyport, MA 01950
(978)499-7606
Fax: (978)499-0686
Website: http://
www.industryventures.com

**Softbank Capital Partners**
10 Langley Rd., Ste. 202
Newton Center, MA 02459
(617)928-9300
Fax: (617)928-9305
E-mail: clax@bvc.com

**Advanced Technology Ventures (Boston)**
281 Winter St., Ste. 350
Waltham, MA 02451
(781)290-0707
Fax: (781)684-0045
E-mail: info@atvcapital.com
Website: http://www.atvcapital.com

**Castile Ventures**
890 Winter St., Ste. 140
Waltham, MA 02451
(781)890-0060
Fax: (781)890-0065
Website: http://www.castileventures.com

**Charles River Ventures**
1000 Winter St., Ste. 3300
Waltham, MA 02451
(781)487-7060
Fax: (781)487-7065
Website: http://www.crv.com

**Comdisco Venture Group (Waltham)**
Totton Pond Office Center
400-1 Totten Pond Rd.
Waltham, MA 02451
(617)672-0250
Fax: (617)398-8099

**Marconi Ventures**
890 Winter St., Ste. 310
Waltham, MA 02451
(781)839-7177

Fax: (781)522-7477
Website: http://www.marconi.com

**Matrix Partners**
Bay Colony Corporate Center
1000 Winter St., Ste.4500
Waltham, MA 02451
(781)890-2244
Fax: (781)890-2288
Website: http://www.matrix
partners.com

**North Bridge Venture Partners**
950 Winter St. Ste. 4600
Waltham, MA 02451
(781)290-0004
Fax: (781)290-0999
E-mail: eta@nbvp.com

**Polaris Venture Partners**
Bay Colony Corporate Ctr.
1000 Winter St., Ste. 3500
Waltham, MA 02451
(781)290-0770
Fax: (781)290-0880
E-mail: partners@polarisventures.com
Website: http://www.polar
isventures.com

**Seaflower Ventures**
Bay Colony Corporate Ctr.
1000 Winter St. Ste. 1000
Waltham, MA 02451
(781)466-9552
Fax: (781)466-9553
E-mail: moot@seaflower.com
Website: http://www.seaflower.com

**Ampersand Ventures**
55 William St., Ste. 240
Wellesley, MA 02481
(617)239-0700
Fax: (617)239-0824
E-mail: info@ampersandventures.com
Website: http://www.ampersand
ventures.com

**Battery Ventures (Boston)**
20 William St., Ste. 200
Wellesley, MA 02481
(781)577-1000
Fax: (781)577-1001
Website: http://www.battery.com

**Commonwealth Capital Ventures, L.P.**
20 William St., Ste.225
Wellesley, MA 02481
(781)237-7373
Fax: (781)235-8627
Website: http://www.ccvlp.com

**Fowler, Anthony & Company**
20 Walnut St.
Wellesley, MA 02481
(781)237-4201
Fax: (781)237-7718

**Gemini Investors**
20 William St.
Wellesley, MA 02481
(781)237-7001
Fax: (781)237-7233

**Grove Street Advisors Inc.**
20 William St., Ste. 230
Wellesley, MA 02481
(781)263-6100
Fax: (781)263-6101
Website: http://www.groves
treetadvisors.com

**Mees Pierson Investeringsmaat B.V.**
20 William St., Ste. 210
Wellesley, MA 02482
(781)239-7600
Fax: (781)239-0377

**Norwest Equity Partners**
40 William St., Ste. 305
Wellesley, MA 02481-3902
(781)237-5870
Fax: (781)237-6270
Website: http://www.norwestvp.com

**Bessemer Venture Partners (Wellesley Hills)**
83 Walnut St.
Wellesley Hills, MA 02481
(781)237-6050
Fax: (781)235-7576
E-mail: travis@bvpny.com
Website: http://www.bvp.com

**Venture Capital Fund of New England**
20 Walnut St., Ste. 120
Wellesley Hills, MA 02481-2175
(781)239-8262
Fax: (781)239-8263

**Prism Venture Partners**
100 Lowder Brook Dr., Ste. 2500
Westwood, MA 02090
(781)302-4000
Fax: (781)302-4040
E-mail: dwbaum@prismventure.com

**Palmer Partners LP**
200 Unicorn Park Dr.
Woburn, MA 01801
(781)933-5445
Fax: (781)933-0698

## Michigan

**Arbor Partners, L.L.C.**
130 South First St.
Ann Arbor, MI 48104
(734)668-9000
Fax: (734)669-4195
Website: http://www.arborpartners.com

**EDF Ventures**
425 N. Main St.
Ann Arbor, MI 48104
(734)663-3213
Fax: (734)663-7358
E-mail: edf@edfvc.com
Website: http://www.edfvc.com

**White Pines Management, L.L.C.**
2401 Plymouth Rd., Ste. B
Ann Arbor, MI 48105
(734)747-9401
Fax: (734)747-9704
E-mail: ibund@whitepines.com
Website: http://www.whitepines.com

**Wellmax, Inc.**
3541 Bendway Blvd., Ste. 100
Bloomfield Hills, MI 48301
(248)646-3554
Fax: (248)646-6220

**Venture Funding, Ltd.**
Fisher Bldg.
3011 West Grand Blvd., Ste. 321
Detroit, MI 48202
(313)871-3606
Fax: (313)873-4935

**Investcare Partners L.P. / GMA Capital LLC**
32330 W. Twelve Mile Rd.
Farmington Hills, MI 48334
(248)489-9000
Fax: (248)489-8819
E-mail: gma@gmacapital.com
Website: http://www.gmacapital.com

**Liberty Bidco Investment Corp.**
30833 Northwestern Highway, Ste. 211
Farmington Hills, MI 48334
(248)626-6070
Fax: (248)626-6072

**Seaflower Ventures**
5170 Nicholson Rd.
PO Box 474
Fowlerville, MI 48836
(517)223-3335
Fax: (517)223-3337
E-mail: gibbons@seaflower.com
Website: http://www.seaflower.com

**Ralph Wilson Equity Fund LLC**
15400 E. Jefferson Ave.
Gross Pointe Park, MI 48230
(313)821-9122
Fax: (313)821-9101
Website: http://www.Ralph
WilsonEquityFund.com
J. Skip Simms, President

## Minnesota

**Development Corp. of Austin**
1900 Eighth Ave., NW
Austin, MN 55912
(507)433-0346
Fax: (507)433-0361
E-mail: dca@smig.net
Website: http://www.spamtownusa.com

**Northeast Ventures Corp.**
802 Alworth Bldg.
Duluth, MN 55802
(218)722-9915
Fax: (218)722-9871

**Medical Innovation Partners, Inc.**
6450 City West Pkwy.
Eden Prairie, MN 55344-3245
(612)828-9616
Fax: (612)828-9596

**St. Paul Venture Capital, Inc.**
10400 Vicking Dr., Ste. 550
Eden Prairie, MN 55344
(612)995-7474
Fax: (612)995-7475
Website: http://www.stpaulvc.com

**Cherry Tree Investments, Inc.**
7601 France Ave. S, Ste. 150
Edina, MN 55435
(612)893-9012
Fax: (612)893-9036
Website: http://www.cherrytree.com

**Shared Ventures, Inc.**
6550 York Ave. S
Edina, MN 55435
(612)925-3411

**Sherpa Partners LLC**
5050 Lincoln Dr., Ste. 490
Edina, MN 55436
(952)942-1070
Fax: (952)942-1071
Website: http://www.sherpapartners.com

**Affinity Capital Management**
901 Marquette Ave., Ste. 1810
Minneapolis, MN 55402
(612)252-9900

Fax: (612)252-9911
Website: http://www.affinitycapital.com

**Artesian Capital**
1700 Foshay Tower
821 Marquette Ave.
Minneapolis, MN 55402
(612)334-5600
Fax: (612)334-5601
E-mail: artesian@artesian.com

**Coral Ventures**
60 S. 6th St., Ste. 3510
Minneapolis, MN 55402
(612)335-8666
Fax: (612)335-8668
Website: http://www.coralventures.com

**Crescendo Venture Management, L.L.C.**
800 LaSalle Ave., Ste. 2250
Minneapolis, MN 55402
(612)607-2800
Fax: (612)607-2801
Website: http://www.crescendo
ventures.com

**Gideon Hixon Venture**
1900 Foshay Tower
821 Marquette Ave.
Minneapolis, MN 55402
(612)904-2314
Fax: (612)204-0913

**Norwest Equity Partners**
3600 IDS Center
80 S. 8th St.
Minneapolis, MN 55402
(612)215-1600
Fax: (612)215-1601
Website: http://www.norwestvp.com

**Oak Investment Partners (Minneapolis)**
4550 Norwest Center
90 S. 7th St.
Minneapolis, MN 55402
(612)339-9322
Fax: (612)337-8017
Website: http://www.oakinv.com

**Pathfinder Venture Capital Funds (Minneapolis)**
7300 Metro Blvd., Ste. 585
Minneapolis, MN 55439
(612)835-1121
Fax: (612)835-8389
E-mail: jahrens620@aol.com

**U.S. Bancorp Piper Jaffray Ventures, Inc.**
800 Nicollet Mall, Ste. 800
Minneapolis, MN 55402

(612)303-5686
Fax: (612)303-1350
Website: http://www.paperjaffrey
ventures.com

**The Food Fund, Ltd. Partnership**
5720 Smatana Dr., Ste. 300
Minnetonka, MN 55343
(612)939-3950
Fax: (612)939-8106

**Mayo Medical Ventures**
200 First St. SW
Rochester, MN 55905
(507)266-4586
Fax: (507)284-5410
Website: http://www.mayo.edu

## Missouri

**Bankers Capital Corp.**
3100 Gillham Rd.
Kansas City, MO 64109
(816)531-1600
Fax: (816)531-1334

**Capital for Business, Inc. (Kansas City)**
1000 Walnut St., 18th Fl.
Kansas City, MO 64106
(816)234-2357
Fax: (816)234-2952
Website: http://
www.capitalforbusiness.com

**De Vries & Co. Inc.**
800 West 47th St.
Kansas City, MO 64112
(816)756-0055
Fax: (816)756-0061

**InvestAmerica Venture Group Inc. (Kansas City)**
Commerce Tower
911 Main St., Ste. 2424
Kansas City, MO 64105
(816)842-0114
Fax: (816)471-7339

**Kansas City Equity Partners**
233 W. 47th St.
Kansas City, MO 64112
(816)960-1771
Fax: (816)960-1777
Website: http://www.kcep.com

**Bome Investors, Inc.**
8000 Maryland Ave., Ste. 1190
St. Louis, MO 63105
(314)721-5707
Fax: (314)721-5135

Website: http://www.gateway
ventures.com

**Capital for Business, Inc. (St. Louis)**
11 S. Meramac St., Ste. 1430
St. Louis, MO 63105
(314)746-7427
Fax: (314)746-8739
Website: http://www.capitalfor
business.com

**Crown Capital Corp.**
540 Maryville Centre Dr., Ste. 120
Saint Louis, MO 63141
(314)576-1201
Fax: (314)576-1525
Website: http://www.crown-
cap.com

**Gateway Associates L.P.**
8000 Maryland Ave., Ste. 1190
St. Louis, MO 63105
(314)721-5707
Fax: (314)721-5135

**Harbison Corp.**
8112 Maryland Ave., Ste. 250
Saint Louis, MO 63105
(314)727-8200
Fax: (314)727-0249

**Heartland Capital Fund, Ltd.**
PO Box 642117
Omaha, NE 68154
(402)778-5124
Fax: (402)445-2370
Website: http://www.heartland
capitalfund.com

**Odin Capital Group**
1625 Farnam St., Ste. 700
Omaha, NE 68102
(402)346-6200
Fax: (402)342-9311
Website: http://www.odincapital.com

## Nevada

**Edge Capital Investment Co. LLC**
1350 E. Flamingo Rd., Ste. 3000
Las Vegas, NV 89119
(702)438-3343
E-mail: info@edgecapital.net
Website: http://www.edgecapital.net

**The Benefit Capital Companies Inc.**
PO Box 542
Logandale, NV 89021
(702)398-3222
Fax: (702)398-3700

**Millennium Three Venture Group LLC**
6880 South McCarran Blvd., Ste. A-11
Reno, NV 89509
(775)954-2020
Fax: (775)954-2023
Website: http://www.m3vg.com

## New Jersey

**Alan I. Goldman & Associates**
497 Ridgewood Ave.
Glen Ridge, NJ 07028
(973)857-5680
Fax: (973)509-8856

**CS Capital Partners LLC**
328 Second St., Ste. 200
Lakewood, NJ 08701
(732)901-1111
Fax: (212)202-5071
Website: http://www.cs-capital.com

**Edison Venture Fund**
1009 Lenox Dr., Ste. 4
Lawrenceville, NJ 08648
(609)896-1900
Fax: (609)896-0066
E-mail: info@edisonventure.com
Website: http://www.edisonventure.com

**Tappan Zee Capital Corp. (New Jersey)**
201 Lower Notch Rd.
PO Box 416
Little Falls, NJ 07424
(973)256-8280
Fax: (973)256-2841

**The CIT Group/Venture Capital, Inc.**
650 CIT Dr.
Livingston, NJ 07039
(973)740-5429
Fax: (973)740-5555
Website: http://www.cit.com

**Capital Express, L.L.C.**
1100 Valleybrook Ave.
Lyndhurst, NJ 07071
(201)438-8228
Fax: (201)438-5131
E-mail: niles@capitalexpress.com
Website: http://www.capitalexpress.com

**Westford Technology Ventures, L.P.**
17 Academy St.
Newark, NJ 07102
(973)624-2131
Fax: (973)624-2008

**Accel Partners**
1 Palmer Sq.
Princeton, NJ 08542

(609)683-4500
Fax: (609)683-4880
Website: http://www.accel.com

**Cardinal Partners**
221 Nassau St.
Princeton, NJ 08542
(609)924-6452
Fax: (609)683-0174
Website: http://www.cardinal
healthpartners.com

**Domain Associates L.L.C.**
One Palmer Sq., Ste. 515
Princeton, NJ 08542
(609)683-5656
Fax: (609)683-9789
Website: http://www.domainvc.com

**Johnston Associates, Inc.**
181 Cherry Valley Rd.
Princeton, NJ 08540
(609)924-3131
Fax: (609)683-7524
E-mail: jaincorp@aol.com

**Kemper Ventures**
Princeton Forrestal Village
155 Village Blvd.
Princeton, NJ 08540
(609)936-3035
Fax: (609)936-3051

**Penny Lane Parnters**
One Palmer Sq., Ste. 309
Princeton, NJ 08542
(609)497-4646
Fax: (609)497-0611

**Early Stage Enterprises L.P.**
995 Route 518
Skillman, NJ 08558
(609)921-8896
Fax: (609)921-8703
Website: http://www.esevc.com

**MBW Management Inc.**
1 Springfield Ave.
Summit, NJ 07901
(908)273-4060
Fax: (908)273-4430

**BCI Advisors, Inc.**
Glenpointe Center W.
Teaneck, NJ 07666
(201)836-3900
Fax: (201)836-6368
E-mail: info@bciadvisors.com
Website: http://www.bci
partners.com

**Demuth, Folger & Wetherill / DFW Capital Partners**
Glenpointe Center E., 5th Fl.
300 Frank W. Burr Blvd.
Teaneck, NJ 07666
(201)836-2233
Fax: (201)836-5666
Website: http://www.dfwcapital.com

**First Princeton Capital Corp.**
189 Berdan Ave., No. 131
Wayne, NJ 07470-3233
(973)278-3233
Fax: (973)278-4290
Website: http://www.lytellcatt.net

**Edelson Technology Partners**
300 Tice Blvd.
Woodcliff Lake, NJ 07675
(201)930-9898
Fax: (201)930-8899
Website: http://www.edelsontech.com

## New Mexico

**Bruce F. Glaspell & Associates**
10400 Academy Rd. NE, Ste. 313
Albuquerque, NM 87111
(505)292-4505
Fax: (505)292-4258

**High Desert Ventures, Inc.**
6101 Imparata St. NE, Ste. 1721
Albuquerque, NM 87111
(505)797-3330
Fax: (505)338-5147

**New Business Capital Fund, Ltd.**
5805 Torreon NE
Albuquerque, NM 87109
(505)822-8445

**SBC Ventures**
10400 Academy Rd. NE, Ste. 313
Albuquerque, NM 87111
(505)292-4505
Fax: (505)292-4528

**Technology Ventures Corp.**
1155 University Blvd. SE
Albuquerque, NM 87106
(505)246-2882
Fax: (505)246-2891

## New York

**New York State Science & Technology Foundation**
**Small Business Technology Investment Fund**
99 Washington Ave., Ste. 1731
Albany, NY 12210

(518)473-9741
Fax: (518)473-6876

**Rand Capital Corp.**
2200 Rand Bldg.
Buffalo, NY 14203
(716)853-0802
Fax: (716)854-8480
Website: http://www.randcapital.com

**Seed Capital Partners**
620 Main St.
Buffalo, NY 14202
(716)845-7520
Fax: (716)845-7539
Website: http://www.seedcp.com

**Coleman Venture Group**
5909 Northern Blvd.
PO Box 224
East Norwich, NY 11732
(516)626-3642
Fax: (516)626-9722

**Vega Capital Corp.**
45 Knollwood Rd.
Elmsford, NY 10523
(914)345-9500
Fax: (914)345-9505

**Herbert Young Securities, Inc.**
98 Cuttermill Rd.
Great Neck, NY 11021
(516)487-8300
Fax: (516)487-8319

**Sterling/Carl Marks Capital, Inc.**
175 Great Neck Rd., Ste. 408
Great Neck, NY 11021
(516)482-7374
Fax: (516)487-0781
E-mail: stercrlmar@aol.com
Website: http://www.serling
carlmarks.com

**Impex Venture Management Co.**
PO Box 1570
Green Island, NY 12183
(518)271-8008
Fax: (518)271-9101

**Corporate Venture Partners L.P.**
200 Sunset Park
Ithaca, NY 14850
(607)257-6323
Fax: (607)257-6128

**Arthur P. Gould & Co.**
One Wilshire Dr.
Lake Success, NY 11020
(516)773-3000
Fax: (516)773-3289

**Dauphin Capital Partners**
108 Forest Ave.
Locust Valley, NY 11560
(516)759-3339
Fax: (516)759-3322
Website: http://www.dauphincapital.com

**550 Digital Media Ventures**
555 Madison Ave., 10th Fl.
New York, NY 10022
Website: http://www.550dmv.com

**Aberlyn Capital Management Co., Inc.**
500 Fifth Ave.
New York, NY 10110
(212)391-7750
Fax: (212)391-7762

**Adler & Company**
342 Madison Ave., Ste. 807
New York, NY 10173
(212)599-2535
Fax: (212)599-2526

**Alimansky Capital Group, Inc.**
605 Madison Ave., Ste. 300
New York, NY 10022-1901
(212)832-7300
Fax: (212)832-7338

**Allegra Partners**
515 Madison Ave., 29th Fl.
New York, NY 10022
(212)826-9080
Fax: (212)759-2561

**The Argentum Group**
The Chyrsler Bldg.
405 Lexington Ave.
New York, NY 10174
(212)949-6262
Fax: (212)949-8294
Website: http://www.argentum
group.com

**Axavision Inc.**
14 Wall St., 26th Fl.
New York, NY 10005
(212)619-4000
Fax: (212)619-7202

**Bedford Capital Corp.**
18 East 48th St., Ste. 1800
New York, NY 10017
(212)688-5700
Fax: (212)754-4699
E-mail: info@bedfordnyc.com
Website: http://www.bedfordnyc.com

**Bloom & Co.**
950 Third Ave.

New York, NY 10022
(212)838-1858
Fax: (212)838-1843

**Bristol Capital Management**
300 Park Ave., 17th Fl.
New York, NY 10022
(212)572-6306
Fax: (212)705-4292

**Citicorp Venture Capital Ltd.
(New York City)**
399 Park Ave., 14th Fl.
Zone 4
New York, NY 10043
(212)559-1127
Fax: (212)888-2940

**CM Equity Partners**
135 E. 57th St.
New York, NY 10022
(212)909-8428
Fax: (212)980-2630

**Cohen & Co., L.L.C.**
800 Third Ave.
New York, NY 10022
(212)317-2250
Fax: (212)317-2255
E-mail: nlcohen@aol.com

**Cornerstone Equity Investors, L.L.C.**
717 5th Ave., Ste. 1100
New York, NY 10022
(212)753-0901
Fax: (212)826-6798
Website: http://www.cornerstone-
equity.com

**CW Group, Inc.**
1041 3rd Ave., 2nd fl.
New York, NY 10021
(212)308-5266
Fax: (212)644-0354
Website: http://www.cwventures.com

**DH Blair Investment Banking Corp.**
44 Wall St., 2nd Fl.
New York, NY 10005
(212)495-5000
Fax: (212)269-1438

**Dresdner Kleinwort Capital**
75 Wall St.
New York, NY 10005
(212)429-3131
Fax: (212)429-3139
Website: http://www.dresdnerkb.com

**East River Ventures, L.P.**
645 Madison Ave., 22nd Fl.

New York, NY 10022
(212)644-2322
Fax: (212)644-5498

**Easton Hunt Capital Partners**
641 Lexington Ave., 21st Fl.
New York, NY 10017
(212)702-0950
Fax: (212)702-0952
Website: http://www.eastoncapital.com

**Elk Associates Funding Corp.**
747 3rd Ave., Ste. 4C
New York, NY 10017
(212)355-2449
Fax: (212)759-3338

**EOS Partners, L.P.**
320 Park Ave., 22nd Fl.
New York, NY 10022
(212)832-5800
Fax: (212)832-5815
E-mail: mfirst@eospartners.com
Website: http://www.eospartners.com

**Euclid Partners**
45 Rockefeller Plaza, Ste. 3240
New York, NY 10111
(212)218-6880
Fax: (212)218-6877
E-mail: graham@euclidpartners.com
Website: http://www.euclidpartners.com

**Evergreen Capital Partners, Inc.**
150 East 58th St.
New York, NY 10155
(212)813-0758
Fax: (212)813-0754

**Exeter Capital L.P.**
10 E. 53rd St.
New York, NY 10022
(212)872-1172
Fax: (212)872-1198
E-mail: exeter@usa.net

**Financial Technology Research Corp.**
518 Broadway
Penthouse
New York, NY 10012
(212)625-9100
Fax: (212)431-0300
E-mail: fintek@financier.com

**4C Ventures**
237 Park Ave., Ste. 801
New York, NY 10017
(212)692-3680
Fax: (212)692-3685
Website: http://www.4cventures.com

**Fusient Ventures**
99 Park Ave., 20th Fl.
New York, NY 10016
(212)972-8999
Fax: (212)972-9876
E-mail: info@fusient.com
Website: http://www.fusient.com

**Generation Capital Partners**
551 Fifth Ave., Ste. 3100
New York, NY 10176
(212)450-8507
Fax: (212)450-8550
Website: http://www.genpartners.com

**Golub Associates, Inc.**
555 Madison Ave.
New York, NY 10022
(212)750-6060
Fax: (212)750-5505

**Hambro America Biosciences Inc.**
650 Madison Ave., 21st Floor
New York, NY 10022
(212)223-7400
Fax: (212)223-0305

**Hanover Capital Corp.**
505 Park Ave., 15th Fl.
New York, NY 10022
(212)755-1222
Fax: (212)935-1787

**Harvest Partners, Inc.**
280 Park Ave, 33rd Fl.
New York, NY 10017
(212)559-6300
Fax: (212)812-0100
Website: http://www.harvpart.com

**Holding Capital Group, Inc.**
10 E. 53rd St., 30th Fl.
New York, NY 10022
(212)486-6670
Fax: (212)486-0843

**Hudson Venture Partners**
660 Madison Ave., 14th Fl.
New York, NY 10021-8405
(212)644-9797
Fax: (212)644-7430
Website: http://www.hudsonptr.com

**IBJS Capital Corp.**
1 State St., 9th Fl.
New York, NY 10004
(212)858-2018
Fax: (212)858-2768

**InterEquity Capital Partners, L.P.**
220 5th Ave.
New York, NY 10001

(212)779-2022
Fax: (212)779-2103
Website: http://www.interequity-capital.com

**The Jordan Edmiston Group Inc.**
150 East 52nd St., 18th Fl.
New York, NY 10022
(212)754-0710
Fax: (212)754-0337

**Josephberg, Grosz and Co., Inc.**
633 3rd Ave., 13th Fl.
New York, NY 10017
(212)974-9926
Fax: (212)397-5832

**J.P. Morgan Capital Corp.**
60 Wall St.
New York, NY 10260-0060
(212)648-9000
Fax: (212)648-5002
Website: http://www.jpmorgan.com

**The Lambda Funds**
380 Lexington Ave., 54th Fl.
New York, NY 10168
(212)682-3454
Fax: (212)682-9231

**Lepercq Capital Management Inc.**
1675 Broadway
New York, NY 10019
(212)698-0795
Fax: (212)262-0155

**Loeb Partners Corp.**
61 Broadway, Ste. 2400
New York, NY 10006
(212)483-7000
Fax: (212)574-2001

**Madison Investment Partners**
660 Madison Ave.
New York, NY 10021
(212)223-2600
Fax: (212)223-8208

**MC Capital Inc.**
520 Madison Ave., 16th Fl.
New York, NY 10022
(212)644-0841
Fax: (212)644-2926

**McCown, De Leeuw and Co. (New York)**
65 E. 55th St., 36th Fl.
New York, NY 10022
(212)355-5500
Fax: (212)355-6283
Website: http://www.mdcpartners.com

**Morgan Stanley Venture Partners**
1221 Avenue of the Americas, 33rd Fl.
New York, NY 10020
(212)762-7900
Fax: (212)762-8424
E-mail: msventures@ms.com
Website: http://www.msvp.com

**Nazem and Co.**
645 Madison Ave., 12th Fl.
New York, NY 10022
(212)371-7900
Fax: (212)371-2150

**Needham Capital Management, L.L.C.**
445 Park Ave.
New York, NY 10022
(212)371-8300
Fax: (212)705-0299
Website: http://www.needhamco.com

**Norwood Venture Corp.**
1430 Broadway, Ste. 1607
New York, NY 10018
(212)869-5075
Fax: (212)869-5331
E-mail: nvc@mail.idt.net
Website: http://www.norven.com

**Noveltek Venture Corp.**
521 Fifth Ave., Ste. 1700
New York, NY 10175
(212)286-1963

**Paribas Principal, Inc.**
787 7th Ave.
New York, NY 10019
(212)841-2005
Fax: (212)841-3558

**Patricof & Co. Ventures, Inc. (New York)**
445 Park Ave.
New York, NY 10022
(212)753-6300
Fax: (212)319-6155
Website: http://www.patricof.com

**The Platinum Group, Inc.**
350 Fifth Ave, Ste. 7113
New York, NY 10118
(212)736-4300
Fax: (212)736-6086
Website: http://www.platinumgroup.com

**Pomona Capital**
780 Third Ave., 28th Fl.
New York, NY 10017
(212)593-3639
Fax: (212)593-3987
Website: http://www.pomonacapital.com

**Prospect Street Ventures**
10 East 40th St., 44th Fl.
New York, NY 10016
(212)448-0702
Fax: (212)448-9652
E-mail: wkohler@prospectstreet.com
Website: http://www.prospectstreet.com

**Regent Capital Management**
505 Park Ave., Ste. 1700
New York, NY 10022
(212)735-9900
Fax: (212)735-9908

**Rothschild Ventures, Inc.**
1251 Avenue of the Americas, 51st Fl.
New York, NY 10020
(212)403-3500
Fax: (212)403-3652
Website: http://www.nmrothschild.com

**Sandler Capital Management**
767 Fifth Ave., 45th Fl.
New York, NY 10153
(212)754-8100
Fax: (212)826-0280

**Siguler Guff & Company**
630 Fifth Ave., 16th Fl.
New York, NY 10111
(212)332-5100
Fax: (212)332-5120

**Spencer Trask Ventures Inc.**
535 Madison Ave.
New York, NY 10022
(212)355-5565
Fax: (212)751-3362
Website: http://www.spencertrask.com

**Sprout Group (New York City)**
277 Park Ave.
New York, NY 10172
(212)892-3600
Fax: (212)892-3444
E-mail: info@sproutgroup.com
Website: http://www.sproutgroup.com

**US Trust Private Equity**
114 W.47th St.
New York, NY 10036
(212)852-3949
Fax: (212)852-3759
Website: http://www.ustrust.com/privateequity

**Vencon Management Inc.**
301 West 53rd St., Ste. 10F
New York, NY 10019
(212)581-8787
Fax: (212)397-4126
Website: http://www.venconinc.com

**Venrock Associates**
30 Rockefeller Plaza, Ste. 5508
New York, NY 10112
(212)649-5600
Fax: (212)649-5788
Website: http://www.venrock.com

**Venture Capital Fund of America, Inc.**
509 Madison Ave., Ste. 812
New York, NY 10022
(212)838-5577
Fax: (212)838-7614
E-mail: mail@vcfa.com
Website: http://www.vcfa.com

**Venture Opportunities Corp.**
150 E. 58th St.
New York, NY 10155
(212)832-3737
Fax: (212)980-6603

**Warburg Pincus Ventures, Inc.**
466 Lexington Ave., 11th Fl.
New York, NY 10017
(212)878-9309
Fax: (212)878-9200
Website: http://www.warburgpincus.com

**Wasserstein, Perella & Co. Inc.**
31 W. 52nd St., 27th Fl.
New York, NY 10019
(212)702-5691
Fax: (212)969-7879

**Welsh, Carson, Anderson, & Stowe**
320 Park Ave., Ste. 2500
New York, NY 10022-6815
(212)893-9500
Fax: (212)893-9575

**Whitney and Co. (New York)**
630 Fifth Ave. Ste. 3225
New York, NY 10111
(212)332-2400
Fax: (212)332-2422
Website: http://www.jhwitney.com

**Winthrop Ventures**
74 Trinity Place, Ste. 600
New York, NY 10006
(212)422-0100

**The Pittsford Group**
8 Lodge Pole Rd.
Pittsford, NY 14534
(716)223-3523

**Genesee Funding**
70 Linden Oaks, 3rd Fl.
Rochester, NY 14625
(716)383-5550
Fax: (716)383-5305

**Gabelli Multimedia Partners**
One Corporate Center
Rye, NY 10580
(914)921-5395
Fax: (914)921-5031

**Stamford Financial**
108 Main St.
Stamford, NY 12167
(607)652-3311
Fax: (607)652-6301
Website: http://www.stamford
financial.com

**Northwood Ventures LLC**
485 Underhill Blvd., Ste. 205
Syosset, NY 11791
(516)364-5544
Fax: (516)364-0879
E-mail: northwood@northwood.com
Website: http://www.north
woodventures.com

**Exponential Business Development Co.**
216 Walton St.
Syracuse, NY 13202-1227
(315)474-4500
Fax: (315)474-4682
E-mail: dirksonn@aol.com
Website: http://www.exponential-ny.com

**Onondaga Venture Capital Fund Inc.**
714 State Tower Bldg.
Syracuse, NY 13202
(315)478-0157
Fax: (315)478-0158

**Bessemer Venture Partners (Westbury)**
1400 Old Country Rd., Ste. 109
Westbury, NY 11590
(516)997-2300
Fax: (516)997-2371
E-mail: bob@bvpny.com
Website: http://www.bvp.com

**Ovation Capital Partners**
120 Bloomingdale Rd., 4th Fl.
White Plains, NY 10605
(914)258-0011
Fax: (914)684-0848
Website: http://www.ovation
capital.com

## North Carolina

**Carolinas Capital Investment Corp.**
1408 Biltmore Dr.
Charlotte, NC 28207
(704)375-3888
Fax: (704)375-6226

**First Union Capital Partners**
1st Union Center, 12th Fl.
301 S. College St.
Charlotte, NC 28288-0732
(704)383-0000
Fax: (704)374-6711
Website: http://www.fucp.com

**Frontier Capital LLC**
525 North Tryon St., Ste. 1700
Charlotte, NC 28202
(704)414-2880
Fax: (704)414-2881
Website: http://www.frontierfunds.com

**Kitty Hawk Capital**
2700 Coltsgate Rd., Ste. 202
Charlotte, NC 28211
(704)362-3909
Fax: (704)362-2774
Website: http://www.kittyhawk
capital.com

**Piedmont Venture Partners**
One Morrocroft Centre
6805 Morisson Blvd., Ste. 380
Charlotte, NC 28211
(704)731-5200
Fax: (704)365-9733
Website: http://www.piedmontvp.com

**Ruddick Investment Co.**
1800 Two First Union Center
Charlotte, NC 28282
(704)372-5404
Fax: (704)372-6409

**The Shelton Companies Inc.**
3600 One First Union Center
301 S. College St.
Charlotte, NC 28202
(704)348-2200
Fax: (704)348-2260

**Wakefield Group**
1110 E. Morehead St.
PO Box 36329
Charlotte, NC 28236
(704)372-0355
Fax: (704)372-8216
Website: http://www.wakefield
group.com

**Aurora Funds, Inc.**
2525 Meridian Pkwy., Ste. 220
Durham, NC 27713
(919)484-0400
Fax: (919)484-0444
Website: http://www.aurora
funds.com

**Intersouth Partners**
3211 Shannon Rd., Ste. 610
Durham, NC 27707
(919)493-6640
Fax: (919)493-6649
E-mail: info@intersouth.com
Website: http://www.intersouth.com

**Geneva Merchant Banking Partners**
PO Box 21962
Greensboro, NC 27420
(336)275-7002
Fax: (336)275-9155
Website: http://www.geneva
merchantbank.com

**The North Carolina Enterprise Fund, L.P.**
3600 Glenwood Ave., Ste. 107
Raleigh, NC 27612
(919)781-2691
Fax: (919)783-9195
Website: http://www.ncef.com

## Ohio

**Senmend Medical Ventures**
4445 Lake Forest Dr., Ste. 600
Cincinnati, OH 45242
(513)563-3264
Fax: (513)563-3261

**The Walnut Group**
312 Walnut St., Ste. 1151
Cincinnati, OH 45202
(513)651-3300
Fax: (513)929-4441
Website: http://www.thewal
nutgroup.com

**Brantley Venture Partners**
20600 Chagrin Blvd., Ste. 1150
Cleveland, OH 44122
(216)283-4800
Fax: (216)283-5324

**Clarion Capital Corp.**
1801 E. 9th St., Ste. 1120
Cleveland, OH 44114
(216)687-1096
Fax: (216)694-3545

**Crystal Internet Venture Fund, L.P.**
1120 Chester Ave., Ste. 418
Cleveland, OH 44114
(216)263-5515
Fax: (216)263-5518
E-mail: jf@crystalventure.com
Website: http://www.crystal
venture.com

**Key Equity Capital Corp.**
127 Public Sq., 28th Fl.
Cleveland, OH 44114
(216)689-3000
Fax: (216)689-3204
Website: http://www.keybank.com

**Morgenthaler Ventures**
Terminal Tower
50 Public Square, Ste. 2700
Cleveland, OH 44113
(216)416-7500
Fax: (216)416-7501
Website: http://www.morgenthaler.com

**National City Equity Partners Inc.**
1965 E. 6th St.
Cleveland, OH 44114
(216)575-2491
Fax: (216)575-9965
E-mail: nccap@aol.com
Website: http://www.nccapital.com

**Primus Venture Partners, Inc.**
5900 LanderBrook Dr., Ste. 2000
Cleveland, OH 44124-4020
(440)684-7300
Fax: (440)684-7342
E-mail: info@primusventure.com
Website: http://www.primusventure.com

**Banc One Capital Partners (Columbus)**
150 East Gay St., 24th Fl.
Columbus, OH 43215
(614)217-1100
Fax: (614)217-1217

**Battelle Venture Partners**
505 King Ave.
Columbus, OH 43201
(614)424-7005
Fax: (614)424-4874

**Ohio Partners**
62 E. Board St., 3rd Fl.
Columbus, OH 43215
(614)621-1210
Fax: (614)621-1240

**Capital Technology Group, L.L.C.**
400 Metro Place North, Ste. 300
Dublin, OH 43017
(614)792-6066
Fax: (614)792-6036
E-mail: info@capitaltech.com
Website: http://www.capitaltech.com

**Northwest Ohio Venture Fund**
4159 Holland-Sylvania R., Ste. 202
Toledo, OH 43623
(419)824-8144

Fax: (419)882-2035
E-mail: bwalsh@novf.com

## Oklahoma

**Moore & Associates**
1000 W. Wilshire Blvd., Ste. 370
Oklahoma City, OK 73116
(405)842-3660
Fax: (405)842-3763

**Chisholm Private Capital Partners**
100 West 5th St., Ste. 805
Tulsa, OK 74103
(918)584-0440
Fax: (918)584-0441
Website: http://www.chisholmvc.com

**Davis, Tuttle Venture Partners (Tulsa)**
320 S. Boston, Ste. 1000
Tulsa, OK 74103-3703
(918)584-7272
Fax: (918)582-3404
Website: http://www.davistuttle.com

**RBC Ventures**
2627 E. 21st St.
Tulsa, OK 74114
(918)744-5607
Fax: (918)743-8630

## Oregon

**Utah Ventures II LP**
10700 SW Beaverton-Hillsdale Hwy.,
Ste. 548
Beaverton, OR 97005
(503)574-4125
E-mail: adishlip@uven.com
Website: http://www.uven.com

**Orien Ventures**
14523 SW Westlake Dr.
Lake Oswego, OR 97035
(503)699-1680
Fax: (503)699-1681

**OVP Venture Partners (Lake Oswego)**
340 Oswego Pointe Dr., Ste. 200
Lake Oswego, OR 97034
(503)697-8766
Fax: (503)697-8863
E-mail: info@ovp.com
Website: http://www.ovp.com

**Oregon Resource and Technology Development Fund**
4370 NE Halsey St., Ste. 233
Portland, OR 97213-1566
(503)282-4462
Fax: (503)282-2976

**Shaw Venture Partners**
400 SW 6th Ave., Ste. 1100
Portland, OR 97204-1636
(503)228-4884
Fax: (503)227-2471
Website: http://www.shawventures.com

## Pennsylvania

**Mid-Atlantic Venture Funds**
125 Goodman Dr.
Bethlehem, PA 18015
(610)865-6550
Fax: (610)865-6427
Website: http://www.mavf.com

**Newspring Ventures**
100 W. Elm St., Ste. 101
Conshohocken, PA 19428
(610)567-2380
Fax: (610)567-2388
Website: http://www.news
printventures.com

**Patricof & Co. Ventures, Inc.**
455 S. Gulph Rd., Ste. 410
King of Prussia, PA 19406
(610)265-0286
Fax: (610)265-4959
Website: http://www.patricof.com

**Loyalhanna Venture Fund**
527 Cedar Way, Ste. 104
Oakmont, PA 15139
(412)820-7035
Fax: (412)820-7036

**Innovest Group Inc.**
2000 Market St., Ste. 1400
Philadelphia, PA 19103
(215)564-3960
Fax: (215)569-3272

**Keystone Venture Capital Management Co.**
1601 Market St., Ste. 2500
Philadelphia, PA 19103
(215)241-1200
Fax: (215)241-1211
Website: http://www.keystonevc.com

**Liberty Venture Partners**
2005 Market St., Ste. 200
Philadelphia, PA 19103
(215)282-4484
Fax: (215)282-4485
E-mail: info@libertyvp.com
Website: http://www.libertyvp.com

**Penn Janney Fund, Inc.**
1801 Market St., 11th Fl.
Philadelphia, PA 19103

(215)665-4447
Fax: (215)557-0820

**Philadelphia Ventures, Inc.**
The Bellevue
200 S. Broad St.
Philadelphia, PA 19102
(215)732-4445
Fax: (215)732-4644

**Birchmere Ventures Inc.**
2000 Technology Dr.
Pittsburgh, PA 15219-3109
(412)803-8000
Fax: (412)687-8139
Website: http://www.birchmerevc.com

**CEO Venture Fund**
2000 Technology Dr., Ste. 160
Pittsburgh, PA 15219-3109
(412)687-3451
Fax: (412)687-8139
E-mail: ceofund@aol.com
Website: http://www.ceoventure
fund.com

**Innovation Works Inc.**
2000 Technology Dr., Ste. 250
Pittsburgh, PA 15219
(412)681-1520
Fax: (412)681-2625
Website: http://www.innovation
works.org

**Keystone Minority Capital Fund L.P.**
1801 Centre Ave., Ste. 201
Williams Sq.
Pittsburgh, PA 15219
(412)338-2230
Fax: (412)338-2224

**Mellon Ventures, Inc.**
One Mellon Bank Ctr., Rm. 3500
Pittsburgh, PA 15258
(412)236-3594
Fax: (412)236-3593
Website: http://www.mellon
ventures.com

**Pennsylvania Growth Fund**
5850 Ellsworth Ave., Ste. 303
Pittsburgh, PA 15232
(412)661-1000
Fax: (412)361-0676

**Point Venture Partners**
The Century Bldg.
130 Seventh St., 7th Fl.
Pittsburgh, PA 15222
(412)261-1966
Fax: (412)261-1718

**Cross Atlantic Capital Partners**
5 Radnor Corporate Center, Ste. 555
Radnor, PA 19087
(610)995-2650
Fax: (610)971-2062
Website: http://www.xacp.com

**Meridian Venture Partners (Radnor)**
The Radnor Court Bldg., Ste. 140
259 Radnor-Chester Rd.
Radnor, PA 19087
(610)254-2999
Fax: (610)254-2996
E-mail: mvpart@ix.netcom.com

**TDH**
919 Conestoga Rd., Bldg. 1, Ste. 301
Rosemont, PA 19010
(610)526-9970
Fax: (610)526-9971

**Adams Capital Management**
500 Blackburn Ave.
Sewickley, PA 15143
(412)749-9454
Fax: (412)749-9459
Website: http://www.acm.com

**S.R. One, Ltd.**
Four Tower Bridge
200 Barr Harbor Dr., Ste. 250
W. Conshohocken, PA 19428
(610)567-1000
Fax: (610)567-1039

**Greater Philadelphia Venture Capital Corp.**
351 East Conestoga Rd.
Wayne, PA 19087
(610)688-6829
Fax: (610)254-8958

**PA Early Stage**
435 Devon Park Dr., Bldg. 500, Ste. 510
Wayne, PA 19087
(610)293-4075
Fax: (610)254-4240
Website: http://www.paearlystage.com

**The Sandhurst Venture Fund, L.P.**
351 E. Constoga Rd.
Wayne, PA 19087
(610)254-8900
Fax: (610)254-8958

**TL Ventures**
700 Bldg.
435 Devon Park Dr.
Wayne, PA 19087-1990
(610)975-3765
Fax: (610)254-4210
Website: http://www.tlventures.com

**Rockhill Ventures, Inc.**
100 Front St., Ste. 1350
West Conshohocken, PA 19428
(610)940-0300
Fax: (610)940-0301

## Puerto Rico

**Advent-Morro Equity Partners**
Banco Popular Bldg.
206 Tetuan St., Ste. 903
San Juan, PR 00902
(787)725-5285
Fax: (787)721-1735

**North America Investment Corp.**
Mercantil Plaza, Ste. 813
PO Box 191831
San Juan, PR 00919
(787)754-6178
Fax: (787)754-6181

## Rhode Island

**Manchester Humphreys, Inc.**
40 Westminster St., Ste. 900
Providence, RI 02903
(401)454-0400
Fax: (401)454-0403

**Navis Partners**
50 Kennedy Plaza, 12th Fl.
Providence, RI 02903
(401)278-6770
Fax: (401)278-6387
Website: http://www.navis
partners.com

## South Carolina

**Capital Insights, L.L.C.**
PO Box 27162
Greenville, SC 29616-2162
(864)242-6832
Fax: (864)242-6755
E-mail: jwarner@capitalinsights.com
Website: http://www.capitalin
sights.com

**Transamerica Mezzanine Financing**
7 N. Laurens St., Ste. 603
Greenville, SC 29601
(864)232-6198
Fax: (864)241-4444

## Tennessee

**Valley Capital Corp.**
Krystal Bldg.
100 W. Martin Luther King Blvd.,
Ste. 212

Chattanooga, TN 37402
(423)265-1557
Fax: (423)265-1588

**Coleman Swenson Booth Inc.**
237 2nd Ave. S
Franklin, TN 37064-2649
(615)791-9462
Fax: (615)791-9636
Website: http://
www.colemanswenson.com

**Capital Services & Resources, Inc.**
5159 Wheelis Dr., Ste. 106
Memphis, TN 38117
(901)761-2156
Fax: (907)767-0060

**Paradigm Capital Partners LLC**
6410 Poplar Ave., Ste. 395
Memphis, TN 38119
(901)682-6060
Fax: (901)328-3061

**SSM Ventures**
845 Crossover Ln., Ste. 140
Memphis, TN 38117
(901)767-1131
Fax: (901)767-1135
Website: http://www.ssm
ventures.com

**Capital Across America L.P.**
501 Union St., Ste. 201
Nashville, TN 37219
(615)254-1414
Fax: (615)254-1856
Website: http://
www.capitalacrossamerica.com

**Equitas L.P.**
2000 Glen Echo Rd., Ste. 101
PO Box 158838
Nashville, TN 37215-8838
(615)383-8673
Fax: (615)383-8693

**Massey Burch Capital Corp.**
One Burton Hills Blvd., Ste. 350
Nashville, TN 37215
(615)665-3221
Fax: (615)665-3240
E-mail: tcalton@masseyburch.com
Website: http://www.masseyburch.com

**Nelson Capital Corp.**
3401 West End Ave., Ste. 300
Nashville, TN 37203
(615)292-8787
Fax: (615)385-3150

## Texas

**Phillips-Smith Specialty Retail Group**
5080 Spectrum Dr., Ste. 805 W
Addison, TX 75001
(972)387-0725
Fax: (972)458-2560
E-mail: pssrg@aol.com
Website: http://www.phillips-smith.com

**Austin Ventures, L.P.**
701 Brazos St., Ste. 1400
Austin, TX 78701
(512)485-1900
Fax: (512)476-3952
E-mail: info@ausven.com
Website: http://www.austinventures.com

**The Capital Network**
3925 West Braker Lane, Ste. 406
Austin, TX 78759-5321
(512)305-0826
Fax: (512)305-0836

**Techxas Ventures LLC**
5000 Plaza on the Lake
Austin, TX 78746
(512)343-0118
Fax: (512)343-1879
E-mail: bruce@techxas.com
Website: http://www.techxas.com

**Alliance Financial of Houston**
218 Heather Ln.
Conroe, TX 77385-9013
(936)447-3300
Fax: (936)447-4222

**Amerimark Capital Corp.**
1111 W. Mockingbird, Ste. 1111
Dallas, TX 75247
(214)638-7878
Fax: (214)638-7612
E-mail: amerimark@amcapital.com
Website: http://www.amcapital.com

**AMT Venture Partners / AMT Capital Ltd.**
5220 Spring Valley Rd., Ste. 600
Dallas, TX 75240
(214)905-9757
Fax: (214)905-9761
Website: http://www.amtcapital.com

**Arkoma Venture Partners**
5950 Berkshire Lane, Ste. 1400
Dallas, TX 75225
(214)739-3515
Fax: (214)739-3572
E-mail: joelf@arkomavp.com

**Capital Southwest Corp.**
12900 Preston Rd., Ste. 700
Dallas, TX 75230
(972)233-8242
Fax: (972)233-7362
Website: http://
www.capitalsouthwest.com

**Dali, Hook Partners**
One Lincoln Center, Ste. 1550
5400 LBJ Freeway
Dallas, TX 75240
(972)991-5457
Fax: (972)991-5458
E-mail: dhook@hookpartners.com
Website: http://www.hookpartners.com

**HO2 Partners**
Two Galleria Tower
13455 Noel Rd., Ste. 1670
Dallas, TX 75240
(972)702-1144
Fax: (972)702-8234
Website: http://www.ho2.com

**Interwest Partners (Dallas)**
2 Galleria Tower
13455 Noel Rd., Ste. 1670
Dallas, TX 75240
(972)392-7279
Fax: (972)490-6348
Website: http://www.interwest.com

**Kahala Investments, Inc.**
8214 Westchester Dr., Ste. 715
Dallas, TX 75225
(214)987-0077
Fax: (214)987-2332

**MESBIC Ventures Holding Co.**
2435 North Central Expressway, Ste. 200
Dallas, TX 75080
(972)991-1597
Fax: (972)991-4770
Website: http://www.mvhc.com

**North Texas MESBIC, Inc.**
9500 Forest Lane, Ste. 430
Dallas, TX 75243
(214)221-3565
Fax: (214)221-3566

**Richard Jaffe & Company, Inc,**
7318 Royal Cir.
Dallas, TX 75230
(214)265-9397
Fax: (214)739-1845

**Sevin Rosen Management Co.**
13455 Noel Rd., Ste. 1670
Dallas, TX 75240

(972)702-1100
Fax: (972)702-1103
E-mail: info@srfunds.com
Website: http://www.srfunds.com

**Stratford Capital Partners, L.P.**
300 Crescent Ct., Ste. 500
Dallas, TX 75201
(214)740-7377
Fax: (214)720-7393
E-mail: stratcap@hmtf.com

**Sunwestern Investment Group**
12221 Merit Dr., Ste. 935
Dallas, TX 75251
(972)239-5650
Fax: (972)701-0024

**Wingate Partners**
750 N. St. Paul St., Ste. 1200
Dallas, TX 75201
(214)720-1313
Fax: (214)871-8799

**Buena Venture Associates**
201 Main St., 32nd Fl.
Fort Worth, TX 76102
(817)339-7400
Fax: (817)390-8408
Website: http://www.buenaventure.com

**The Catalyst Group**
3 Riverway, Ste. 770
Houston, TX 77056
(713)623-8133
Fax: (713)623-0473
E-mail: herman@thecatalystgroup.net
Website: http://www.thecatalyst
group.net

**Cureton & Co., Inc.**
1100 Louisiana, Ste. 3250
Houston, TX 77002
(713)658-9806
Fax: (713)658-0476

**Davis, Tuttle Venture Partners (Dallas)**
8 Greenway Plaza, Ste. 1020
Houston, TX 77046
(713)993-0440
Fax: (713)621-2297
Website: http://www.davistuttle.com

**Houston Partners**
401 Louisiana, 8th Fl.
Houston, TX 77002
(713)222-8600
Fax: (713)222-8932

**Southwest Venture Group**
10878 Westheimer, Ste. 178

Houston, TX 77042
(713)827-8947
(713)461-1470

**AM Fund**
4600 Post Oak Place, Ste. 100
Houston, TX 77027
(713)627-9111
Fax: (713)627-9119

**Ventex Management, Inc.**
3417 Milam St.
Houston, TX 77002-9531
(713)659-7870
Fax: (713)659-7855

**MBA Venture Group**
1004 Olde Town Rd., Ste. 102
Irving, TX 75061
(972)986-6703

**First Capital Group Management Co.**
750 East Mulberry St., Ste. 305
PO Box 15616
San Antonio, TX 78212
(210)736-4233
Fax: (210)736-5449

**The Southwest Venture Partnerships**
16414 San Pedro, Ste. 345
San Antonio, TX 78232
(210)402-1200
Fax: (210)402-1221
E-mail: swvp@aol.com

**Medtech International Inc.**
1742 Carriageway
Sugarland, TX 77478
(713)980-8474
Fax: (713)980-6343

## Utah

**First Security Business Investment Corp.**
15 East 100 South, Ste. 100
Salt Lake City, UT 84111
(801)246-5737
Fax: (801)246-5740

**Utah Ventures II, L.P.**
423 Wakara Way, Ste. 206
Salt Lake City, UT 84108
(801)583-5922
Fax: (801)583-4105
Website: http://www.uven.com

**Wasatch Venture Corp.**
1 S. Main St., Ste. 1400
Salt Lake City, UT 84133
(801)524-8939

Fax: (801)524-8941
E-mail: mail@wasatchvc.com

## Vermont

**North Atlantic Capital Corp.**
76 Saint Paul St., Ste. 600
Burlington, VT 05401
(802)658-7820
Fax: (802)658-5757
Website: http://www.north
atlanticcapital.com

**Green Mountain Advisors Inc.**
PO Box 1230
Quechee, VT 05059
(802)296-7800
Fax: (802)296-6012
Website: http://www.gmtcap.com

## Virginia

**Oxford Financial Services Corp.**
Alexandria, VA 22314
(703)519-4900
Fax: (703)519-4910
E-mail: oxford133@aol.com

**Continental SBIC**
4141 N. Henderson Rd.
Arlington, VA 22203
(703)527-5200
Fax: (703)527-3700

**Novak Biddle Venture Partners**
1750 Tysons Blvd., Ste. 1190
McLean, VA 22102
(703)847-3770
Fax: (703)847-3771
E-mail: roger@novakbiddle.com
Website: http://www.novakbiddle.com

**Spacevest**
11911 Freedom Dr., Ste. 500
Reston, VA 20190
(703)904-9800
Fax: (703)904-0571
E-mail: spacevest@spacevest.com
Website: http://www.spacevest.com

**Virginia Capital**
1801 Libbie Ave., Ste. 201
Richmond, VA 23226
(804)648-4802
Fax: (804)648-4809
E-mail: webmaster@vacapital.com
Website: http://www.vacapital.com

**Calvert Social Venture Partners**
402 Maple Ave. W
Vienna, VA 22180

Organizations, Agencies, & Consultants

(703)255-4930
Fax: (703)255-4931
E-mail: calven2000@aol.com

**Fairfax Partners**
8000 Towers Crescent Dr., Ste. 940
Vienna, VA 22182
(703)847-9486
Fax: (703)847-0911

**Global Internet Ventures**
8150 Leesburg Pike, Ste. 1210
Vienna, VA 22182
(703)442-3300
Fax: (703)442-3388
Website: http://www.givinc.com

**Walnut Capital Corp. (Vienna)**
8000 Towers Crescent Dr., Ste. 1070
Vienna, VA 22182
(703)448-3771
Fax: (703)448-7751

## Washington

**Encompass Ventures**
777 108th Ave. NE, Ste. 2300
Bellevue, WA 98004
(425)486-3900
Fax: (425)486-3901
E-mail: info@evpartners.com
Website: http://www.encom
passventures.com

**Fluke Venture Partners**
11400 SE Sixth St., Ste. 230
Bellevue, WA 98004
(425)453-4590
Fax: (425)453-4675
E-mail: gabelein@flukeventures.com
Website: http://www.flukeventures.com

**Pacific Northwest Partners SBIC, L.P.**
15352 SE 53rd St.
Bellevue, WA 98006
(425)455-9967
Fax: (425)455-9404

**Materia Venture Associates, L.P.**
3435 Carillon Pointe
Kirkland, WA 98033-7354
(425)822-4100
Fax: (425)827-4086

**OVP Venture Partners (Kirkland)**
2420 Carillon Pt.
Kirkland, WA 98033
(425)889-9192
Fax: (425)889-0152
E-mail: info@ovp.com
Website: http://www.ovp.com

**Digital Partners**
999 3rd Ave., Ste. 1610
Seattle, WA 98104
(206)405-3607
Fax: (206)405-3617
Website: http://www.digitalpartners.com

**Frazier & Company**
601 Union St., Ste. 3300
Seattle, WA 98101
(206)621-7200
Fax: (206)621-1848
E-mail: jon@frazierco.com

**Kirlan Venture Capital, Inc.**
221 First Ave. W, Ste. 108
Seattle, WA 98119-4223
(206)281-8610
Fax: (206)285-3451
Website: http://www.kirlanventure.com

**Phoenix Partners**
1000 2nd Ave., Ste. 3600
Seattle, WA 98104
(206)624-8968
Fax: (206)624-1907

**Voyager Capital**
800 5th St., Ste. 4100
Seattle, WA 98103
(206)470-1180
Fax: (206)470-1185
E-mail: info@voyagercap.com
Website: http://www.voyagercap.com

**Northwest Venture Associates**
221 N. Wall St., Ste. 628
Spokane, WA 99201
(509)747-0728
Fax: (509)747-0758
Website: http://www.nwva.com

## Wisconsin

**Venture Investors Management, L.L.C.**
University Research Park
505 S. Rosa Rd.
Madison, WI 53719
(608)441-2700
Fax: (608)441-2727
E-mail: roger@ventureinvestors.com
Website: http://www.venture
investers.com

**Capital Investments, Inc.**
1009 West Glen Oaks Lane, Ste. 103
Mequon, WI 53092
(414)241-0303
Fax: (414)241-8451
Website: http://
www.capitalinvestmentsinc.com

**Future Value Venture, Inc.**
2745 N. Martin Luther King
Dr., Ste. 204
Milwaukee, WI 53212-2300
(414)264-2252
Fax: (414)264-2253
E-mail: fvvventures@aol.com
William Beckett, President

**Lubar and Co., Inc.**
700 N. Water St., Ste. 1200
Milwaukee, WI 53202
(414)291-9000
Fax: (414)291-9061

**GCI**
20875 Crossroads Cir., Ste. 100
Waukesha, WI 53186
(262)798-5080
Fax: (262)798-5087

# Glossary of Small Business Terms

**Absolute liability**
Liability that is incurred due to product defects or negligent actions. Manufacturers or retail establishments are held responsible, even though the defect or action may not have been intentional or negligent.

**ACE**
See Active Corps of Executives

**Accident and health benefits**
Benefits offered to employees and their families in order to offset the costs associated with accidental death, accidental injury, or sickness.

**Account statement**
A record of transactions, including payments, new debt, and deposits, incurred during a defined period of time.

**Accounting system**
System capturing the costs of all employees and/or machinery included in business expenses.

**Accounts payable**
See Trade credit

**Accounts receivable**
Unpaid accounts which arise from unsettled claims and transactions from the sale of a company's products or services to its customers.

**Active Corps of Executives (ACE)**
A group of volunteers for a management assistance program of the U.S. Small Business Administration; volunteers provide one-on-one counseling and teach workshops and seminars for small firms.

**ADA**
See Americans with Disabilities Act

**Adaptation**
The process whereby an invention is modified to meet the needs of users.

**Adaptive engineering**
The process whereby an invention is modified to meet the manufacturing and commercial requirements of a targeted market.

**Adverse selection**
The tendency for higher-risk individuals to purchase health care and more comprehensive plans, resulting in increased costs.

**Advertising**
A marketing tool used to capture public attention and influence purchasing decisions for a product or service. Utilizes various forms of media to generate consumer response, such as flyers, magazines, newspapers, radio, and television.

**Age discrimination**
The denial of the rights and privileges of employment based solely on the age of an individual.

**Agency costs**
Costs incurred to insure that the lender or investor maintains control over assets while allowing the borrower or entrepreneur to use them. Monitoring and information costs are the two major types of agency costs.

**Agribusiness**
The production and sale of commodities and products from the commercial farming industry.

**America Online**
An online service which is accessible by computer modem. The service features Internet access, bulletin boards, online periodicals, electronic mail, and other services for subscribers.

**Americans with Disabilities Act (ADA)**
Law designed to ensure equal access and opportunity to handicapped persons.

**Annual report**
Yearly financial report prepared by a business that adheres to the requirements set forth by the Securities and Exchange Commission (SEC).

**Antitrust immunity**
Exemption from prosecution under antitrust laws. In the transportation industry, firms with antitrust immunity are permitted under certain conditions to set schedules and sometimes prices for the public benefit.

**Applied research**
Scientific study targeted for use in a product or process.

**Asians**
A minority category used by the U.S. Bureau of the Census to represent a diverse group that includes Aleuts, Eskimos, American Indians, Asian Indians, Chinese, Japanese, Koreans, Vietnamese, Filipinos, Hawaiians, and other Pacific Islanders.

**Assets**
Anything of value owned by a company.

**Audit**
The verification of accounting records and business procedures conducted by an outside accounting service.

**Average cost**
Total production costs divided by the quantity produced.

**Balance Sheet**
A financial statement listing the total assets and liabilities of a company at a given time.

**Bankruptcy**
The condition in which a business cannot meet its debt obligations and petitions a federal district court either for reorganization of its debts (Chapter 11) or for liquidation of its assets (Chapter 7).

**Basic research**
Theoretical scientific exploration not targeted to application.

**Basket clause**
A provision specifying the amount of public pension funds that may be placed in investments not included on a state's legal list (see separate citation).

**BBS**
See Bulletin Board Service

**BDC**
See Business development corporation

**Benefit**
Various services, such as health care, flextime, day care, insurance, and vacation, offered to employees as part of a hiring package. Typically subsidized in whole or in part by the business.

**BIDCO**
See Business and industrial development company

**Billing cycle**
A system designed to evenly distribute customer billing throughout the month, preventing clerical backlogs.

**Birth**
See Business birth

**Blue chip security**
A low-risk, low-yield security representing an interest in a very stable company.

**Blue sky laws**
A general term that denotes various states' laws regulating securities.

**Bond**
A written instrument executed by a bidder or contractor (the principal) and a second party (the surety or sureties) to assure fulfillment of the principal's obligations to a third party (the obligee or government) identified in the bond. If the principal's obligations are not met, the bond assures payment to the extent stipulated of any loss sustained by the obligee.

**Bonding requirements**
Terms contained in a bond (see separate citation).

**Bonus**
An amount of money paid to an employee as a reward for achieving certain business goals or objectives.

**Brainstorming**
A group session where employees contribute their ideas for solving a problem or meeting a company objective without fear of retribution or ridicule.

**Brand name**

The part of a brand, trademark, or service mark that can be spoken. It can be a word, letter, or group of words or letters.

**Bridge financing**

A short-term loan made in expectation of intermediateterm or long-term financing. Can be used when a company plans to go public in the near future.

**Broker**

One who matches resources available for innovation with those who need them.

**Budget**

An estimate of the spending necessary to complete a project or offer a service in comparison to cash-on-hand and expected earnings for the coming year, with an emphasis on cost control.

**Bulletin Board Service (BBS)**

An online service enabling users to communicate with each other about specific topics.

**Business and industrial development company (BIDCO)**

A private, for-profit financing corporation chartered by the state to provide both equity and long-term debt capital to small business owners (see separate citations for equity and debt capital).

**Business birth**

The formation of a new establishment or enterprise. The appearance of a new establishment or enterprise in the Small Business Data Base (see separate citation).

**Business conditions**

Outside factors that can affect the financial performance of a business.

**Business contractions**

The number of establishments that have decreased in employment during a specified time.

**Business cycle**

A period of economic recession and recovery. These cycles vary in duration.

**Business death**

The voluntary or involuntary closure of a firm or establishment. The disappearance of an establishment or enterprise from the Small Business Data Base (see separate citation).

**Business development corporation (BDC)**

A business financing agency, usually composed of the financial institutions in an area or state, organized to assist in financing businesses unable to obtain assistance through normal channels; the risk is spread among various members of the business development corporation, and interest rates may vary somewhat from those charged by member institutions. A venture capital firm in which shares of ownership are publicly held and to which the Investment Act of 1940 applies.

**Business dissolution**

For enumeration purposes, the absence of a business that was present in the prior time period from any current record.

**Business entry**

See Business birth

**Business ethics**

Moral values and principles espoused by members of the business community as a guide to fair and honest business practices.

**Business exit**

See Business death

**Business expansions**

The number of establishments that added employees during a specified time.

**Business failure**

Closure of a business causing a loss to at least one creditor.

**Business format franchising**

The purchase of the name, trademark, and an ongoing business plan of the parent corporation or franchisor by the franchisee.

**Business license**

A legal authorization issued by municipal and state governments and required for business operations.

**Business name**

Enterprises must register their business names with local governments usually on a "doing business as" (DBA) form. (This name is sometimes referred to as a "fictional name.") The procedure is part of the business licensing process and prevents any other business from using that same name for a similar business in the same locality.

**Business norms**
See Financial ratios

**Business permit**
See Business license

**Business plan**
A document that spells out a company's expected course of action for a specified period, usually including a detailed listing and analysis of risks and uncertainties. For the small business, it should examine the proposed products, the market, the industry, the management policies, the marketing policies, production needs, and financial needs. Frequently, it is used as a prospectus for potential investors and lenders.

**Business proposal**
See Business plan

**Business service firm**
An establishment primarily engaged in rendering services to other business organizations on a fee or contract basis.

**Business start**
For enumeration purposes, a business with a name or similar designation that did not exist in a prior time period.

**Cafeteria plan**
See Flexible benefit plan

**Capacity**
Level of a firm's, industry's, or nation's output corresponding to full practical utilization of available resources.

**Capital**
Assets less liabilities, representing the ownership interest in a business. A stock of accumulated goods, especially at a specified time and in contrast to income received during a specified time period. Accumulated goods devoted to production. Accumulated possessions calculated to bring income.

**Capital expenditure**
Expenses incurred by a business for improvements that will depreciate over time.

**Capital gain**
The monetary difference between the purchase price and the selling price of capital. Capital gains are taxed at a rate of 28% by the federal government.

**Capital intensity**
The relative importance of capital in the production process, usually expressed as the ratio of capital to labor but also sometimes as the ratio of capital to output.

**Capital resource**
The equipment, facilities and labor used to create products and services.

**Caribbean Basin Initiative**
An interdisciplinary program to support commerce among the businesses in the nations of the Caribbean Basin and the United States. Agencies involved include: the Agency for International Development, the U.S. Small Business Administration, the International Trade Administration of the U.S. Department of Commerce, and various private sector groups.

**Catastrophic care**
Medical and other services for acute and long-term illnesses that cost more than insurance coverage limits or that cost the amount most families may be expected to pay with their own resources.

**CDC**
See Certified development corporation

**CD-ROM**
Compact disc with read-only memory used to store large amounts of digitized data.

**Certified development corporation (CDC)**
A local area or statewide corporation or authority (for profit or nonprofit) that packages U.S. Small Business Administration (SBA), bank, state, and/or private money into financial assistance for existing business capital improvements. The SBA holds the second lien on its maximum share of 40 percent involvement. Each state has at least one certified development corporation. This program is called the SBA 504 Program.

**Certified lenders**
Banks that participate in the SBA guaranteed loan program (see separate citation). Such banks must have a good track record with the U.S. Small Business Administration (SBA) and must agree to certain conditions set forth by the agency. In return, the SBA agrees to process any guaranteed loan application within three business days.

**Champion**
An advocate for the development of an innovation.

**Channel of distribution**
The means used to transport merchandise from the manufacturer to the consumer.

**Chapter 7 of the 1978 Bankruptcy Act**
Provides for a court-appointed trustee who is responsible for liquidating a company's assets in order to settle outstanding debts.

**Chapter 11 of the 1978 Bankruptcy Act**
Allows the business owners to retain control of the company while working with their creditors to reorganize their finances and establish better business practices to prevent liquidation of assets.

**Closely held corporation**
A corporation in which the shares are held by a few persons, usually officers, employees, or others close to the management; these shares are rarely offered to the public.

**Code of Federal Regulations**
Codification of general and permanent rules of the federal government published in the Federal Register.

**Code sharing**
See Computer code sharing

**Coinsurance**
Upon meeting the deductible payment, health insurance participants may be required to make additional health care cost-sharing payments. Coinsurance is a payment of a fixed percentage of the cost of each service; copayment is usually a fixed amount to be paid with each service.

**Collateral**
Securities, evidence of deposit, or other property pledged by a borrower to secure repayment of a loan.

**Collective ratemaking**
The establishment of uniform charges for services by a group of businesses in the same industry.

**Commercial insurance plan**
See Underwriting

**Commercial loans**
Short-term renewable loans used to finance specific capital needs of a business.

**Commercialization**
The final stage of the innovation process, including production and distribution.

**Common stock**
The most frequently used instrument for purchasing ownership in private or public companies. Common stock generally carries the right to vote on certain corporate actions and may pay dividends, although it rarely does in venture investments. In liquidation, common stockholders are the last to share in the proceeds from the sale of a corporation's assets; bondholders and preferred shareholders have priority. Common stock is often used in firstround start-up financing.

**Community development corporation**
A corporation established to develop economic programs for a community and, in most cases, to provide financial support for such development.

**Competitor**
A business whose product or service is marketed for the same purpose/use and to the same consumer group as the product or service of another.

**Computer code sharing**
An arrangement whereby flights of a regional airline are identified by the two-letter code of a major carrier in the computer reservation system to help direct passengers to new regional carriers.

**Consignment**
A merchandising agreement, usually referring to secondhand shops, where the dealer pays the owner of an item a percentage of the profit when the item is sold.

**Consortium**
A coalition of organizations such as banks and corporations for ventures requiring large capital resources.

Glossary

**Consultant**
An individual that is paid by a business to provide advice and expertise in a particular area.

**Consumer price index**
A measure of the fluctuation in prices between two points in time.

**Consumer research**
Research conducted by a business to obtain information about existing or potential consumer markets.

**Continuation coverage**
Health coverage offered for a specified period of time to employees who leave their jobs and to their widows, divorced spouses, or dependents.

**Contractions**
See Business contractions

**Convertible preferred stock**
A class of stock that pays a reasonable dividend and is convertible into common stock (see separate citation). Generally the convertible feature may only be exercised after being held for a stated period of time. This arrangement is usually considered second-round financing when a company needs equity to maintain its cash flow.

**Convertible securities**
A feature of certain bonds, debentures, or preferred stocks that allows them to be exchanged by the owner for another class of securities at a future date and in accordance with any other terms of the issue.

**Copayment**
See Coinsurance

**Copyright**
A legal form of protection available to creators and authors to safeguard their works from unlawful use or claim of ownership by others. Copyrights may be acquired for works of art, sculpture, music, and published or unpublished manuscripts. All copyrights should be registered at the Copyright Office of the Library of Congress.

**Corporate financial ratios**
The relationship between key figures found in a company's financial statement expressed as a numeric value. Used to evaluate risk and company performance. Also known as Financial averages, Operating ratios, and Business ratios.

**Corporation**
A legal entity, chartered by a state or the federal government, recognized as a separate entity having its own rights, privileges, and liabilities distinct from those of its members.

**Cost containment**
Actions taken by employers and insurers to curtail rising health care costs; for example, increasing employee cost sharing (see separate citation), requiring second opinions, or preadmission screening.

**Cost sharing**
The requirement that health care consumers contribute to their own medical care costs through deductibles and coinsurance (see separate citations). Cost sharing does not include the amounts paid in premiums. It is used to control utilization of services; for example, requiring a fixed amount to be paid with each health care service.

**Cottage industry**
Businesses based in the home in which the family members are the labor force and family-owned equipment is used to process the goods.

**Credit Rating**
A letter or number calculated by an organization (such as Dun & Bradstreet) to represent the ability and disposition of a business to meet its financial obligations.

**Customer service**
Various techniques used to ensure the satisfaction of a customer.

**Cyclical peak**
The upper turning point in a business cycle.

**Cyclical trough**
The lower turning point in a business cycle.

**DBA**
See Business name

**Death**
See Business death

**Debenture**

A certificate given as acknowledgment of a debt (see separate citation) secured by the general credit of the issuing corporation. A bond, usually without security, issued by a corporation and sometimes convertible to common stock.

**Debt**

Something owed by one person to another. Financing in which a company receives capital that must be repaid; no ownership is transferred.

**Debt capital**

Business financing that normally requires periodic interest payments and repayment of the principal within a specified time.

**Debt financing**

See Debt capital

**Debt securities**

Loans such as bonds and notes that provide a specified rate of return for a specified period of time.

**Deductible**

A set amount that an individual must pay before any benefits are received.

**Demand shock absorbers**

A term used to describe the role that some small firms play by expanding their output levels to accommodate a transient surge in demand.

**Demographics**

Statistics on various markets, including age, income, and education, used to target specific products or services to appropriate consumer groups.

**Demonstration**

Showing that a product or process has been modified sufficiently to meet the needs of users.

**Deregulation**

The lifting of government restrictions; for example, the lifting of government restrictions on the entry of new businesses, the expansion of services, and the setting of prices in particular industries.

**Desktop Publishing**

Using personal computers and specialized software to produce camera-ready copy for publications.

**Disaster loans**

Various types of physical and economic assistance available to individuals and businesses through the U.S. Small Business Administration (SBA). This is the only SBA loan program available for residential purposes.

**Discrimination**

The denial of the rights and privileges of employment based on factors such as age, race, religion, or gender.

**Diseconomies of scale**

The condition in which the costs of production increase faster than the volume of production.

**Dissolution**

See Business dissolution

**Distribution**

Delivering a product or process to the user.

**Distributor**

One who delivers merchandise to the user.

**Diversified company**

A company whose products and services are used by several different markets.

**Doing business as (DBA)**

See Business name

**Dow Jones**

An information services company that publishes the Wall Street Journal and other sources of financial information.

**Dow Jones Industrial Average**

An indicator of stock market performance.

**Earned income**

A tax term that refers to wages and salaries earned by the recipient, as opposed to monies earned through interest and dividends.

**Economic efficiency**

The use of productive resources to the fullest practical extent in the provision of the set of goods and services that is most preferred by purchasers in the economy.

**Economic indicators**

Statistics used to express the state of the economy. These include the length of the average work week, the rate of unemployment, and stock prices.

**Economically disadvantaged**
See Socially and economically disadvantaged

**Economies of scale**
See Scale economies

**EEOC**
See Equal Employment Opportunity Commission

**8(a) Program**
A program authorized by the Small Business Act that directs federal contracts to small businesses owned and operated by socially and economically disadvantaged individuals.

**Electronic mail (e-mail)**
The electronic transmission of mail via phone lines.

**E-mail**
See Electronic mail

**Employee leasing**
A contract by which employers arrange to have their workers hired by a leasing company and then leased back to them for a management fee. The leasing company typically assumes the administrative burden of payroll and provides a benefit package to the workers.

**Employee tenure**
The length of time an employee works for a particular employer.

**Employer identification number**
The business equivalent of a social security number. Assigned by the U.S. Internal Revenue Service.

**Enterprise**
An aggregation of all establishments owned by a parent company. An enterprise may consist of a single, independent establishment or include subsidiaries and other branches under the same ownership and control.

**Enterprise zone**
A designated area, usually found in inner cities and other areas with significant unemployment, where businesses receive tax credits and other incentives to entice them to establish operations there.

**Entrepreneur**
A person who takes the risk of organizing and operating a new business venture.

**Entry**
See Business entry

**Equal Employment Opportunity Commission (EEOC)**
A federal agency that ensures nondiscrimination in the hiring and firing practices of a business.

**Equal opportunity employer**
An employer who adheres to the standards set by the Equal Employment Opportunity Commission (see separate citation).

**Equity**
The ownership interest. Financing in which partial or total ownership of a company is surrendered in exchange for capital. An investor's financial return comes from dividend payments and from growth in the net worth of the business.

**Equity capital**
See Equity; Equity midrisk venture capital

**Equity financing**
See Equity; Equity midrisk venture capital

**Equity midrisk venture capital**
An unsecured investment in a company. Usually a purchase of ownership interest in a company that occurs in the later stages of a company's development.

**Equity partnership**
A limited partnership arrangement for providing start-up and seed capital to businesses.

**Equity securities**
See Equity

**Equity-type**
Debt financing subordinated to conventional debt.

**Establishment**
A single-location business unit that may be independent (a single-establishment enterprise) or owned by a parent enterprise.

**Establishment and Enterprise Microdata File**
See U.S. Establishment and Enterprise Microdata File

**Establishment birth**
See Business birth

**Establishment Longitudinal Microdata File**
See U.S. Establishment Longitudinal Microdata File

**Ethics**
See Business ethics

**Evaluation**
Determining the potential success of translating an invention into a product or process.

**Exit**
See Business exit

**Experience rating**
See Underwriting

**Export**
A product sold outside of the country.

**Export license**
A general or specific license granted by the U.S. Department of Commerce required of anyone wishing to export goods. Some restricted articles need approval from the U.S. Departments of State, Defense, or Energy.

**Failure**
See Business failure

**Fair share agreement**
An agreement reached between a franchisor and a minority business organization to extend business ownership to minorities by either reducing the amount of capital required or by setting aside certain marketing areas for minority business owners.

**Feasibility study**
A study to determine the likelihood that a proposed product or development will fulfill the objectives of a particular investor.

**Federal Trade Commission (FTC)**
Federal agency that promotes free enterprise and competition within the U.S.

**Federal Trade Mark Act of 1946**
See Lanham Act

**Fictional name**
See Business name

**Fiduciary**
An individual or group that hold assets in trust for a beneficiary.

**Financial analysis**
The techniques used to determine money needs in a business. Techniques include ratio analysis, calculation of return on investment, guides for measuring profitability, and break-even analysis to determine ultimate success.

**Financial intermediary**
A financial institution that acts as the intermediary between borrowers and lenders. Banks, savings and loan associations, finance companies, and venture capital companies are major financial intermediaries in the United States.

**Financial ratios**
See Corporate financial ratios; Industry financial ratios

**Financial statement**
A written record of business finances, including balance sheets and profit and loss statements.

**Financing**
See First-stage financing; Second-stage financing; Thirdstage financing

**First-stage financing**
Financing provided to companies that have expended their initial capital, and require funds to start full-scale manufacturing and sales. Also known as First-round financing.

**Fiscal year**
Any twelve-month period used by businesses for accounting purposes.

**504 Program**
See Certified development corporation

**Flexible benefit plan**
A plan that offers a choice among cash and/or qualified benefits such as group term life insurance, accident and health insurance, group legal services, dependent care assistance, and vacations.

**FOB**
See Free on board

**Format franchising**
See Business format franchising; Franchising

**401(k) plan**
A financial plan where employees contribute a percentage of their earnings to a fund that is invested in stocks, bonds, or money markets for the purpose of saving money for retirement.

**Four Ps**
Marketing terms referring to Product, Price, Place, and Promotion.

**Franchising**
A form of licensing by which the owner-the franchisor- distributes or markets a product, method, or service through affiliated dealers called franchisees. The product, method, or service being marketed is identified by a brand name, and the franchisor maintains control over the marketing methods employed. The franchisee is often given exclusive access to a defined geographic area.

**Free on board (FOB)**
A pricing term indicating that the quoted price includes the cost of loading goods into transport vessels at a specified place.

**Frictional unemployment**
See Unemployment

**FTC**
See Federal Trade Commission

**Fulfillment**
The systems necessary for accurate delivery of an ordered item, including subscriptions and direct marketing.

**Full-time workers**
Generally, those who work a regular schedule of more than 35 hours per week.

**Garment registration number**
A number that must appear on every garment sold in the U.S. to indicate the manufacturer of the garment, which may or may not be the same as the label under which the garment is sold. The U.S. Federal Trade Commission assigns and regulates garment registration numbers.

**Gatekeeper**
A key contact point for entry into a network.

**GDP**
See Gross domestic product

**General obligation bond**
A municipal bond secured by the taxing power of the municipality. The Tax Reform Act of 1986 limits the purposes for which such bonds may be issued and establishes volume limits on the extent of their issuance.

**GNP**
See Gross national product

**Good Housekeeping Seal**
Seal appearing on products that signifies the fulfillment of the standards set by the Good Housekeeping Institute to protect consumer interests.

**Goods sector**
All businesses producing tangible goods, including agriculture, mining, construction, and manufacturing businesses.

**GPO**
See Gross product originating

**Gross domestic product (GDP)**
The part of the nation's gross national product (see separate citation) generated by private business using resources from within the country.

**Gross national product (GNP)**
The most comprehensive single measure of aggregate economic output. Represents the market value of the total output of goods and services produced by a nation's economy.

**Gross product originating (GPO)**
A measure of business output estimated from the income or production side using employee compensation, profit income, net interest, capital consumption, and indirect business taxes.

**HAL**
See Handicapped assistance loan program

**Handicapped assistance loan program (HAL)**
Low-interest direct loan program through the U.S. Small Business Administration (SBA) for handicapped persons. The SBA requires that these persons demonstrate that their disability is such that it is impossible for them to secure employment, thus making it necessary to go into their own business to make a living.

**Health maintenance organization (HMO)**
Organization of physicians and other health care professionals that provides health services to subscribers and their dependents on a prepaid basis.

**Health provider**
An individual or institution that gives medical care. Under Medicare, an institutional provider is a hospital, skilled nursing facility, home health agency, or provider of certain physical therapy services.

**Hispanic**
A person of Cuban, Mexican, Puerto Rican, Latin American (Central or South American), European Spanish, or other Spanish-speaking origin or ancestry.

**HMO**
See Health maintenance organization

**Home-based business**
A business with an operating address that is also a residential address (usually the residential address of the proprietor).

**Hub-and-spoke system**
A system in which flights of an airline from many different cities (the spokes) converge at a single airport (the hub). After allowing passengers sufficient time to make connections, planes then depart for different cities.

**Human Resources Management**
A business program designed to oversee recruiting, pay, benefits, and other issues related to the company's work force, including planning to determine the optimal use of labor to increase production, thereby increasing profit.

**Idea**
An original concept for a new product or process.

**Import**
Products produced outside the country in which they are consumed.

**Income**
Money or its equivalent, earned or accrued, resulting from the sale of goods and services.

**Income statement**
A financial statement that lists the profits and losses of a company at a given time.

**Incorporation**
The filing of a certificate of incorporation with a state's secretary of state, thereby limiting the business owner's liability.

**Incubator**
A facility designed to encourage entrepreneurship and minimize obstacles to new business formation and growth, particularly for high-technology firms, by housing a number of fledgling enterprises that share an array of services, such as meeting areas, secretarial services, accounting, research library, on-site financial and management counseling, and word processing facilities.

**Independent contractor**
An individual considered self-employed (see separate citation) and responsible for paying Social Security taxes and income taxes on earnings.

**Indirect health coverage**
Health insurance obtained through another individual's health care plan; for example, a spouse's employersponsored plan.

**Industrial development authority**
The financial arm of a state or other political subdivision established for the purpose of financing economic development in an area, usually through loans to nonprofit organizations, which in turn provide facilities for manufacturing and other industrial operations.

**Industry financial ratios**
Corporate financial ratios averaged for a specified industry. These are used for comparison purposes and reveal industry trends and identify differences between the performance of a specific company and the performance of its industry. Also known as Industrial averages, Industry ratios, Financial averages, and Business or Industrial norms.

**Inflation**
Increases in volume of currency and credit, generally resulting in a sharp and continuing rise in price levels.

**Informal capital**
Financing from informal, unorganized sources; includes informal debt capital such as trade credit or loans from friends and relatives and equity capital from informal investors.

**Initial public offering (IPO)**
A corporation's first offering of stock to the public.

**Innovation**
The introduction of a new idea into the marketplace in the form of a new product or service or an improvement in organization or process.

**Intellectual property**
Any idea or work that can be considered proprietary in nature and is thus protected from infringement by others.

**Internal capital**
Debt or equity financing obtained from the owner or through retained business earnings.

**Internet**
A government-designed computer network that contains large amounts of information and is accessible through various vendors for a fee.

**Intrapreneurship**
The state of employing entrepreneurial principles to nonentrepreneurial situations.

**Invention**
The tangible form of a technological idea, which could include a laboratory prototype, drawings, formulas, etc.

**IPO**
See Initial public offering

**Job description**
The duties and responsibilities required in a particular position.

**Job tenure**
A period of time during which an individual is continuously employed in the same job.

**Joint marketing agreements**
Agreements between regional and major airlines, often involving the coordination of flight schedules, fares, and baggage transfer. These agreements help regional carriers operate at lower cost.

**Joint venture**
Venture in which two or more people combine efforts in a particular business enterprise, usually a single transaction or a limited activity, and agree to share the profits and losses jointly or in proportion to their contributions.

**Keogh plan**
Designed for self-employed persons and unincorporated businesses as a tax-deferred pension account.

**Labor force**
Civilians considered eligible for employment who are also willing and able to work.

**Labor force participation rate**
The civilian labor force as a percentage of the civilian population.

**Labor intensity**
The relative importance of labor in the production process, usually measured as the capital-labor ratio; i.e., the ratio of units of capital (typically, dollars of tangible assets) to the number of employees. The higher the capital-labor ratio exhibited by a firm or industry, the lower the capital intensity of that firm or industry is said to be.

**Labor surplus area**
An area in which there exists a high unemployment rate. In procurement (see separate citation), extra points are given to firms in counties that are designated a labor surplus area; this information is requested on procurement bid sheets.

**Labor union**
An organization of similarly-skilled workers who collectively bargain with management over the conditions of employment.

**Laboratory prototype**
See Prototype

**LAN**
See Local Area Network

**Lanham Act**
Refers to the Federal Trade Mark Act of 1946. Protects registered trademarks, trade names, and other service marks used in commerce.

**Large business-dominated industry**
Industry in which a minimum of 60 percent of employment or sales is in firms with more than 500 workers.

**LBO**
See Leveraged buy-out

**Leader pricing**
A reduction in the price of a good or service in order to generate more sales of that good or service.

**Legal list**
A list of securities selected by a state in which certain institutions and fiduciaries (such as pension funds, insurance companies, and banks) may invest. Securities not on the list are not eligible for investment. Legal lists typically restrict investments to high quality securities meeting certain specifications. Generally, investment is limited to U.S. securities and investment-grade blue chip securities (see separate citation).

**Leveraged buy-out (LBO)**
The purchase of a business or a division of a corporation through a highly leveraged financing package.

**Liability**
An obligation or duty to perform a service or an act. Also defined as money owed.

**License**
A legal agreement granting to another the right to use a technological innovation.

**Limited partnerships**
See Venture capital limited partnerships

**Liquidity**
The ability to convert a security into cash promptly.

**Loans**
See Commercial loans; Disaster loans; SBA direct loans; SBA guaranteed loans; SBA special lending institution categories Local Area Network (LAN) Computer networks contained within a single building or small area; used to facilitate the sharing of information.

**Local development corporation**
An organization, usually made up of local citizens of a community, designed to improve the economy of the area by inducing business and industry to locate and expand there. A local development corporation establishes a capability to finance local growth.

**Long-haul rates**
Rates charged by a transporter in which the distance traveled is more than 800 miles.

**Long-term debt**
An obligation that matures in a period that exceeds five years.

**Low-grade bond**
A corporate bond that is rated below investment grade by the major rating agencies (Standard and Poor's, Moody's).

**Macro-efficiency**
Efficiency as it pertains to the operation of markets and market systems.

**Managed care**
A cost-effective health care program initiated by employers whereby low-cost health care is made available to the employees in return for exclusive patronage to program doctors.

**Management Assistance Programs**
See SBA Management Assistance Programs

**Management and technical assistance**
A term used by many programs to mean business (as opposed to technological) assistance.

**Mandated benefits**
Specific treatments, providers, or individuals required by law to be included in commercial health plans.

**Market evaluation**
The use of market information to determine the sales potential of a specific product or process.

**Market failure**
The situation in which the workings of a competitive market do not produce the best results from the point of view of the entire society.

**Market information**
Data of any type that can be used for market evaluation, which could include demographic data, technology forecasting, regulatory changes, etc.

**Market research**
A systematic collection, analysis, and reporting of data about the market and its preferences, opinions, trends, and plans; used for corporate decision-making.

**Market share**
In a particular market, the percentage of sales of a specific product.

**Marketing**
Promotion of goods or services through various media.

**Master Establishment List (MEL)**
A list of firms in the United States developed by the U.S. Small Business Administration; firms can be selected by industry, region, state, standard metropolitan statistical area (see separate citation), county, and zip code.

**Maturity**
The date upon which the principal or stated value of a bond or other indebtedness becomes due and payable.

**Medicaid (Title XIX)**
A federally aided, state-operated and administered program that provides medical benefits for certain low income persons in need of health and medical care who are eligible for one of the government's welfare cash payment programs, including the aged, the blind, the disabled, and members of families with dependent children where one parent is absent, incapacitated, or unemployed.

**Medicare (Title XVIII)**
A nationwide health insurance program for disabled and aged persons. Health insurance is available to insured persons without regard to income. Monies from payroll taxes cover hospital insurance and monies from general revenues and beneficiary premiums pay for supplementary medical insurance.

**MEL**
See Master Establishment List

**MESBIC**
See Minority enterprise small business investment corporation

**MET**
See Multiple employer trust

**Metropolitan statistical area (MSA)**
A means used by the government to define large population centers that may transverse different governmental jurisdictions. For example, the Washington, D.C. MSA includes the District of Columbia and contiguous parts of Maryland and Virginia because all of these geopolitical areas comprise one population and economic operating unit.

**Mezzanine financing**
See Third-stage financing

**Micro-efficiency**
Efficiency as it pertains to the operation of individual firms.

**Microdata**
Information on the characteristics of an individual business firm.

**Mid-term debt**
An obligation that matures within one to five years.

**Midrisk venture capital**
See Equity midrisk venture capital

**Minimum premium plan**
A combination approach to funding an insurance plan aimed primarily at premium tax savings. The employer self-funds a fixed percentage of estimated monthly claims and the insurance company insures the excess.

**Minimum wage**
The lowest hourly wage allowed by the federal government.

**Minority Business Development Agency**
Contracts with private firms throughout the nation to sponsor Minority Business Development Centers which provide minority firms with advice and technical assistance on a fee basis.

**Minority Enterprise Small Business Investment Corporation (MESBIC)**
A federally funded private venture capital firm licensed by the U.S. Small Business Administration to provide capital to minority-owned businesses (see separate citation).

**Minority-owned business**
Businesses owned by those who are socially or economically disadvantaged (see separate citation).

**Mom and Pop business**
A small store or enterprise having limited capital, principally employing family members.

**Moonlighter**
A wage-and-salary worker with a side business.

**MSA**
See Metropolitan statistical area

**Multi-employer plan**
A health plan to which more than one employer is required to contribute and that may be maintained through a collective bargaining agreement and required to meet standards prescribed by the U.S. Department of Labor.

**Multi-level marketing**
A system of selling in which you sign up other people to assist you and they, in turn, recruit others to help them. Some entrepreneurs have built successful companies on this concept because the main focus of their activities is their product and product sales.

**Multimedia**
The use of several types of media to promote a product or service. Also, refers to the use of several different types of media (sight, sound, pictures, text) in a CD-ROM (see separate citation) product.

**Multiple employer trust (MET)**
A self-funded benefit plan generally geared toward small employers sharing a common interest.

**NAFTA**
See North American Free Trade Agreement

**NASDAQ**
See National Association of Securities Dealers Automated Quotations

**National Association of Securities Dealers Automated Quotations**
Provides price quotes on over-the-counter securities as well as securities listed on the New York Stock Exchange.

**National income**
Aggregate earnings of labor and property arising from the production of goods and services in a nation's economy.

**Net assets**
See Net worth

**Net income**
The amount remaining from earnings and profits after all expenses and costs have been met or deducted. Also known as Net earnings.

**Net profit**
Money earned after production and overhead expenses (see separate citations) have been deducted.

**Net worth**
The difference between a company's total assets and its total liabilities.

**Network**
A chain of interconnected individuals or organizations sharing information and/or services.

**New York Stock Exchange (NYSE)**
The oldest stock exchange in the U.S. Allows for trading in stocks, bonds, warrants, options, and rights that meet listing requirements.

**Niche**
A career or business for which a person is well-suited. Also, a product which fulfills one need of a particular market segment, often with little or no competition.

**Nodes**
One workstation in a network, either local area or wide area (see separate citations).

**Nonbank bank**
A bank that either accepts deposits or makes loans, but not both. Used to create many new branch banks.

**Noncompetitive awards**
A method of contracting whereby the federal government negotiates with only one contractor to supply a product or service.

**Nonmember bank**
A state-regulated bank that does not belong to the federal bank system.

**Nonprofit**
An organization that has no shareholders, does not distribute profits, and is without federal and state tax liabilities.

**Norms**
See Financial ratios

**North American Free Trade Agreement (NAFTA)**
Passed in 1993, NAFTA eliminates trade barriers among businesses in the U.S., Canada, and Mexico.

**NYSE**
See New York Stock Exchange

Glossary

### Occupational Safety & Health Administration (OSHA)
Federal agency that regulates health and safety standards within the workplace.

### Optimal firm size
The business size at which the production cost per unit of output (average cost) is, in the long run, at its minimum.

### Organizational chart
A hierarchical chart tracking the chain of command within an organization.

### OSHA
See Occupational Safety & Health Administration

### Overhead
Expenses, such as employee benefits and building utilities, incurred by a business that are unrelated to the actual product or service sold.

### Owner's capital
Debt or equity funds provided by the owner(s) of a business; sources of owner's capital are personal savings, sales of assets, or loans from financial institutions.

### P & L
See Profit and loss statement

### Part-time workers
Normally, those who work less than 35 hours per week. The Tax Reform Act indicated that part-time workers who work less than 17.5 hours per week may be excluded from health plans for purposes of complying with federal nondiscrimination rules.

### Part-year workers
Those who work less than 50 weeks per year.

### Partnership
Two or more parties who enter into a legal relationship to conduct business for profit. Defined by the U.S. Internal Revenue Code as joint ventures, syndicates, groups, pools, and other associations of two or more persons organized for profit that are not specifically classified in the IRS code as corporations or proprietorships.

### Patent
A grant made by the government assuring an inventor the sole right to make, use, and sell an invention for a period of 17 years.

### PC
See Professional corporation

### Peak
See Cyclical peak

### Pension
A series of payments made monthly, semiannually, annually, or at other specified intervals during the lifetime of the pensioner for distribution upon retirement. The term is sometimes used to denote the portion of the retirement allowance financed by the employer's contributions.

### Pension fund
A fund established to provide for the payment of pension benefits; the collective contributions made by all of the parties to the pension plan.

### Performance appraisal
An established set of objective criteria, based on job description and requirements, that is used to evaluate the performance of an employee in a specific job.

### Permit
See Business license

### Plan
See Business plan

### Pooling
An arrangement for employers to achieve efficiencies and lower health costs by joining together to purchase group health insurance or self-insurance.

### PPO
See Preferred provider organization

### Preferred lenders program
See SBA special lending institution categories

### Preferred provider organization (PPO)
A contractual arrangement with a health care services organization that agrees to discount its health care rates in return for faster payment and/or a patient base.

### Premiums
The amount of money paid to an insurer for health insurance under a policy. The premium is generally paid periodically (e.g., monthly), and often is split between the employer and the employee. Unlike deductibles and coinsurance or copayments,

premiums are paid for coverage whether or not benefits are actually used.

**Prime-age workers**
Employees 25 to 54 years of age.

**Prime contract**
A contract awarded directly by the U.S. Federal Government.

**Private company**
See Closely held corporation

**Private placement**
A method of raising capital by offering for sale an investment or business to a small group of investors (generally avoiding registration with the Securities and Exchange Commission or state securities registration agencies). Also known as Private financing or Private offering.

**Pro forma**
The use of hypothetical figures in financial statements to represent future expenditures, debts, and other potential financial expenses.

**Proactive**
Taking the initiative to solve problems and anticipate future events before they happen, instead of reacting to an already existing problem or waiting for a difficult situation to occur.

**Procurement**
A contract from an agency of the federal government for goods or services from a small business.

**Prodigy**
An online service which is accessible by computer modem. The service features Internet access, bulletin boards, online periodicals, electronic mail, and other services for subscribers.

**Product development**
The stage of the innovation process where research is translated into a product or process through evaluation, adaptation, and demonstration.

**Product franchising**
An arrangement for a franchisee to use the name and to produce the product line of the franchisor or parent corporation.

**Production**
The manufacture of a product.

**Production prototype**
See Prototype

**Productivity**
A measurement of the number of goods produced during a specific amount of time.

**Professional corporation (PC)**
Organized by members of a profession such as medicine, dentistry, or law for the purpose of conducting their professional activities as a corporation. Liability of a member or shareholder is limited in the same manner as in a business corporation.

**Profit and loss statement (P & L)**
The summary of the incomes (total revenues) and costs of a company's operation during a specific period of time. Also known as Income and expense statement.

**Proposal**
See Business plan

**Proprietorship**
The most common legal form of business ownership; about 85 percent of all small businesses are proprietorships. The liability of the owner is unlimited in this form of ownership.

**Prospective payment system**
A cost-containment measure included in the Social Security Amendments of 1983 whereby Medicare payments to hospitals are based on established prices, rather than on cost reimbursement.

**Prototype**
A model that demonstrates the validity of the concept of an invention (laboratory prototype); a model that meets the needs of the manufacturing process and the user (production prototype).

**Prudent investor rule or standard**
A legal doctrine that requires fiduciaries to make investments using the prudence, diligence, and intelligence that would be used by a prudent person in making similar investments. Because fiduciaries make investments on behalf of third-party beneficiaries, the

standard results in very conservative investments. Until recently, most state regulations required the fiduciary to apply this standard to each investment. Newer, more progressive regulations permit fiduciaries to apply this standard to the portfolio taken as a whole, thereby allowing a fiduciary to balance a portfolio with higher-yield, higher-risk investments. In states with more progressive regulations, practically every type of security is eligible for inclusion in the portfolio of investments made by a fiduciary, provided that the portfolio investments, in their totality, are those of a prudent person.

**Public equity markets**
Organized markets for trading in equity shares such as common stocks, preferred stocks, and warrants. Includes markets for both regularly traded and nonregularly traded securities.

**Public offering**
General solicitation for participation in an investment opportunity. Interstate public offerings are supervised by the U.S. Securities and Exchange Commission (see separate citation).

**Quality control**
The process by which a product is checked and tested to ensure consistent standards of high quality.

**Rate of return**
The yield obtained on a security or other investment based on its purchase price or its current market price. The total rate of return is current income plus or minus capital appreciation or depreciation.

**Real property**
Includes the land and all that is contained on it.

**Realignment**
See Resource realignment

**Recession**
Contraction of economic activity occurring between the peak and trough (see separate citations) of a business cycle.

**Regulated market**
A market in which the government controls the forces of supply and demand, such as who may enter and what price may be charged.

**Regulation D**
A vehicle by which small businesses make small offerings and private placements of securities with limited disclosure requirements. It was designed to ease the burdens imposed on small businesses utilizing this method of capital formation.

**Regulatory Flexibility Act**
An act requiring federal agencies to evaluate the impact of their regulations on small businesses before the regulations are issued and to consider less burdensome alternatives.

**Research**
The initial stage of the innovation process, which includes idea generation and invention.

**Research and development financing**
A tax-advantaged partnership set up to finance product development for start-ups as well as more mature companies.

**Resource mobility**
The ease with which labor and capital move from firm to firm or from industry to industry.

**Resource realignment**
The adjustment of productive resources to interindustry changes in demand.

**Resources**
The sources of support or help in the innovation process, including sources of financing, technical evaluation, market evaluation, management and business assistance, etc.

**Retained business earnings**
Business profits that are retained by the business rather than being distributed to the shareholders as dividends.

**Revolving credit**
An agreement with a lending institution for an amount of money, which cannot exceed a set maximum, over a specified period of time. Each time the borrower repays a portion of the loan, the amount of the repayment may be borrowed yet again.

**Risk capital**
See Venture capital

**Risk management**
The act of identifying potential sources of financial loss and taking action to minimize their negative impact.

**Routing**
The sequence of steps necessary to complete a product during production.

**S corporations**
See Sub chapter S corporations

**SBA**
See Small Business Administration

**SBA direct loans**
Loans made directly by the U.S. Small Business Administration (SBA); monies come from funds appropriated specifically for this purpose. In general, SBA direct loans carry interest rates slightly lower than those in the private financial markets and are available only to applicants unable to secure private financing or an SBA guaranteed loan.

**SBA 504 Program**
See Certified development corporation

**SBA guaranteed loans**
Loans made by lending institutions in which the U.S. Small Business Administration (SBA) will pay a prior agreed-upon percentage of the outstanding principal in the event the borrower of the loan defaults. The terms of the loan and the interest rate are negotiated between theborrower and the lending institution, within set parameters.

**SBA loans**
See Disaster loans; SBA direct loans; SBA guaranteed loans; SBA special lending institution categories

**SBA Management Assistance Programs**
Classes, workshops, counseling, and publications offered by the U.S. Small Business Administration.

**SBA special lending institution categories**
U.S. Small Business Administration (SBA) loan program in which the SBA promises certified banks a 72-hour turnaround period in giving its approval for a loan, and in which preferred lenders in a pilot program are allowed to write SBA loans without seeking prior SBA approval.

**SBDB**
See Small Business Data Base

**SBDC**
See Small business development centers

**SBI**
See Small business institutes program

**SBIC**
See Small business investment corporation

**SBIR Program**
See Small Business Innovation Development Act of 1982

**Scale economies**
The decline of the production cost per unit of output (average cost) as the volume of output increases.

**Scale efficiency**
The reduction in unit cost available to a firm when producing at a higher output volume.

**SCORE**
See Service Corps of Retired Executives

**SEC**
See Securities and Exchange Commission

**SECA**
See Self-Employment Contributions Act

**Second-stage financing**
Working capital for the initial expansion of a company that is producing, shipping, and has growing accounts receivable and inventories. Also known as Second-round financing.

**Secondary market**
A market established for the purchase and sale of outstanding securities following their initial distribution.

**Secondary worker**
Any worker in a family other than the person who is the primary source of income for the family.

**Secondhand capital**
Previously used and subsequently resold capital equipment (e.g., buildings and machinery).

**Securities and Exchange Commission (SEC)**
Federal agency charged with regulating the trade of securities to prevent unethical practices in the investor market.

**Securitized debt**
A marketing technique that converts long-term loans to marketable securities.

**Seed capital**
Venture financing provided in the early stages of the innovation process, usually during product development.

**Self-employed person**
One who works for a profit or fees in his or her own business, profession, or trade, or who operates a farm.

**Self-Employment Contributions Act (SECA)**
Federal law that governs the self-employment tax (see separate citation).

**Self-employment income**
Income covered by Social Security if a business earns a net income of at least $400.00 during the year. Taxes are paid on earnings that exceed $400.00.

**Self-employment retirement plan**
See Keogh plan

**Self-employment tax**
Required tax imposed on self-employed individuals for the provision of Social Security and Medicare. The tax must be paid quarterly with estimated income tax statements.

**Self-funding**
A health benefit plan in which a firm uses its own funds to pay claims, rather than transferring the financial risks of paying claims to an outside insurer in exchange for premium payments.

**Service Corps of Retired Executives (SCORE)**
Volunteers for the SBA Management Assistance Program who provide one-on-one counseling and teach workshops and seminars for small firms.

**Service firm**
See Business service firm

**Service sector**
Broadly defined, all U.S. industries that produce intangibles, including the five major industry divisions of transportation, communications, and utilities; wholesale trade; retail trade; finance, insurance, and real estate; and services.

**Set asides**
See Small business set asides

**Short-haul service**
A type of transportation service in which the transporter supplies service between cities where the maximum distance is no more than 200 miles.

**Short-term debt**
An obligation that matures in one year.

**SIC codes**
See Standard Industrial Classification codes

**Single-establishment enterprise**
See Establishment

**Small business**
An enterprise that is independently owned and operated, is not dominant in its field, and employs fewer than 500 people. For SBA purposes, the U.S. Small Business Administration (SBA) considers various other factors (such as gross annual sales) in determining size of a business.

**Small Business Administration (SBA)**
An independent federal agency that provides assistance with loans, management, and advocating interests before other federal agencies.

**Small Business Data Base**
A collection of microdata (see separate citation) files on individual firms developed and maintained by the U.S. Small Business Administration.

**Small business development centers (SBDC)**
Centers that provide support services to small businesses, such as individual counseling, SBA advice, seminars and conferences, and other learning center activities. Most services are free of charge, or available at minimal cost.

**Small business development corporation**
See Certified development corporation

**Small business-dominated industry**
Industry in which a minimum of 60 percent of employment or sales is in firms with fewer than 500 employees.

**Small Business Innovation Development Act of 1982**
Federal statute requiring federal agencies with large extramural research and development budgets to

allocate a certain percentage of these funds to small research and development firms. The program, called the Small Business Innovation Research (SBIR) Program, is designed to stimulate technological innovation and make greater use of small businesses in meeting national innovation needs.

**Small business institutes (SBI) program**
Cooperative arrangements made by U.S. Small Business Administration district offices and local colleges and universities to provide small business firms with graduate students to counsel them without charge.

**Small business investment corporation (SBIC)**
A privately owned company licensed and funded through the U.S. Small Business Administration and private sector sources to provide equity or debt capital to small businesses.

**Small business set asides**
Procurement (see separate citation) opportunities required by law to be on all contracts under $10,000 or a certain percentage of an agency's total procurement expenditure.

**Smaller firms**
For U.S. Department of Commerce purposes, those firms not included in the Fortune 1000.

**SMSA**
See Metropolitan statistical area

**Socially and economically disadvantaged**
Individuals who have been subjected to racial or ethnic prejudice or cultural bias without regard to their qualities as individuals, and whose abilities to compete are impaired because of diminished opportunities to obtain capital and credit.

**Sole proprietorship**
An unincorporated, one-owner business, farm, or professional practice.

**Special lending institution categories**
See SBA special lending institution categories

**Standard Industrial Classification (SIC) codes**
Four-digit codes established by the U.S. Federal Government to categorize businesses by type of economic activity; the first two digits correspond to major groups such as construction and manufacturing, while the last two digits correspond to subgroups such as home construction or highway construction.

**Standard metropolitan statistical area (SMSA)**
See Metropolitan statistical area

**Start-up**
A new business, at the earliest stages of development and financing.

**Start-up costs**
Costs incurred before a business can commence operations.

**Start-up financing**
Financing provided to companies that have either completed product development and initial marketing or have been in business for less than one year but have not yet sold their product commercially.

**Stock**
A certificate of equity ownership in a business.

**Stop-loss coverage**
Insurance for a self-insured plan that reimburses the company for any losses it might incur in its health claims beyond a specified amount.

**Strategic planning**
Projected growth and development of a business to establish a guiding direction for the future. Also used to determine which market segments to explore for optimal sales of products or services.

**Structural unemployment**
See Unemployment

**Sub chapter S corporations**
Corporations that are considered noncorporate for tax purposes but legally remain corporations.

**Subcontract**
A contract between a prime contractor and a subcontractor, or between subcontractors, to furnish supplies or services for performance of a prime contract (see separate citation) or a subcontract.

**Surety bonds**
Bonds providing reimbursement to an individual, company, or the government if a firm fails to complete

a contract. The U.S. Small Business Administration guarantees surety bonds in a program much like the SBA guaranteed loan program (see separate citation).

**Swing loan**
See Bridge financing

**Target market**
The clients or customers sought for a business' product or service.

**Targeted Jobs Tax Credit**
Federal legislation enacted in 1978 that provides a tax credit to an employer who hires structurally unemployed individuals.

**Tax number**
A number assigned to a business by a state revenue department that enables the business to buy goods without paying sales tax.

**Taxable bonds**
An interest-bearing certificate of public or private indebtedness. Bonds are issued by public agencies to finance economic development.

**Technical assistance**
See Management and technical assistance

**Technical evaluation**
Assessment of technological feasibility.

**Technology**
The method in which a firm combines and utilizes labor and capital resources to produce goods or services; the application of science for commercial or industrial purposes.

**Technology transfer**
The movement of information about a technology or intellectual property from one party to another for use.

**Tenure**
See Employee tenure

**Term**
The length of time for which a loan is made.

**Terms of a note**
The conditions or limits of a note; includes the interest rate per annum, the due date, and transferability and convertibility features, if any.

**Third-party administrator**
An outside company responsible for handling claims and performing administrative tasks associated with health insurance plan maintenance.

**Third-stage financing**
Financing provided for the major expansion of a company whose sales volume is increasing and that is breaking even or profitable. These funds are used for further plant expansion, marketing, working capital, or development of an improved product. Also known as Third-round or Mezzanine financing.

**Time deposit**
A bank deposit that cannot be withdrawn before a specified future time.

**Time management**
Skills and scheduling techniques used to maximize productivity.

**Trade credit**
Credit extended by suppliers of raw materials or finished products. In an accounting statement, trade credit is referred to as "accounts payable."

**Trade name**
The name under which a company conducts business, or by which its business, goods, or services are identified. It may or may not be registered as a trademark.

**Trade periodical**
A publication with a specific focus on one or more aspects of business and industry.

**Trade secret**
Competitive advantage gained by a business through the use of a unique manufacturing process or formula.

**Trade show**
An exhibition of goods or services used in a particular industry. Typically held in exhibition centers where exhibitors rent space to display their merchandise.

**Trademark**
A graphic symbol, device, or slogan that identifies a business. A business has property rights to its trademark from the inception of its use, but it is still prudent to register all trademarks with the Trademark Office of the U.S. Department of Commerce.

**Translation**
See Product development

**Treasury bills**
Investment tender issued by the Federal Reserve Bank in amounts of $10,000 that mature in 91 to 182 days.

**Treasury bonds**
Long-term notes with maturity dates of not less than seven and not more than twenty-five years.

**Treasury notes**
Short-term notes maturing in less than seven years.

**Trend**
A statistical measurement used to track changes that occur over time.

**Trough**
See Cyclical trough

**UCC**
See Uniform Commercial Code

**UL**
See Underwriters Laboratories

**Underwriters Laboratories (UL)**
One of several private firms that tests products and processes to determine their safety. Although various firms can provide this kind of testing service, many local and insurance codes specify UL certification.

**Underwriting**
A process by which an insurer determines whether or not and on what basis it will accept an application for insurance. In an experience-rated plan, premiums are based on a firm's or group's past claims; factors other than prior claims are used for community-rated or manually rated plans.

**Unfair competition**
Refers to business practices, usually unethical, such as using unlicensed products, pirating merchandise, or misleading the public through false advertising, which give the offending business an unequitable advantage over others.

**Unfunded accrued liability**
The excess of total liabilities, both present and prospective, over present and prospective assets.

**Unemployment**
The joblessness of individuals who are willing to work, who are legally and physically able to work, and who are seeking work. Unemployment may represent the temporary joblessness of a worker between jobs (frictional unemployment) or the joblessness of a worker whose skills are not suitable for jobs available in the labor market (structural unemployment).

**Uniform Commercial Code (UCC)**
A code of laws governing commercial transactions across the U.S., except Louisiana. Their purpose is to bring uniformity to financial transactions.

**Uniform product code (UPC symbol)**
A computer-readable label comprised of ten digits and stripes that encodes what a product is and how much it costs. The first five digits are assigned by the Uniform Product Code Council, and the last five digits by the individual manufacturer.

**Unit cost**
See Average cost

**UPC symbol**
See Uniform product code

**U.S. Establishment and Enterprise Microdata (USEEM) File**
A cross-sectional database containing information on employment, sales, and location for individual enterprises and establishments with employees that have a Dun & Bradstreet credit rating.

**U.S. Establishment Longitudinal Microdata (USELM) File**
A database containing longitudinally linked sample microdata on establishments drawn from the U.S. Establishment and Enterprise Microdata file (see separate citation).

**U.S. Small Business Administration 504 Program**
See Certified development corporation

**USEEM**
See U.S. Establishment and Enterprise Microdata File

**USELM**
See U.S. Establishment Longitudinal Microdata File

**VCN**
See Venture capital network

Glossary

**Venture capital**
Money used to support new or unusual business ventures that exhibit above-average growth rates, significant potential for market expansion, and are in need of additional financing to sustain growth or further research and development; equity or equity-type financing traditionally provided at the commercialization stage, increasingly available prior to commercialization.

**Venture capital company**
A company organized to provide seed capital to a business in its formation stage, or in its first or second stage of expansion. Funding is obtained through public or private pension funds, commercial banks and bank holding companies, small business investment corporations licensed by the U.S. Small Business Administration, private venture capital firms, insurance companies, investment management companies, bank trust departments, industrial companies seeking to diversify their investment, and investment bankers acting as intermediaries for other investors or directly investing on their own behalf.

**Venture capital limited partnerships**
Designed for business development, these partnerships are an institutional mechanism for providing capital for young, technology-oriented businesses. The investors' money is pooled and invested in money market assets until venture investments have been selected. The general partners are experienced investment managers who select and invest the equity and debt securities of firms with high growth potential and the ability to go public in the near future.

**Venture capital network (VCN)**
A computer database that matches investors with entrepreneurs.

**WAN**
See Wide Area Network

**Wide Area Network (WAN)**
Computer networks linking systems throughout a state or around the world in order to facilitate the sharing of information.

**Withholding**
Federal, state, social security, and unemployment taxes withheld by the employer from employees' wages; employers are liable for these taxes and the corporate umbrella and bankruptcy will not exonerate an employer from paying back payroll withholding. Employers should escrow these funds in a separate account and disperse them quarterly to withholding authorities.

**Workers' compensation**
A state-mandated form of insurance covering workers injured in job-related accidents. In some states, the state is the insurer; in other states, insurance must be acquired from commercial insurance firms. Insurance rates are based on a number of factors, including salaries, firm history, and risk of occupation.

**Working capital**
Refers to a firm's short-term investment of current assets, including cash, short-term securities, accounts receivable, and inventories.

**Yield**
The rate of income returned on an investment, expressed as a percentage. Income yield is obtained by dividing the current dollar income by the current market price of the security. Net yield or yield to maturity is the current income yield minus any premium above par or plus any discount from par in purchase price, with the adjustment spread over the period from the date of purchase to the date of maturity.

# Index

*Listings in this index are arranged alphabetically by business plan type, then alphabetically by business plan name. Users are provided with the volume number in which the plan appears.*

Index

Index